HEBREW SYNTAX

𝕴ntroductory 𝕳ebrew 𝕲rammar

HEBREW SYNTAX

BY

REV. A. B. DAVIDSON, LL.D., D.D.

LATE PROFESSOR OF HEBREW AND OLD TESTAMENT EXEGESIS
NEW COLLEGE, EDINBURGH

THIRD EDITION

EDINBURGH
T. & T. CLARK, 38 GEORGE STREET

PRINTED IN GREAT BRITAIN BY
LEWIS REPRINTS LTD.
MEMBER OF BROWN KNIGHT & TRUSCOTT GROUP
LONDON AND TONBRIDGE
FOR
T. & T. CLARK, EDINBURGH

ISBN 0 567 21007 3

FIRST EDITION 1894
SECOND EDITION 1896
THIRD EDITION 1901
Latest Impression 1981

PREFACE TO THE SECOND EDITION

THE need after a comparatively short time for a new Edition of this *Syntax* encourages the belief that the book is being found serviceable by students and teachers. In the present Edition a few changes have been introduced into the body of the book, and some errors in the Index of passages have been corrected.

The main principles of Syntax are printed in larger type, and the less common, poetical or anomalous, usages thrown into the form of notes. The illustrative examples, at least the earlier ones in each case, have been taken as much as possible from the classical prose, but references have been multiplied, partly in order that the principle illustrated may be seen in various connexions, and partly under the impression that the references might be useful in forming exercises for Prose Composition; and the

purposes of composition have been had in view in the form given to a number of the sections.

Several points in Syntax are still involved in some obscurity, such as the use of the Imperfect, and its interchange with other tenses, especially in poetry ; and the use of the Jussive, particularly in later writings. What has been said on these points, if it do nothing more, will make intelligible the state of the question regarding them. For fuller details Canon Driver's special work on the *Tenses* should be consulted.

From the assumption, perhaps, that the Predicate is the principal element in the sentence, Arabic Grammars usually begin Syntax with the Verb, and this order has been followed in some recent Hebrew Grammars. It may be disputed which order is the more logical in analysing the sentence. The order here followed, Pronoun, Noun, Verb, and Sentence, was adopted partly for the sake of simplicity, and partly to make the book run somewhat parallel to the *Introductory Grammar*, in the hope that the two might occasionally be read simultaneously. In order to avoid repetition, treatment of Infinitive and Participle, which have both a nominal and verbal character. was postponed till the sections

on the Government of the Verb had been completed.

I am under great obligations to Mr. Charles Hutchison, M.A., formerly Hebrew Tutor, New College, Edinburgh, who read over the proofs of the first edition, and to several students and reviewers who have made useful suggestions.

EDINBURGH, *February* 1896.

TABLE OF CONTENTS

HEBREW SYNTAX

SYNTAX OF THE PRONOUN

PERSONAL PRONOUNS

§ 1. In their full form the Personal pron. are employed only in the Nom. case. In the oblique cases (Gen., Acc.) they are attached in the form of suffixes to other words. On the Cases, cf. § 18, Gr. § 17.

When a pron. in the oblique case is repeated for the sake of emphasis, it is put in the absolute form. *Gen.* as suff. 1 K. 21. 19 דָּמְךָ גַּם אַתָּה *thine own* blood. 2 S. 17. 5 מַה־בְּפִיו גַּם־הוּא *what is in his* mouth also. Nu. 14. 32, 2 S. 19. 1, Jer. 27. 7, Ez. 23. 43, Ps. 9. 7, Pr. 23. 15. Or gen. with prep. 1 S. 25. 24 בִּי־אֲנִי הֶעָוֹן on *me* be the guilt. 1 K. 1. 26, Ezr. 7. 21. In the acc. Gen. 27. 34 בָּרֲכֵנִי גַם־אָנִי bless *me* too. Pr. 22. 19. So when emphasis falls on noun in the oblique case. Gen. 4. 26 לְשֵׁת גַּם־הוּא *to Seth* also. Gen. 10. 21.—Cf. these exx. Gen. 30. 20 ; 41. 10, 1 Chr. 23. 13.

Rem. 1. Occasionally oblique case has full form. 2 K. 9. 18 עַד הֵם if reading right, cf. *v.* 20. Neh. 4. 17 אֵין אֲנִי the pron. being co-ordinated with the following nouns. Cases like Is. 18. 2 are different, מִן־הוּא being = מֵאֲשֶׁר הוּא (היה) *since it* was. Nah. 2. 9 מִימֵי הִיא = מִימֵי אֲשֶׁר הִיא *since the days she was,* i.e. *all her days,* cf. 2 K. 7. 7. Such a sense is usually מִימֶיהָ (1 S. 25. 28, 1 K. 1. 6, Job 27. 6 ; 38. 12), and the text is doubtful. Jer. 46. 5 הֵמָּה חַתִּים is a clause, חַתִּים pred. and המה subj., though the consn. is more

I

usual with finite form than with ptcp. Jud. 9. 48, 2 S.
21. 4, Lam. 1. 10, Neh. 13. 23. Ps. 89. 48 אֲנִי stands for
emphasis first: remember, *I, what transitoriness!* But cf.
v. 51. In 1 Chr. 9. 22 הֵמָּה seems really *obj.* to verb as in
Aram. Ezr. 5. 12. So Moab. Stone, l. 18.

    Rem. 2. When 3 p. pr. is used neuterly for *it*, it may be
mas. or fem. In Pent., where הוּא is common, the gend. is
matter of pointing, Ex. 1. 16; and everywhere the pron. is
apt by attraction to take the gend. of pred., Deu. 4. 6;
30. 20, Ez. 10. 15, Ps. 73. 16, Job 31. 11, Jer. 10. 3.
The *fem.*, however, is usual when pron. refers back to
some action or circumstance just spoken of, particularly if
suff., Jos. 10. 13, Jud. 14. 4, Gen. 24. 14 וּבָהּ אֵדַע *and thereby* (the circumstance) shall I know. Is. 47. 7 לֹא זָכַרְתְּ אַחֲרִיתָהּ
thou thoughtest not on the issue *of it* (the conduct described).
Gen. 42. 36; 47. 26, · Ex. 10. 11, Nu. 14. 41; 23. 19, 1 S.
11. 2, 1 K. 11. 12. So the verb, Jud. 11. 39 וַתְּהִי חֹק *and it
became* a rule. Is. 7. 7; 14. 24.

    Rem. 3. By a common gramm. negligence the *mas.*
pron., esp. as suff., is used of *fem.* subjects. Is. 3. 16
וּבְרַגְלֵיהֶם תְּעַכַּסְנָה make a tinkling *with their feet*. Gen. 26. 15;
31. 9; 32. 16; 33. 13, Ex. 1. 21, Nu. 27. 7, 1 S. 6. 7, 10,
Am. 4. 1, Ru. 1. 8, 22, Song 4. 2; 6. 8.

    § 2. The oblique cases of the Pers. pron. appear in the
form of suffixes to nouns, verbs, and particles. (*a*) Suffixes
to nouns are in *gen.*, and are equivalent to our possessive
pron. Gen. 4. 1 אִשְׁתּוֹ *his* wife, 4. 10 אָחִיךָ *thy* brother.
This gen. is usually gen. of subj., as above, but may be gen.
of obj., Gen. 16. 5 חֲמָסִי *my* wrong (that done me). 18. 21.
Cf. § 23, R. 1.

    If several nouns be coupled by *and*, suff. must be repeated
with each. Deu. 32. 19 בָּנָיו וּבְנֹתָיו *his* sons *and* daughters.
Gen. 38. 18 חֹתָמְךָ וּפְתִילְךָ וּמַטְּךָ *thy* seal *and* string *and*
staff. Exceptions are very rare even in poetry. Ex. 15. 2,
2 S. 23. 5.

    The suff. of prep. and other particles, which are really

nouns, must also be considered in *gen.* Gen. 3. 17 בַּעֲבוּרֶךָ
for *thy* sake, 39. 10 אֶצְלָהּ beside *her* (at *her* side).

(*b*) The verbal suff. is in acc. of direct *obj.* Gen. 3. 13
הַנָּחָשׁ הִשִּׁיאַנִי the serpent beguiled *me.* 4. 8 וַיַּהַרְגֵהוּ and
slew *him.* See § 73, R. 4. The suff. to אֵת is also acc. Gen.
40. 4 וַיְשָׁרֶת אֹתָם he served *them.* 41. 10.

§ 3. The adj. being but feebly developed the relation of a
noun to its material, quality, and the like is often expressed
by the gen. הַר קֹדֶשׁ hill of holiness, *holy* hill. In such
cases the suff. is gen. to the whole expression. Ps. 2. 6
הַר קָדְשִׁי *my* holy-hill. Is. 2. 20 אֱלִילֵי זְהָבוֹ *his* idols-of-
gold. 13. 3; 30. 22, 23; 53. 5. On constructions like Lev.
6. 3 מִדּוֹ בַד *his linen garment,* see Nomin. Appos.

The noun with suff., forming a definite expression, the
qualifying adj. has the Art. Gen. 43. 29 הֲזֶה אֲחִיכֶם הַקָּטֹן
is this *your youngest brother.*

Rem. 1. The suff. to some particles which have a certain
verbal force, as הִנֵּה *behold,* יֵשׁ *there is,* אַיִן *there is not,* עוֹד *still,*
are partly verbal in form (Gr. § 49). But suff. of 1st pers.
is בְּעוֹדִי in the sense *while I have being,* Ps. 104. 33; 146. 2,
and מֵעוֹדִי *since I had being,* Gen. 48. 15 (Nu. 22. 30). In
ordinary sense Ps. 139. 18.

Rem. 2. These uses of the suff. are to be noted. Ex.
2. 9 אֶתֵּן אֶת־שְׂכָרֵךְ I will give *thy hire,* *i.e.* give *thee* hire.
Gen. 30. 18, Jud. 4. 9 לֹא תִהְיֶה תִּפְאַרְתְּךָ the glory shall not be
thine. Gen. 39. 21 וַיִּתֵּן חִנּוֹ gave *him* favour. Ez. 27. 15
rendered *thee* tribute. Nu. 12. 6, text doubtful. Ps. 115.
7? Job 6. 10, Hos. 2. 8 (her wall = a wall against her).

Rem. 3. 1 S. 30. 17 לְמָחֳרָתָם *their following day,* the use
of suff. is unique in Heb., though something analogous is
common in Ar. The text is dubious.

DEMONSTRATIVE PRONOUNS

§ 4. The Demons. pron. זֶה and הוּא are used as in Eng.
Jud. 4. 14 זֶה הַיּוֹם *this* is the day. Gen. 41. 28 הוּא הַדָּבָר

that is the thing. Deu. 1. 1 אֵלֶּה הַדְּבָרִים *these* are the words. On their use as adj. § 32, and R. 3.

In usage זֶה refers to a subject when first mentioned, or when about to be mentioned (= the following), while הוּא refers back to a subj. already spoken of. Jud. 7. 4, of whom I shall say זֶה יֵלֵךְ אִתְּךָ הוּא יֵלֵךְ *this one* shall go with thee, *that one* shall go. Gen. 42. 14 הוּא אֲשֶׁר דִּבַּרְתִּי *that* is what I said to you. 32. 3; 44. 17. So the common prophetic phrase בַּיּוֹם הַהוּא on *that day* (time just spoken of), Is. 4. 2.

The pron. זֶה is used almost as a noun in all the three cases. Gen. 29. 27 שְׁבֻעַ זֹאת the week *of this one*. 1 K. 21. 2. Gen. 2. 23 לְזֹאת יִקָּרֵא *this* shall be called. 1 S. 21. 12, 1 K. 22. 17. Is. 29. 11 קְרָא־נָא זֶה read *this* (writing). 2 S. 13. 17 שִׁלְחוּ־נָא אֶת־זֹאת send *this person* away ; and *mas.* with same contemptuous sense, 1 K. 22. 27 (1 S. 21. 16). 2 K. 6. 20 פְּקַח אֶת־עֵינֵי־אֵלֶּה open the eyes *of these men*. Gen. 29. 33. Pron. הוּא is not used in this way, though cf. 1 K. 20. 40.

Rem. 1. When *this, that* are used neuterly while הוּא is perhaps more common than *fem.* (Gen. 42. 14, Am. 7. 6), זֹאת is much oftener used than *mas.* Gen. 42. 18 זֹאת עֲשׂוּ וִחְיוּ do *this* and ye shall live. 42. 15 בְּזֹאת *by this* shall ye be proved. Is. 5. 25 בכל־זאת for (amidst) *all this*. Is. 9. 11, 20 ; 10. 4, Hos. 7. 10, Am. 7. 3. The *mas.*, however, is not unusual, esp. in the sense of *such*, Gen. 11. 6, 2 K. 4. 43. The distinction between *this* and *that* stated above is usually preserved, but *this* thing, *these* things seem exclusively used. Gen. 24. 9 ; 15. 1 ; 20. 8.

§ 5. When זֶה is repeated it is equivalent to *this ... that*, *the one ... the other*. Is. 6. 3 וְקָרָא זֶה אֶל־זֶה and *the one* called to *the other*. 1 K. 3. 23 זֹאת אֹמֶרֶת וְזֹאת ... אֹמֶרֶת *this one* says ... *and the other* says. Jos. 8. 22 אֵלֶּה מִזֶּה

וְאֵלֶּה מִזֶּה *some* on this side *and some* on that side. Ex.
14. 20, 2 S. 2. 13, 1 K. 20. 29; 22. 20, Ps. 20. 8; 75. 8, Job
1. 16, Dan. 12. 2. Comp. 1 K. 20. 40 thy servant עֹשֵׂה הֵנָּה
וְהֵנָּה was busy *with this and that*, where *gen.* as Deu. 25. 16
עֹשֵׂה אֵלֶּה.

§ 6. As in other languages, the Demons. have come to be
treated as adjectives. They necessarily make their noun
definite, and then conform so much to the usage of adj. as
themselves to take the Art. Is. 4. 2 בַּיּוֹם הַהוּא *on that day*.
Occasionally, however, Art. is wanting, Gen. 19. 33 בַּלַּיְלָה
הוּא *that night*, 30. 16; 32. 23, 1 S. 19. 10, Ps. 12. 8. The
Art. is always wanting when Demons. adj. qualifies a noun
determined by a suff. Ex. 10. 1 אֹתֹתַי אֵלֶּה *these my signs*.
With another adj. or several Demons. stands last. Gen.
41. 35. See § 32. The form הַלָּזֶה *yonder* is generally used
as adj. Gen. 24. 65; 37. 19, Jud. 6. 20, 1 S. 17. 26, 2 K.
4. 25; as pron. Dan. 8. 16.

Rem. 1. In some cases the Demons., as a substantive
definite of itself, seems to stand in appos. with the defined
noun, Ps. 104. 25, Ezr. 3. 12, Song 7. 8. Text of 1 K. 14.
14 is obscure, and 2 K. 6. 33, 1 Chr. 21. 17 are doubtful.
With proper names, Ex. 32. 1 זֶה מֹשֶׁה, Jud. 5. 5. With
noun defined by suff., Josh 9. 12, 13, Hab. 1. 11. The
noun is rarely undefined, Ps. 80. 15 זֹאת גֶּפֶן *this vine*, Mic.
7. 12 (text uncertain). Phenic. says קבר ז *this grave*, and
הקבר ז. Cf. Moab. St. l. 3 הבמת זאת *this high place*. In Ar.
Demons. being a noun, stands in appos., before the noun if
defined by Art., and after if a proper name or defined by
suff.

Rem. 2. The Demons., particularly זה, is used with in-
terrogatives to add emphasis or vividness to the question.
Gen. 27. 21 הַאַתָּה זֶה בְּנִי *art thou* my son Esau? See § 7c.
In the same way force is added to adverbial and particularly *temporal* expressions. 1 K. 19. 5 וְהִנֵּה־זֶה מַלְאָךְ *and lo!*
an angel. 1 Kings 17. 24 עַתָּה זֶה יָדַעְתִּי *now indeed* I know!

2 K. 5. 22 have *just* come to me. Gen. 27. 36 זֶה פַעֲמַיִם *now* twice; 31. 38 זֶה עֶשְׂרִים שָׁנָה *twenty years now*. 31. 41; 43. 10; 45. 6, Nu. 22. 28, Deu. 8. 2, Jud. 16. 15, 1 S. 29. 3, 2 S. 14. 2, Job 19. 3.

Rem. 3. The form זוּ is often a *relative* in poetry (as in Aram., Eth.). Like אֲשֶׁר it suffers no change for gend. and number. Job 19. 19 וְזֶה אָהַבְתִּי נֶהְפְּכוּ־בִי and *they-whom* I loved are turned against me. Ps. 74. 2; 78. 54; 104, 8; Pr. 23. 22, Job 15. 17. The form זוּ (Ps. 132. 12 זוֹ) is still oftener used. Ex. 15. 13, Is. 42. 24; 43. 21, Ps. 9. 16; 10. 2; 17. 9; 31. 5; 32. 8; 68. 29; 143. 8.

Rem. 4. The Demons. unites with prepp. to form adverbial expressions. See Lex. On its union with כ to express *such*, cf. § 11, R. 1e.

INTERROGATIVE PRONOUN

§ 7. The pron. מִי *who?* is used of persons, mas. and fem.; and מָה *what?* of things. Both are invariable for gend. and number.

(*a*) The pron. מִי may be used in the three cases. Gen. 3. 11 מִי הִגִּיד לְךָ *who* told thee? 24. 65; 33. 5, Is. 6. 8. The gen., Gen. 24. 23 בַּת־מִי אַתְּ *whose* daughter art thou? 32. 18 לְמִי אַתָּה *to whom* belongest thou? 1 S. 12. 3; 24. 15, Ps. 27. 1. And acc., Is. 6. 8 אֶת־מִי אֶשְׁלַח *whom* shall I send? 1 S. 28. 11, 2 K. 19. 22. The acc. is always preceded by אֵת. Like other words מִי may be repeated to particularise or distribute. Ex. 10. 8 מִי וָמִי הַהֹלְכִים *who all* are they that are to go?

(*b*) The neut. מָה is also used in all the cases. Gen 31. 36 מַה־פִּשְׁעִי *what is* my offence? 32. 28, 2 K. 9. 18. The gen. by prep., Gen. 15. 8 בַּמָּה אֵדַע *by what* shall I know? Rarely after a noun, Jer. 8. 9 wisdom *of what* (what sort of w.)? Nu. 23. 3. The acc., Gen. 4. 10 מֶה עָשִׂיתָ *what* hast thou done? 15. 2. The אֵת is not used before

what. In Jer. 23. 33 אֶת־מַה־מַשָּׂא *rd·* הַמַּשָּׂא אַתֶּם *ye are the burden.*

With adj. and verbs מה has the sense of *how.* Gen. 28. 17 מַה־נּוֹרָא *how terrible!* 2 K. 4. 43 מָה אֶתֵּן זֶה לִפְנֵי מֵאָה אִישׁ *how shall I set* such a thing before a hundred people? Ex. 10. 26, Job 9. 2, Ps. 133. 1.

(*c*) The interrog. pron. strengthen themselves by זֶה &c. to add vividness to the question. 1 S. 17. 55 בֶּן־מִי־זֶה הַנַּעַר *whose* son (I wonder) is the lad? 1 S. 10. 11 מַה־זֶּה הָיָה לְבֶן־קִישׁ *what in the world* has come over the son of Kish? Gen. 3. 13; 27. 20, Jud. 18. 24, 2 S. 12. 23, Ps. 24. 8.

§ 8. In the indirect sentence the interrog. remains without change. Gen. 21. 26 לֹא יָדַעְתִּי מִי עָשָׂה I do not know *who did it.* 43. 22, Jud. 13. 6, 1 S. 17. 56. The interrog. are also used as indef. pron., *whoever, whoso, whatever, aught.* Jud. 7. 3 מִי יָרֵא · · · יָשֹׁב *whoever is afraid* let him return. Ex. 32. 26 מִי לַיהוה אֵלָי *whoever is for Je.,* Unto me (let him come)! 2 S. 18. 12 שִׁמְרוּ מִי have a care *whoever ye be!* Ex. 24. 14, Is. 54. 15.—1 S. 19. 3 וְרָאִיתִי מָה וְהִגַּדְתִּי לָךְ and if I observe *aught* I will tell thee. 2 S. 18. 23 וִיהִי־מָה אָרוּץ *be what may* I will run! Nu. 23. 3, Job 13. 13; 26. 7, Pr. 9. 13. In some sentences of this form, however, the strict interrog. sense is probably still to be retained. Deu. 20. 5, Jud. 10. 18; 21. 5, Is. 50. 8. The form מִי אֲשֶׁר is also used, Ex. 32. 33, 2 S. 20. 11, cf. מַה־שֶּׁ Ecc. 1. 9.

Rem. 1. The neut. מה may be used of persons if their circumstances or relations be inquired of, as 1 S. 29. 3 *what* are these Hebrews? On the other hand, מי is used of things when the idea of a person is involved, Jud. 13. 17 *who* is thy name? (as usual in Syr.), but generally *what* in this case, Gen. 32. 28. Mic. 1. 5, cf. 1 S. 18. 18 (*rd.* חַיַּי *my clan*), 2 S. 7. 18, Gen. 33. 8, Jud. 9. 28. Some cases are peculiar, and suggest a provincial or colloquial use of מי for מה; *e.g.* Ru. 3. 16 מִי־אַתְּ בִּתִּי with Jud. 18. 18 מָה אַתֶּם, Am. 7. 2, 5

מי יקום יעקב *how* shall J. stand? Is. 51. 19. The Mass. on Mic. 6. 5 states that the Orientals use מי for מה.

Rem. 2. In phrases like מַה־בֶּצַע *what profit?* Gen. 37. 26, the original consn. was probably What is the profit? (appos. at least is not allowable in Ar.). Ps. 30 10, Is. 40. 18, Mal. 3. 14, Ps. 89. 48, Job 26. 14. In a number of cases the words are separated, Jer. 2. 5 מַה־מָּצְאוּ בִי עָוֶל *what evil?* and second word might be adverb. acc. 1 S. 26. 18; 20. 10, 2 S. 19. 29; 24. 13, 1 K. 12. 16. The similar use of מי is against acc., Deu. 3. 24; 4. 7, Jud. 21. 8, 2 S. 7. 23, 1 Chr. 17. 21.—Song 5. 9 מה מְדּוֹד *what sort of beloved?* is no evidence for *gen.*, which cannot be the relation of the words.

Rem. 3. These uses of מה are to be noted. Jud. 1. 14 מַה־לָּךְ *what hast thou?* i.e. what ails thee? what dost thou mean, want, &c.? Gen. 21. 17, 1 S. 11. 5, Jon. 1. 6.—Jud. 11. 12 מַה־לִּי וָלָךְ? *what have I to do with thee?* 2 S. 16. 10; 19. 23. 2 K. 9. 18, 19 מַה־לְּךָ וּלְשָׁלוֹם. Cf. Jer. 2. 18, Ps. 50. 16. Without *and* with second word, Hos. 14. 9. Passages like 1 K. 12. 16, 2 Chr. 10. 16, Song 8. 4, show how מה naturally passes over to be a negative, *not.* (Ar.).

Rem. 4. The expression אֵי זֶה is an interrog. adj. *which? what?* Jon. 1. 8 אֵי מִזֶּה עַם אַתָּה *of what people* art thou? 2 S. 15. 2 אֵי מִזֶּה עִיר אַתָּה *of what city?* 1 K. 13. 12; 22. 24, 2 K. 3. 8, 2 Chr. 18. 23, Is. 66. 1, Jer. 6. 16, Job 38. 19, 24, Ecc. 11. 6. The *fem.*, Jer. 5. 7 אֵי לָזֹאת *for what?* In many cases אֵי זֶה is merely *where?*

THE RELATIVE PRONOUN

§ 9. The word אֲשֶׁר is of uncertain derivation. Its usage differs according as it is preceded by what we call the antecedent, or is not.

When the antecedent is expressed אשר seems a conjunctive word, serving to connect the antecedent with what we call the relative clause. In this case אשר, besides being uninflected, is incapable of entering into regimen, admitting neither prep. nor את of acc., but possibly stands in apposi-

tion with the antecedent. It is neither subj. nor obj. of the
relative clause. The subj. or obj. of this clause is a pronoun
referring back to the antecedent, and agreeing with it in
gend., numb., and person. This pronoun may be expressed,
but is often merely understood when no ambiguity would
arise from its omission.

(*a*) When the retrospective pron. is subj. it may be
expressed in a nominal sentence, as Gen. 9. 3 אֲשֶׁר כָּל־רֶמֶשׂ
הוּא־חַי every creeping thing *which is alive*. But it is
oftener omitted. Gen. 3. 3 הָעֵץ אֲשֶׁר בְּתוֹךְ הַגָּן the tree
which is in the midst of the garden. In a verbal sent. the
pron. is represented by the verbal inflection, as 15. 7 אֲנִי יְיָ
אֲשֶׁר הוֹצֵאתִיךָ I am Je. *which brought thee out*. The
separate pron. is hardly ever expressed, 2 K. 22. 13.

(*b*) When the pron. is the obj. (in a verbal clause) it is
often expressed. Gen. 45. 4 אֲנִי יוֹסֵף אֲשֶׁר מְכַרְתֶּם אֹתִי
I am Jos. *whom ye sold*. Ps. 1. 4 כַּמֹּץ אֲשֶׁר תִּדְּפֶנּוּ רוּחַ
like the chaff *which the wind drives*. Gen. 21. 2, Jer. 28. 9;
44. 3, Ex. 6. 5, 2 K. 19. 4 (if not 2 acc. as 1 S. 21. 3). But
often omitted. Deu. 13. 7 אֱלֹהִים אֲשֶׁר לֹא יָדַעְתָּ gods
whom thou hast not known. Gen. 2. 8; 6. 7; 12. 1, Jud.
11. 39; 16. 30, 1 S. 7. 14; 10. 2, 2 S. 15. 7.

(*c*) When the retrospective pron. is gen. by noun or prep.
Deu. 28. 49 גּוֹי אֲשֶׁר לֹא־תִשְׁמַע לְשֹׁנוֹ a nation *whose tongue*
thou shalt not understand. Gen. 24. 3, the Canaanite אֲשֶׁר
אָנֹכִי יוֹשֵׁב בְּקִרְבּוֹ *in whose midst* I dwell. 28. 13 הָאָרֶץ
אֲשֶׁר אַתָּה שֹׁכֵב עָלֶיהָ the land *upon which* thou liest. Gen.
38. 25, Ex. 4. 17, Nu. 22. 30, Deu. 1. 22, Ru. 2. 12. Here the
pron. requires to be expressed.

After words of time the prep. and suff. is very much
omitted, so that אֲשֶׁר is equivalent to *when*. Gen. 45. 6,
Deu. 4. 10, Jud. 4. 14, 2 S. 19. 25 עַד הַיּוֹם אֲשֶׁר בָּא until
the day *when* (in which) he came in peace. 1 K. 22. 25,
cf. Gen. 6. 4; 40. 13.

(*d*) With adverbs of place.   Gen. 13. 3 הַמָּקוֹם אֲשֶׁר הָיָה
שָׁם אָהֳלֹה the place *where* was his tent.   20. 13 כָּל־הַמָּקוֹם
אֲשֶׁר נָבוֹא שָׁמָּה every place *whither* we shall come.   3. 23
הָאֲדָמָה אֲשֶׁר לֻקַּח מִשָּׁם the ground *whence* he was taken.
Gen. 19. 27; 31. 13; 35. 15; 40. 3, Ex. 20. 21, 2 S. 15. 21.—
Ex. 21. 13, Nu. 14. 24, Deu. 30. 3.—Gen. 24. 5.   The adverbial
there, &c., may be omitted, Gen. 35. 13, esp. when the antecedent noun has prep.

Rem. 1.   The part. אֲשֶׁר is usually separated from the pron.
or adverb of the rel. clause by one or more words (see exx.
above), but there are exceptions esp. in nominal sentences,
Gen. 2. 11, Deu. 8. 9; 19. 17, 1 S. 9. 10.   Sometimes אֲשֶׁר
and pron. have an emphasis which must be brought out by
expressing a pronom. antecedent.   Jer. 32. 19 אֲשֶׁר עֵינֶיךָ
thou whose eyes.   Is. 42. 24 זוּ חָטָאנוּ לוֹ Is it not Je.? *he*
against *whom* we have sinned.   Hos. 14. 4, Ez. 11. 12,
Neh. 2. 3; cf. Dan. 2. 37; 4. 6.

Rem. 2.   The expression of the separate pron. in nominal
sent. occurs mostly when the pred. is an adj. or ptcp., *e.g.*
Gen. 9. 3; it is less necessary when pred. is an adverb or a
prep. with its gen. after the verb *to be*, as Gen. 3. 3.   When
the nominal sent. is positive the pron. usually precedes the
pred., Gen. 9. 3, Lev. 11. 26, 39, Num. 9. 13; 14. 8, 27,
Deu. 20. 20, 1 S. 10. 19, 2 K. 25. 19, Jer. 27. 9, Ez. 43. 19,
Ru. 4. 15, Neh. 2. 18, Ecc. 7. 26, cf. Jer. 5. 15.   When the
sent. is neg. the pron. follows the pred.   Gen. 7. 2; 17. 12,
Nu. 17, 5, Deu. 17. 15; 20. 15, Jud. 19. 12, 1 K. 8. 41.
Although the expression of pron. in nominal sent. is genuine
Shemitic idiom, it is still mainly in later writings that it
occurs.

Rem. 3.   It is rare that אֲשֶׁר takes prep. or אֵת when
antecedent is expressed.   Neither Is. 47. 12 nor 56. 4 is a
case.   Is. 56. 4 בַּאֲשֶׁר is under preceding verb *choose*, cf. 66.
3, 4.   In 47. 12 the prep. is carried on from previous clause,
in that which, &c., the complement of יֹנַעַת being unexpressed.   Zech. 12. 10 (text obscure).   In other cases אֲשֶׁר
is distant from anteced. and אֵת resumptive, Lev. 22. 15 *that*

which they offer. Ez. 23. 40, Jer. 38. 9 might be, *in that* they have thrown.

§ 10. The word אֲשֶׁר often includes a pronominal ante-cedent, *i.e.* it is equivalent to *he-who, that-which, they-who, whom,* or indefinitely *one-who,* &c. In this case it is sus-ceptible of government like a substantive, admitting prep. and אֵת of acc. When used in this way אֲשֶׁר has the case which, according to our mode of thought, the pronom. antecedent would have. Gen. 7. 23 וַיִּשָּׁאֶר נֹחַ וַאֲשֶׁר אִתּוֹ בַּתֵּבָה and N. was left, and *they-who* were with him. 43. 16 וַיֹּאמֶר לַאֲשֶׁר עַל־בֵּיתוֹ he said *to him-who* was over his house. 44. 1 וַיְצַו אֶת־אֲשֶׁר עַל־בֵּיתוֹ and he commanded *him-who* was, &c. 31. 1 וּמֵאֲשֶׁר לְאָבִינוּ *of that-which* is our father's. 9. 24 וַיֵּדַע אֵת אֲשֶׁר־עָשָׂה לוֹ בְּנוֹ he knew *what* his son had done to him. 2 K. 6. 16 רַבִּים אֲשֶׁר אִתָּנוּ מֵאֲשֶׁר אוֹתָם more are *they-who are* with us *than they-who are* with them (later for אִתָּם). Jud. 16. 30 the dead whom he slew in death רַבִּים מֵאֲשֶׁר הֵמִית בְּחַיָּיו were more *than those-whom* he slew in his life. Gen. 15. 4; 27. 8; 47. 24, Ex. 4. 12; 20. 7; 33. 19, Lev. 27. 24, Nu. 22. 6, Jos. 10. 11, 1 S. 15. 16, 2 K. 10. 22, Is. 47. 13; 52. 15, Ru. 2. 2, 9. Ez. 23. 28 בְּיַד אֲשֶׁר שָׂנֵאת into the hand *of those-whom* thou hatest.

Rem. 1. The consn. in this case is quite the same as in § 9. The so-called rel. clause is complete in itself apart from אֲשֶׁר, which has no resemblance to the rel. pron. of classical languages. Cf. Lev. 27. 24, Ru. 2. 2, Nu. 5. 7. Cases like Gen. 31. 32 עִם אֲשֶׁר *with whomsoever,* are unusual, cf. Gen. 44. 9.

Rem. 2. In § 10 the retrospective pronoun is greatly omitted except when gen., cf. Lev. 5. 24; 27. 24, Ru. 2. 2, Is. 8. 23; and even prep. and gen. are sometimes omitted where they would naturally stand, Is. 8. 12; 31. 6—par-ticularly with verb *to say, e.g.* Hos. 2. 14; 13. 10.

Rem. 3. The adverbial complement *there, thither,* &c., is omitted after the compound עַל אֲשֶׁר‎, בְּכֹל אֲשֶׁר‎, אֶל אֲשֶׁר‎, מֵאֲשֶׁר‎, &c., in designations of *place,* Ex. 5. 11; 32. 34, Jos. 1. 16, Jud. 5. 27, 1 S. 14. 47; 23. 13, 2 S. 7. 9; 8. 6; 15. 20, 1 K. 18. 12, 2 K. 8. 1. In Gen. 21. 17 *there* is expressed in the nominal sent. (Ar. ḥaithu *hua*).

Rem. 4. On use of זֶה‎, &c. as Rel. § 6, R. 3, and on Art. as Rel. § 22, R. 4.

OTHER PRONOMINAL EXPRESSIONS

§ 11. The want of a reflexive pronoun is supplied in various ways. (*a*) By the use of reflexive forms of the verb (Niph., Hith.). Gen. 3. 10 וָאִירָא וָאֵחָבֵא‎ I was afraid, *and hid myself.* 45. 1 לֹא יָכֹל לְהִתְאַפֵּק‎ he was unable *to control himself.* 3. 8; 45. 1; 42. 7, 1 S. 18. 4; 28. 8, 1 K. 14. 2; 20. 38; 22. 30.

(*b*) By the ordinary personal pron., simple or suff. Is. 7. 14 יִתֵּן אֲדֹנָי הוּא‎ *the Lord Himself* will give. Ex. 32. 13 אֲשֶׁר נִשְׁבַּעְתָּ לָהֶם בָּךְ‎ to whom thou didst swear *by thyself.* Jer. 7. 19 הַאֹתִי הֵם מַכְעִסִים הֲלֹא אֹתָם‎ do they provoke *me?* is it not *themselves,* &c. Gen. 3. 7; 33. 17, Ex. 5. 7, 11, Is. 3. 9; 49. 26; 63. 10, Hos. 4. 14, Pr. 1. 18, Job 1. 12.

(*c*) By a separate word, esp. נֶפֶשׁ‎. Am. 6. 8 נִשְׁבַּע י׳ בְּנַפְשׁוֹ‎ Je. has sworn *by himself.* 1 S. 18. 1, 3. Plur., Jer. 37. 9. So קֶרֶב, לֵב‎ *heart.* Gen. 8. 21 וַיֹּאמֶר י׳ אֶל לִבּוֹ‎ and Je. *thought with himself.* 18. 12 וַתִּצְחַק שׂ׳ בְּקִרְבָּהּ‎ Sarah laughed *within herself.* Gen. 24. 45, 1 S. 1. 13; 27. 1, 1 K. 12. 26, Hos. 7. 2. Also פָּנִים‎ *face, presence, self,* esp. in later style. 2 S. 17. 11 וּפָנֶיךָ הֹלְכִים בַּקְּרָב‎ *thou thyself* going into battle (*rd.* perh. בְּקִרְבָּם‎ *among them*). Ez. 6. 9 וְנָקֹטּוּ בִפְנֵיהֶם‎ they shall loathe *themselves.* Ex. 33. 14, Deu. 4. 37, Ez. 20. 43; 36. 31, Job 23. 17. In ref. to *things,* עֶצֶם‎ *bone, self-same, self.* Ex. 24. 10; chiefly PC. and Ez. Gen. 7. 13, Ez. 24. 2.

Rem. 1. Some other quasi-pronominal expressions are these: (a) *Some, several,* may be expressed by plur. Gen. 24. 55 יָמִים *some* days (a time); 40. 4 (cf. 27. 44; 29. 20 יָמִים אֲחָדִים *a few* days). Ez. 38. 17. By prep. מִן with noun. Gen. 30. 14 give me מִדּוּדָאֵי בְנֵךְ *some of* thy son's mandrakes. Jer. 19. 1 מִזִּקְנֵי הָעָם *some of* the elders. Ex. 17. 5, Ps. 137. 3, and often in later style.

(b) *Any, every* by כֹּל. Deu. 16. 21 an Ashera כָּל־עֵץ *any* (kind of) *wood. Any one, one,* by אִישׁ. Gen. 13. 16 אִם יוּכַל אִישׁ *if one* were able. *Anything,* דָּבָר Gen. 18. 14. *No, none,* by לֹא...אִישׁ; *nothing,* לֹא...דָּבָר, the *neg.* placed before the verb. Gen. 45. 1 לֹא עָמַד אִישׁ *none* stood. Hos. 2. 12 אִישׁ לֹא יַצִּילֶנָּה *none* shall deliver her. 2 K. 10. 25 אִישׁ אַל־יֵצֵא *let no one* go out. Ex. 16. 19. Deu. 2. 7 לֹא חָסַרְתָּ דָּבָר thou didst want *nothing*; 22. 26, 2 S. 17. 19, 1 K. 18. 21. Sometimes strengthened by כֹל, 2 S. 18. 13. Cf. Gen. 3. 1, thou shalt eat of *no tree.* Ex. 12. 48. The phrase לֹא...מְאוּמָה *nothing*, 1 S. 12. 4, cf. Gen. 22. 12.

(c) *This . . . that, the one . . . the other,* by זֶה...זֶה Is. 6. 3 (§ 5), or אֶחָד...אֶחָד, Ex. 17. 12, 1 K. 3. 25. *One another* by אִישׁ...אָחִיו or אִישׁ...רֵעֵהוּ, Gen. 13. 11; 11. 3, Ex. 16. 15; 32. 27, Is. 3. 5; *fem.* Ex. 26 3, 5, Ez. 1. 23, Is. 34. 16.

(d) *Each* distributively by אִישׁ, Jud. 9. 55 וַיֵּלְכוּ אִישׁ לִמְקֹמוֹ Jud. 7. 7, 1 S. 8. 22; 10. 25, 2 S. 6. 19, the noun usually sing., but usually *plur.* with *tents,* Jud. 7. 8 שִׁלַּח אִישׁ לְאֹהָלָיו the men of Israel he dismissed, *every one to his tents.* 1 Sam. 13. 2.—Also by אֶחָד Is. 6. 2, Jud. 8. 18. When אִישׁ would be in the gen. it is placed as *casus pendens* with a retrospective suff. Gen. 42. 35 הִנֵּה־אִישׁ צְרוֹר־כַּסְפּוֹ *every man's* bundle of money; 15. 10; 41. 12; 42. 25, Nu. 17. 17. So Gen. 9. 5 מִיַד אִישׁ אָחִיו at the hand of *every man's* brother, unless אִישׁ אחיו had become a single expression like *one another,* and the phrase mean at the *hand of one another.* Comp. Zech. 7. 10 do not plot רָעַת אִישׁ אחיו the hurt *of one another,* cf. 8. 17 for the sense.

(e) *Such* is expressed by כְּ with זֶה or suff. Gen. 44. 7 כַּדָּבָר הַזֶה *such a thing,* כדברים האלה *such things.* 41. 38 כָּזֶה *such a one.* Jer. 5. 9 גּוֹי אשר כזה *such a nation.* Gen. 44. 15 אִישׁ אשר כָּמֹנִי *such as I,* 2 S. 9. 8,—2 S. 17. 15

כָּזֹאת וכזאת *such and such a thing.* Jos. 7. 20, 2 K. 5. 4 ;
9. 12, cf. 1 K. 14. 5. For *so and so* (person) Ru. 4. 1. Cf.
1 S. 21. 3, 2 K. 6. 8.

(*f*) The pronouns *mine, ours, yours, theirs*, &c., must be
expressed by prep. and suff. Is. 43. 1 לִי אַתָּה thou art *mine* ;
Gen. 48. 5. Gen. 26. 20 הַמִּים לָנוּ the water is *ours*. Jer.
44. 28 they shall know דְּבַר מִי יָקוּם מִמֶּנִּי וּמֵהֶם whose word
shall stand, *mine or theirs.*

SYNTAX OF THE NOUN

GENDER OF THE NOUN

§ 12. Of the two genders, mas. and fem., the mas. is the prevailing one, and by a natural inaccuracy the writer often falls into it even when speaking of a fem. subject, especially in using suffixes. § 1, R. 3. The distinctive fem. termination *a*, i.e. *at* (Gr. § 16, R. *b*) is generally used in adj. and ptcp. referring to a fem. subject.

In the case of living creatures, distinction of gender is indicated—

(*a*) By the fem. termination, as אַיִל *a hart*, fem. אַיֶּלֶת, עֶלֶם *a youth*, fem. עַלְמָה, עֵגֶל *a calf*, fem. עֶגְלָה.

(*b*) By different words, as אָב *father*, אֵם *mother*, חֲמוֹר *he-ass*, אָתוֹן *she-ass*, אַיִל *ram*, רָחֵל *ewe*, עֶבֶד *servant*, אָמָה *maid*.

(*c*) Or the same word may be used for both genders, and differentiated only in construction, as Hos. 13. 8 דֹּב שַׁכּוּל *a bear* robbed of her whelps, 2 K. 2. 24 שְׁתַּיִם דֻּבִּים *two bears*. So גְּמַלִּים *camels*, mas. Gen. 24. 63, fem. 32. 16; אֱלֹהִים *goddess?* 1 K. 11. 5. The grammatical difference, however, does not seem always meant to express a real difference of gend., cf. Jer. 2. 24. Anciently נַעַר appears to have been of common gend.

(*d*) Or a word of one gend. may be used as name of the class or genus, without distinction of individuals, as כֶּלֶב *dog*, זְאֵב *wolf*, mas.; אַרְנֶבֶת *hare*, יוֹנָה *dove*, fem.

§ 13. Of inanimate things the following classes are usually fem. (Gr. § 16):—

(*a*) Proper names of countries and cities, as בָּבֶל *Babylon*, צִדוֹן *Sidon*. Words like מוֹאָב *Moab*, &c., when used as name of the people, are usually mas., but fem. when the name of the country, and also when used for the population as a collective personified (§ 116, R. 5). So the word בַּת *daughter* of inhabitants or people, as בַּת בָּבֶל, בַּת צִיוֹן.

(*b*) Common names of definite places, as districts, quarters of the earth, &c., as עִיר *city*, תֵּבֵל *the world*, כִּכָּר *the circle* (of the Jordan), שְׁאוֹל *hades* (mas. as personified Is. 14. 9), תֵּימָן the *south*, צָפוֹן *north*, Is. 43. 6. But there are exceptions.

(*c*) The names of *instruments, utensils* used by man, and members of the body, particularly such as are double, as חֶרֶב *sword*, כּוֹס *cup*, נַעַל *shoe*; עַיִן *eye*, אֹזֶן *ear*, רֶגֶל *foot*, &c. So of animals, קֶרֶן *horn*. Again there are exceptions, as אַף *nose, nostril*, עֹרֶף *neck*, פֶּה *mouth*.

(*d*) The names of the elements, natural powers and unseen forces, as אֵשׁ *fire*, נֶפֶשׁ *soul*, רוּחַ *wind, spirit* (usually), שֶׁמֶשׁ *the sun* (usually), but יָרֵחַ *moon*, is mas.

§ 14. Some other classes of nouns are fem. 1. Abstract nouns, as אֱמֶת *truth*, גְּבוּרָה *strength*, צְדָקָה *righteousness*, though there is often also a mas. form, as עֵזֶר and עֶזְרָה *help*, נָקָם and נְקָמָה *vengeance*. So adj. and ptcp. used nominally, as we should say as neuters, as רָעָה *evil* (physical), Hos. 5. 9 נֶאֱמָנָה a *sure thing*, Am. 3. 10 נְכֹחָה what is *straightforward*, Mic. 3. 9 הַיְשָׁרָה. And often in the plur. Gen. 42. 7 קָשׁוֹת *harsh things, harshly*, Is. 32. 4, 8 צָחוֹת *clear things, plainly*, נְדִיבוֹת *liberal things*. Zeph. 3. 4. The mas. plur. is sometimes used in poetry, Ps. 16. 6, 11, Pr. 8. 6 נְגִידִים. Cf. Is. 26. 10; 28. 22; 30. 10; 42. 9; 43. 18; 48. 6; 58. 11; 59. 9; 64. 2, Nu. 22. 18; 24. 13, Jos. 2. 23; 3. 5, 2 S. 2. 26, 2 K. 8. 4; 25. 28.

2. Collectives, which are often *fem.* of ptcp., as אֹרְחָה

a caravan (from אֹרַח *a traveller*), גּוֹלָה *captivity* (גּוֹלֶה *one going captive*), יֹשֶׁבֶת *inhabitants*, Is. 12. 6, אֹיֶבֶת *enemy* (of a people), דַּלָּה *the lower classes*, 2 K. 24. 14, Jer. 40. 7, plur. Jer. 52. 15, 16. Cf. Mic. 4. 6, Zeph. 3. 19, Ez. 34. 4.

3. The *fem.*, however, sometimes is used as *nomen unitatis* when the mas. is collect., as אֳנִי *fleet*, 1 K. 9. 26, אֳנִיָּה *a ship*, Jon. 1. 3, 4; שֵׂעָר *the hair*, 2 S. 14. 26, שַׂעֲרָה *a hair*, Jud. 20. 16, 1 K. 1. 52, but probably coll. Job 4. 15; שִׁירָה *a song*, Is. 5. 1, mas. generally coll. 1 K. 5. 12, though also singular, *e.g.* Is. 26. 1. So מֶרְכָּבָה *a chariot*, Gen. 41. 43 with מֶרְכָּב 1 K. 5. 6. Perhaps פְּשִׁתָּה *wick*, Is. 42. 3; 43. 17, cf. Hos. 2. 7, 11, *flax*.

Rem. 1. Sometimes when a parallel is seen in lifeless things to some organ or feature of living creatures the fem. is used, as יָרֵךְ *the thigh*, *loins* (sing. and plur.), יַרְכְתַיִם *the sides*, furthest back parts, of a locality ; מֵצַח *forehead, front*, מִצְחָה *shin-front, greave*. And in a wider way, יוֹנֵק *suckling*, *child*, יוֹנֶקֶת *sucker, shoot*. So such words as *horns, feet* when transferred to things are used in plur. with fem. termination.

Rem. 2. The fem. is used where other languages would use the neut., *e.g.* זֹאת *this*, שְׁתֵּי אֵלֶּה *these two things*, Is. 47. 9; אַחַת מֵהֵנָּה *one of these things*, 1 Chr. 21. 10; particularly in ref. to something previously mentioned, Is. 22. 11; 37. 26; 41. 20; 43. 13; 46. 11; 47. 7; 48. 16; 60. 22. See § 109, R. 2. Occasionally the plur. seems used as a neut., where fem. might have stood, Job 22. 21 בָּהֶם=בָּה *thereby*. Ez. 33. 18, Is. 30. 6. The passages Is. 38. 16; 64. 4 are obscure.

NUMBER

§ 15. Of the three numbers the *dual* is now little used. On its use cf. Gr. § 16, R. *a*.

The plur. of compound expressions like בֵּית אָב *a father-house* or *clan*, גִּבּוֹר חַיִל *a man of valour* (wealth), is formed variously.

1. בֵּית אָבוֹת plur. of second.   1 S. 31. 9 בֵּית עֲצַבֵּיהֶם
their idol temples.   1 K. 12. 31, 2 K. 17. 29, 32, Mic. 2. 9,
Dan. 11. 15, Ps. 120. 1, &c. שִׁיר הַמַּעֲלוֹת?

2. גִּבּוֹרֵי חַיִל plur. of first.   Jer. 8. 14 עָרֵי הַמִּבְצָר *fenced
cities,* Is. 56. 6 בְּנֵי הַנֵּכָר *strangers,* cf. *v.* 3.   1 S. 22. 7, 1 Chr.
5. 24; 7. 2, 9, 2 Chr. 8. 5; 14. 5.

3. גִּבּוֹרֵי הַחֲיָלִים plur. of both.   Gen. 42. 35 צְרֹרוֹת
כַּסְפֵּיהֶם *their bundles of money.*   1 K. 13. 32 בָּתֵּי הַבָּמוֹת.
1 K. 15. 20, 2 K. 9. 1 (cf. sing. Am. 7. 14); 23. 19; 25. 23, 26,
Is. 42. 22, Jer. 5. 17; 40. 7, Mic. 1. 16, 1 Chr. 5. 24; 7. 5, 7,
11, 40.   Cf. Neh. 10. 37.

§ 16. Many words are used only in plur.   (*a*) Such words
as express the idea of something composed of parts, *e.g.* of
several features, as פָּנִים *face,* צַוָּארִים *neck* (also sing.), or of
tracts of space or time, שָׁמַיִם *heaven,* מַיִם *water,* עֲבָרִים
region on the other side, Is. 7. 20; חַיִּים *life,* עוֹלָמִים *eternity,*
Is. 45. 17, נְצָחִים *id.,* נְעוּרִים *time of youth,* זְקֻנִים *time of old
age,* &c.   Comp. סְפָרִים *a letter* (also sing.), 2 K. 20. 12, Jer.
29. 25.

(*b*) Abstract nouns.   As סַנְוֵרִים *blindness,* בְּתוּלִים
virginity, מֵישָׁרִים *uprightness,* כִּפֻּרִים *atonement,* זְנוּנִים
whoredom, שִׁלֻּמִים *requital,* תַּהְפֻּכוֹת *perversity,* &c.   The
plur. in this case may express the idea of a combination of
the elements or characteristics composing the thing, or of
the acts realising it.

(*c*) The plur. of *eminence* or excellence (majesty) also
expresses an intensification of the idea of the sing.; *e.g.*
אֱלֹהִים *God,* and analogically קְדוֹשִׁים *Holy One,* Hos. 12. 1,
Pr. 30. 3, עֶלְיוֹנִים *Most High,* Dan. 7. 18; so ptcp. referring
to God, Is. 54. 5, Ps. 149. 2, Job 35. 10.   Similar words are
אֲדֹנִים *lord, master,* בְּעָלִים *owner,* cf. Is. 10. 15, Pr. 10. 26.
So תְּרָפִים *Teraphim,* even of one image.   On the consn.
of such plur. cf. § 31, and § 116, R. 4.

§ 17. Many words in sing. have a collective meaning, and do duty for the plur., as בָּקָר cattle, צֹאן sheep, goats, טַף children, רֶמֶשׂ creeping things, עוֹף birds, בְּהֵמָה cattle, beasts, &c., רֶכֶב chariots. Almost any word may be used in the sing. as collective, as אִישׁ men, נֶפֶשׁ persons, עֵץ trees, Gen. 3. 8, שׁוֹר oxen, Gen. 49. 6, אַרְבֶּה locusts, עִיר cities, אֶבֶן stones. 1 K. 22. 47 הַקָּדֵשׁ hierodouli, 2 K. 11. 10 הַחֲנִית spears (beside a plur.), 2 K. 25. 1. 1 K. 16. 11 רֵעֵהוּ his comrades (beside a plur.), 1 Chr. 20. 8. Particularly in enumerations, where the emphasis is on the number, and it is sufficient to state the *kind* or class of thing enumerated, *e.g.* חָלָל slain, 2 S. 23. 8, נַעֲרָה בְתוּלָה *young virgins*, Jud. 21. 12, מֶלֶךְ kings, 1 K. 20. 1 (more usual Jud. 1. 7), גֶּפֶן vines, Is. 7. 23, מָשָׁל proverbs, 1 K. 5. 12 ; and expressions like עֹשֵׂה מִלְחָמָה *warriors*, 2 Chr. 26. 13, רֹעֵה צֹאן Gen. 47. 3, cf. 2 K. 24. 14, הַסַּבָּל *the burden bearers*, Neh. 4. 4 (1 K. 5. 29 *rd.* perhaps סֵבֶל). It is, however, chiefly words that express *classes* of persons or things that are used in the sing., and words of *time, weight,* and *measure.* Cf. § 37.

Rem. 1. The plur. is quite natural in such instances as עֵצִים *timber* (pieces of wood), חִטִּים *wheat in grain*, 2 S. 17. 28 (חִטָּה *wheat in crop*, Ex. 9. 32). So שְׂעֹרִים and שְׂעֹרָה *barley*, &c.

Rem. 2. The plur. seems often used to heighten the idea of the sing., 1 S. 2. 3 דֵּעוֹת *knowledge*, Jud. 11. 36 *vengeance*, 2 S. 4. 8, Is. 27. 11 *understanding*, 40. 14 ; Ps. 16. 11 *joy*, Ps. 49. 4 ; 76. 11 ; 88. 9 *abomination*, Pr. 28. 20, Job 36. 4. Cf. § 16*b*. In poetry the plur. comes to be used for sing. without difference of meaning, Gen. 49. 4 *bed* sing. and plur., 1 Chr. 5. 1, Ps. 63. 7 ; 46. 5 ; 132. 5, Job 6. 3 (seas).

Rem. 3. The plur. is sometimes used to express the idea in a general and indefinite way. Jud. 12. 7 בְּעָרֵי גִלְעָד *in* (one of) *the cities* of Gilead, 1 S. 17. 43 *staves*, 2 K. 22. 20 *thy graves*, Job 17. 1, Gen. 21. 7, Ex. 21. 22, Zech. 9. 9, Neh. 6. 2. The word דִּבְרֵי *matters of* seems to convey the same meaning, Ps. 65. 4.

Rem. 4. Such words as *hand, head, mouth, voice,* &c., when the organ or thing is common to a number of persons, are generally used in the sing. Jud. 7. 16 put the trumpets into *the hand* of them all, *v.* 19, Gen. 19. 10. Jud. 7. 25 the *head* of Oreb and Zeeb, cf. 8. 28; 9. 57, Jos. 7. 6, Dan. 3. 27. Ps. 17. 10 *their mouth,* Ps. 78. 36 *tongue,* 144. 8. So to clap כַּף *the hands* 2 K. 11. 12, Is. 55. 12. So perhaps נְבֵלָה and פֶּגֶר *carcases,* Is. 5. 25, 1 S. 17. 46, cf. πτῶμα Rev. 11. 8. But cf. *heads* Job 2. 12, and usually *eyes,* though cf. Gen. 44. 21.

Rem. 5. The idea of universality is sometimes expressed by the use of both genders, Is. 3. 1 מַשְׁעֵן וּמַשְׁעֵנָה *every stay,* Deu. 7. 14. Also by the use of contrasted expressions, as Zech. 7. 14 עֹבֵר וָשָׁב *passing* or *returning,* 9. 8, and the common עָצוּר וְעָזוּב *restrained* or *free,* Deu. 32. 36, 1 K. 14. 10; 21. 21, 2 K. 9. 8; 14. 26. Cf. Noeld. *Carm. Arab.* 42. 4.

Rem. 6. The coll. בקר *cattle* is used in plur. Neh. 10. 37, but צֹאנֵנוּ is to be read in same verse. The parall. to 2 Chr. 4. 3, viz. 1 K. 7. 24, reads differently. Plur. of רכב *chariots,* Song. 1. 9. In Am. 6. 12 *rd.* perhaps בַּבָּקָר יָם.

THE CASES

§ 18. The cases are not marked by means of terminations except in rare instances. They must be supposed, however, to exist, and an accurate analysis of construction will take them into account. The cases are three, Nom., Gen., and Acc. When a word is governed by prep. לְ *to,* the dative is sometimes spoken of, and the abl. when it is governed by prep. מִן *from,* &c.; but this is inaccurate application of classical terminology.

1. *The Nom.*—The nom. has no particular termination (Gr. § 17). The personal pronouns are only used in nom., their oblique cases appearing as suffixes. The nom. is often *pendens,* being resumed by pronoun (§ 106).

2. *The Gen.*—(*a*) All words after a cons. state are in gen.,

as סוּס הָאִישׁ *the man's* horse. (*b*) All words governed by a prep. are in gen., as לְרוּחַ הַיּוֹם *at the cool* of the day; *cool* is gen. by prep., and *day* is gen. by *cool*. (*c*) All suffixes to nouns and prep. are to be considered in gen., as סוּסוֹ *his* horse (h. of him), אֶצְלָהּ beside *her* (at the side of her). (*d*) Sometimes a clause assumes the place of a gen. to a preceding noun, the clause being equivalent to the infin. or *nomen actionis.* Is. 29. 1 קִרְיַת חָנָה דָוִד *thou city* where David dwelt (of David's dwelling).

3. *The Acc.*—There are traces of a case ending in *a*. (*a*) The acc. may be directly governed by a verb, וַיִּקַּח אֶת־הָאָדָם he took *the man.* The verbal suffixes are usually direct obj., וַיַּנִּחֵהוּ and put *him.* (*b*) The acc. may be of the kind called adverbial or modal, as in designations of place, time, &c., in statements of the *condition* of subj. or obj. during an action, or in limitations of the incidence of an action, or the extent of the application of a quality (§ 70, § 24, R. 5). (*c*) So-called prepp. like אַחֲרֵי *behind*, אֵצֶל *beside*, &c., are really nouns in this kind of acc., except when preceded by another prep., as מֵאַחֲרֵי *from behind*, when, of course, they are in the gen. (*d*) Many times clauses with כִּי *that*, אֶת־אֲשֶׁר ,אֲשֶׁר *how that*, assume the place of a virtual acc. to a preceding verb.

4. The *construct* is not a case but a state of the noun. The cons. is the governing noun in a genitive-relation; its state or difference of form from the abs. or ordinary form is due to the closeness of the connection between it and its gen. The cons. may be in any case, as *nom.* וּזֲהַב הָאָרֶץ הַהִיא טוֹב *and the gold* of that land *is good ;* or gen. בְּתוֹךְ הַגָּן *in the midst* of the garden, where *midst* is gen. by prep.; or acc. לִשְׁמֹר דֶּרֶךְ עֵץ הַחַיִּים *to keep the way* of the tree of life, where *way* is acc. after *keep*, and cons. before its gen. *tree*, &c.

The cons. occasionally ends in *i*, more rarely in *o* or *u*. In Eth. the vowel *a* marks the cons.

DETERMINATION. THE ARTICLE

§ 19. There is no indef. art. in Heb., the noun if indef. remains without change.   Job 1. 1 אִישׁ הָיָה there was *a man*.   1 K. 3. 24 קְחוּ־לִי חֶרֶב fetch me *a sword*.

The predicate naturally is indeterminate and without Art. Gen. 3. 1 הַנָּחָשׁ הָיָה עָרוּם the serpent was *cunning*.   2. 12, 25 ; 3. 6 ; 29. 2, 2 S. 18. 7.   The inf. or *nomen actionis* retains too much of the verbal nature to admit the Art.   Occasionally הַדַּעַת *the knowing* occurs.   Gen. 2. 9, Jer. 22. 16.   And *fem.* verbal nouns approach more closely the real noun, and occasionally take Art.   Ps. 139. 12 כַּחֲשֵׁכָה כָּאוֹרָה *the darkness* is as *the light*.

Rem. 1. The numeral אֶחָד *one* is sometimes used almost like an indef. art., esp. in later style.   Ex. 16. 33, 1 S. 7. 9, 12, 1 K. 19. 4 ; 22. 9, 2 K. 7. 8 ; 8. 6.   Or it has the sense of *a certain* ; Jud. 9. 53 ; 13. 2, 1 S. 1. 1, 1 K. 13. 11, 2 K. 4. 1.   The words אִישׁ *man*, אִשָּׁה *woman* prefixed to another term appear to express indefiniteness, אִישׁ נביא *a prophet*, Jud. 6. 8 ; 4. 4, 2 S. 14. 5 ; 15. 16, 1 K. 3. 16 ; 7. 14 ; 17. 9. Eth. uses *man, woman* in the same way.

---

[1] The inflection of an Ar. noun ‘*abd* “servant” may illustrate the cases.

SING.

	Abs.	with Art.	Cons. and Gen.
N.	‘abd*un* a serv.	’el ‘abd*u* the ser.	‘abd*u* lmalik*i* the s. of the king.
G.	‘abd*in*	’el ‘abd*i*	‘abd*i* lmalik*i*.
A.	‘abd*an*	’el ‘abd*a*	‘abd*a* lmalik*i*.

DUAL.

N.	‘abd*âni*	’el ‘abd*âni*	‘abd*â* lmalik*i*.
G.A.	abd*aini*	’el ‘abd*aini*	‘abd*ayi* lmalik*i*

PLURAL.

N.	‘abd*ûna*	’el ‘abd*ûna*	‘abd*û* lmalik*i*.
G.A.	‘abd*îna*	’el ‘abd*îna*	‘abd*î* lmalik*i*.

The regular plur. given here to ‘*abd* does not exist in usage.   After a vowel both the Alif and the vowel of the Art. are elided in pronunciation.

Rem. 2. The inf. לָמוּט is probably strengthened form of לָמוּט Ps. 66. 9; 121. 3. In 1 K. 10. 19 שֶׁבֶת seems a noun, Am. 6. 3. Jer. 5. 13 הַדִּבֵּר the Art. might be relative, either *he who* speaks, or *that which* he speaks (§ 22, R. 4), both little natural. Scarcely more likely, *the* " He has said " (the phrase they use). Sep. הַדְּבָר.

Rem. 3. In some cases the subj. and pred. are *coextensive*, and pred. has Art. Gen. 2. 11 הוּא הַסֹּבֵב *it is that which goeth round*. Particularly with ptcps. Gen. 42. 6 *he* was *the seller;* 45. 12, Deu. 3. 21; 8. 18; 9. 3, 2 S. 5. 2, 1 Chr. 11. 2.

Rem. 4. Certain archaic terms, originally appellatives, have acquired the force of proper names, as שְׁאוֹל *hades*, תֵּבֵל *the* inhabited *world*, תְּהוֹם *the* primary *ocean* (plur. with Art. Is. 63. 13, of waters of Red Sea, Ps. 106. 9), and do not take Art. And so some other terms used in poetry, which greatly dispenses with the Art., as רוֹזְנִים *princes*, Ps. 2. 2, אֱנוֹשׁ *man*, Ps. 8. 5, שָׂדַי *field*, Ps. 8. 8, צַלְמָוֶת *darkness, midnight*, Ps. 23. 4, תּוּשִׁיָּה *wisdom, power*, Is. 28. 29, Job 6. 13. Also רְאֵם *wild ox*, even in a comparison, Ps. 92. 11. So the divine names עֶלְיוֹן, שַׁדַּי, אֱלֹהַּ.

§ 20. Words may be determinate in themselves or from construction, and with these the Art. is not used. Words def. of themselves are—(*a*) *Proper* names of persons, countries, cities, rivers, &c., as יהוה *Jehovah*, מֹשֶׁה *Moses*, מוֹאָב *Moab*, צֹר *Tyre*, פְּרָת *Euphrates*. (*b*) The personal and other pronouns, Ex. 20. 2 אָנֹכִי יהוה *I* am the Lord, Gen. 29. 27 שְׁבַע זֹאת the week of *this one*, 41. 28 הוּא הַדָּבָר *that* is the thing, 3. 11 מִי הִגִּיד *who* told thee?—Words determined by construction are—nouns in the cons. state before a *definite* gen., whether this gen. be a proper name, a pron. (separate or suffix), a noun defined by Art., or itself a cons. determined by a definite gen. (Gen. 3. 24). Ru. 1. 3 אִישׁ נָעֳמִי *the* husband of Naomi. Gen. 24. 23 בַּת מִי אַתְּ *the* daughter of whom (whose d.) art thou? 2. 25 הָאָדָם וְאִשְׁתּוֹ the man and *his wife*. 2. 19 חַיַּת הַשָּׂדֶה *the* beast of

the field.   3. 24 דֶּרֶךְ עֵץ הַחַיִּים the way of the tree of life,
6. 18 נְשֵׁי בָנֶיךָ.

Rem. 1. Proper names of persons are always without
the Art., and so names of peoples called after a personal
ancestor, as Moab, Edom.   Many names of places, rivers,
&c., however, were originally appellatives and sometimes
retain the Art., as הַלְּבָנוֹן Lebanon (the white mountain?),
הַיַּרְדֵּן Jordan (the river?), הַגִּבְעָה Gibeah (the hill), הָעַי Ai (the
mound).   Usage fluctuates.

Rem. 2. The def. gen. makes the whole expression definite.   But this rule seems to have exceptions, the cons.
remaining indef.   This is the case at any rate with prop.
names, as 1 S. 4. 12 אִישׁ בִּנְיָמִין a man of Benjamin, Josh.
7. 21 a Babylonish garment, Jud. 10. 1, Deu. 22. 19, and
apparently in other cases, Lev. 14. 34 a house, Gen. 9. 20,
Jer. 13. 4.   It is to be assumed in general, however, that
the def. gen. determines the whole expression.   Thus Heb.
may say הַזָּהָב the gold (so called generic Art. § 22), i.e.
gold, and so Gen. 41. 42 רְבִד הַזָּהָב the chain of the gold, i.e.
a chain of gold; the kind of definiteness, whatever it be,
extends over the expression.   Song 1. 13, 14; 4. 3.   Cf.
1 S. 25. 36 מִשְׁתֵּה הַמֶּלֶךְ the banquet of the king, i.e. a royal
banquet; Jud. 8. 18 royal children.   The use of Art. fluctuates, Song 1. 11, 13.

Rem. 3. In compound proper names the Art. maintains
its usual place.   1 S. 5. 1 אֶבֶן הָעֵזֶר Ebenezer.   And so with
gentilics, Jud. 6. 11, 24 אֲבִי הָעֶזְרִי the Abiezrite, 1 S. 17. 58
בֵּית הַלַּחְמִי the Bethlehemite.   6. 14.

Rem. 4. A number of cases occur of Art. with cons. or
noun with suff.   (a) In some cases the text is faulty, being
filled up by explanatory glosses from the marg.   Gen. 24. 67
omit Sarah his mother.   Jos. 3. 11 om. הברית, so v. 14, and
v. 17 ברית י'.   Jos. 8. 11 om. war (13. 5, cf. § 29, R. 5).
Jer. 25. 26 rd. הממלכות abs. and om. earth (Sep.), Ez. 45. 16
om. earth (Sep.).   Jer. 32. 12 הַסֵּפֶר הַמִּקְנָה can hardly be
appos. the bill, the sale; probably ungrammatical explicitum
from marg. for it of Sep.   1 Chr. 15. 27 rd. probably בַּמַּשָּׂא
וְהַשֹּׁעֲרִים (Berth.), cf. vv. 22, 23.   2 Chr. 8. 16 cf. Ex. 9. 18,

2 S. 19. 25. Is. 36. 8, 16 הַמֶלֶךְ אַשּׁוּר is correct in 2 K. 18. 23, 31, and hardly belongs to the original text. Jer. 48. 32 הַגֶּפֶן שִׂבְמָה is *voc.* and perhaps protected by Lam. 2. 13 הַבַּת ירושלם; otherwise Is. 16. 9.—1 S. 26. 22, 2 K. 7. 13 are corrected by Mass. More serious faults of text, 2 S. 24. 5 (Dr. *in loc.*), Ez. 46. 19, Dan. 8. 13.

(*b*) Jos. 13. 9 " Medeba unto Dibon " is appos. to *the Mishor*, explaining it. Ez. 47. 15 might be the way *to* Hethlon, cf. Hos. 6. 9, but text dubious. Gen. 31. 13 אנכי האל בית־אל can hardly be, I am the God *at* Bethel (acc.). Cases like 2 S. 2. 32; 9. 4, &c., are not parallel, and Num. 22. 5 is no doubt to be read: the river (Euph.), *unto* the land of the children, &c. 2 K. 23. 17 (possibly הוּא קֶבֶר). 1 K. 14. 24, Art. may have slipped in mechanically after כל. Jud. 16. 14 possibly הָאָרֶג, חִיתֶד being subsequent gloss. Ezr. 8. 29 perhaps הַלְּשָׁכוֹת, " house of God " being in loose appos., and " weigh " a virtual verb of motion (carry to and weigh). Ps. 123. 4 (לַשְׁאֲנַנִּים? as second clause). Nu. 21. 14, 2 S. 10. 7, 1 K. 16. 24, &c., are cases of appos.

With suff. Lev. 27. 23 הָעֶרְכְּךָ, the phrase is technical and suff. otiose. Jos. 8. 33 הַחֶצְיוֹ *the* (other) half of it. Is. 24. 2 כַּגְּבִרְתָּהּ in assonance with the other words. Mic. 2. 12 possibly הַדֹּבֵר וּתְ'. 2 K. 15. 16 after כל. Jos. 7. 21, Pr. 16. 4, Ezr. 10. 14.

§ 21. Determination by Art.—With individual persons or things the Art. is used when they are *known*, and definite to the mind for any reason, *e.g.*—

(*a*) From having been already mentioned. Gen. 18. 7 בֶּן־הַבָּקָר וַיִּקַּח בֶּן־בָּקָר he took *a* calf; *v.* 8 he took אֲשֶׁר עָשָׂה בֶּן־הַבָּקָר *the* calf which he had got ready.

(*b*) Or from being the only one of their kind, as הַשֶּׁמֶשׁ *the* sun, הַיָּרֵחַ *the* moon; *the* earth, *the* high priest, *the* king, &c.

(*c*) Or, though not the only one of the class, when usage has elevated into distinctive prominence a particular individual of the class, as הַנָּהָר *the* river (Euphrates) הַבַּעַל

the lord (Baal), הַשָּׂטָן *the* adversary (Satan), Job 1. 6, Zech. 3. 1, הַיְאֹר *the* stream (Nile, cf. Am. 8. 8, the stream of Egypt), הַכִּכָּר *the* circle (of Jordan), הַבַּיִת *the* house (Temple), Mic. 3. 12, Ps. 30. 1, הָאֱלֹהִים *the* (true) God.

(*d*) Or when the person or thing is an *understood* element or feature in the situation or circumstances. Gen. 24. 20, she emptied her pail אֶל־הַשֹּׁקֶת into *the trough* (of course existing where there were flocks to water). 35. 17 וַתֹּאמֶר הַמְיַלֶּדֶת and *the midwife* (naturally present) said, 38. 28. So 18. 7 *the boy*; 22. 6 *the fire* and *the knife*; 26. 8 *the window.* Ex. 2. 15 *the* well (beside every encampment). Jud. 3. 25 *the* key. 1 S. 19. 13, 2 S. 18. 24, Pr. 7. 19 *the* goodman. Eng. also uses the def. Art. in such cases; at other times it employs the unemphatic possessive pron. Gen. 24. 64, she lighted מֵעַל הַגָּמָל from *her camel*; *v.* 65 she took הַצָּעִיף *her veil*; 47. 31 *his bed.* Jud. 3. 20, 2 S. 19. 27, 1 K. 13. 13, 27, 2 K. 5. 21.

(*e*) It is a peculiar extension of this usage when, in narratives particularly, persons or things appear definite to the imagination of the speaker—the person just from the part he played, and the thing from the use made of it. In this case Eng. uses the indef. Art. 2 S. 17. 17 וְהָלְכָה הַשִּׁפְחָה וְהִגִּידָה and *a wench* always went and told them. 1 S. 9. 9 כֹּה אָמַר הָאִישׁ thus spoke *a man* when he went, &c. Jos. 2. 15 וַתּוֹרִדֵם בַּחֶבֶל and she let them down with *a rope.* Ex. 17. 14 כְּתֹב זֹאת בַּסֵּפֶר write this in *a book*; 1 S. 10. 25, Jer. 32. 10, Job 19. 23.—Deu. 15. 17, Ex. 21. 20 with *a rod*, Nu. 22. 27, Jos. 8. 29 on *a tree*, Jud. 4. 18 *a* rug, *v.* 21 *a* tent-pin, *v.* 19 *a* milk bottle, 6. 38 *a* cupful, 9. 48; 16. 21 (3. 31?). So probably Is. 7. 14 הָעַלְמָה *a maid.* Gen. 9. 23 *a* garment (less naturally *his, i.e.* Noah's). Deu. 22. 17, Jud. 8. 25, 1 S. 21. 10 (some passages may belong to *d*). So with rel. cl. Ps. 1. 1, Jer. 49. 36.

(*f*) The person addressed is naturally def. to the mind, and the so-called vocative often has the Art. 1 K. 18. 26 הַבַּעַל עֲנֵנוּ *O Baal*, hear us! 2 K. 9. 5 אֵלֶיךָ הַשָּׂר unto thee, *Captain*! Jud. 6. 12 יְ עִמְּךָ גִּבּוֹר הֶחָיִל Je. is with thee, *O man of valour*. Jud. 3. 19, 1 S. 17. 58, 2 S. 14. 4, Hos. 5. 1, Jer. 2. 31, Is. 42. 18, Jo. 1. 2, Zech. 3. 8. The noun with Art. is probably in appos. to *thou, ye* understood. Cf. Job 19. 21, Mal. 3. 9, Mic. 1. 2.—2 K. 9. 31, Is. 22. 16; 47. 8; 54. 1, 11, Zeph. 2. 12.

Rem. 1. In such cases as הַיּוֹם *to-day*, הַלַּיְלָה *to-night*, הַפַּעַם *this time*, Gen. 2. 23, הַשָּׁנָה *this year* Jer. 28. 16, the definiteness is due to the fact that the times belong to the speaker's present and are before him. Jud. 13. 10 בַּיּוֹם *that* (a former) *day* is defined by the circumstance that occurred on it.

Rem. 2. To *e* belongs the phrase וַיְהִי הַיּוֹם occurring 1 S. 1. 4; 14. 1, 2 K. 4. 8, 11, 18, Job 1. 6, 13; 2. 1. Probably: and it fell *on a day* (lit. *the* day, viz. that on which it fell, &c.). Others make הַיּוֹם *subj.*, and *the day was*, *i.e.* there fell *a day*. The vav impf. following is less natural on this view, but the explanation of Art. is the same.—Gen. 28. 11 *a* place prob. belongs to *e*; it is hardly *heilige Stätte* (like Ar. maqam) either here or 2 K. 5. 11.

§ 22. It is on the same principle as in § 21 that classes of persons, creatures, or things have the Art. The classes are *known* just from the fact of their having distinct characteristics. But, further, in such cases the individual possesses all the characteristics which distinguish the class, and the class is seen in any individual. Hence the use of the *sing.* is common.

(*a*) The sing. of gentilic nouns is so used, as Gen. 13. 7 הַכְּנַעֲנִי *the* Canaanite, 15. 21. Of course also the plur. with Art., rarely without, though פְּלִשְׁתִּים Philistines, is more common; cf. 2 S. 21. 12.

(*b*) So adjectives and ptcps., as הַצַּדִּיק *the righteous*,

הָרָשָׁע *the wicked.* Ptcp., Jos. 8. 19 הָאוֹרֵב *the ambush,* 1 S.
13. 17 הַמַּשְׁחִית *the active warriors,* Gen. 14. 13 הַפָּלִיט *the
fugitive* (if these do not belong to § 21 *e,* and be defined by
the action they perform). The Art. is frequently omitted in
poetry. Here also *plur.* is common. Ps. 1. 4–6.

(*c*) The various classes of creatures, as Gen. 8. 7 הָעֹרֵב
a raven, v. 8 *a* dove. Esp. in comparisons. Jud. 14. 6 כְּשַׁסַּע
הַגְּדִי *as one rends a* kid. 2 S. 17. 10 כְּלֵב הָאַרְיֵה *like the
heart of a* lion. Ps. 33. 17 שֶׁקֶר הַסּוּס לִתְשׁוּעָה *a horse* is
vain for deliverance. So Ecc. 7. 26 הָאִשָּׁה *a* woman
(*i.e.* women). 1 S. 26. 20 *a* partridge, Jud. 7. 5 as *a* dog
laps, 1 S. 17. 34, Am. 3. 12; 5. 19. 2 K. 8. 13 מָה עַבְדְּךָ
הַכֶּלֶב *what is thy servant, the dog* (thy dog of a s.)?

(*d*) So other well-known objects, such as the precious
metals and stones, and, in general, any well-known article,
though usage fluctuates here; Gen. 2. 11 אֲשֶׁר שָׁם הַזָּהָב
where there is gold. Am. 2. 6, Gen. 13. 2, 2 Chron. 2. 13, 14.
Gen. 11. 3 *the* brick, *the* asphalt, *the* mortar. 1 K. 10. 27,
Is. 28. 7.

(*e*) And, in general, in comparisons—the thing to which
comparison is made naturally being known and distinct
before the mind. Is. 1. 18 אִם־יִהְיוּ חֲטָאֵיכֶם כַּשָּׁנִים כַּשֶּׁלֶג
יַלְבִּינוּ *if your sins be like crimson,* they shall be white
like snow. 10. 14 וַתִּמְצָא כַקֵּן יָדִי *and my hand hath found
like a nest* the wealth of the nations. Nu. 11. 12, Jud. 16. 9,
1 K. 14. 15, 2 S. 17. 3, Hos. 6. 4, Deu. 1. 44, Is. 34. 4; 51. 8;
53. 6, 7, Mic. 4. 12. See the exx. in *c.*

Rem. 1. Any object or thing well known receives the
Art., *e.g.* affections or diseases, Gen. 19. 11 הַסַּנְוֵרִים *blindness,* Zech. 12. 4 *madness,* &c., 2 S. 1. 9 הַשָּׁבָץ *dizziness?*
Lev. 13. 12 *leprosy.* So plagues, calamities, as *blasting,
mildew,* &c. Am. 4. 9, Hag. 2. 17, Deu. 28. 21, 22, cf. Ex.
5. 3, 2 K. 6. 18. So moral qualities as *faithfulness* Is. 11.
5, &c. Also physical elements as *fire* in the frequent *burn*

בָּאֵשׁ *with fire*, &c.; *darkness* Is. 9. 1.   In all these cases, however, usage fluctuates, the Art. being most frequent with prefixed prep.

Rem. 2. In comparisons use of Art. fluctuates.   But generally: when the thing to which comparison is made stands simply the Art. is used (see exx. in § 22 *e*); and so when a clause follows which merely states or explains the point in the comparison, Ps. 1. 4; 49. 13, Is. 61. 10, 11, Hos. 6. 4.   But when an epithet or clause is added which describes the object not generally but in a particular aspect or condition, the Art. is not used.   Is. 13. 14; 16. 2; 29. 5; 41. 2, Hos. 2. 5; 4. 16.   The usage fluctuates particularly in poetry.

Rem. 3. Poetry often omits Art. where prose would use it, Ps. 2. 2, 8, 10 מַלְכֵי אֶרֶץ kings of *the earth*, 72. 17 לִפְנֵי שֶׁמֶשׁ before *the sun*, *v.* 5, 7.   So in archaic or semi-poetical phrases like *earth and heaven* Gen. 2. 4, Ps. 148. 13, Gen. 14. 19; *beast of the earth* Gen. 1. 24, cf. Ps. 50. 10; 104. 11, 20, Is. 56. 9.   In prose also the Art. is omitted with expressions familiar, Ex. 27. 21 אֹהֶל מוֹעֵד *tent of meeting* (as we say "to church," cf. John 6. 59 ἐν συναγωγῇ), 1 K. 16. 16 שַׂר צָבָא *commander in chief*.   So *king*, 1 K. 21. 10, 13 to curse God *and king*, cf. 1 K. 16. 18, Am. 7. 13.   Gen. 24. 11 לְעֵת עֶרֶב *at evening time*, Deu. 11. 12 *to year's end*, 4. 47.   Also such words as *head, hand, foot, face, mouth*.   Is. 37. 22 shake ראֹשׁ *the head*, Mic. 7. 16 יד עַל־פֶּה put *the hand upon the mouth*.   Job 21. 5, Pr. 11. 21; 16. 5.   Gen. 32. 31 *face to face*, Nu. 12. 8 *mouth to mouth*.   2 S. 23. 6 בְּיָד *with the hand*, Is. 28. 2, Neh. 13. 21, 2 Chr. 25. 20.   Is. 1. 6 from *foot-sole to head*.   Jer. 2. 27 to turn עֹרֶף *the back*.   The words *heart, soul, eyes*, &c., when in gen. by an adj., usually want the Art. Ps. 7. 11 upright *of heart*.   Is. 24. 7, Ps. 95. 10 (Deu. 20. 6 Art.).   Ps. 101. 5, Job 3. 20, Jud. 18. 25, cf. Ps. 37. 14, Job 30. 25.

In particular the word כֹל before such words without Art. may mean *all, the whole*.   Is. 1. 5 כָּל־ראֹשׁ *the whole head*, 9. 11 *the whole mouth*, 2 K. 23. 3 the *whole heart . . . soul*, Ez. 36. 5.   And even in other cases, Is. 28. 8 *all tables*.   So phrases like כָּל־חַי *all living*, כָל־בָּשָׂר *all flesh*.—The phrase

פֹּעֲלֵי אָוֶן is usually anarthrous (Ps. 125. 5 Art.). And certain terms are used with a kind of technical brevity, *e.g.* גְּבוּל *boundary*, Jos. 13. 23, *breadth*, &c. (in measurements), 2 Chr. 3. 3. So "gate," "court," &c. (§ 32, R. 2). Cf. Mal. 1. 10, 11.

Rem. 4. In later writings particularly the Art. is used like a rel. pron., as subj. or obj. to a verb and with prep. Jos. 10. 24, 1 Chr. 26, 28 ; 29, 8. 17, 2 Chr. 1. 4 (older usage Jud. 5. 27, Ru. 1. 16), 29. 36, Ezr. 8. 25 ; 10. 14, 17 (Jud. 13. 8 might be ptcp. without *m.*). Ez. 26. 17 also as accented is perf.

The art. with ptcp. is usual (§ 99), and a number of cases accented as perf. of י"ע verbs are certainly *fem. ptcp.*, how-ever the accentuation is to be explained, *e.g.* Gen. 18. 21 their cry הַבָּאָה *which is come* ; 46. 27, Is. 51. 10, Ru. 1. 22 ; 4. 3. Gen. 21. 3 הַנּוֹלַד־לוֹ is ptcp. 1 K. 11. 9, Is. 56. 3 are also probably ptcps., and should be so pointed, unless the pointing is to be explained as following the type of ל"א verb, cf. 1 K. 17. 14 תִּכְלֶה. Dan. 8. 1 being late is doubtful. 1 S. 9. 24 for הֶעָלֶיהָ *that which is upon it, rd.* probably הָאַלְיָה *the* (fat) *tail* (Hitz. הֶעָלֶיהָ as imp. hiph.?). Jos. 10. 24 is anomalous in spelling, and possibly should be read הַהֹלְכִים.—Ar. occa-sionally joins Art. to finite verb, the ass *alyujadda'u which has its ears cut off.* Of course it is said that Art. is for *alladhi* the rel.

THE GENITIVE. CONSTRUCT

§ 23. In the compound expression formed by the Gen. and the preceding cons. state, as בֶּן־הַמֶּלֶךְ *the son of the king*, the first word is hurriedly passed over, and con-sequently shortened where possible (Gr. § 17), and the accent falls on the last half of the expression. The first half of the expression is called in Oriental grammar *the annexed*, the second half *that to which annexion is made*, and the relation between them *annexion*.

The gen. may be a noun (subst. or adj.), a pronoun, or a clause. The cons. must be a noun (subst. or adj.). The use

of the gen. is very wide. It expresses almost any relation
between two nouns, corresponding often to the semi-
adjectival use of nouns in our own language, as tree-fruit,
fruit-tree, seed-corn, water-pot, except that the order of
words is reversed, fruit of tree, tree of fruit, &c. The gen.
may be said to be either gen. of the *subject* or gen. of the
object, and this distinction applies to pron. suffixes, which are
also in the gen. Gen. 27. 41 יְמֵי אֵבֶל אָבִי the days of
mourning for my father; 3. 24 דֶּרֶךְ עֵץ הַחַיִּים the way *to
the tree* of life; 42. 19 שֶׁבֶר רַעֲבוֹן בָּתֵּיכֶם *corn* (needful) *for
the famine* of your houses; 2 S. 8. 10 אִישׁ מִלְחֲמוֹת תֹּעִי
engaged in *wars with Toi*; Is. 9. 6 קִנְאַת י׳ תַּעֲשֶׂה־זֹּאת
the zeal of Je. will do this; 26. 11 יֶחֱזוּ קִנְאַת־עָם they shall
see thy *zeal for the people* (Ps. 69. 10). Gen. 16. 5 חֲמָסִי
עָלֶיךָ *my wrong* (that done me) be on thee; 29. 13 שֵׁמַע
יַעֲקֹב the news *about Jacob* (2 S. 4. 4). Is. 32. 2 סֵתֶר זֶרֶם
a covert *from the rain*. Ps. 60. 10 מוֹאָב סִיר רַחְצִי *Moab* is
my wash-pot. Is. 56. 7 בֵּית תְּפִלָּתִי *my house of prayer*. Gen.
44. 2 כֶּסֶף שִׁבְרוֹ *his corn-money*. Gen. 18. 20, Is. 23. 5, Am.
8. 10, Ob. 10, Hab. 2. 17.

Rem. 1. The gen. of the subject may be (*a*) the *possessor*
of any object, as Jer. 7. 4 הֵיכַל יהוה *the temple of Je.*; Gen.
4. 1 אִשְׁתּוֹ *his wife*. (*b*) The *subject* to which any quality or
attribute belongs, 1 K. 5. 10 חָכְמַת שְׁלֹמֹה the wisdom *of
Solomon*; 10. 9 אַהֲבַת י׳ the love *of Je.* (*c*) The *agent* in any
action, especially after *pass.* ptcp., Is. 53. 4 מֻכֵּה אלהים
stricken *of God*; or the instrument, Is. 22. 2 לֹא חַלְלֵי חֶרֶב וְלֹא
מֵתֵי מִלְחָמָה not slain *by the sword* nor *dead through war*. Cf.
on Particip. § 98. The gen. of the object is the converse
of this, and may be : (*a*) the *possession* of a possessor, Gen.
42. 30 אֲדֹנֵי הארץ the lord *of the country*. (*b*) The *quality* or
attribute belonging to any subject, 1 K. 20. 31 מַלְכֵי חֶסֶד
kings *of clemency*, Is. 30. 18 אֱלֹהֵי מִשְׁפָּט a God *of justice*.
(*c*) The *object* of any action, particularly after active ptcp.,

Isa. 5. 18 מֹשְׁכֵי הֶעָוֹן *dragging on iniquity,* v. 23 מַצְדִּיקֵי רָשָׁע *justifying the wicked.*

§ 24. The genius of the language is not favourable to the formation of adjectives, and the gen. is used in various ways as explicative of the preceding noun, indicating its material, qualities, or relations. (*a*) When the gen. is identical with the cons., merely expressing for ex. its name, as Gen. 2. 15 בַּן־עֵדֶן the *garden of Eden*; 15. 18 נְהַר־פְּרָת the *river of Euphrates*; Is. 41. 14 תּוֹלַעַת יַעֲקֹב thou *worm (of) Jacob*; Is. 37. 22 בַּת יְרוּשָׁלָ͏ם the *daughter of Jerus.* Or the class to which it belongs, Is. 9. 5 פֶּלֶא יוֹעֵץ a *wonder of a counsellor*; Hos. 13. 2 זֹבְחֵי אָדָם *men who sacrifice*; Gen. 16. 12 פֶּרֶא אָדָם a *wild ass of man*; Is. 1. 4 זֶרַע מְרֵעִים a *race of malefactors.* 1 K. 10. 15, Is. 29. 19, Mic. 5. 4, Pr. 15. 20, 2 Chr. 2. 7.

(*b*) When the gen. is the *material*; Gen. 24. 22 נֶזֶם זָהָב a *ring of gold*; Ex. 20. 24 מִזְבַּח אֲדָמָה an *altar of earth.* Gen. 3. 21, Jud. 7. 13, 1 K. 6. 36, Is. 2. 20, Ps. 2. 9. Or the *commodity* or article in measure, weight, or number, Jud. 6. 19 אֵיפַת קֶמַח an *ephah of meal*, Gen. 21. 14, 1 S. 16, 20; 17. 17, Hos. 3. 2.—The consn. by Apposition is very common in this case, § 29. See also the Numerals, §§ 36, 37.

(*c*) When the gen. is an *attribute* or quality, 1 K. 20. 31 מַלְכֵי חֶסֶד *clement* kings; Jud. 11. 1 גִּבּוֹר חַיִל a *valiant hero*; Lev. 19. 36 מֹאזְנֵי צֶדֶק *right* balances; Is. 43. 28 שָׂרֵי קֹדֶשׁ *holy* princes, and very often in later writings. Or more generally: Is. 51. 11 שִׂמְחַת עוֹלָם *everlasting* joy; Zech. 11. 4 צֹאן הַהֲרֵגָה the *flock (destined) for slaughter*; Is. 13. 3 עַלִּיזֵי גַאֲוָתִי my *proud exulters* (Zeph. 3. 11). Is. 13. 8; 22. 2; 28. 4; 32. 2, Ex. 29. 29, Ps. 5. 7; 23. 2, Pr. 1. 9; 5. 19, Zeph. 3. 4. Jer. 20. 17 *with child always.*—The equivalence of this gen. to the adj. appears from the loose constructions, Deu. 25. 15 אֶבֶן שְׁלֵמָה וָצֶדֶק a *full* and *right*

weight; 1 S. 30. 22 כֹּל אִישׁ רָע וּבְלִיַּעַל every *bad* and *worthless* man.

(*d*) Under the explicative gen. may also be classed the gen. of restriction or specification. Adj. and ptcp. are construed with a gen. which specifies the extent or point of their application: Is. 6. 5 אִישׁ טְמֵא־שְׂפָתַיִם a man *unclean of lips*; Ex. 32. 9 עַם־קְשֵׁה־עֹרֶף הוּא they are a *stiffnecked people*; Gen. 24. 16 וְהַנַּעַר טֹבַת מַרְאֶה מְאֹד and the girl was *very pretty*; 2 S. 9. 13 פִּסֵּחַ שְׁתֵּי רַגְלָיו lame *in his two feet*; 1 S. 25. 3 הָאִשָּׁה טוֹבַת שֶׂכֶל וִיפַת תֹּאַר וְהָאִישׁ רַע מַעֲלָלִים the woman was *of great discretion*, and *beautiful in form*, but the man was *evil in his doings*. Gen. 12. 11; 26. 7; 29. 17; 39. 6; 41. 2–6, Ex. 4. 10; 6. 12, Deu. 9. 6, 13, Jud. 3. 15; 18. 25, 1 S. 2. 5; 22. 2, 2 S. 4. 4, Is. 1. 4, 30; 3. 3; 19. 10; 20. 4 (*rd.* חֲשׂוּפַי); 29. 24; 54. 6, Am. 2. 16, Ps. 24. 4, Job 3. 20; 9. 4, Lam. 1. 1, Song 5. 8.

Rem. 1. The gen. of material, a ring *of gold*, is not *partitive*, but explicative—a ring which is gold.

Rem. 2. The gen. of *quality*, &c., forms along with its cons. a single conception, hence the suff. goes to the gen. Ps. 2. 6 הַר קָדְשִׁי *my holy hill*, Deu. 1. 41, Is. 2. 20; 9. 3; 30. 22; 31. 7; 64. 9. 10, Zeph. 3. 11, Job 18. 7.   Cf. § 27.

Rem. 3. The gen. of attribute or quality is very common with certain nouns, אִישׁ, אִשָּׁה *man, woman*, בֵּן, בַּת *son, daughter*, בַּעַל *owner, possessor*.   Ex. 4. 10 אִישׁ דְּבָרִים a *good speaker*, Job 11. 2 אִ' שְׂפָתַיִם a *babbler*, 2 S. 16. 7 אִ' דָּמִים a *bloodshedder*, Pr. 25. 24 אֵשֶׁת מִדְיָנִים a *brawling* woman.   Gen. 9. 20; 25. 27, 2 S. 18. 20, 1 K. 2. 26, Ps. 140. 12.—Pr. 11. 16; 12. 4; 12. 19; 28. 5; 29. 1, 8, Ru. 3. 11, Zeph. 3. 4.

1 S. 14. 52 בֶּן־חַיִל *mighty man*, 26. 16 בְּנֵי מָוֶת *deserving death*, 1. 16 בַּת בְּלִיַּעַל a *worthless person*.   Nu. 17. 25, Deu. 3. 18, Jud. 18. 2, 2 S. 3. 34, 2 K. 14. 14, Is. 5. 1; 14. 12, Jer. 48. 45, Jon. 4. 10, Job 5. 7; 28. 8.—Mic. 4. 14, Mal. 2. 11, Ecc. 12. 4.   And in stating *age*, 1 S. 4. 15 בֶּן־תִּשְׁעִים וּשְׁמֹנֶה שָׁנָה 98 years old.   Gen. 50. 26, Nu. 32. 11, Josh. 24. 29, Jud. 2. 8, Gen. 17. 17.

3

Gen. 37. 19 בַּעַל הַחֲלֹמוֹת the *dreamer*, 2 K. 1. 8 שְׂעַר 'ב *hairy*, Pr. 23. 2 נֶפֶשׁ 'ב *of large appetite*. Gen. 14. 13, Ex. 24. 14, Is. 41. 15; 50. 8 (adversary), Jer. 37. 13, Nah. 1. 2, Pr. 18. 9; 22, 24; 24. 8, Neh. 6. 18, Ecc. 7. 12, Dan. 8. 6 (*two-horned*).—1 S. 28. 7, 1 K. 17. 17, Nah. 3. 4.—In 2 S. 1. 6 פרשים seems to mean *war-horses*, but cf. Dr. or Well. on *v.* 18.

Rem. 4. Adverbs and particles being really nouns may stand virtually in the gen., 1 K. 2. 31 דְּמֵי חִנָּם *causeless* blood-shed, Nu. 29. 6 עֹלַת הַתָּמִיד *the continual* burnt-offering, Ez. 39. 14, 'אַנְשֵׁי ת, Deu. 26. 5 מְתֵי מְעָט *a few* men, Jer. 13. 27 אַחֲרֵי מָתַי after *how long*. 2 S. 24. 24, Hab. 2. 19, Ez. 30. 16 (if read. right). And of course such particles as בִּלְתִּי, אַיִן &c. may themselves take a gen. after them.

Rem. 5. The consn. in (*d*) is the usual one in Heb., of the type *integer vitæ*; the *acc.* of limitation after adj. and ptcp. is uncommon, *e.g.* Is. 40. 20 הַמִּסְכָּן תְּרוּמָה he who is poor *in oblation*, Job 15 10 כַּבִּיר מֵאָבִיךָ יָמִים older *in days*. But this is not liked, cf. 30. 1 younger לְיָמִים *in days*, so 32. 4. The prep. בְּ is generally used of members of the body (Am. 2. 15) when the *gen.* is not employed, cf. Ps. 125. 4 (Pr. 17. 20). Cf. § 71, R. 3. Ar. on the other hand regards this gen. as *improper* (unreal) annexion, being substitute for acc. of limitation.

Rem. 6. Proper names are occasionally followed by a gen., as Ur of the Chaldees Gen. 11. 31, Aram of the two rivers Gen. 24. 10, Gath of the Philistines Am. 6. 2, Gibeah of Saul Is. 10. 29, Mizpeh of Gilead Jud. 11. 29, &c. Most proper names were originally appellatives, and in other cases there were several places of the same name, but in such a case as *Zion of the Holy One* of Israel Is. 60. 14, the last fact does not apply, and the first had certainly been long forgotten. Cf. *thy sun v.* 20, Jer. 15. 9, Nu. 31. 12, Ezr. 3. 7. Most languages so construe proper names. Wright, Ar. Gr. ii. § 79.

The common י' צְבָאוֹת is probably breviloquence for י' אֱלֹהֵי צ' 2 S. 5. 10, Am. 3. 13 and often.

§ 25. A clause may occasionally take the place of the gen. Such a clause will be what we call relative (in Heb.

rel. or descriptive), particularly in designations of *time* and *place:* Gen. 40. 3 מְקוֹם אֲשֶׁר יוֹסֵף אָסוּר שָׁם *the place where* J. was confined; Is. 29. 1 קִרְיַת חָנָה דָוִד *thou city where* D. dwelt; 1 S. 25. 15 כָּל־יְמֵי הִתְהַלַּכְנוּ אִתָּם *all the days* we were conversant with them; Ex. 4. 13 שְׁלַח־נָא בְּיַד־תִּשְׁלַח send *by the hand of him* whom thou wilt send (send by means of some one else); 6. 28 בְּיוֹם דְּבֶּר יהוה *on the day* Je. spoke. Gen. 39. 20, Deu. 32. 35, 2 S. 15. 21, 1 K. 21. 19, Jer. 22. 12; 36. 2; 48. 36, Hos. 1. 2; 2. 1, Ps. 4. 8; 18. 1; 56. 4, 10; 59. 17; 65. 5; 81. 6; 90. 15; 102. 3; 104. 8; 137. 8, 9; 138. 3; 146. 5, Pr. 8. 32, Lev. 13. 46; 14. 46, Nu. 3. 1; 9. 18, Job 6. 17, 2 Chr. 29. 27.

§ 26. In annexion the determining *Art.* is prefixed to the gen. Both members of the expression are usually indef. when the Art. is wanting, and both usually def. when it is present. Gen. 42. 30 אֲדֹנֵי הָאָרֶץ *the* lord of *the* country; 24. 22 נֶזֶם זָהָב *a* ring of gold. Of course proper names and all pron., whether separate or suffixal, are def. of themselves. § 20. A number of constructs may follow one another, each depending on the one after it as its gen. Gen. 47. 9 יְמֵי שְׁנֵי חַיֵּי אֲבֹתַי the *days* of the *years* of the *lives* of my fathers; 1 K. 2. 5 לִשְׁנֵי שָׂרֵי צְבָאוֹת ישראל to the *two captains* of the *hosts* of Is. Gen. 41. 10, Lev. 10. 14, Nu. 6. 13, Josh. 4. 5, 2 K. 10. 6, Is. 10. 12; 21. 17, 1 Chr. 9. 13 (if חַיִל be read. Perhaps לְ has fallen out before מְלָאכֶת).

§ 27. As in annexion the two members form a single expression, nothing (except the *Art.* to the gen. and the ה of direction to the cons.) can come between them. (*a*) An adj. qualifying either of the members must stand outside the expression. Jo. 3. 4 יוֹם י' הַגָּדוֹל *the great day* of the Lord, Gen. 27. 15 בִּגְדֵי עֵשָׂו בְּנָהּ הַגָּדֹל הַחֲמֻדֹת *the best garments* of *her elder son* Esau; Gen. 10. 21 אֲחִי יֶפֶת הַגָּדוֹל *the elder brother* of Japheth; 44. 14 וַיָּבֹא בֵּיתָה יוֹסֵף he came *to the*

house of J.; 28. 2; 43. 17; 46. 1, Deu. 4. 41, 1 K. 19. 15.—
Deu. 3. 24; 11. 7; 1 S. 25. 25, Is. 36. 9.

(*b*) For the same reason not more than one cons. can
stand before the same gen. For ex. *the sons and daughters
of the man* cannot be expressed thus: בְּנֵי וּבְנוֹת הָאִישׁ,
because the form בְּנֵי, not being dependent, is without
reason. Various forms are adopted. (1) בְּנֵי הָאִישׁ וּבְנוֹתָיו·
הַבָּנִים וְהַבָּנוֹת (אֲשֶׁר) לָאִישׁ (3).   בְּנֵי הָאִישׁ וְהַבָּנוֹת (2).
The first is lightest and most usual. Gen. 41. 8 the magicians
of Eg. and her wise men (= the mag. and wise men of E.),
Jud. 8. 14 the princes of Succoth and her elders (= the pr.
and el. of S.). The second is occasional. Gen. 40. 1 מַשְׁקֵה
מֶלֶךְ־מ׳ וְהָאֹפֶה *the butler* of the king of E. *and the baker*;
Ps. 64. 7 וְקֶרֶב אִישׁ וְלֵב עָמֹק *the breast* of each *and the heart*
is deep. The third, circumscription of gen. by prep. לְ, is
common, and gains ground in the later stages of the
language. Gen. 40. 5 הַמַּשְׁקֶה וְהָאֹפֶה אֲשֶׁר לְמֶלֶךְ מ׳.—
This circumscription must be had recourse to also when the
first member of a gen. relation is to be preserved indef., the
second being def. 1 S. 16. 18 בֵּן לְיִשַׁי *a* son of Jesse; cf.
20. 27 בֶּן־יִשַׁי *the* son of Jesse (David), 1 K. 2. 39 שְׁנֵי־עֲבָדִים
לְשִׁמְעִי *two slaves* of Shimei, Gen. 41. 12. See more fully
Rem. 5, below.

§ 28. Such words as כֹּל *all*, רֹב *multitude, many*, are
nouns, and are followed by gen. Gen. 8. 9 כָּל־הָאָרֶץ *all*
(of) *the earth*, Ps. 51. 3 כְּרֹב רַחֲמֶיךָ *according to thy many*
mercies. So the numerals. Gen. 40. 12 שְׁלֹשֶׁת יָמִים *three*
days. See § 29 Apposition, and § 36 *seq.* Numerals. On
Adj. in gen. by their noun, cf. § 32, R. 5.

Rem. 1. The cons. before a clause (§ 25) is scarcely a
mere *formal* shortening of the word due to the closeness of
connexion. It has syntactical meaning, the clause being
equivalent to inf. cons. with suff. ; *e.g.* 1 S. 25. 15 = כָּל־יְמֵי

הִתְהַלֶּכְנוּ (Pr. 6. 22), Ps. 4. 8 = מֵעֵת רֹב דְּגָנָם (Hos. 4. 7;
10. 1, Deu. 7. 7). In other cases there is om. of rel. pr.

More like a mere formal shortening is the use of the
cons. before prepp. In poetry and the higher style chiefly
the ptcps. (and nouns) of verbs that govern by a prep. are put
in cons. before the prep. The real consn. in this case is by
prep. and the cons. is secondary, as appears from Jud. 8. 11
מַשְׁכִּימֵי בַבֹּקֶר; הַשְׁכוּנֵי בָאֳהָלִים (so Sep.) with *Art.* — Is. 5. 11
9. 2 שִׂמְחַת בַּקָּצִיר; 28. 9 גְּמוּלֵי מֵחָלָב, Jud. 5. 10, 2 S. 1. 21, Is.
14. 19; 56. 10 (inf.), Jer. 8. 16, Ez. 13. 2, Ps. 2. 12, Job 24. 5.

The few cases of shortening before *vav copul.* seem due
to assonance, Ez. 26. 10 (cf. Jer. 4. 29), Is. 33. 6, or to the
ear being accustomed to the cons. form before words closely
connected, Is. 35. 2. In Is. 51. 21 the coming word יין seems
to influence the preceding " drunken." Jer. 33. 22 מְשָׁרְתַי אֹתִי
is altogether anomalous (cf. *v.* 21); Hag. 2. 17.

Rem. 2. On indef. cons. before def. gen. cf. § 20, R. 2.

Rem. 3. Sometimes an adj. is used nominally and brought
within the chain of constructs. Is. 28. 16, a corner-stone
יְקְרַת *of preciousness* of a foundation; perhaps *v.* 1, 4 flower
נֹבֵל of *a faded-thing* (faded flower), Jer. 4. 11 *wind of dry-
ness.* In some cases the Abs. seems retained in a phrase.
Is. 28. 1 גִּיא שְׁמָנִים הֲלוּמֵי יִין *the fat valley* of those stricken
down of wine; *v.* 3 גֵּאוּת. Ps. 68. 22, Pr. 21. 6? Text is
doubtful, Is. 63. 11, the words " Moses," " his people,"
being wanting in Sep. Ez. 6. 11 רְעוֹת wanting in Sep. Is.
32. 13 קְרִיָה עַלִּיזָה may be loose subord. in acc. On Is. 19. 8,
cf. Rem. 1.—The consn. 2 S. 1. 9, כָּל עוֹד נַפְשִׁי בִי (Job 27. 3,
Hos. 14. 3), where כֹל seems separated from its gen., is uncertain. The כֹל appears rather to be used adverbially,
wholly, in whole, cf. Ecc. 5. 15 (Ps. 39. 6; 45. 14) and the
Chald. כָּל קֳבֵל דְּ Dan. 2. 8, 41, &c.

Rem. 4. An instance of two cons. before a gen. is Ez.
31. 16, but Sep. wants וּטוֹב. Dan. 1. 4 is scarcely an ex.,
cf. Is. 29. 12. Occasionally the first word seems to stand
loosely in Abs., Is. 55. 4; less necessarily 53. 3, 4. In
the broader or emphatic style, when one cons. would be
followed by several gen., it is repeated before each. Gen.
24. 3, *God* of heaven *and God* of earth; 11. 29; 14. 19, Jon.

24. 2, though usage fluctuates, Gen. 14. 22; 28. 5, Ex. 3.
6, 16 with 4. 5, 1 K. 18. 36.   There is nothing unusual in
several gen. after one cons.   Deu. 5. 19; 8. 8; 32. 19, Jud.
1. 7, 9, Is. 1. 11, 28; 37. 3; 64. 10, Ps. 5. 7, Pr. 3. 4.
On the other hand Deu. 8. 7, 15, &c., are ex. of loose
rhetorical accumulation of terms.   Cf. Deu. 3. 5, 1 K. 4. 13.

Rem. 5. Circumscription of the gen. is used: 1. When
it is needful to preserve the indefiniteness of first word.
1 S. 16. 18 בֵּן לְיִשַׁי *a son* of Jesse, 1 S. 17. 8, 1 K. 2. 39, Gen.
41. 12, Nu. 25. 14, Song 8. 1.   Similarly the so-called לְ of
authorship, מִזְמוֹר לְדָוִד *a psalm of D.*, or simply לְדָוִד *by David.*
2. When it is desired to retain for the first noun the somewhat greater distinctiveness given by the Art.   Gen. 25. 6;
29. 9; 47. 4, Jud. 6. 25, 1 S. 21. 8, 1 K. 4. 2, 2 K. 5. 9, Ps.
116. 15; 118. 20.   3. When it is necessary to retain a
definite designation or expression in its completeness.   1 K.
15. 23 סֵפֶר דִּבְרֵי הַיָּמִים לְמַלְכֵי יה׳ the book *of the Chronicles of
the Kings* of Judah, 2 K. 11. 4 *the centurions*, Ru. 2. 3
חֶלְקַת הַשָּׂדֶה לְבֹעַז *the field-portion* (property) of Boaz, 2 S.
23. 11 the *field-portion* (piece of country); cf. 2 K. 9. 25,
Nu. 27. 16; 30. 2, Gen. 41. 43, Jos. 19. 51, 2 S. 2. 8, 2 Chr.
8. 10.   Sometimes also with words not declinable, as *Teraphim* Gen. 31. 19.   And in general to express the gen.
relation *of, belonging to*, in consns. where the *case* could not
be used.   Am. 5. 3 *of, in, the house* of Isr., 1 K. 14. 13, Jer.
22. 4, Am. 9. 1, Ezr. 10. 14, 1 Chr. 3. 1, 5; 7. 5.   4. For
the same reason the circumscription is usual in dates and
with numerals.   Gen. 7. 11 in the 600 year לְחַיֵּי נֹחַ *of the life*
of N., 1 K. 3. 18 בַּיּוֹם הַשְּׁלִישִׁי לְלָדְתִּי, Gen. 16. 3, 1 K. 14. 25,
and often.   Cf. on dates, § 38c.   The circums. occurs,
however, without significance and gains in later style, Ps.
123. 4, 1 S. 20. 40, Jer. 12. 12 חֶרֶב לַיהוה the sword of Je.
5. The gen. suff. is circumscribed in the same way, perhaps
with some emphasis.   1 K. 1. 33 הַפִּרְדָּה אֲשֶׁר לִי *my* mule ; cf.
v. 38, Ru. 2. 21, Lam. 1. 10, cf. 3. 44.   So the curious
אִשָּׁה לִי *my wife* (a w. of mine) 2 Chr. 8. 11.   After suff.
Song 1. 6 כַּרְמִי שֶׁלִּי *my own* vineyard, Ps. 132. 11, 12.

Rem. 6. A noun in appos. with a cons. is sometimes
attracted into construction.   1 S. 28. 7 אֵשֶׁת בַּעֲלַת אוֹב *a woman*

possessing an Ob.   Is. 23. 12 ; 37. 22 'צ בת בְּתוּלַת *the virgin*,
the daughter of Zion.   Jer. 14. 17, Deu. 21. 11.   And sometimes a noun in cons. is suspended by being repeated before
its gen., or by the interposition of a synonym in appos.
Gen. 14. 10 חמר בארות בְּאֵרֹת *pits*, pits of bitumen.   Nu. 3. 47,
Deu. 33. 19, Jud. 5. 22 ; 19. 22, 2 S. 20. 19, 2 K. 10. 6 ;
17. 13 (Kere), Jer. 46. 9 (if text right), Ps. 78. 9, Job 20. 17,
Dan. 11. 14.   1 K. 20. 14 is different, and Ps. 35. 16 obscure.

NOMINAL APPOSITION

§ 29. With a certain simplicity and concreteness of
thought the Hebrew said: The altar is brass, the table is
wood, instead of the altar is *brazen*, the table is *of wood*.
Similarly he said: The ark is three storeys, the altar is
stones, instead of *consists of* three storeys.   So: the homer is
barley; the famine is three years; his judgments are
righteousness; I am peace. When, therefore, two nouns
stand related to one another in meaning in such a way
that they may form the subj. and pred. in a simple
judgment or proposition, as, *the altar is brass*, they may be
made to express one complex idea by being placed in
apposition, *the altar, the brass*, for the altar *of* brass, or, the
brazen altar ; a homer, barley, for *of* or *in* barley. In the
former case *altar* is the principal thing, and *brass* is *explanation*; in the other *barley* is principal, and said to be the
permutative (substitute or exchange) for the measure.   In
many cases appos. is used as in other languages, as, *I, the
Lord; his servants, the prophets*, &c.   Apposition is used—

(*a*) In the case of the person or thing and its name.   2 S.
3. 31 דָּוִד הַמֶּלֶךְ *the king David*; Nu. 34. 2 כְּנַעַן הָאָרֶץ
the land Canaan; 1 Chr. 5. 9 פְּרָת הַנָּהָר *the river Euphrates*,
Gen. 14. 6 שֵׂעִיר בְּהַרְרָם *in their mountain Seir*.   Gen. 24. 4,
1 S. 3. 1 ; 4. 1, 1 K. 4. 1 ; 16. 21, 24, Ezr. 8. 21 ; 9. 1.   In such
cases as Nu. 34. 2, 1 Chr. 5. 9 the *gen.* is more common,
though apposition may seem more logical.

If the personal name be second the *nota acc.* אֵת or prep. if before the appellative has to be repeated. Gen. 24. 4 לִבְנִי לְיִצְחָק *to my son Isaac*; 21. 10. Gen. 4. 2 וַתֹּסֶף לָלֶדֶת אֶת־אָחִיו אֶת־הֶבֶל *bore his brother Abel*; and אֵת is usual before the proper name even when the appell. wants it, particularly if any word come between them. Is. 7. 6; 8. 2, Gen. 22. 20, 21; 48. 13, Ex. 1. 11; Jud. 3. 15, 1 K. 11. 14. On the other hand, there is no repetition of אֵת or prep. with appell. when second. Gen. 16. 3 אֶת־הָגָר שִׁפְחָתָהּ took *H. her maid*; 11. 31; 12. 5; 14. 16; 20. 14; 24. 59. Gen. 4. 8 וַיָּקָם אֶל־הֶבֶל אָחִיו rose up against *Ab. his brother.*—Gen. 11. 28, Jud. 8. 27, 2 S. 7. 8, 10, Is. 22. 20. Cf. Gen. 43. 28, 2 S. 11. 17.

(*b*) The person or thing and its *class.* 1 K. 7. 14 אִשָּׁה אַלְמָנָה a *woman, a widow* (widow woman); 2 K. 9. 4 הַנַּעַר הַנָּבִיא the *prophetical youth* (not, the youthful prophet); Ex. 24. 5 זְבָחִים שְׁלָמִים *sacrifices* (of) *peace-offerings* (gen. ׳שׁ later). Deu. 22. 23, 1 S. 2. 13, 2 S. 10. 7. Gen. 21. 20 a *shooter, a bowman,* and 6. 17 *the flood, waters*; the second word merely explains the archaic or unusual first.

(*c*) The thing and its *material,* which may also be considered the individual and its general class. 2 K. 16. 17 הַבָּקָר הַנְּחֹשֶׁת the *brazen oxen*; Deu. 16. 21 אֲשֵׁרָה כָל־עֵץ an *Ashera* (of) *any wood*; Ex. 39. 17 הָעֲבֹתֹת הַזָּהָב the *cords* (of) *gold*; Ex. 28. 17 four טוּרִים אֶבֶן *rows* (of) *stones* (*gen.* 39. 10); 2 Chr. 4. 13, two *rows pomegranates,* Ez. 22. 18, 1 Chr. 15. 19, Zech. 4. 10.—1 Chr. 28. 18 הַכְּרוּבִים זָהָב the *cher.* (*of, in*) *gold,* Lev. 6. 3. In 2 K. 16. 14 *rd.* perh. *abs.* הַמִּזְבֵּחַ; but cf. 23. 17.

(*d*) The measure, weight, or number, and the thing measured, weighed, or counted. 2 K. 7. 1, 16, 18 סְאָה סֹלֶת וְסָאתַיִם שְׂעֹרִים a *seah flour* and *two seahs barley,* Gen. 18. 6, Ru. 2. 17 כְּאֵיפָה שְׂעֹרִים about *an ephah* of *barley.* Ex.

29. 40 רְבִעִית הַהִין יַיִן the *fourth of a hin* of *wine;* ib. a *tenth* of *fine flour*, Nu. 15. 4, Ex. 9. 8; 16. 33, Nu. 22. 18, 1 K. 18. 32, Lev. 6. 13.—Gen. 41. 1 שְׁנָתַיִם יָמִים *two years* of *time*, 2 S. 13. 23. 2 S. 24. 13 שֶׁבַע שָׁנִים רָעָב 7 *years* of *famine;* ib. שְׁלֹשֶׁת יָמִים דֶּבֶר 3 *days* of *pestilence*. Gen. 29. 14, Nu. 11. 20, Deu. 21. 13, 2 K. 15. 13; Gen. 45. 11, 1 Chr. 21. 12, Ez. 38. 17, Dan. 11. 13. 2 K. 3. 4 100,000 *rams, wool* (fleeces), but 1 S. 16. 20 is not an *ass-load* of bread, but an *ass laden with b.* (text dubious).—1 K. 16. 24 בְּכִכְּרַיִם כֶּסֶף for *two talents* of *silver*, 2 K. 5. 23, cf. v. 17; 1 S. 17. 5.

With different order, Neh. 2. 12 אֲנָשִׁים מְעַט *men, few*, Is. 10. 7; Nu. 9. 20 יָמִים מִסְפָּר *days, a number* (many), 2 S. 8. 8; 24. 24, 1 K. 5. 9. Ex. 27. 16 *a curtain* of 20 *cubits*.

(*e*) Even the thing and its quality (regarded as its substance or class), or anything which, being characteristic, may serve as specification or explanation of it. 1 K. 22. 27 מַיִם לַחַץ *water* of *distress* (scanty as in stress); Ps. 60. 5 יַיִן תַּרְעֵלָה *wine* of *reeling*; Pr. 22. 21 אֲמָרִים אֱמֶת *words* of *truth*, Zech. 1. 13, Is. 3. 24 *work* of *crisping*, Dan. 8. 13. Ez. 18. 6 אִשָּׁה נִדָּה. 1 K. 6. 7.

The usage receives large extension in the predicative form. Gen. 11. 1 the earth *was one tongue;* 14. 10 the vale *was pits, pits* (full of p.), Is. 5. 12 their feast *is harp*, &c., Ps. 45. 9 all thy garments *are myrrh and cassia*, Ezr. 10. 13 the season *was rains*. Gen. 13. 10, 2 S. 17. 3, 1 K. 10. 6, Is. 7. 24; 65. 4, Jer. 24. 2; 48. 38, Mic. 5. 4, Ez. 2. 8; 27. 36, Zech. 8. 13, Ps. 10. 5; 19. 10; 25. 10; 55. 22; 92. 9; 109. 4; 110. 3; 111. 7; 120. 7, Pr. 3. 17; 8. 30, Job 3. 4; 5. 24; 8. 9, 2 Chr. 9. 5, Dan. 9. 23 (cf. 10. 11).

Rem. 1. The order *Dav. the king* occurs 2 K. 8. 29; 9. 15, and in later style 1 Chr. 24. 31, &c. In 2 S. 13. 39 *rd.* (רוח) וַתֵּכֶל רוּחַ הַמֶּלֶך for דוד). In other cases the usual order is *Isaiah the prophet* Is. 39. 3, *Abiathar the priest* 1 S. 30. 7.

Hos. 5. 13 *king Jareb* is obscure ; Pr. 31. 1 perhaps *L. king of Massa.*

Rem. 2. Repetition of prep. &c. before proper name has exceptions, Gen. 24. 12, 1 S. 25. 19 (but Sep. om. Nabal, cf. *v.* 25), Job 1. 8. With *my, thy, his people Israel* om. is more common.

Rem. 3. In most of the cases *a—e* the *gen.* may be used (§ 24), 1 K. 7. 10, 2 K. 5. 5, 1 Chr. 29. 4, 2 Chr. 8. 18 ; 9. 9, 13. Cf. Ez. 47. 4 מֵי מַתְנִים with מַיִם בִּרְכַּיִם.

Rem. 4. In cases like 1 Chr. 28. 18 הַכְּרוּבִים זָהָב where object is def. and material indef. the latter might be in *acc.* of specification, cher. *in* gold ; Lev. 6. 3 *linen garment* (*g. in* linen) ; and so cases like Gen. 18. 6 three *seahs fine flour,* though appos. is more natural. Ar. has four ways of connexion : appos. ; the prep. *min, of* (explicative); the *gen.;* and *acc.* of specif. Such passages as Ps. 71. 7 מַחֲסִי עֹז *my strong refuge,* Ez. 16. 27 דַּרְכֵּךְ זִמָּה *thy lewd way,* Hab. 3. 8, 2 S. 22. 33, seem cases of appos., the noun being explanatory. Of course the second noun is not gen., but an acc. of limitation is less natural and expressive, and cases like Ps. 38. 20 שֹׂנְאַי שֶׁקֶר, 35. 19; 69. 5 ; 119. 86, Ez. 13. 22 are of a different class (§ 70, 71, R. 2). Lev. 26. 42 בְּרִיתִי יַעֲקוֹב, &c., Jer. 33. 20 ב' הַיּוֹם start from the gen. *the cov.* (of) *with Jacob,* and when the annexion is broken by the suff. the second noun is loosely left without prep., cf. Jer. 33. 21. An *acc.* of specification with proper name or def. noun is improbable. With Ezr. 2. 62, Neh. 7. 64, comp. Jer. 52. 20.

Rem. 5. Some cases of apparent appos. are due to errors of text. Josh. 3. 14 om. הברית, 8. 11 om. המלחמה, cf. *v.* 10, as explanatory margins. Jos. 13. 5 הארץ הגבלי might be like Nu. 34. 2 (but Sep. otherwise). Jud. 8. 32 perhaps עפרת like 6. 24. Is. 11. 14 *rd.* בְּכָתֵף. Jer. 8. 5 om. *Jerus.* and Ez. 45. 16 om. הארץ, both with Sep.

Rem. 6. The word כל *all* instead of taking gen. is often placed in appos., 2 S. 2. 9 יִשְׂרָאֵל כֻּלֹּה, Is. *all of it,* 1 K. 22. 28, Is. 9. 8 ; 14. 29, 31, Jer. 13. 19, Mic. 2. 12 ; often in Ezek., 11 15 ; 14. 5 ; 20. 40, &c. The archaic form of suff., as 2 S. 2. 9, is common, Is. 15. 3 ; 16. 7, Jer. 2. 21 ; 8. 6, 10 ;

20. 7 (15. 10 *rd.* בְּלָהֶם קְלָלוּנִי or בְּלַהֶם ?).—In such phrases as 1 S. 4. 10 וַיָּנֻסוּ אִישׁ לְאֹהָלָיו *each* is in appos. to subj. in the verb (*pl. tents* except Jud. 20. 8, 2 K. 14. 12 K'th.). In prose the plur. verb mostly precedes, but in higher style often follows, Is. 13. 8, 14.

Rem. 7. An anticipative pron. sometimes precedes the subj. or obj., which then stands in appos. with the pron. ; Ex. 2. 6 וַתִּרְאֵהוּ אֶת־הַיֶּלֶד *and she saw him, the child*, Ez. 10. 3 בְּבֹאוֹ הָאִישׁ *when he came, the man*. Ex. 7. 11 ; 35. 5, Lev. 13. 57, Josh. 1. 2, 1 K. 21. 13 (2 K. 16. 15), Jer. 31. 1, Ez. 3. 21 ; 42. 14 (text?) ; 44. 7, Ps. 83. 12, Pr. 5. 22, Song 3. 7, 1 Chr. 5. 26 ; 9. 22, Ezr. 3. 12 ; 9. 1, Dan. 11. 11, 27. —In 1 K. 19. 21 Sep. wants " the flesh," and in Jer. 9. 14 " this people." The usage is common in Aram., and prevails in later style ; it appears in Pr. 1–9, 10–22, but not in 25–29.

Rem. 8. When the same word is repeated in appos. *intensity* of various kinds is expressed ; *e.g.* the superl. of adj., 1 S. 2. 3 *very proudly*, Is. 6. 3 *most holy*, Ecc. 7. 24 *very deep*. With nouns Gen. 14. 10, Ex. 8. 10, 2 K. 3. 16 *pits, pits* (sheer pits), Jud. 5. 22, Jo. 4. 14.—With words of time the idea of continuity, constancy, Deu. 14. 22 שָׁנָה שָׁנָה *year* by *year*. Often with prep. בְּ, Deu. 15. 20 שָׁנָה בְשָׁנָה, 1 S. 1. 7, Nu. 24. 1, Jud. 16. 20, 2 K. 17. 4. Comp. Deu. 2. 27 *always by the road*, 16. 20 *always righteousness*. Ex. 23. 30, Deu. 28. 43.

(2) With Numerals the idea of *distribution ;* Gen. 7. 2 *seven, seven (by sevens)*, 7. 3, 9, 15, Josh. 3. 12, Is. 6. 2 ; sometimes with *and*, 2 S. 21. 20, 1 Chr. 20. 6. Gen. 32. 17 *each flock* separately ; 2 K. 17. 29 ; 25. 15.

(3) When words are joined by *and* the idea of *variety* is expressed ; Deu. 25. 13, 14 *stone and stone* (divers weights), Ps. 12. 3, 1 Chr. 12. 34, Pr. 20. 10. The usage is very common in later style to express *respective, various, several*, 1 Chr. 28. 14 the *respective services ; v.* 15 the *several lampstands ; v.* 16 the *various tables*. 1 Chr. 26. 13, 2 Chr. 8. 14 ; 11. 12 ; 19. 5, &c., Ezr. 10. 14, Neh. 13. 24, Est. 1. 8, 22, and often. With כל prefixed, Est. 2. 11, 2 Chr. 11. 12 (also post-Biblical).

THE ADJECTIVE

§ 30. The adj. as attribute, being virtually in apposition
to the noun, is placed after it, and agrees with it in gend.,
numb., and case. Gen. 21. 8 וַיַּעַשׂ מִשְׁתֶּה גָדוֹל he made
a great feast; 20. 9 הֵבֵאתָ עָלַי חֲטָאָה גְדֹלָה thou hast
brought on me *a great sin*; Is. 5. 9 בָּתִּים רַבִּים לְשַׁמָּה *many
houses* shall be desolate. It also agrees in determination,
being without the Art. if its noun be indef., but having the
Art. if the noun be determined in any way (by Art., def.
gen. or suff.). Gen. 21. 8; 20. 9 above. 2 K. 4. 9 אִישׁ
אֱלֹהִים קָדוֹשׁ *a holy man* of God; 1 S. 12. 22 שְׁמוֹ הַגָּדוֹל
his great name; 17. 13 שְׁלֹשֶׁת בְּנֵי יִשַׁי הַגְּדֹלִים *the* three
eldest sons of Jesse; Is. 8. 7 מֵי הַנָּהָר הָעֲצוּמִים *the many
waters* of the River. If there be several adj. the concord of
all is the same; Is. 27. 1 בְּחַרְבּוֹ הַקָּשָׁה וְהַגְּדוֹלָה וְהַחֲזָקָה
with his *sore* and *great* and *strong sword*.

The concord of the adj. when *pred.* is the same as when
it is qualificative, though liable to be less exact. The
position of pred. in the sentence is also variable (§ 103 seq.).
The pred. is usually indefinite.

§ 31. The adj. having no dual is used in *plur.* with dual
nouns; Is. 35. 3 בִּרְכַּיִם כֹּשְׁלוֹת *failing knees;* 42. 7 לִפְקֹחַ
עֵינַיִם עִוְרוֹת to open *blind eyes*; Ex. 17. 12 וִידֵי מֹשֶׁה כְּבֵדִים
the hands of M. were *heavy* (*hand* mas. only here, cf. Ez.
2. 9). Gen. 29. 17, 1 S. 3. 2, Ps. 18. 28; 130. 2, Pr. 6. 17, 18.

With collectives agreement may be grammatical in the
sing., or *ad sensum* in the *plur.;* 1 S. 13. 15 הָעָם הַנִּמְצָאִים
עִמּוֹ the people *that were present* with him; but in *v.* 16
הָעָם הַנִּמְצָא. § 115.

With the plur. of eminence the adj. is usually sing.; Is.
19. 4 אֲדֹנִים קָשֶׁה *a harsh master*. Ps. 7. 10 אֱלֹהִים צַדִּיק
righteous God; but in some parts of the Hex. (E) plur.,

Josh. 24. 19 אלהים קְדשִׁים *a holy* God (cf. pl. vb. Gen. 20. 13; 35. 7). So 1 S. 17. 26 א׳ חַיִּים *the living* God, Deu. 5. 23, Jer. 23. 36, but also א׳ חַי 2 K. 19. 4, 16. Cf. *Teraphim* of single image, 1 S. 19. 13, 16. Gen. 31. 34 (E), where Ter. is treated as pl., may be doubtful.

§ 32. The demonstrative adj. הוּא, זֶה *this, that,* have the same concord as other adj. But (1) they necessarily make their noun def., הָאִישׁ הַזֶּה *this man,* הַיָּמִים הָהֵם *those days,* and have themselves the Art. (2) In the case of nouns determined by pron. suff. they are in Appos. *without* the Art., Ex. 10. 1 אֹתֹתַי אֵלֶּה *these my signs ;* and so always. (3) With another adj. or several they stand last, 1 K. 3. 6 הַחֶסֶד הַגָּדוֹל הַזֶּה *this great* goodness (*v.* 9); Deu. 1. 19 הַמִּדְבָּר הַגָּדוֹל וְהַנּוֹרָא הַהוּא *that great and terrible* wilderness; Gen. 41. 35 הַשָּׁנִים הַטֹּבוֹת הַבָּאֹת הָאֵלֶּה *these good coming* years.

Rem. 1. Occasionally the adj. precedes the noun, particularly רַב in plur. (sing. Is. 21. 7; 63. 7, Ps. 31. 20; 145. 7), Jer. 16. 16, Ps. 32. 10; 89. 51, Pr. 7. 26; 31. 29, Neh. 9. 28, 1 Ch. 28. 5. Ez. 24. 12 (fem. cons.) might suggest that in some instances of the sing. the adj. is used *nominally.*—Is. 28. 21 the adj. may be pred., *strange is* his work. In other cases the adj. is independent and the consn. apposition, Is. 23. 12 *thou violated one,* virgin, &c.; 53. 11 perhaps the place of צַדִּיק is due to attraction of vb. יַצְדִּיק; 10. 30 also apposition, *thou poor one,* Anathoth (Ew. *al.* would rd. עֲנִיָּה imp. *answer her*). Jer. 3. 7, 10 בגודה is almost a proper name, *Treacherous,* her sister.

Rem. 2. Sometimes the noun is defined and adj. without the Art. (1) Numerals as אֶחָד *one,* and words similarly used as אַחֵר *another,* רבים *many,* being def. of themselves, may dispense with Art. Gen. 42. 19 (Art. *v.* 33), 1 S. 13. 17, 2 K. 25. 16, Jer. 24. 2, Ez. 10. 9; Gen. 43. 14, Jer. 22. 26, Ez. 39. 27. (2) In some cases the adj. is *acc.* of condition, or at any rate of the nature of pred. Gen. 37. 2, Nu. 14, 37,

1 S. 2. 23 (Sep. wants), Is. 57. 20 (11. 9?), Ez. 4. 13;
34. 12, Hag. 1. 4, Ps. 18. 18; 92. 12.—Is. 17. 6 prob. *rd.*
סְעִפֵי הַפּ'.   (3) Possibly euphony in some cases led to om. of
Art. 2 S. 6. 3, unless *new cart* expressed a single idea (cf
Mic. 2. 7) to which Art. was prefixed.   (4) Other exx. Jer.
2. 21, where Hitz. suggests that סוֹרֵי הַגֶּפֶן may = הַסּוּרִים לְגֶפֶן,
1 S. 15. 9 where *rd.* נִבְזֶה וְנִמְאָס (cf. 1 K. 19. 11) at any rate.
Dan. 8. 13; 11. 31.   So formulas like חַיִּים אֱלֹהִים, א' חַי *the
living* God.

In other cases the adj. is defined and noun without Art.
(1) Numerals and similar words like כֹּל, having a certain
definiteness of their own, may communicate it to their noun,
which then dispenses with Art.   Gen. 21. 29; 41. 26, Nu.
11. 25, cf. 2 S. 20. 3, Gen. 1. 21; 9. 10.   (2) Certain half-
technical terms came to be def. of themselves, as *court, gate,
entrance,* &c. (§ 22, R. 4): *court* 1 K. 7. 12, 2 K. 20. 4
(K're), Ez. 40. 28, 31 (47. 16 text obscure); *gate* Ez. 9. 2,
Zech. 14. 10 (Neh. 3. 6, gate is cons.); *entrance* Jer. 38. 14.
So *way* 1 S. 12. 23, Jer. 6. 16 (cf. Jud. 21. 19); *day,* particularly with ordinals, Gen. 1. 31, Ex. 12. 15; 20. 10;
Deu. 5. 14, Lev. 19. 6; 22. 27; cf. Is. 43. 13 מֵהַיּוֹם = מִיּוֹם.
(3) Other exx. 1 S. 6. 18; 16. 23, 2 S. 12. 4, Jer. 6. 20;
17. 2 (Ps. 104. 18); 32. 14 (text obscure), Zech. 4. 7, Neh.
9. 35, Ps. 62. 4, Ez. 21. 19 (text uncertain).   2 K. 20. 13
rather as Jer. 6. 20 than as Song 7. 10.   1 S. 19. 22 *rd.*
perhaps הַפֶּרֶךְ (Sep.) for הַנִּרֵל.   (4) With ptcp. Jud. 21. 19,
Jer. 27. 3; 46. 16 (Zech. 11. 2).

Rem. 3.   The usage § 32 (2) goes throughout all stages
of the language, Gen. 24. 8, Ex. 11. 8, Deu. 5. 26; 11. 18,
Josh. 2. 14, 20, Jud. 6. 14, 1 K. 8. 59; 10. 8; 22. 23, Jer.
31. 21, Ezr. 2. 65, Neh. 6. 14; 7. 67, 2 Chr. 18. 22; 24. 18,
Dan. 10. 17.—Josh. 2. 17 is doubly anomalous (cf. Jud. 16.
28).   The demons. is without Art. sometimes in the phrase
בַּלַּיְלָה הוּא *on that night,* Gen. 19. 33; 30. 16; 32. 23, 1 S.
19. 10, cf. Ps. 12. 8 (§ 6, R. 1).   1 S. 2. 23 text dubious.—
On the other hand 2 K. 1. 2; 8. 8, 9 *rd.* חֳלִי (cf. Jer. 10. 19).
In 1 S. 17. 17 *num.* may define לֶחֶם (1 S. 14. 29?).   In 1 S.
17. 12 text faulty.

The order § 32 (3) may be changed when adj. is em-

phatic, 2 Chr. 1. 10, or when other specifications are linked
to it, Jer. 13. 10.

Rem. 4. When two adj. qualify a *fem.* noun the second
is sometimes left in *mas.* 1 K. 19. 11 רוח גדולה וחזק a *great*
and *strong* wind, Jer. 20. 9 (1 S. 15. 9). And in cases of a
commodity and its measure or number the adj. may agree
with the commodity as the main thing, 1 S. 17. 17 *this ephah
of parched corn; v.* 28.

Rem. 5. The adj. is sometimes used nominally and put
by the noun in *gen.*; 2 K. 18. 17 חֵיל כָּבֵד a *great force,* Is.
22. 24 כָּל־כְּלֵי הַקָּטָן all vessels *of the smallest,* Song 7. 10
יֵין הַטּוֹב wine *of the best.* Deu. 19. 13; 27. 25, Jer. 22. 17
(cf. 2 K. 24. 4), Nu. 5. 18, 2 K. 25. 9 (Am. 6. 2?), Zech.
14. 4, Ps. 73. 10; 74. 15 (cf. Ex. 14. 27); 78. 49; 109. 2,
2 Chr. 4. 10, Ecc. 1. 13; 8. 10.—Other exx. of adj. used
nominally, Gen. 30. 35, 37 (exposing *the white*), Deu. 28. 48
(and *nakedness*), Josh. 3. 4 (*a distance*), Jud. 9. 16; 14. 14
(*sweetness*), Josh. 24. 14, 2 K. 10. 15 (perh. om. אֵת), Jer.
2. 25; 15. 15; 30. 12, Is. 28. 4 (flower *of a fading thing*),
v. 16, Ps. 111. 8, Job 33. 27 (perverted *right*).—Conversely
the noun may be put in gen. by the adj. used nominally,
often with superlative meaning, Jud. 5. 29 (the *wisest*), Is.
19. 11; 35. 9, Ez. 7. 24; 28. 7. Ex. 15. 16, 1 S. 16. 7;
17. 40, Jer. 15. 15, Ps. 46. 5; 65. 5. Pr. 16. 19, שְׁפַל might
be inf.

Rem. 6. The adj. when it expresses the characteristic
attribute of the noun is sometimes used instead of it; Is.
24. 23 הַלְּבָנָה the *moon* (*the white*), הַחַמָּה the *sun* (*the hot*),
30. 16 קַל the *horse* (*swift*), Jer. 8: 16, Mal. 3. 11 הָאֹכֵל *the
consumer* (*locust*). Mostly in poetry and less common than
in Ar.

THE ADJECTIVE. COMPARISON

§ 33. The language possesses no elative form of the adj.
Comparison is made by the simple form, followed by prep.
מִן, Gen. 3. 1 עָרוּם מִכֹּל חַיַּת הַשָּׂדֶה *more cunning than* all
the beasts; Deu. 11. 23 גּוֹיִם גְּדֹלִים מִכֶּם nations *greater*

than you; Hos. 2. 9 כִּי טוֹב לִי אָז מֵעָתָּה it was *better* for me then *than* now; 1 S. 9. 2 גָּבֹהַּ מִכָּל־הָעָם *taller*. Jud. 14. 18, 1 S. 24. 18, 2 S. 19. 8. With *better* the subj. is often a clause (inf.), Gen. 29. 19, Ps. 118. 8, 9, Pr. 21. 3, 9 (§ 89).

(*b*) The quality (*tertium comp.*) is often expressed by a verb, Gen. 41. 40 אֶגְדַּל מִמֶּךָ I *will be greater* than thou; 29. 30 וַיֶּאֱהַב אֶת־רָחֵל מִלֵּאָה he *loved* R. *more than* L., 2 S. 1. 23 מִנְּשָׁרִים קַלּוּ מֵאֲרָיוֹת גָּבֵרוּ they *were swifter than* eagles and *stronger* than lions. Gen. 19. 9 עַתָּה נָרַע לְךָ מֵהֶם now will we *treat thee worse* than them. Gen. 37. 4; 48. 19, Deu. 7. 7, Jud. 2. 19, 1 S. 18. 30, 2 S. 6. 22; 18. 8; 20. 5, 6, 1 K. 5. 10, 11; 10. 23; 14. 9.

§ 34. The superlative is expressed by the simple adj. with Art., or followed by gen. of a noun or pron., 1 S. 17. 14 וְדָוִד הוּא הַקָּטָן and David was *the youngest;* 18. 17 בִּתִּי הַגְּדוֹלָה *my eldest* (elder) daughter, Deu. 21. 3. — 2 K. 10. 6 גְּדֹלֵי הָעִיר *the greatest men* of the city; Jer. 6. 13 מִקְּטַנָּם וְעַד־גְּדוֹלָם from *the least of them*, &c. Gen. 9. 24; 10. 21; 29. 16; 42. 13; 43. 29, Jud. 6. 15; 15. 2, 1 S. 9. 21, Mic. 7. 4, Jon. 3. 5, 2 Chr. 21. 17, Ps. 45. 13, Job 30. 6 (§ 32, R. 5). Absolute superlativeness is expressed by מְאֹד *very* (a noun in *acc.*), Jud. 3. 17 בָּרִיא מְאֹד *very fat*, Gen. 12. 14; 41. 31, which may be intensified by prep. עַד, 1 K. 1. 4 הַנַּעֲרָה יָפָה עַד־מְאֹד the girl was *extremely pretty*, 2 S. 2. 17, Gen. 27. 33; in later style בִּמְאֹד מְאֹד Ez. 9. 9; or מ' is repeated without prep., Nu. 14. 7.

Rem. 1. In *form* a few words correspond to the Ar. elative ('afḍalu), as אַכְזָר *cruel*, אַכְזָב *deceptive*, אֵיתָן *perennial*. But in Ar. many adj. of this form have no compar. sense, *'aḥmaru, red;* *'aḥmaqu, foolish*.

Rem. 2. The adj. or verb with מן may often be rendered by *too*, or *rather than*. Gen. 18. 14 הֲיִפָּלֵא מֵי' דָּבָר is anything *too hard for* Je.? (Deu. 17. 8, Jer. 32. 17, 27), Jud. 7. 2, רב מִתִּתִּי *too many for me to give*, 1 K. 8. 64 קטן מֵהָכִיל *too small*

to contain, Gen. 4. 13 גָדוֹל מִנְּשׂוֹא *too great to bear*, Ps. 61. 3 the rock יָרוּם מִמֶּנִּי *too high for me*, Is. 49. 6 *too light to be*, Ex. 18. 18, 1 K. 19. 7, Gen. 26. 16; 36. 7, Ru. 1. 12, Hab. 1. 13, Ps. 139. 12 *too dark for thee* (to see). So with מֵעַט Isa. 7. 13 is wearying men *too little?* Nu. 16. 9.—Hos. 6. 6 knowledge of God *rather than burnt-offerings*; Ps. 52. 5 evil *rather than good*, Hab. 2. 16, 2 S. 19. 44, where perhaps *rd.* בְּכוֹר for בדוד, first-born *rather than thou* (Sep.).

Rem. 3. The word expressing the quality is occasionally omitted, Is. 10. 10 (greater or more) *than those of Jer.*, Job 11. 17 (clearer) *than noon*. In Mic. 7. 4; Is. 40. 17; 41. 24, Ps. 62. 10, מהבל the prep. is partitive or explicative, *of* (consisting of) vanity.

Rem. 4. The consn. with מִן is sometimes virtually a superlative, 1 S. 15. 33 תִּשְׁכַּל מִנָּשִׁים אִמֶּךָ *the most bereaved* of women (lit. bereaved above w.).—A superl. sense is expressed by joining a noun with its own *pl.* in the gen., Gen. 9. 25 a *slave of slaves* (lowest slave), Ex. 26 33 *holy of holies* (most holy), Is. 34. 10 *eternity of eternities* (all eternity), Ecc. 1. 2 *vanity of vanities* (absolute vanity), Song 1. 1, Ez. 16. 7, Deu. 10. 17. 1 K. 8. 27, though such phrases had at first sometimes a lit. sense.

Rem. 5. Just as the simple adj. the abstract noun with gen. conveys superl. meaning, as טוּב *the best*, Gen. 45. 18, Is. 1. 19, מֵיטַב *the best* 1 S. 15. 9, 15, מִבְחַר *the choicest* Ex. 15. 4, Deu. 12. 11, רֹאשׁ, רֵאשִׁית *the chiefest*, Nu. 24. 20, Am. 6. 1, 6.

Rem. 6. A kind of superl. sense is given to a word by connecting it with the divine name. Probably the idea was that God *originated* the thing (as Ar.), or that it belonged to Him, and was therefore extraordinary. Sometimes the meaning appears to be " in God's estimation," Gen. 10. 9. Cf. Jon. 3. 3 עִיר גְּדוֹלָה לֵאלֹהִים (Acts 7. 20); Ps. 36. 7; 68. 16; 80. 11; 104. 16, Song 8. 6, 1 Chr. 12. 23.—1 S. 14. 15; 26. 12 (Gen. 30. 8 seems different).

THE NUMERALS

§ 35. The numeral *one* is an adj., having the usual place and concord (§ 30). 1 S. 2. 34 בְּיוֹם אֶחָד *in one* day, 1 K. 18. 23 הַפָּר הָאֶחָד *the one* ox, Gen. 11. 6 שָׂפָה אַחַת *one* speech, 32. 9 הַמַּחֲנֶה הָאַחַת *the one* camp. 11. 1.

Rem. 1. In later style *one* sometimes precedes its noun, Neh. 4. 11, Dan. 8. 13, Nu. 31. 28, Song 4. 9.

Rem. 2. It is also construed nominally, followed (*a*) by gen., Gen. 22. 2 אַחַד הֶהָרִים *one* of the mountains, 2 S. 2. 1, Job 2. 10; (*b*) by prep. מִן, Gen. 3. 22 אַחַד מִמֶּנּוּ *one* of us, 2. 21. The short form usual in this case (Lev. 13. 2, Nu. 16. 15, 1 S. 9. 3, 1 K. 19. 2; 22. 13, 2 K. 6. 12; 9. 1, &c.; cf. otherwise 1 S. 16. 18; 26. 22, 2 S. 2. 21, &c.) might be *cons.* before prep. (§ 28, R. 1), but in some cases at least it must be a form of *abs.*, Gen. 48. 22, 2 S. 17. 22, Is. 27. 12, Zech. 11. 7. (*c*) It is itself governed in gen. by its noun (§ 32, R. 5), Lev. 24. 22, 2 K. 12, 10, Is. 36. 9. (*d*) With prep. מִן before it, it is a strong *any*; Lev. 4. 2 מֵאַחַת מֵהֵנָּה *any* of these things, Lev. 5. 13, Deu. 15. 7, Ez. 18. 10 (text obscure). So in Ar. after a neg.

§ 36. The Numerals 2–10 are nouns, being followed by the thing enumerated either in Appos. (permutative, § 29), or in the gen. (explicative, § 24). Or, chiefly in later style, the thing may precede and the Num. follow in Appos. The thing enumerated is *plur.*

(*a*) With *indef.* nouns or expressions (cons. with indef. gen.) the Num. is mostly *abs.* and the noun in Appos. Gen. 29. 34 שְׁלֹשָׁה בָנִים *three sons.* 24. 10 עֲשָׂרָה גְמַלִּים *ten camels.* 1 K. 3. 16 שְׁתַּיִם נָשִׁים *two women.* Deu. 19. 2 שָׁלוֹשׁ עָרִים *three cities.* 31. 10 שֶׁבַע שָׁנִים *seven years.* There are exceptions, 2 K. 5. 22; and in the case of *two* the cons. is more common than abs. even before indef. noun. There are also two general exceptions—(1) With יָמִים *days* the cons. is usual; Jud. 19. 4 שְׁלֹשֶׁת יָמִים *three days.* Deu.

5. 13; 16. 4, 8, 13, but cf. 2 K. 2. 17. (2) So before *other* Num. 1 S. 25. 2 שְׁלֹשֶׁת אֲלָפִים *three thousand.* Jos. 8. 12 חֲמֵשֶׁת אֲלָפִים *five thousand.* 1 K. 5. 30 שְׁלֹשׁ מֵאוֹת *three hundred,* Jud. 4. 13.—Jos. 1. 11; 2. 16; 3. 2; 6. 3; 7. 3; 8. 12, Jud. 3. 29; 4. 6; 15. 11, 1 S. 26. 2. Cf. Rem. 1.

(*b*) With noun determined by Art. or def. gen. the Num. is mostly in *cons.* with gen. of noun. Deu. 10. 4 עֲשֶׂרֶת הַדְּבָרִים *the ten words.* Jos. 10. 16 חֲמֵשֶׁת הַמְּלָכִים *the five kings.* Jud. 3. 3 חֲמֵשֶׁת סַרְנֵי פְלִשְׁתִּים *the five lords* of the Ph. 1 S. 16. 10 שִׁבְעַת בָּנָיו *his seven sons.* Gen. 40. 12, 18, Nu. 23. 4, Jud. 14. 12; 18. 7, 1 S. 17. 13 (20. 20?), 2 S. 21. 22; 23. 16, 1 K. 21. 13, 2 K. 25. 18. There are exceptions, cf. 1 S. 17. 14. Cases like Am. 1. 3, 6, 9, &c., are according to § 20, R. 2.

(*c*) The Num. may follow the noun in Appos.—mostly in later style. 1 Chr. 12. 39 יָמִים שְׁלוֹשָׁה *three days.* Dan. 1. 12. 1 Chr. 22. 14; 25. 5, 2 Chr. 3. 12; 4. 8, Neh. 2. 11, Dan. 1. 5, 15, Ezr. 8. 15, cf. Jos. 21 *pass.* Ex. in earlier books are comparatively rare, Gen. 32. 15, 16. In 1 S. 1. 24 *rd* בְּפַר מְשֻׁלָּשׁ.

Rem. 1. Additional ex. of *a.* Gen. 30. 20; 45. 23; 47. 2, Deu. 16. 9, 16; 17. 6, Jos. 6. 4, Jud. 9. 34; 16. 8, 1 S. 1. 8; 25. 5, 2 S. 21. 6, 1 K. 5. 28; 7. 4, 30; 10. 19; 17. 12; 18. 23; 21. 10, 2 K. 2. 24, Jer. 2. 13. There are exceptions, 1 K. 11. 16.

Rem. 2. The position of the Num. before the noun is almost exclusive in earlier writings, and is common at all times. This is true of all Num., whether units or higher numbers. The position after the noun occurs in Kings, is not unusual in P., and becomes very usual in Chr., Ezr., Neh., Dan., &c.[1]

---

[1] Sven Herner, *Syntax der Zahlwörter im Alt. Test.*, Lund, 1893. This careful Treatise pays particular attention to the literary age of the various usages.

Rem. 3. The *gend.* is sometimes inexact. Gen. 7. 13
(due to mas. form of noun), cf. Ex. 26. 26; Job 1. 4, Ez.
7. 2, Zech. 3. 9, 1 Chr. 3. 20, Ez. 45. 3 Kth.—The noun is
sometimes sing. after units in the case of words used col-
lectively, 2 K. 8. 17; 22. 1 (year), 25. 17 (cubit), Ex. 21. 37
(בקר, צאן), cf. Gen. 46. 27; and in cases where the thing
weighed or measured is omitted (§ 37, R. 4). Gen. 24. 22,
Jud. 17. 10, 1 S. 10. 4; 17. 17; 21. 4, Ex. 16. 22. In Ez.
45. 1 *rd.*, breadth *twenty* thousand.

Rem. 4. The Num. 2, 3, 4, 7 may take suffixes, as שְׁנֵינוּ
we two, both of us, שְׁלָשְׁתָּם *they three*, &c. Nu. 12. 4, 1 S.
25, 43, 2 S. 21. 9, Ez. 1. 8, Dan. 1. 17, cf. 2 K. 1. 10 *his*
fifty.—The *order* is to be observed : Gen. 9. 19 שְׁלֹשָׁה אֵלֶּה
these three, 1 K. 3. 18 שְׁתַּיִם אֲנַחְנוּ *we two*. Gen. 22. 23, Deu.
19. 9, 1 S. 20. 42. So *gen.* Ex. 21. 11, 2 S. 21. 22, Is. 47, 9.

Rem. 5. The language says *two three*, &c. (without *or*),
as Engl. 2 K. 9. 32, Is. 17. 6, Am. 4. 8.

§ 37. Numerals above the units mostly have the noun in
plur. (except collectives and words of *time, measure,* and
weight). They stand in Appos., and mainly precede their
noun—but may follow (chiefly in later style). When they
follow, the noun is *plur.*, even though otherwise employed in
sing.

(*a*) The Num. 11–19. Gen. 37. 9 אַחַד עָשָׂר כּוֹכָבִים
eleven stars. 2 S. 9. 10 חֲמִשָּׁה עָשָׂר בָּנִים *fifteen sons*. Jos.
4. 8 שְׁתֵּי עֶשְׂרֵה אֲבָנִים *twelve stones*. Gen. 32. 23; 42. 13,
Ex. 15. 27; 24. 4, Deu. 1. 23, Jud. 3. 14, 2 S. 2. 30; 9. 10;
19. 18, 1 K. 18. 31, 2 K. 14. 21. Ex. 27. 15, Nu. 17. 14; 29.
14, 15, Jos. 15. 41.

(*b*) The tens, 20–90. Jud. 12. 14 אַרְבָּעִים בָּנִים *forty
sons*. Gen. 18. 24 חֲמִשִּׁים צַדִּיקִם *fifty righteous*. Exceptional
order, Gen. 32. 15, 16 אֲתֹנֹת עֶשְׂרִים *twenty she-asses*, &c.
Gen. 18. 26, 28, Ex. 15. 27; 21. 32, Jud. 1. 7; 8. 30; 10. 4;
12. 14; 14. 11–13, 2 S. 3. 20; 9. 10, 2 K. 2. 16; 10. 1; 13. 7;
15, 20, Ez. 42. 2; 45. 12.

(*c*) Numbers composed of tens and units, *e.g.* 23, are treated as a single number *twenty-and-three*; and as they stand in Appos. the unit remains in the *Abs.* (cases like 2 K. 2. 24 are exceptional). The *gend.* of the unit is, of course, determined by the noun: Jud. 10. 2 עֶשְׂרִים וְשָׁלשׁ שָׁנָה *23 years.* The order *three-and-twenty* also occurs—chiefly in later style. It also belongs to later style to separate the elements of the Num., repeating the noun with each, as *twenty year and three years,* or the reverse order (mainly with the word *year*).

Jud. 7. 3 עֶשְׂרִים וּשְׁנַיִם אֶלֶף *22 thousand* (cf. Rem. 1). Nu. 7. 88 ע' וְאַרְבָּעָה פָּרִים *24 oxen.* Nu. 35. 6, Jos. 19. 30; 21. 39, Jud. 10. 3; 20. 15, 35, 46, 2 K. 10. 14, Ez. 11. 1, 1 Chr. 2. 22; 12. 29.—Gen. 11. 24, Ex. 38. 24, Nu. 3. 39, 43; 26. 22; 31. 38, Jud. 20. 21.—Gen. 5. 15; 12. 4; 23. 1; 25. 7. Cf. Gen. 5 *pass.*, Gen. 11. 13–25. Lev. 12. 4, 5 (repet. of *days*), cf. Num. 31. 32 *seq.* (thousand).

(*d*) The usage is the same with מֵאָה *hundred,* מָאתַיִם, מֵאוֹת (all in abs.; cons. מְאַת in later style); and אֶלֶף *thousand,* אֲלָפִים, אֲלָפִים (cons. אַלְפֵי occasional, Ex. 32. 28, Job 1. 3). 1 K. 18. 4 מֵאָה נְבִיאִים *100 prophets.* Jud. 15. 4 שְׁלשׁ־מֵאוֹת שׁוּעָלִים *300 foxes.* 1 K. 3. 4 אֶלֶף עֹלוֹת *1000 burnt-offerings.* 2 K. 3. 4 מֵאָה אֶלֶף אֵילִים *100,000 rams* (Rem. 1). 2 K. 18. 23 אַלְפַּיִם סוּסִים *2000 horses.* Ex. of *hundred*: Jud. 7. 22, 1 S. 17. 7; 18. 25; 25. 18; 30. 21, 2 S. 3. 14; 8. 4; 14. 26; 16. 1, 1 K. 7. 20; 10. 17; 11. 3, Jos. 7. 21. Ex. of *thousand*: 1 S. 13. 5; 17. 5, 1 K. 5. 6, Job 42. 12.

(*e*) While, however, the Num. 11 and upward are construed with plur., except with collectives and words of *time, weight,* and *measure,* there is a natural tendency in enumerations to regard the thing enumerated as forming a *class* or genus, and to use the sing.; cf. § 17. Ex. 24. 4, Jud. 21. 12, 2 S. 8. 4; 23. 8, 1 K. 5. 12; 9. 14, 2 K. 24. 14. Comp. 1 K.

10. 16 ,ith 17, and 2 K. 2. 16 with 17; Ex. 26. 19 with 36. 24. The sing. is chiefly used with things which one is accustomed to count; the sing. *king*, 1 K. 20. 1, 16, is unusual. Rem. 1.

(*f*) When the expression is def. the Art. usually goes with the noun, and the Num. is def. of itself. Jud. 7. 7 שְׁלֹשׁ אֶת־אֶלֶף מֵאוֹת הָאִישׁ *the 300 men* (Rem. 1). 17. 3 וּמֵאָה מָאתַיִם הָאֲנָשִׁים *the 1100* (shekels) *of silver.* 1 S. 30. 21 הַכֶּסֶף *the 200 men.* Gen. 18. 28, Deu. 9. 25, Jos. 4. 20, Jud. 7. 22; 18. 17, 1 K. 7. 44, 2 Chr. 25. 9, Ex. 26. 19; 36. 24.

Rem. 1. Words used in sing. in the cases *a—d* are יוֹם *days*, שָׁנָה *years*, אִישׁ *men* (esp. of troops), אֶלֶף *thousands*, אַמָּה *cubits* (often pl.), בַּת, כֹּר (measures), כִּכָּר *talents* (also pl.), שֶׁקֶל, גֵּרָה (oftenest pl.) &c.; and collect. as רַגְלִי *infantry*, רֶכֶב *chariots*, נֶפֶשׁ *persons*, בקר *cattle*, צֹאן *sheep.* Usage fluctuates; cf. § 17.—Adj. and words in Appos. may agree grammatically in sing. 1 S. 22, 18, 1 K. 20. 16, or *ad sensum* in pl. Jud. 18. 16, 1 K. 1. 5.

Rem. 2. In *eleven* the forms עַשְׁתֵּי עָשָׂר, עֲשָׂ', ע', עֶשְׂרֵה occur Deu. 1. 3, Jer. 1. 3; 39. 2, Ez. 26. 1, but chiefly belong to later style. In *twelve* the forms שְׁנֵים עָשָׂר, שְׁתֵּים עֶשְׂרֵה are usual, the cons. שְׁנֵי &c., comparatively rare.

Rem. 3. The form *twenty-and-three* (in *c*) is the older order and the one usual at all times, *i.e.* the larger number first and the two joined by *and.* The same order is usual when there are higher numbers, thus: hundreds *and* tens *and* units; thousands *and* hundreds *and* tens, &c. It is characteristic of later style (occasionally in Kings) to put the smaller number first or omit the *and.* Cf. Ezr. 2 or Neh. 7 *pass.*, Nu. 4. 36, 1 K. 10. 14. The repet. *20 year and 3 years* or reverse order is almost peculiar to P.[1]

Rem. 4. Words readily understood in expressions of weight, measure, or date are often omitted, as *shekel, ephah, day*, Gen. 24. 22 עֲשָׂרָה זָהָב *ten* (shekels) *gold*, Ru. 3. 15 שֵׁשׁ שְׂעֹרִים *six* (ephahs) *of barley*, Gen. 20. 16; 45. 22, 1 S. 10. 3, 4;

---

[1] According to Herner, § 12, only 1 K. 6. 1 outside of P.

17. 17, 1 K. 10. 16. On om. of *day*, § 38*c*. The consn. Ex. 26. 2 אַרְבַּע בָּאַמָּה four *by the cubit*, four cubits, is common in later style. Ez. 40. 5, Zech. 5. 2, 1 Chr. 11. 23.

Rem. 5. Numerals as independent nouns may take the Art. Gen. 18. 29 הָאַרְבָּעִים *the forty*. 2 K. 1. 13 הַחֲמִשִּׁים הַשְּׁלִישִׁי *the third fifty; v. 14 the former* (pl.) *fifties*; with suff. *v.* 10. Gen. 14. 9, Nu. 3. 46, Deu. 19. 9, 2 S. 23. 18 seq. In most other cases the Num. is without Art., though there are exceptions. Jos. 4. 4 שְׁנֵים הֶעָשָׂר אִישׁ *the twelve men*, Nu. 16. 35, Ex. 28. 10.

Rem. 6. After *eleven* and upwards the *sing.* noun, particularly of material or commodity, is probably in *acc.* of specification. § 71.

§ 38. The Ordinals.—(*a*) The ordinals *first—tenth* are adj. and used regularly (Gr. § 48. 2). Jud. 19. 5 בַּיּוֹם הָרְבִיעִי *on the fourth day*. 2 K. 18. 9 בַּשָּׁנָה הָרְבִיעִית. So always in stating the number of the *month* (cf. *c*), 1 Chr. 27. 2–13.

(*b*) From *eleventh* upwards the Card. numbers do duty for ordinals, and Art. is not generally used with the noun. Deu. 1. 3 בְּאַרְבָּעִים שָׁנָה *in the fortieth year*. 2 K. 25. 27 בִּשְׁנֵים עָשָׂר חֹדֶשׁ *in the twelfth month*. Ex. 16. 1, Deu. 1. 2, 3, 2 K. 25. 27, Jer. 25. 3, 1 Chr. 24. 12–18; 25. 18–31.

(*c*) In stating dates there are some peculiarities. 1. The *gen.* "of the month" is circumscribed by prep., לַחֹדֶשׁ, and *day* is often omitted. Ex. 16. 1 בַּחֲמִשָּׁה עָשָׂר יוֹם לַחֹדֶשׁ *on the fifteenth day of the month*. 2 K. 25. 27 בְּעֶשְׂרִים וְשִׁבְעָה לַחֹדֶשׁ *on the 27th of the month*. Even the Card. 1–10 are greatly used in this case, mostly with om. of *day*. 2 K. 25. 8 בְּשִׁבְעָה לַחֹדֶשׁ *on the seventh*. Deu. 1. 3 בְּאֶחָד לַחֹדֶשׁ *on the first*. Gen. 8. 5, Lev. 23. 32, Ez. 1. 1, Zech. 7. 1, cf. 2 Chr. 29. 17, Ezr. 3. 6.

2. The word *year* is very often put in cons. before the whole phrase, Num. and year. 2 K. 8. 25 בִּשְׁנַת שְׁתֵּים עֶשְׂרֵה שָׁנָה *in the year of twelve years* (the twelfth year),

1 K. 16. 8, 15, 29, 2 K. 8. 25; 14. 23; 15. 13, 17, 23, 27; 25. 8. And with *year* understood : 1 K. 15. 25, 28 בִּשְׁנַת שְׁתַּיִם *the year of two* years (second year). 1 K. 16. 10; 22. 41, 2 K. 3. 1; 15. 30, 32; 18. 10; 24. 12, Zech. 7. 1, Ezr. 5. 13, Neh. 1. 1, Dan. 1. 21 ; 2. 1.

Rem. 1. The adj. אחד *one* is very often used for *first*, Gen. 2. 11 seq.; 4. 19, Ex. 1. 15, Nu. 11. 26, 2 S. 4. 2, Ru. 1. 4.

Rem. 2. The word *year* is also construed with gen. of the *def.* Ordinal. 2 K. 17. 6 בִּשְׁנַת הַתְּשִׁיעִית *in the year of the ninth* year. 2 K. 25. 1, Jer. 32. 1, Ezr. 7. 8, Neh. 2. 1 ; 5. 14.—In *c* the form בֶּעָשׂוֹר לַחֹדֶשׁ is used for *on the tenth* of the m. (spelling plenary except Ex. 12. 3).

Rem. 3. The Art. seems used with the Num. in cases where the whole expression is def., as Lev. 25, 10, 11 *the fiftieth year* (of jubilee), Deu. 15. 9 *the seventh year* (of manumission), 1 K. 19. 19 ; but occasionally in other cases, Ex. 12. 18, Nu. 33, 38, 1 K. 6. 38, 1 Chr. 24. 16; 25. 19; 27. 15. Its place varies, 1 K. 19. 19 שְׁנֵים הֶעָשָׂר with 1 Chr. 25. 19 הַשְׁנַיִם עָשָׂר.

Rem. 4. *Distributives.*—(*a*) These may be expressed by Card. with לְ *to* : 1 K. 10. 22 אַחַת לְשָׁלֹשׁ שָׁנִים once *to* = *every three years.* Ex. 16. 22, 1 K. 5. 2, Ez. 1. 6. (*b*) By repeating the Num. Gen. 7. 2, 3, 9, 15, Ex. 17. 12, 1 K. 18. 13, Ez. 40. 10. § 29, R. 8. Very often the whole phrase is repeated, Is. 6. 2 *six wings, six wings* to each, Jos. 3. 12, Nu. 13. 2; 34. 18, Ex. 36. 30.

Rem. 5. *Multiplicatives* are expressed variously.—Thus: *as much as* you, they, &c., by כָּכֶם, כָּהֶם, 2 S. 24. 3, Jer. 36. 32, Deu. 1. 11.—*double* by מִשְׁנֶה, used in Appos. either before or after the noun, Gen. 43. 12 (after), 15 (before), Ex. 16. 5, 22. Also by שְׁנַיִם, Ex. 22. 3, 6, 8, *twofold.*—By the *du. fem.* of Num., as 2 S. 12. 6 אַרְבַּעְתָּיִם *fourfold.* Gen. 4. 15 שִׁבְעָתָיִם *sevenfold.* Is. 30. 26, Ps. 12. 7. Or by simple Card. Lev. 26. 21, 24, cf. Gen. 4. 24.—By יָדוֹת (hands), Gen. 43. 34 *fivefold,* Dan. 1. 20 *tenfold.* Comp. Gen. 26. 12 מֵאָה שְׁעָרִים *a hundredfold.*

Times is expressed by פַּעַם (beat). Gen. 2. 23 הַפַּעַם *this time*. Jos. 6. 3 אַחַת פ' *one time*. Neh. 13. 20 וּשְׁתַּיִם פ' *once or twice*. Gen. 27. 36; 43. 10 פַּעֲמַיִם *two times*. Ex. 23. 17 שָׁלֹשׁ פְּעָמִים *three times*, &c. Gen. 33. 3, Nu. 14. 22, 2 K. 13. 19, Job 19. 3, Neh. 4. 6.—2 S. 24. 3 מֵאָה פעמים *100 times*. Deu. 1. 11 אלף פעמים *1000 times*, 1 K. 22. 16.—The word *time* may be omitted. 2 K. 6. 10 אַחַת, שְׁתַּיִם *once, twice*. 1 K. 10. 22, Job 40. 5. Also בְּאַחַת, בִּשְׁתַּיִם 1 S. 18. 21, Job 33. 14, Nu. 10. 4. With similar omission, שֵׁנִית *a second time*, Gen. 41. 5, Is. 11. 11; שְׁלִישִׁת *a third time*, 1 S. 3. 8, *a seventh time* 1 K. 18. 44.—Other words for *times* are רְגָלִים Ex. 23. 14, Nu. 22. 28, 32, 33; and מֹנִים Gen. 31. 7.

Rem. 6. *Fractions.*—Apart from חֲצִי *half*, 1 K. 16. 21, &c., fractions are formed: (*a*) by separate words, as רֹבַע *a fourth*, Nu. 23. 10, 2 K. 6. 25; חֹמֶשׁ *a fifth*, Gen. 47. 26. The analogy has not been followed in other cases (cf. Ar. *tholth* a third). The form רֶבַע also, 1 S. 9. 8. For a *tenth* עִשָּׂרֹן (pl. 'עֶשׂ), peculiar to P. The *tithe* is מַעֲשֵׂר. (*b*) By the *fem.* of Ordin. as שְׁלִשִׁית *a third*, 2 S. 18. 2, 2 K. 11. 5, Ez. 5. 2, 12; רְבִעִית *a fourth*, Nu. 15. 4, Neh. 9. 3. So the others, Gen. 47. 24, Lev. 5. 11, 16, 24, Ez. 4. 11; 45. 13. Above *tenth* the Card. must be used, Neh. 5. 11, *the one per cent*. The noun of measure, weight, &c., usually has the Art. after the fraction, Ex. 26. 16, Nu. 15. 4; 28. 14, 1 K. 7. 31, 32, 2 K. 6. 25, Ez. 45. 13; 46. 14.

Obs.—In prose composition these general rules may be safely followed. 1. Place all numerals *before* their noun. 2. The units take their noun in *pl.*; before an indef. noun they are in the abs., except *two*; before a def. noun in cons.; also in cons. before the word *days* and before other numerals. 3. The numbers 11–19 have fixed forms (Gr. § 48), but the *second* form of 11 and 12 may be neglected. 4. The numbers 11 and upwards take their noun in *pl.*, except collectives, and words of *time, weight*, and *measure*, though usage is not uniform, § 37, R. 1. 5. Compound numbers like 23 form one number *twenty-and-three* (in this order), the unit in abs., but its gender regulated by the noun. So in greater numbers the largest first, and each class joined by *and*, as 6000 *and* 300 *and* 50 *and* four. 6. The rules for Ordinals, § 38.

SYNTAX OF THE VERB

THE PERFECT

§ 39. The simple perf. is used to express an action completed either in reality or in the thought of the speaker.

The perf. is used to express completed actions where
Eng. also uses past tenses.—(*a*) Like the Eng. past tense, to
denote an action completed at a time indicated by the
narrative, as Gen. 4. 26 הוּחַ֫ל אָז *then it was begun* (began
men); or completed in the indefinite past, Job 1. 1 הָיָה אִישׁ
there was a man.   Gen. 3. 1; 15. 18; 22. 1; 29. 9; 31. 20.
Even if the finished action may have extended over a period
of time, unless it is desired to mark this specially, the simple
perf. is employed; Gen. 14. 4, twelve years עָבְ֫דוּ *they served*,
1 K. 14. 21, and often.

(*b*) Like the Eng. perf. with *have*, to denote an action
finished in the past but continuing in its effects into pres.;
Gen. 4. 6 פָנֶ֫יךָ נָפְלוּ לָ֫מָּה *why has* (is) *thy face fallen?*   Is.
1. 4 אֶת־יְ עָֽזְבוּ *they have forsaken* the Lord.   In this case
the pres. must sometimes be used in Eng., Ps. 2. 1 לָ֫מָּה
גוֹיִם רָֽגְשׁוּ *why do* the nations *rage?* Ps. 1. 1.   Or to denote
an action *just* finished, or finished within an understood
period; Gen. 4. 10 עָשִׂ֫יתָ מֶה *what hast thou done?*   1 S.
12. 3 לָקָ֫חְתִּי מִי אֶת־שׁוֹר *whose ox have I taken?*   Gen.
3. 22; 12. 18; 22. 12; 26. 22; 46. 31, Ex. 5. 14, Nu. 22. 34,
Jud. 10. 10; 11. 7, 1 S. 14. 29.

(*c*) Like the Eng. pluperf. to indicate that one of two
actions was completed before the other.   This use is most
common in dependent (relative or conjunctive) clauses.   Gen.

2. 8, he put there אֶת־הָאָדָם אֲשֶׁר יָצָר the man *whom he had made*; 6. 6 וַיִּנָּחֶם י׳ כִּי עָשָׂה אֶת־הָאָדָם repented *that he had made* man. Gen. 2. 5, 22; 3. 23; 18. 8, 33; 19. 27; 26. 15, 18; 28. 11, Nu. 22. 2, 1 S. 6. 19; 7. 14; 28. 20, 1 K. 5. 15; 11. 9. With modal force, Gen. 40. 15 *should have put*, 1 S. 17. 26 *should have defied*. After הִנֵּה, Gen. 19. 28 the smoke *was gone up*, Deu. 9. 16, Jud. 6. 28.

When the dependent clause is introduced by *and* the subj. usually precedes the verb; Gen. 20. 4 וַאֲבִי׳ לֹא קָרַב אֵלֶיהָ *and* Abimelek *had not approached*. 31. 19, 34, Jud. 6. 21, 1 S. 9. 15; 25. 21; 28. 3, 2 S. 18. 18, 1 K. 1. 41, 2 K. 9. 16.

(*d*) In hypothetical sentences the perf. is employed both in protasis and apodosis where Lat. subj. would be used. Jud. 13. 23 לוּ חָפֵץ לַהֲמִיתֵנוּ לֹא לָקַח עֹלָה *if he had wanted* to kill us *he would not have taken* a burnt-offering. Gen. 43. 10, Nu. 22. 33, Jud. 8. 19; 14. 18, Is. 1. 9. So in other supposed cases; Gen. 26. 10 one of the people כִּמְעַט שָׁכַב *might readily have lain*, 2 K. 13. 19. Also in Opt. sent. in ref. to past, Nu. 14. 2, and fut., Is. 48. 18; 63. 19. Cf. Cond. and Opt. Sent. §§ 130, 134.

Rem. 1. Though it may be doubtful whether the shades of meaning expressed by our tenses were present to the eastern mind, it is of great consequence to observe them in translation. The direct sent. 1 K. 21. 14 סֻקַּל נָבוֹת וַיָּמֹת N. *has been stoned and is dead*, when made dependent by כִּי v. 15, must be rendered, *that* N. *had been stoned and was dead*. In Is. 53. 5, 6 the perf. must be translated in three ways: all we *were* (had) *gone astray*; the Lord *caused to fall* on him; by his stripes *we have been healed*. Job 1. 21, the Lord gave . . . *hath taken*. In Ps. 30. perf. has all its various uses: *v.* 4 *hast brought up*; *v.* 7 *I said*; *v.* 8 *hadst made to stand* . . . *didst hide*; *v.* 12 *hast turned* (or possibly *didst turn*). Ezr. 1. 7. So inchoative perf., Ps. 97. 1 י׳ מָלָךְ *is become king*; 2 K. 15. 1 *became king*, and often.

§ 40. The perf. expresses actions regarded as completed, where Eng. rather uses the present.—(*a*) In the case of stative verbs, *i.e.* verbs expressing mainly a mental or physical condition, as *to know, remember, refuse, trust, rejoice, hate, love, desire, be just*, &c.; *to be, be high, great, small, deep, clean, full, be old, many*, &c. Eng. by its pres. expresses the condition, Heb. rather the act which has resulted in it. Gen. 27. 2 זָקַנְתִּי לֹא יָדַעְתִּי יוֹם מוֹתִי *I am old, I know not*, &c.; Jud. 14. 16 רַק שְׂנֵאתַנִי וְלֹא אֲהַבְתָּנִי *thou only hatest me, and lovest me not*; Gen. 42. 31 לֹא הָיִינוּ מְרַגְּלִים *we are not spies*. Stative verbs, however, often occur in such a way that their perf. must be rendered by a past tense; Gen. 28. 16 *I knew*, 34. 19 *he delighted*, 37. 3 *loved*, Jud. 8. 34 *remembered*. The connexion shows to what time the completed act belongs.

(*b*) In a class of actions which are completed just in the act of giving them expression. This usage appears chiefly with verbs denoting to speak, as verbs of swearing, declaring, advising, and the like, or their equivalents in gesture. Deu. 26. 3 הִגַּדְתִּי הַיּוֹם *I profess* this day; 2 S. 17. 11 כִּי יָעַצְתִּי *I advise*; 2 S. 19. 8 בַּיהוָה נִשְׁבַּעְתִּי *I swear* by the Lord Gen. 22. 16, Nu. 14. 20, Deu. 4. 26; 26. 17; 30. 15, 18, 19, 1 S. 17. 10, 2 S. 16. 4 *I worship*, 19. 30, 1 K. 2. 42 *I hear* (obey), 2 K. 9. 3 *I anoint*, Jer. 22. 5; 42. 19, Ez. 36. 7, Ps. 129. 8; 130. 1, Pr. 17. 5. Song 2. 7 *I adjure*. So the frequent אָמַר י' *saith* Je., or כֹּה א' י' *thus saith*. In some cases impf. יֹאמַר is used, hardly as a frequent. but as a present. This occurs in the midst of a speech, Is. 1. 11, 18; 33. 10; 40. 1, 25; 41. 21, Ps. 12. 6. Both forms Is. 66. 9.

(*c*) In a class of actions which, being of frequent occurrence, have been proved by experience (perf. of experience). Jer. 8. 7 the turtle and swallow שָׁמְרוּ אֶת־עֵת בֹּאָנָה *observe* the time of their coming; Job 7. 9 כָּלָה עָנָן וַיֵּלַךְ *the cloud*

dissolves and vanishes. Is. 40. 7, 8, Am. 5. 8, Ps. 84. 4 *findeth,*
layeth, Pr. 1. 7 *despise,* 14. 19 *bow*; 22. 12, 13.

Rem. 1. Exx. of stative verbs. זכר *remember,* Nu. 11. 5,
Jer. 2. 2; מֵאֵן *refuse,* Ex. 7. 14, Nu. 22, 13, Deu. 25. 7;
בטח *trust,* 2 K. 18. 19, 20; שמח *rejoice,* 1 S. 2. 1, Is. 9. 2;
חפץ *to wish,* Deu. 25. 8, Is. 1. 11; צדק *be just,* Gen. 38. 26,
Ps. 19. 10; נבה *be high,* Is. 3. 16; 55. 9; גדל *be great,* Gen.
19. 13; קטן *be small,* Gen. 32. 11; עמק *be deep,* Ps. 92. 6;
טהר *be clean,* Pr. 20. 9; מלא *be full,* Is. 2. 6, Mic. 3. 8;
אבל *to mourn,* Is. 33. 9, Joel. 1. 9; אבה *be willing,* Deu.
25. 7; מאס *loathe,* Am. 5. 21, Job 7. 16; שׂבע *be sated,* Is.
1. 11; רבב *be many,* Ps. 3. 2 (רבה = become many); קוּה *hope,*
Ps. 130. 5, &c.

§ 41. The perf. is used to express actions which a lively
imagination conceives as completed, but for which the fut. is
more usual in Eng.—(*a*) The perf. of certainty. Actions
depending on a resolution of the will of the speaker (or of
others whose mind is known), or which appear inevitable
from circumstances, or which are confidently expected, are
conceived and described as having taken place. This use is
common in promises, threats, bargaining, and the like. Is.
42. 1 הֵן עַבְדִּי נָתַתִּי רוּחִי עָלָיו behold my servant, *I will
put* my spirit upon him; Is. 6. 5 אוֹי־לִי כִי־נִדְמֵיתִי woe is
me *for I am undone*; Ru. 4. 3 חֶלְקַת הַשָּׂדֶה מָכְרָה נָעֳמִי
Naomi *is selling* the field-portion. Gen. 15. 18; 17. 20;
30. 13, Nu. 17. 27, 28, Jud. 15. 3, 1 S. 2. 16; 14. 10; 15. 2,
2 S. 24. 23, 1 K. 3. 13, 2 K. 5. 20, Is. 30. 19, Jer. 4. 13; 31.
5, 6, Ps. 6. 9, 10; 20. 7; 36. 13; 37. 38. In these last exx.
and many others the tense may be called the perf. of
confidence.

(*b*) It often happens, esp. in the higher style, that in the
midst of descriptions of the fut. the imagination suddenly
conceives the act as accomplished, and interjects a perf.
amidst a number of imperfs. Job 5. 20, 23 *hath redeemed*

(4. 10); Hos. 5. 5 Judah *is fallen*. This usage receives an extension among the prophets, whose imagination so vividly projects before them the event or scene which they predict that it appears realised.   Is. 5. 13 גָּלָה עַמִּי מִבְּלִי־דָעַת my people *is gone into captivity*; 9. 5 כִּי יֶלֶד יֻלַּד־לָנוּ for *a child has been born to us*; 9. 1 הַהֹלְכִים בַּחֹשֶׁךְ רָאוּ אוֹר גָּדוֹל they who walked in darkness *have seen great light*. Is. 5. 14; 9. 2 seq., 10. 28; 11. 8, 9; 28. 2, Hos. 4. 6; 10. 7, 15, Jer. 4. 29, Am. 5. 2.   The prophetic perf. is sometimes scarcely to be distinguished from perf. of confidence, Ps. 22. 22, 30.

(*c*) The perf. is used in the sense of the *future perf.* to indicate that an action though fut. is finished in relation to another fut. action.   Gen. 24. 19 עַד אִם־כִּלּוּ לִשְׁתֹּת *until they* (shall) *have done* drinking; 2 S. 5. 24 כִּי אָז יָצָא י׳ לְפָנֶיךָ for then Je. *will have gone forth*.   Gen. 28. 15; 43. 9; 48. 6, 1 S. 1. 28, 2 K. 7. 3; 20. 9, Is. 4. 4; 6. 11; 16. 12, Jer. 8. 3, Mic. 5. 2, Ru. 2. 21.

> Rem. 1. The prophetic perf. may be distinguished from the ordinary perf. by the fact that it is not maintained consistently, but interchanges with *impfs.* or *vav conv. perfs.*, the prophet abandoning his ideal position and returning to the actual, and so falling into the ordinary *fut.* tenses, *e.g.* Is. 5. 14–17.   The prophetic passage may begin with *perf.*, Is. 5. 13, which is frequently introduced by כִּי *for*, לָכֵן *therefore*, or other particles, Is. 3. 8; 9. 5; or it may begin with *vav impf.*, Is. 2. 9.   When further clauses with *and* are added, if the ideal position be sustained, the natural secution, *vav impf.*, may be used, Is. 9. 5, Ps. 22. 30, or simple *perf.* if verb be disconnected with *and*, Is. 5. 16.   But frequently the ideal position is deserted and the ordinary *fut.* tenses, the *impf.* or *vav perf.*, are employed, Is. 5. 14, cf. *v.* 17, Ps. 85, 11, 12.   Cf. Is. 13. 9, 10; 14. 24; 35, 2, 6; 46. 13; 47. 9; 52. 15; 60. 4.
>
> Rem. 2. It seems but a variety of (*c*) when the perf. is used in questions expressing any lively feeling, as astonishment, indignation, incredulity, or the like.   The speaker

imagines the act done, and expresses it in a tone convey-
ing his feeling regarding it. Gen. 18. 12 *shall I have* (had)
pleasure! 21. 7 *who would have said?* Ex. 10. 3; 16. 28,
Jud. 9. 9 *shall I have abandoned*! Nu. 23. 10, 23, 1 S. 26. 9,
2 K. 20. 9, Jer. 30. 21, Ez. 18. 19, Hab. 2. 18, Ps. 10. 13;
11. 3; 39. 8; 80. 5, Job 12. 9. Cf. interchange of perf. and
impf. Hab. 1. 2, 3, Ps. 60. 11.

Rem. 3. Owing to the want of participles expressing
past time, the perf. has to be used in attributive or circumstantial clauses referring to past. Gen. 44. 4 לֹא הִרְחִיקוּ *not
having gone far*; 44. 12 הֵחֵל *beginning* at the eldest; 48. 14
guiding his hands, Gen. 21. 14; Nu. 30. 12 *without checking*,
Deu. 21. 1, Jud. 6. 19; 20. 31, 1 S. 30. 2, 1 K. 13. 18, Job
11. 16 waters *passed away*; Is. 3. 9 *without concealment*.
And so to express an action prior to the main action spoken
of, Ps. 11. 2. Very compressed is the language, Jud. 9. 48
מַה רְאִיתֶם עָשִׂיתִי what *ye have seen me do*. If *me* had been
expressed the consn. would have been an ordinary Ar. one.
Lam. 1. 10, Neh. 13. 23; cf. impf. 2 S. 21. 4, Is. 3. 15.

Rem. 4. Another verb following on perf. is usually
appended with *vav impf.*, but in animated speech asyndetous
perfs. are often accumulated. Deu. 32, 15, Jud. 5. 27, Is.
18. 5; 25. 12; 30. 33, Lam. 2. 16.

Rem. 5. In some instances perf. appears to express a
wish (precative perf.). Job 21. 16 the counsel רָחֲקָה *be far*!
22. 18. Lam. 1. 21 הֵבֵאתָ *bring thou*, where structure of
verse requires ref. to fut; 3. 56 seq., where *v.* 55 continues
54; Ps. 18. 47. Is. 43. 9 נִקְבְּצוּ may be form of imper., and
Ps. 7. 7 צִוִּיתָ a circumst. clause. It would be strange if Heb.
altogether wanted this usage, which is common to all the
Shem. languages in some shape. Wright, ii. 3, Dillm.
p. 406 foot, Noeldeke, p. 181, Del. Assyr. Gr. § 93. The
position of the verb is freer in Heb., as is usual in comparison of Ar. The usage may be allied to perf. of confidence
(Ps. 10. 16; 22. 22; 31. 6; 57. 7; 116. 16), the strong
wish causing the act to be conceived as accomplished.

THE SIMPLE IMPERFECT

§ 42. The simple impf. expresses an action incomplete or unfinished. Such an action may be conceived as nascent, or entering on execution (pres.), progressing, or moving on towards execution (impf.), or as ready, or about to enter upon execution (fut.). Connected with the last use is the use of impf. to express a great variety of actions which are *dependent* on something preceding, whether it be the will or desire of the speaker (juss., opt.), or his judgment or permission (potential), or on some other action, or on particles expressing *purpose* and the like (subjunctive).

The uses of the impf. are very various, and some of them rarer in prose writing; those usual in ordinary prose may be mentioned first.

§ 43. (*a*) The impf. expresses a *future* action, whether from the point of the speaker's present, or from any other point assumed. 1 S. 24. 21 יָדַעְתִּי כִּי מָלֹךְ תִּמְלוֹךְ I know *that thou shalt be king*; 2 K. 3. 27 וַיִּקַּח אֶת־בְּנוֹ אֲשֶׁר יִמְלֹךְ he took his son *who was to be king*; Gen. 2. 17; 3. 4; 6. 7; 37. 8; 43. 25 *were to eat*, 1 K. 7. 7, 2 K. 13. 14 *was to die*.

(*b*) The impf. is employed to express actions which are contingent or depending on something preceding. The shades of sense of impf. in this use of it are manifold, corresponding to Eng. *will* (of volition), *shall* (of command), *may* and *can* (of possibility or permission), *am to*, in the present; and to *would, should, might, could, was to*, in the past or indirect speech. Particularly (1) in interrogative sentences; (2) in dependent clauses with כִּי *that* and the like; and (3) after particles like אֵיךְ *how*! אוּלַי *perhaps*, &c., and conditional particles like אִם *if*. Gen. 3. 2 מִפְּרִי עֵץ־הַגָּן נֹאכֵל *we may eat*; 3. 3 לֹא תֹאכְלוּ מִמֶּנּוּ *ye shall not eat of it*; Gen. 43. 7 הֲיָדוֹעַ נֵדַע כִּי יֹאמַר *were we then to know that he would say*? 27. 45 לָמָה אֶשְׁכַּל שְׁנֵיכֶם *why should I*

be bereaved of you both? 44. 8 נִגְנֹב וְאֵיךְ *and how should we steal!* 2. 19 לוֹ מַה־יִּקְרָא לִרְאֹת to see *what he would call* it; Jud. 9. 28 נַעַבְדֶנּוּ כִּי שְׁכֶם מִי־ who is Shechem *that we should serve him?* Job 9. 29 אֶרְשָׁע אָנֹכִי *I am* (have) *to be guilty!* Gen. 44. 34; 47. 15, Ex. 3. 11, Deu. 7. 17, Jud. 8. 6; 17. 8, 9 *wherever he might find*, 1 S. 18. 18; 20. 2, 5 *should sit*, 23. 13, 2 S. 2. 22; 3. 33 *should* Abner (*was A. to*) *die!* 6. 9, 2 K. 8. 13, Ps. 8. 5, Job 7. 17. With אוּלַי Gen. 16. 2; 24. 5, Nu. 23. 27, 1 S. 6. 5, 1 K. 18. 5, 2 K. 19. 4, Am. 5. 15. With אִם *if*, Gen. 18. 26, 28, 30; 30. 31, Jud. 4. 8, Am. 6. 9. See Cond. Sent.—With Job 9. 29 cf. 10. 15; 12. 4, 1 S. 14. 43; 28. 1.

(c) In particular impf. follows *final* (telic) conjunctions, as לְמַעַן *in order that*, אֲשֶׁר *that*, לְבִלְתִּי *that not*, פֶּן *lest.* Ex. 4. 5 יַאֲמִינוּ לְמַעַן *that they may believe*; Deu. 4. 40 אֲשֶׁר לָךְ יִיטַב *that it may be well* with thee (cf. next clause); Gen. 3. 3 תְּמֻתוּן פֶּן־ בּוֹ תִגְּעוּ לֹא ye shall not touch it *lest ye die.* Ex. 20. 20, 2 S. 14. 14. See Final Sent.

Rem. 1. The expression יוֹדֵעַ מִי *who knows?* differs little from *perhaps*, and is followed by impf., 2 S. 12. 22, Jo. 2. 14, Jon. 3. 9. In Est. 4. 14 אִם is supplied before the verb.

§ 44. Frequentative impf.—The impf. expresses actions of general occurrence, such actions being independent of time. That which is nascent or ready to occur passes easily over into that which is of frequent or indefinite occurrence. This use of impf. is common in proverbial sayings, in comparisons, in the expression of social and other customs, and particularly of actions which, having a certain moral character, are viewed as universal, but also of actions which are or were customary in given circumstances without being necessary.

(a) Of actions for which Eng. uses the present. Gen.

5

10. 9 עַל־כֵּן יֵאָמַר כְּנִמְרֹד therefore *it is said*, as Nimrod ;
6. 21 מִכָּל־מַאֲכָל אֲשֶׁר יֵאָכֵל take of all food *which is eaten*
(edible); Pr. 10. 1 בֵּן חָכָם יְשַׂמַּח־אָב a wise son *makes a
father glad*. Particularly with כֵּן *so*, כַּאֲשֶׁר *as*, and similar
words. 1 S. 24. 14 כַּאֲשֶׁר יֹאמַר מְשַׁל הַקַּדְמֹנִי מֵרְשָׁעִים יֵצֵא
רֶשַׁע *as says* the proverb, Out of the evil *cometh forth evil*;
Jud. 7. 5 כַּאֲשֶׁר יָלֹק הַכֶּלֶב *as a dog laps*; Gen. 29. 26
לֹא־יֵעָשֶׂה כֵן בִּמְקוֹמֵנוּ *it is not so done* in our country. Sometimes this *is not* has the nuance of *ought not*. Gen. 20. 9
מַעֲשִׂים אֲשֶׁר לֹא־יֵעָשׂוּ deeds which *ought not to be done*,
cf. 34. 7, 2 S. 13. 12.—Gen. 50. 3, Ex. 33. 11, Deu. 1. 31, 44 ;
2. 11, 20 ; 28. 29, Jud. 11. 40 ; 14. 10, 1 S. 5. 5 ; 19. 24, 2 S.
5. 8 ; 13. 18 ; 19. 4, Am. 3. 7, 12, Hos. 2. 1 (cannot be counted).
Of a universal truth, Ex. 23. 8, Deu. 16. 19 a gift *blinds*, 1 S.
16. 7, 2 S. 11. 25 the sword *devours*, 1 K. 8. 46 no one *who
sinneth not*, Ps. 1. 3–6. Of a characteristic or habit, Gen.
44. 5, Ex. 4. 14 *speaks* (can speak), Deu. 10. 17, 1 S. 23. 22,
2 S. 19. 36, 2 K. 9. 20 *drives* furiously, Is. 13. 17, 18 (the
Medes), 28. 27, 28, Ps. 1. 2, Job 9. 11–13. But also of an
event repeated or general within a limited area. 1 S. 9. 6
כָל אֲשֶׁר יְדַבֵּר בֹּא יָבֹא *whatever he speaks comes true*; 1 K.
22. 8 לֹא יִתְנַבֵּא עָלַי טוֹב *he never prophesies* good about
me. Ex. 13. 15 ; 18. 15, 2 K. 6. 12, Hos. 4. 8, 13 ; 7. 1–3,
14–16 ; 13. 2 *kiss* calves, Am. 2. 7, 8, Is. 1. 23 ; 14. 8, Mic.
3. 11.

(*b*) Of actions customary or general in the past. Gen. 2. 6
וְאֵד יַעֲלֶה and a mist *used to go up*. 1 S. 2. 19 וּמְעִיל קָטֹן
תַּעֲשֶׂה־לּוֹ אִמּוֹ and a little robe his mother *used to make for
him*. 2 Chr. 9. 21 once every three years תָּבוֹאנָה אֳנִיּוֹת
תַּרְשִׁישׁ *came* the ships of Tarsh. This impf. may *distribute*
an action over its details or particulars ; Gen. 2. 19 וְכֹל אֲשֶׁר
יִקְרָא־לוֹ הָאָדָם *whatever he called it*. Particularly under the
influence of a negative; 1 S. 13. 19 וְחָרָשׁ לֹא יִמָּצֵא a smith

was not to be found; Gen. 2. 25 וְלֹא יִתְבֹּשָׁשׁוּ *they were not* (at any time) *ashamed*; 1 S. 1. 13 שְׂפָתֶיהָ נָעוֹת וְקוֹלָהּ לֹא יִשָּׁמֵעַ her lips moved, *but her voice was not heard*. Ex. 21. 36, 1 K. 8. 8, 27 (cf. 22. 8 in *a*); 18. 10, 2 K. 23. 9 (contrast neg. impf. and pos. perf.), Jer. 13. 7. Cf. Rem. 1.

Rem. 1. Other exx. Gen. 6. 4; 29. 2; 31. 39, Ex. 8. 20, Nu. 11. 5. 9, Deu. 2. 11, 20, Jud. 5. 8; 6. 4, 5; 17. 6, 1 S. 1. 7; 13. 18; 14. 47 (*rd.* perhaps יְיֹשִׁעַ); 18. 5; 23. 13; 25. 28, 2 S. 1. 22 *never returned*; 2. 28 *did not engage in the pursuit*; 12. 3, 31; 17. 17; 20. 18; 23. 10, 1 K. 5. 25, 28; 6. 8; 10. 5; 17. 6; 18. 10; 21. 6, 2 K. 3. 25; 4. 8; 13. 20, Jer. 36. 18, Ps. 106. 43, Job 1. 5, 1 Chr. 20. 3.

Rem. 2. This impf. is used, *e.g.*, 1. in describing a boundary line and naming its *successive* points, Jos. 16. 8, interchanging with *vav perf.*, 15. 3 and often. 2. In describing the course of an ornamentation, 1 K. 7. 15, 23 *ran round*, 2 Chr. 4. 2. 3. In stating the amount of metal that went to *each* of a class of articles, 1 K. 10. 16, 2 Chr. 9. 15; and so of the number of victims offered in a great sacrifice, 1 K. 3. 4, cf. 10. 5. 4. In describing the quantity which a vessel, &c., contained, 1 K. 7. 26. So the details of collecting and disbursing moneys, 2 K. 12. 12–17.—In 2 K. 8. 29 (9. 15) the preceding *plur.* " wounds " perhaps distributes the verb *wounded* (*perf.* 2 Chr. 22. 6), just as *the rest* does Joab's action, 1 Chr. 11. 8, and *all the cities* David's, 1 Chr. 20. 3, and *all the land* the effect of the flies, Ex. 8. 20, cf. Deu. 11. 24. So 2 S. 23. 10 of the people returning in parties or successively (*v.* 9 their dispersion). Jer. 52. 7, Ezr. 9. 4.

Rem. 3. Allied to § 44*a* above is the use of impf. to form attributive or adjectival clauses, descriptive of the subj. or obj. of a previous sentence. The restricted sphere of the ptcp. enlarges this usage. Gen. 49. 27 בנ' זְאֵב יִטְרָף Benj. is *a ravening wolf*; Is. 40. 20 עֵץ לֹא־יִרְקַב a tree *that doth not rot*; Hos. 4. 14 עָם לֹא־יָבִין *an undiscerning* people; Is. 51. 2 שָׂרָה תְּחוֹלֶלְכֶם S. *your mother* (*who bears* you); *v.* 12 man *that dies* (*mortal* man). 55. 13, Ps. 78. 6, Job 8. 12, cf. Ex. 12. 34,

Nu. 11. 33, Zeph. 3. 17. Is. 30. 14 *unsparingly*, Ps. 26. 1
without wavering. Particularly in comparisons. Job 9. 26
כְּנֶשֶׁר יָטוּשׂ as *an eagle swooping*; 7. 2 as a servant *that
longeth*. Deu. 32. 11, Hos. 11. 10, Is. 62. 1, Jer. 23. 29.

§ 45. To express single unfinished or enduring actions in
the *pres.* or *past* the ptcp. is usually employed in prose, with
a different shade of meaning. The impf., however, is often
used after certain particles, as אָז *then*, טֶרֶם *not yet*, בְּטֶרֶם
before. Ex. 15. 1 אָז יָשִׁיר מֹשֶׁה *then sang* Moses; Gen. 19. 4
טֶרֶם יִשְׁכָּבוּ *they were not yet lain down* when, &c. 27. 33
וָאֹכַל בְּטֶרֶם תָּבוֹא and I ate *before thou camest*. Deu. 4. 41,
Jos. 8. 30; 10. 12; 22. 1, 1 K. 3. 16; 9. 11; 11. 7; 16. 21,
2 K. 12. 18; 15. 16.—Gen. 2. 5; 24. 45, 1 S. 3. 3.—Jud. 14. 18,
1 S. 2. 15, 2 K. 6. 32, Jer. 1. 5. So sometimes after עַד, Jos.
10. 13, Ps. 73. 17. See Temporal Sent.

Rem. 1. The use of impf. with interrog. is peculiar. The
interrogation not only brings the action into the present, but
seems to give such force to the verb that the *finite* tense
may be used. Gen. 32. 30 why תִּשְׁאַל *dost thou ask*? 37. 15
מַה־תְּבַקֵּשׁ *what dost thou seek*? comp. the answer אָנֹכִי מְבַקֵּשׁ.
So question and answer Gen. 16. 8. 2 K. 20. 14 מֵאַיִן יָבֹאוּ
whence came they? with the answer בָּאוּ *they came*. Gen.
44. 7, Ex. 2. 13; 3. 3, Jud. 17. 9; 19. 17, 1 S. 1. 8; 17. 8;
28. 16, 2 S. 1. 3, 1 K. 21. 7, Job 1. 7; 2. 2; 15. 7, Is.
45. 9, 10. In some cases the questions may be freq., Is.
40. 27. Perhaps also with other strong particles, like
הִנֵּה 1 S. 21. 15, Gen. 37. 7? And necessarily when ptcp.
is resolved into a *neg.* clause, Jud. 20. 16, Lev. 11. 47.

Rem. 2. Such particles as *then* create a space or period
with which the action is contemporaneous, into which the
speaker throws himself, cf. 2 K. 8. 22 where *then* = *at that*
(general) *time*. In poetry the usage is extended, and appears
with such words as *day*, *time*. Job 3. 3 perish יוֹם אִוָּלֶד בּוֹ the
day on which *I was* (am) *born*! 6. 17, Deu. 32. 35. In
other cases it may be doubtful whether contemporaneousness
or immediate subsequence be expressed: Job 3. 11 why *died*

(die) I not *from the womb*, came I not out of the belly *and expired?* cf. *v.* 13. The pointing וָאָגוֵע would have been good prose (Jer. 20. 17), and so would *perf.* in first clause (Jer. 20. 18), but the one tense protects the other. Cf. the reverse order of events, Nu. 12. 12.

In elevated style this usage of impf. is common. The speaker does not bring the past into his own present, he transports himself back into the past, with the events in which he is thus face to face. Ex. 15. 5 the depths יְכַסְיֻמוּ *covered* (cover) *them*; Deu. 32. 10 יִמְצָאֵהוּ *found* (findeth) *him*; Ps. 80. 9 a vine from Eg. תַּפִּיעַ *thou bringest, thou drivest out* the nations; Job 4. 15. 16 a breath יַחֲלֹף תְּסַמֵּר *passes*, my hair *stands up; it stops*, &c. So an instantaneous effect is graphically expressed. Ex. 15. 12 thou didst stretch thy hand תִּבְלָעֵמוֹ אֶרֶץ the earth *swallows them*, *v.* 14 the nations heard יִרְגָּזוּן *they are terrified*. Is. 41. 5, Hab. 3. 10, Ps. 46. 7; 77. 17; 69. 33; 78. 20. The Eng. pres. best renders this impf., our historical pres. being a similar usage. Nu. 23. 7 Balak יַנְחֵנִי *bringeth me*. Ps. 18. 7; 104. 6–8. Hitz. (Ps. 18. 4) so explains 1 K. 21. 6 כִּי אֲדַבֵּר; כִּי is recitativum. If reading right, Jud. 2. 1 אַעֲלֶה must rather express progressive bringing up. So perhaps 2 S. 15. 37 יָבוֹא *proceeded*. In 1 K. 7. 8 יַעֲשֶׂה is wanting in Sep.

Rem. 3. In the prophetic and higher style the impf. is often used of single actions where prose would express itself differently. There is also frequent interchange of perf. and impf., *e.g.* Is. 5. 12; 9. 17; 10. 28; 13. 10; 14. 24; 18. 5; 19. 6, 7; 42. 25; 43. 17; 49. 13, 17; 51. 6; 60. 4, Hos. 7. 1; 12. 11, Ps. 26. 4, 5; 52. 9; 93. 3. In early writing these changes have meaning, but in later poetry, especially in the historical psalms and Job, the significance is not always apparent, and the changes look part of an unconscious traditional style. Some scholars, however, diminish the difficulty by the assumption that the impf. often stands for *vav impf.* See § 51, R. 5.

Rem. 4. The impf. is frequently used for imper., even in the 2nd pers. Deu. 7. 5; 13. 5, Am. 7. 12, Hab. 3. 2, Ps. 17. 8; 64. 2; 71. 2, 20, 21; 140. 2.

THE CONVERSIVE TENSES. PERF. AND IMPF. WITH
STRONG VAV

§ 46. The conversive tenses seem the result of two
things: first, the feeling of the *connexion* of two actions, and
that the second belongs to the sphere of the first, a connexion expressed by *vav*; and, second, that effort of the
lively imagination already noticed under the simple tense-
forms (§ 41 *b*, § 45, R. 2, 3), by which an impf. is interjected
among perfs., and conversely, a perf. among impfs. These
lively transportations of the imagination, which appear only
occasionally in the case of the simple tenses, have in this
instance given rise to two distinct fixed tense-expressions,
the *vav conv. impf.* and the *vav conv. perf.* In usage the
former has become the historical or narrative tense, and the
latter the usual expression for the fut. or freq. when connected with preceding context by *and*. The actual *genesis*
of these two tense-forms belongs, however, to a period lying
behind the present state of the language. They are now
virtually *simple* forms, having the meaning of the preceding
tenses, impf. or perf., and it is doubtful if it is legitimate to
analyse them, and treat *vav impf.* for ex. as *and* with an
impf. in any of the senses which it might have if standing
alone.—It is the shortened forms of impf. that are usually
employed with *vav*, when these exist; but this is by no
means universal.

IMPERFECT WITH STRONG VAV. VAV CONV. IMPF.

§ 47. *Vav conv. impf.* follows a simple perf. in any of the
senses of the perf. In usage, however, it has become a
tense-form in these meanings of the perf. in narrative style,
though no perf. immediately precedes. If the connexion of
vav and impf. be broken through anything such as a neg.
or other word coming between, the discourse returns to the

simple *perf.* Gen. 1. 5 וַיִּקְרָא לָאוֹר ... וְלַחֹשֶׁךְ קָרָא. Gen. 4. 4, 5 וַיִּשַׁע י׳ אֶל־הֶבֶל וְאֶל־קַיִן לֹא שָׁעָה *and* Je. *had respect* to Abel, *but* to Cain *he had not respect.*

As to the kind of connexion between the preceding and *vav impf.* the latter may express either what is strictly consequential, or what is merely successive in time, or what is only successive in the mind of the speaker. In the last case the event or fact expressed by *vav impf.* may really be identical with the preceding event, and a repetition of it, or synchronous with it, or even anterior to it; the speaker expresses them in the order in which they occur to him, so that the *and* is merely connective, though the form retains its conversive meaning. Gen. 40. 23 לֹא זָכַר ... וַיִּשְׁכָּחֵהוּ *he remembered not* Joseph, *and forgat him*; Jud. 16. 10 הֵתַלְתָּ בִּי וַתְּדַבֵּר אֵלַי כְּזָבִים thou *hast cheated* me, *and to'd* me lies. With *vav perf.*, Jud. 14. 12 אִם הַגֵּד תַּגִּידוּ לִי וּמְצָאתֶם if ye *will tell it* me, *and find it out.* After עָשֹׂה *to do, vav impf.* is often merely explanatory, 1 K. 18. 13. אֵת אֲשֶׁר עָשִׂיתִי וָאַחְבִּא what *I did and hid*, &c. Gen. 31. 26, Ex. 1. 18; 19. 4, Jud. 9. 16, 1 K. 2. 5, 2 Chr. 2. 2, cf. Neh. 13. 17. 2 S. 14. 5 I am a widow וַיָּמָת אִישִׁי *and my husband is dead.* Jud. 2. 21 אֲשֶׁר עָזַב יהו׳ וַיָּמֹת which Joshua *left and died.* So *vav impf.* often merely sums up the result of a preceding narrative, Jud. 3. 30 וַתִּכָּנַע מוֹאָב *so* Moab *was subdued*; 8. 28.

§ 48. (*a*) *Vav impf.* continues a perf. in sense of Eng. past; and it is usual in this sense in narrative, although no perf. actually precedes. Gen. 3. 13 הַנָּחָשׁ הִשִּׁיאַנִי וָאֹכֵל the serpent *deceived me, and I ate.* 4. 1; 7. 19, 1 S. 15. 24. With neg., Gen. 4. 5 unto Cain לֹא שָׁעָה וַיִּחַר לְקַיִן מְאֹד he had not respect, *and C. was very angry.* Gen. 8. 9, Jer. 20. 17, Job 3. 10; 32. 3 did not find an answer *and condemn* (so as to condemn). With interrog., Gen. 12. 19.—When

vav is separated from verb, Gen. 31. 33 וַיָּבֹא . . . וְלֹא מָצָא,
41. 21, Jud. 6. 10.

(*b*) It continues perf. in sense of Eng. perf. with *have*.
Gen. 3. 17 כִּי שָׁמַעְתָּ לְקוֹל אִשְׁתְּךָ וַתֹּאכַל *hast hearkened
and eaten*. 16. 5 וָאֵקַל *and I am despised*; 32. 31. With
interr., Deu. 4. 33 הֲשָׁמַע עָם קוֹל אֱ' וַיֶּחִי *has a people heard
the voice of God and lived?* With neg. 1 S. 15. 19 וְלָמָּה
לֹא־שָׁמַעְתָּ בְּקוֹל יְ' וַתַּעַט *why hast thou not obeyed, but
hast flown* upon the spoil? 1 S. 19. 17, Job 9. 4.—Jos. 4. 9
he set up 12 stones וַיִּהְיוּ שָׁם *and they are there* to this day.
Ís. 50. 7, Jer. 8. 6. Gen. 32. 5, 1 S. 19. 5.

(*c*) In the sense of plup. Gen. 39. 13 כִּי עָזַב בִּגְדוֹ וַיָּנָס
had left his garment *and fled*; 31. 34 וְרָחֵל לָקְחָה . . . וַתְּשִׂמֵם
וַתֵּשֶׁב עֲלֵיהֶם . . . now R. *had taken* the Teraphim, *and put
them* in the camel's saddle, *and sitten down upon them*. Gen.
27. 1; 26. 18, Ex. 15. 19, Nu. 21. 26, Jos. 10. 1, Jud. 4. 11,
1 S. 30. 1, 2, 2 S. 18. 18, 1 K. 2. 41. Is. 39. 1 כִּי חָלָה וַיֶּחֱזָק
heard *that he had been sick, and was better*.

(*d*) After hypothetical or conditional perf. 1 S. 25. 34
לוּלֵי מִהַרְתְּ וַתָּבֹאִי (so *rd*.) unless thou hadst made haste
and come; Ex. 20. 25 כִּי חַרְבְּךָ הֵנַפְתָּ עָלֶיהָ וַתְּחַלְלֶהָ *hast
thou lifted up* thy iron upon it, *thou hast polluted it*. Pr. 11. 2
בָּא זָדוֹן וַיָּבֹא קָלוֹן *has pride come*, shame *has come* (when
pride comes then, &c.), cf. 18. 3.—Nu. 5. 27, Ps. 139. 11, Pr.
18. 22, Job 9. 16; 23. 13. In Opt. Sent. Jos. 7. 7, Is. 48. 18.

Rem. 1. The *contrast* in such passages as Gen. 32. 31
רָאִיתִי אֱ' וַתִּנָּצֵל נַפְשִׁי I have seen God *and* (yet) *my life is preserved* hardly lies in the *vav*, but is suggested by the two
events. 2 S. 3. 8. Neither is it probable that the *vav*
expresses an *inference*; Job 2. 3 וַתְּסִיתֵנִי is not, *and so* (so
that) *thou settest me on*. The ref. is rather to Satan's
insinuation, ch. 1. 9 seq.

Rem. 2. It is questionable whether *vav impf*. has the

sense of plup. except in continuance of a perf. of that
meaning. When *and* introduces something *anterior* to the
general narrative, it is usually disconnected with the verb,
which is then preceded by its subj. (§ 39 *c*). There are a few
peculiar cases, Ex. 32. 29, 1 S. 14. 24, 1 K. 13. 12, Is. 39. 1,
Jer. 39. 11, Zech. 7. 2, Neh. 2. 9. There is nothing to show
that Ex. 32. 29 is anterior, it seems parallel to *v.* 26, 27.
In 1 S. 14. 24 Sep. has a different text in which וַיֹּאֶל stands
quite regularly. In 1 K. 13. 12 the sense requires hiph.
וַיַּרְאוּ *and they showed.* Possibly Is. 39. 1 should *rd.* as 2 K.
20. 12 כִּי שָׁמַע, though the mere fact of a different reading is
not conclusive. See Driver's exhaustive note p. 84.

§ 49 (*a*) Vav impf. continues a perf. of experience,
expressing a common truth. Is. 40. 24 נָשַׁף בָּהֶם וַיִּבָשׁוּ he
blows upon them, *and they wither*; Job 7. 9 כָּלָה עָנָן וַיֵּלַךְ
the cloud wastes away *and vanishes.* Nah. 3. 16, Job 14. 2;
24. 2, 11. So in continuance of a ptcp. with this meaning.
Am. 5. 8 הַקּוֹרֵא לְמֵי הַיָּם וַיִּשְׁפְּכֵם who calleth the waters
of the sea, *and poureth them*; 9. 5.—Gen. 49. 17, 1 S. 2. 6,
Jer. 10. 13, Am. 6. 3, Mic. 7. 3, Nah. 1. 4, Ps. 34. 8, cf. *v.* 21,
Job 12. 18, 22–25, Pr. 21. 22.

(*b*) In continuance of prophetic perf. Is. 9. 5 בֵּן נִתַּן־לָנוּ
וַתְּהִי . . . וַיִּקְרָא a son has been given us, *and* the government
is laid upon his shoulder, *and they have called.* Ps. 22. 30
אָכְלוּ וַיִּשְׁתַּחֲווּ all the fat of the earth *have eaten and
worshipped.* In such cases the *fut.* is almost necessary in
Engl. owing to our different way of thinking. Is. 5. 25;
24. 18; 48. 20, 21, Mic. 2. 13, Jer. 8. 16, Ps. 20. 9. After
perf. of confidence, Ps. 109. 28. With no preceding perf., but
stating the issue of actions just described, Is. 2. 9 וַיִּשַּׁח
אָדָם וַיִּשְׁפַּל־אִישׁ therefore men *are brought down, and man
humbled* (punishment, not practice as A.V.), cf. 5. 15; 44.
12, 13. Job 5. 15, 16; 36. 7. Or confident expectation, Ps.
64. 8–10 וַיֹּרֵם *hath shot at them,* &c. 94. 22, 23; 37. 40.

§ 50. (*a*) Vav impf. continues any verbal form as inf. or ptcp. which is used in a sense equivalent to a perf., and even a simple impf. having reference to past time. Gen. 39. 18 בַּהֲרִימִי קוֹלִי וָאֶקְרָא when I lifted up my voice *and cried*; 35. 3 לָאֵל הָעֹנֶה אֹתִי וַיְהִי עִמָּדִי who answered me, *and was with me*. See exx. § 96, and R. 2, and § 100 *e*. Gen. 27. 33; 28. 6, 1 K. 18. 18, Ps. 50. 16 (past is reviewed).—Ps. 3. 5 קוֹלִי אֶל־יְ' אֶקְרָא וַיַּעֲנֵנִי I cried aloud unto Je., *and he heard me*. Ps. 52. 9; 95. 10, 1 S. 2. 29, 1 K. 20, 33, Deu. 2. 12, Jer. 52. 7, Hos. 11. 4, cf. Gen. 37. 18.

(*b*) Vav impf. may naturally follow anything which forms a starting-point for a development, though not a verb, such as a statement of time, a *casus pendens*, or the like. Gen. 22. 4 בַּיּוֹם הַשְּׁלִישִׁי וַיִּשָּׂא אֶת־עֵינָיו on the third day *he lifted up* his eyes; Is. 6. 1 בִּשְׁנַת מוֹת הַמֶּלֶךְ וָאֶרְאֶה. 1 S. 4. 20; 21. 6, Hos. 11. 1, Ps. 138. 3. 1 K. 15. 13 וְגַם אֶת־מ' אִמּוֹ וַיְסִרֶהָ מִגְּבִירָה and also Maacha his mother *he removed* from being dowager, 12. 17. Hos. 13. 6 כְּמַרְעִיתָם וַיִּשְׂבָּעוּ the more their pasture, *the more they ate themselves full*. Gen. 22. 24, 2 K. 16. 14, Jer. 6. 19, Mic. 2. 13, Ex. 14. 20. After הִנֵּה Nu. 22. 11. In 2 S. 11. 12 וּמִמָּחֳרָת begins *v*. 13. Similarly after a clause stating the ground or reason. 1 S. 15. 23 יַעַן מָאַסְתָּ . . . וַיִּמְאָסְךָ מִמֶּלֶךְ because thou hast rejected the word of Je. *he has rejected* thee from being king. 1 K. 10. 9, Is. 45. 4; 48. 5, Job 36. 9, Ps. 59. 16 (Hitz. וַיִּלִינוּ), cf. 1 S. 2. 16. Pr. 25. 4 (inf. abs.).

And vav impf. regularly continues another vav impf., as Nu. 22. 21, 22 וַיָּקָם בִּל' . . . וַיֵּלֶךְ . . . וַיַּחֲבשׁ . . . וַיִּחַר־אַף א' *and* Balaam *arose and saddled* his ass, *and went* . . . *and* the anger of God *was kindled*.

§ 51. In such sentences as *and in course of time Cain brought*, or, *and when they were in the field Cain rose up*, *i.e.* when the circumstances, temporal or adverbial, under which the action was performed are stated, the language

prefers to use co-ordinate clauses, prefixing וַיְהִי *and it was.*
Gen. 4. 3 וַיְהִי מִקֵּץ יָמִים וַיָּבֵא קַיִן *and it was* in course of
time *that* (and) *Cain brought*; 4. 8 וַיְהִי בִּהְיוֹתָם בַּשָּׂדֶה
וַיָּקָם ק' *and it was* when they were in the field *that C. rose
up.* This construction is the usual one in prose narrative.
See for variety of usage Gen. 12. 11, 14; 19. 34; 21. 22;
22. 20; 24. 52; 26. 8; 27. 1; 29. 13; 41. 8, Jud. 1. 14; 11. 4,
1 S. 10. 11; 11. 11 end, 2 S. 2. 23.

Rem. 1. Such a sentence as *and when they saw her they
praised her* may be made in various ways. 1. . . . וַיְהִי כִּרְאוֹתָם
וַיִּרְאוּ. . . . 3. . . . וַיְהַלְלוּ . . . כִּרְאוֹתָם . . . 2. וַיְהַלְלוּ. . .
The first is usual; the second with inf. back in the clause is
classical, *e.g.* Gen. 32. 26; 34. 7 (35. 9); the third not
unusual with *see, hear,* and *finish* כְּכַלּוֹת (24. 19; 30. 1; 37.
21, Ex. 34. 33, 2 S. 11. 27), but also in other cases. Other
forms are rarer, *e.g.* Gen. 27. 34 וַיְהַלְלוּ . . . כִּרְאוֹתָם without
and (cf. 2 S. 15. 10); or mainly late, as וַיְהַלְלוּ . . . וְכִרְאוֹתָם or
וְכִר' . . . הַלְלוּ with *and* at the beginning.

The secution to ויהי is not always vav impf., though this
is usual. These forms appear 1. וַיְהִי . . . וַיָּבֵא ק'. 2. ויהי
. . . וַיָּבֵא ק'. Exx. 4. ויהי . . . וְהִנֵּה ק'. 3. . . . וְקֵץ הֵבִיא ויהי
. . . הֵבִיא ק'. Exx.
of 2, Gen. 40. 1, Ex. 16. 27, Deu. 9. 11, Jos. 10. 27, 1 S.
18. 30, 1 K. 11. 4; 14. 25; 15. 29; 17. 17. Of 3, Gen.
7. 10; 15. 12; 22. 1, Ex. 12. 29, 1 S. 18. 1, 2 S. 3. 6, 2 K.
2. 9. In 4 הנה is usually followed by ptcp. or nominal sent.

Rem. 2. Ex. of vav impf. after stative verb, Is. 3. 16,
are haughty and walk; Ps. 16. 9. The impf. after אָ֑ז, &c.
referring to the past (§ 45) is also continued by vav impf.
Jos. 8. 30, 31; 10. 12; 22. 1, 1 K. 3. 16; 11. 7 perf., 2 K.
12. 18. On the other hand, the secution of fut. perf.
(§ 41 c) is usually vav perf. or simple impf., Jud. 9. 9, 1 S.
26. 9, Is. 4. 4; 55. 10, 11, Gen. 26. 10; 43. 9. So very
often the proph. perf. (§ 41 b) and perf. of confidence is continued by vav perf., the ideal position not being maintained.
Gen. 9. 13; 17. 20, Nu. 24. 17, Deu. 15. 6, 2 K. 5. 20,
Is. 2. 11; 43. 14.

Rem. 3. In the brief language of poetry vav impf. some-

times expresses a dependence which is usually expressed by
כִּֿי.   Is. 51. 12, 13 מִי־אַתְּ וַתִּֿירְאִי who art thou *that thou fearest?*
Ps. 144. 3 with 8. 5.   Cf. Is. 49. 7.

Rem. 4. Vav impf. express the *ingress* or entrance upon
realisation of the second action in connection with the
first.   But the second is confined to the sphere of the first,
and has not independent duration, as an unconnected impf.
might have.   Thus אָמַר וַיְהִי *he said, and it was*, is all bounded
by one circle, so that *and it was* becomes in usage the
expression of a finished fact, taking on the quality of the
preceding perf.   Hence vav impf. comes to stand inde-
pendently in the sense of the perf.   It may be interjected
like the perf. amidst other forms (§ 41 *b*), Ps. 55. 18, 19,
Hab. 1. 10, or stand unconnected with immediately preceding forms, Ps. 8. 6 *and thou didst let him want*, adding
merely another fact ; cf. 2 S. 19. 2, where *mourns* is a larger
idea than " weeps " which it embraces (unless " mourns "
were understood of successive fits of lamentation).   The
fact expressed by vav. impf. may be completed really or only
ideally.   Jer. 38. 9 *and he is dead* (must die) of hunger ;
Job 10. 8 *and thou hast swallowed me up* ; 10. 22 *and it has
shone* (its light is) as darkness.   Cf. the instructive pass.
Nu. 12. 12.

In such poetical passages as Job 4. 5 ; 6. 21 ; 14. 10,
where vav impf. appears to follow a present, it is not the
vav impf. but the preceding verbs that are peculiar.   The
vigorous poetical style expresses the completed acts *touch,
see, die*, by the impf. (pres.), cf. 14. 10 *b*.—It is not always
easy to perceive the significance of the changes in secution ;
cf. Am. 9. 5 with Ps. 104. 32, Hos. 8. 13, Mic. 6. 16, Ps. 42. 6
with *v*. 12, Job 7. 17, 18 ; 9. 20, Ps. 52. 9.

Rem. 5. The use of the impf., particularly in poetry, can
hardly be accounted for by supposing that it expresses in
every case some meaning distinctively belonging to the
simple impf.   This difficulty has induced some scholars to
assume that the vav conv. forms may be broken up and
still retain the conversive sense.   Hitz. proceeds on these
principles : 1. vav and the verb may be separated, so that
קָטְלוּ . . . וְ = וְקָטְלוּ vav perf. ; and יַקְטִיל . . . וְ, יַקְטִיל . . . וְ =

יִקְטֹל, and so יִקְטֹל . . . וְ = וַיִּקְטֹל. Job. 5. 11; 28. 25, Is.
29. 16, Ps. 22. 22; 27. 10; 44. 10, Job 3. 25 b; 4. 11,
Jer. 44. 22.[1] 2. The simple impf. forms without vav may
be equivalent to the convers. forms where the latter might
have stood, viz. at the *head* of the clause, so that יַקְטִיל,
יִקְטֹל = וַיִּקְטֹל and יִקְטֹל = וַיִּקְטֹל, Ps. 8. 7; 18. 12; 44. 11; 81.
8; 138. 3; 139. 13, Hos. 6. 1. 3. The simple impf. forms
(without vav in the clause) may be equivalent to the convers.
forms in the middle of a clause, just because there the vav
conv. forms could not stand, the vav necessarily falling
away! Ps. 32. 5; 60. 12; 114. 3. Cf. Hitzig on Ps. 32. 5;
30. 9; 39. 4; 116. 3, Jer. 15. 6; 44. 22.

The exx. cited by Ew. indicate that he proceeds virtually
on the same principles. 1. Ps. 69. 22 impf. disjoined from
vav (in secution to vav impf.). 2. Ps. 78. 15 no vav but
impf. at head of the clause where vav conv. impf. might
have stood. So *v.* 26, 49, 50. 3. Ps. 81. 7 no vav in
the clause and impf. (after perf.) not at the head. So
Ps. 106. 18; 107. 6, 13. Driver admits of two cases: 1.
Separation of vav by tmesis, but only with strictly *modified*
form (יַקְטֵל &c.). And 2. strictly modified form at head of
clause without vav. If the principle be admitted at all,
however, it will be necessary to go further, because the
strictly modified forms are so few, and even they are not
always employed.

In regard to 1, 3 of Hitz. above, it is certain that the
presence or absence of a preceding vav has no effect on the
usage of impf. in the middle of a clause.

It is not unnatural that in rapid and vigorous speech the
vav might drop off when the verb stands at the head of a
clause, particularly among other vav impf. forms, as Ps. 78.
15, 26. Comp. Ps. 106. 17 with Nu. 16. 32; 26. 10; Hos.
6. 1, Pr. 7. 7. Cf. Ps. 18. 12, 14, 16, 38, 39, 44, with the
same verses in 2 S. 22.

Rem. 6. In some cases vav impf. is pointed as simple
vav, *e.g.* Is. 10. 13 וְאָסִיר, וְאוֹרִיד, 43. 28 וַאֲחַלֵּל, 48. 3; 51. 2;

---

[1] Hitz. extends the principle to prose, *e.g.* Deu. 2. 12, Jos. 15. 63, 2 S.
2. 28 (on Job 20. 19).

57. 17; 63. 3–5, Zech. 8. 10, Ps. 104. 32; 107. 26–29. In most of these cases the peculiarity belongs to the *first* pers. In some of them the vav has evidently conversive force, *e.g.* Is. 43. 28; 51. 2; in others, *e.g.* Is. 10. 13, it may be doubtful whether the impf. be not a graphic pres. or freq. There seems no doubt that according to the Massor. tradition the strong vav received in some instances a lighter pronunciation. On similar light vav with Juss. cf. § 65, R. 6.

Rem. 7. Strong vav is also used with Cohort. This form had no doubt originally a wider sense as an intensive. In some cases a certain force or liveliness may still appear in coh. with vav. conv., *e.g.* Gen. 41. 11 וַנַּחַלְמָה *and why! we dreamed*, 32. 6, Ps. 3. 6; but often any additional emphasis is not to be detected, the form being partly rhythmical, 2 S. 22. 24, or probably, since coh. and juss. make up a single tense-form, partly used as the natural parallel to the juss. forms of vav impf. The use of strong vav with coh. is sporadic. It is rare in the prophets, and most common in the personal narratives in Ezr., Neh., and Dan.

PERFECT WITH STRONG VAV. VAV CONV. PERF.

§ 52. *Vav perf.* follows a simple impf. in any of its uses, and has the same use. It has, however, in practice become a tense-form, used in the sense of impf., particularly as fut. and freq., although no impf. precedes. When a neg. or other word must come between the *vav* and perf., the discourse returns to the simple impf. Is. 11. 6 וְגָר זְאֵב עִם־כֶּבֶשׂ וְנָמֵר עִם־גְּדִי יִרְבָּץ *and* the wolf *shall dwell* with the lamb, *and* the leopard *shall lie down* with the kid; Hos. 2. 9 וּבִקְשָׁתַם וְלֹא תִמְצָא *and she shall seek them, and shall not find* them. Gen. 12. 12, 1 S. 1. 11.

§ 53. (*a*) *Vav perf.* continues impf. in the sense of *fut.*, and its use in this sense is general, although no impf. immediately precedes. 1 K. 22. 22 אֵצֵא וְהָיִיתִי רוּחַ שֶׁקֶר *I will go out and be* a lying spirit; Jud. 6. 16 אֶהְיֶה עִמָּךְ

וְהָכִּיתָ I *will be* with thee, *and thou shalt smite* Midian. With interrog. Ex. 2. 7 הַאֵלֵךְ וְקָרָאתִי shall I go *and call*? Jud. 15. 18, Ru. I. 11, I S. 23. 2. With neg. Jer. 22. 10 לֹא יָשׁוּב עוֹד וְרָאָה he shall no more return, *and see* his native land. Gen. 18. 18; 24. 7, 38, 40; 40. 13, 19; 46. 33; 50. 25.

(*b*) It continues the impf. when it is contingent or dependent on something foregoing, and in general in the senses mentioned § 43 *b*. *E.g.* of volition, I S. 17. 32 עַבְדְּךָ יֵלֵךְ וְנִלְחַם thy servant *will go and fight*. Of command, Ex. 20. 24 מִזְבַּח אֲדָמָה תַּעֲשֶׂה־לִּי וְזָבַחְתָּ an altar of earth *shalt thou make me, and sacrifice* upon it; *v.* 9.—Gen. 37. 26 what gain כִּי נַהֲרֹג אֶת־אָחִינוּ וְכִסִּינוּ אֶת־דָּמוֹ *that we should kill* our brother, *and cover* his blood? I S. 29. 8.—Gen. 27. 12 אוּלַי יְמֻשֵּׁנִי וְהָיִיתִי כִמְתַעְתֵּעַ perhaps he *may feel me, and I shall be* as one that mocks him. 2 K. 19. 4, Nu. 22. 11, 2 S. 16. 12.—2 K. 14. 10 וְלָמָּה תִתְגָּרֶה בְּרָעָה וְנָפַלְתָּה why *shouldst thou provoke* misfortune *and fall*? Jer. 40. 15.—Gen. 39. 9 אֵיךְ אֶעֱשֶׂה . . . וְחָטָאתִי how *should I do* this great evil *and sin*! 2 S. 12. 18 how *shall we tell* him, *and he will take on* (how if . . . he will, &c.).—Jud. 1. 12 אֲשֶׁר יַכֶּה קִ׳ס וּלְכָדָהּ . . . וְנָתַתִּי לוֹ whoever *smites* Kirjath Sepher, *and takes it*, I will give, &c. Gen. 44. 9. After עַד אֲשֶׁר, עַד Gen. 29. 8, Jud. 16. 2, I S. I. 22, 2 S. 10. 5, Hos. 5. 15. After בְּטֶרֶם Ex. I. 19, I S. 2. 15 in a *freq.* sense. See Cond. Sent.

(*c*) It continues an impf. following telic particles. Gen. 32. 12 פֶּן־יָבֹא וְהִכַּנִי lest he come *and smite me*. Is. 28. 13 לְמַעַן יֵלְכוּ וְכָשְׁלוּ וְנִשְׁבָּרוּ that they may go, *and fall and be broken*, &c. With וְלֹא *that not* Deu. 19. 10; 23. 15.—Gen. 3. 22; 19. 19, Ex. I. 10, Deu. 4. 16, 19; 6. 15, I S. 9. 5, Is. 6. 10, Hos. 2. 5, Am. 5. 6.—Gen. 12. 13, Nu. 15. 40, Deu. 4. 1; 6. 18.

Rem. 1. It is rarer that impf. with simple *vav* is used instead of *vav perf.* after the particles in *b*, *c*, as Ps. 2. 12 פֶּן־יֶאֱנַף וְתֹאבְדוּ lest he be angry *and ye perish*. In most of the cases the verbs are parallel (just as in very many other cases they are asyndetous), *e.g.* Is. 40. 27 (לָמָּה); Ex. 23. 12, Is. 41. 20 (לְמַעַן). And אוּלַי *perhaps* has often almost the force of a wish, and vav with impf. expresses purpose. Jer. 20. 10 (cohor.), Nu. 22. 6, 1 K. 18. 5.

§ 54. Vav perf. continues an impf. expressing what is customary or general (freq. impf.) in pres. or past. (*a*) Ex. 1. 19 בְּטֶרֶם תָּבוֹא הַמְיַלֶּדֶת וְיָלָדוּ before the midwife *comes they are delivered*; Hos. 7. 7 כֻּלָּם יֵחַמּוּ כַּתַּנּוּר וְאָכְלוּ they all *get heated* like an oven, *and devour* their judges; Is. 36. 6 אֲשֶׁר יִסָּמֵךְ אִישׁ עָלָיו וּבָא בְכַפּוֹ on which *one leans, and it goes* into his hand; Am. 5. 19 כַּאֲשֶׁר יָנוּס הָאִישׁ מִפְּנֵי הָאֲרִי וּפְגָעוֹ הַדֹּב as *a man flees* from a lion, *and a bear meets him.* Ex. 18. 16, Deu. 5. 21; 11. 10, Is. 29. 8, 11, 12, Jer. 17. 5–8; 20. 9, Ez. 29. 7, Mic. 2. 1, 2, Pr. 4. 16; 16. 29; 18. 10, 17.

(*b*) Very commonly in the past. Gen. 2. 6 וְאֵד יַעֲלֶה . . . וְהִשְׁקָה a mist used to go up, *and water*; 2. 10 וּמִשָּׁם יִפָּרֵד וְהָיָה from there it separated itself, *and became* four heads; 1 S. 2. 19, 20, and a little robe תַּעֲשֶׂה־לּוֹ אִמּוֹ וְהַעֲלְתָה לוֹ his mother used to make for him, *and bring it up to him* every year. Gen. 6. 4; 29. 2, 3; 31. 8; 38. 9, Ex. 17. 11, Nu. 21. 8, 9, 1 K. 18. 10. This use of *vav perf.* is very common in graphic descriptions of past events that were customary or habitual, and in giving the details of a scene. Gen. 29. 2, 3 (watering of the flocks), Ex. 33. 7–11 (procedure with the Tabernacle), Jud. 2. 18, 19 (what happened when a Judge was raised up), Jud. 6. 2–6 (details of a Midianite raid), 1 S. 1. 4–7 (Elkanah's case with his two wives), 1 S. 2. 13–16 (practice of the priests), 1 S. 17. 34–36 (David's

experiences with wild beasts), Am. 4. 7, 8 (a drought), 1 K.. 5. 6–8 (Solomon's menage).

Rem. 1. (1) The story is generally introduced by וַיְהִי *and it used to be*, followed by אִם or כִּי with perf. (simple perf. Nu. 11. 8), sometimes without והיה (Jud. 2. 18); or by freq. impf. Ex. 33. 7. (2) Details are often introduced or a new start made in the narrative by והיה. (3) When vav is disjoined from the verb the simple freq. impf. is employed. (4) The writer does not always consistently continue vav perf. or freq. impf., but falls into simple narrative with vav impf., &c., 1 S. 2. 16, Jud. 6. 4; 12. 5, 6. The passage 1 S. 17. 34 seq. is freq., וַיָּקָם having the force of a vigorous supposition (when he rose up).

The use of vav perf. as freq. is exceedingly free; it may occur in any connexion, introducing an additional trait or an entirely new fact. Is. 6. 3 וְקָרָא זֶה אֶל־זֶה *and one cried* (continuously) to the other; 2 S. 12. 16 וּבָא וְלָן וְשָׁכַב *and he went in and lay all night* (the child died on 7th day). 1 S. 7. 16 וְהָלַךְ *and he used to go* yearly (following a historical narrative); 1 K. 9. 25 וְהֶעֱלָה שׁ׳ *and* Sol. *offered* thrice a year (a new point). 1 S. 16. 23; 27. 9, 1 K. 4. 7, 2 K. 3. 4, cf. Gen. 37. 3.

§ 55. Vav perf. continues verbal forms belonging to the sphere of impf., or equivalent to it in meaning, as (*a*) imper., coh., juss.; (*b*) infin.; (*c*) ptcp.

(*a*) 1 S. 8. 22 שְׁמַע בְּקוֹלָם וְהִמְלַכְתָּ listen to their voice, *and appoint a king*; 1 K. 2. 31 פְּגַע־בּוֹ וּקְבַרְתּוֹ fall upon him, *and bury him*. Gen. 6. 14; 19. 2; 45. 19, Ex. 18. 19–22, 1 S. 12. 24; 15. 3, 18, 2 S. 19. 34, 1 K. 2. 36; 17. 13, Jer. 25. 15. So after inf. abs. as general imper. (§ 88 *b*), Deu. 1. 16; 31. 26, Jer. 32. 14. Cohort., Gen. 31. 44 נִכְרְתָה בְרִית וְהָיָה לְעֵד let us make a cov. *and it shall be a witness*; Ru. 2. 7. After juss., Ex. 5. 7 הֵם יֵלְכוּ וְקֹשְׁשׁוּ תֶבֶן let them go themselves, *and gather straw*. 1 K. 1. 2; 22. 13. Gen. 1. 14; 28. 3.

(*b*) Infin.—In ref. to fut., 2 K. 18. 32 עַד־בֹּאִי וְלָקַחְתִּי

6

till I come *and take* you; Jud. 8. 7 בְּתֵת י' אֶת־זֶבַח בְּיָדִי
וְדַשְׁתִּי when Je. gives Zebah into my hand *I will thrash*, &c.
Gen. 27. 45, Ex. 1. 16; 7. 5, Jud. 6. 18, 1 S. 10. 2, 8, 1 K.
2. 42, 2 K. 10. 2, 3. So inf. abs. for finite verb, Is. 5. 5; 31. 5.
After inf. in *freq.* sense, Am. 1. 11 עַל־רָדְפוֹ אָחִיו וְשִׁחֵת
רַחֲמָיו *and stifled his compassions*; Jer. 7. 9, 10 הֲגָנֹב רָצֹחַ
וְנָאֹף . . . וּבָאתֶם do ye steal, murder, commit adultery . . .
and then come and stand before me! 23. 14.

(c) Ptcp.—In ref. to fut., Ex. 7. 17 . . . הִנֵּה אָנֹכִי מַכֶּה
וְנֶהֶפְכוּ לְדָם behold *I will smite* the waters, *and they shall
be turned* into blood. So *v.* 27, 28; 8. 17; 17. 6, Deu. 4. 22,
Jos. 1. 13, 1 S. 14. 8, 1 K. 2. 2; 13. 2, 3; 20. 36, Jer. 21. 9;
25. 9. In a contingent or freq. sense, Ex. 21. 12 מַכֵּה אִישׁ
וָמֵת any one who smites a man *so that he dies*; 2 S. 14. 10
הַמְדַבֵּר אֵלַיִךְ וַהֲבֵאתוֹ אֵלַי whoever speaks to thee *bring
him to me* (it is scarcely necessary to read והבאתו, cf. Jer.
2. 27, Song 5. 9, Jos. 2. 17, 20). 1 S. 2. 13, 14 כָל־אִישׁ זֹבֵחַ זֶבַח
וּבָא נַעַר הַכֹּהֵן whenever any one sacrificed the priest's man
would come . . . v. 14. Nu. 21. 8, 2 S. 17. 17, Mic. 3. 5.

§ 56. Vav perf. may follow anything which supplies the
ground or condition of a new development. Hence it forms
the apodosis to temporal, causal, and conditional sentences
or their equivalents, *casus pendens*, &c. Gen. 3. 5 בְּיוֹם
אֲכָלְכֶם וְנִפְקְחוּ עֵינֵיכֶם on the day ye eat *your eyes shall be
opened.* Obad. 8. Hos. 1. 4 עוֹד מְעַט וּפָקַדְתִּי yet a little,
and I will visit; and often with עוֹד, Ex. 17. 4, Is. 10. 25;
21. 16; 29. 17, cf. 16. 14; 18. 5, 1 S. 2. 31, 1 K. 13. 31.—Is.
6. 7 נָגַע זֶה עַל־שְׂפָתֶיךָ וְסָר עֲוֺנֶךָ this has touched thy
lips, *and* thine iniquity *shall depart.* Ps. 25. 11 לְמַעַן שִׁמְךָ
וְסָלַחְתָּ י' for thy name's sake *pardon.* Is. 3. 16, 17; 37. 29,
Nu. 14. 24, Jud. 11. 8, 1 K. 20. 28, 2 K. 19. 28.—*Casus pendens*,
Is. 9. 4 כִּי כָל־סְאוֹן סֹאֵן . . . וְהָיְתָה for every boot of him
that trampeth in the fray . . . *shall be* for burning; 10. 26

וּמַטְּהוּ עַל־הַיָּם וּנְשָׂאוֹ and his rod upon the sea, *he shall lift it up.* Nu. 14. 31, 1 S. 25, 27, 2 S. 14. 10. After הִנֵּה. Nu. 14. 40 הִנֶּנּוּ וְעָלִינוּ; Jer. 23. 39 הִנְנִי וְנָשִׁיתִי (so *rd.* וּנְשָׂאתִי=). Ez. 34. 11. Cf. Gen. 47. 23. In all the above uses of vav the apod. has a certain emphasis.

And, of course, vav perf. continues another vav perf. Gen. 3. 22 פֶּן־יִשְׁלַח . . . וְלָקַח . . . וְאָכַל . . . וָחָי. Deu. 11. 18-20.

§ 57. When there is an adverbial clause the phrase וְהָיָה *and it shall be,* or, *was* (freq.), is often prefixed, particularly when the actions are *fut.* or *frequentative.* Ex. 22. 26 וְהָיָה כִּי־יִצְעַק אֵלַי וְשָׁמַעְתִּי *and when he shall cry* unto me, *I will hear*; Nu. 21. 9 וְהָיָה אִם־נָשַׁךְ אֶת־אִישׁ וְהִבִּיט . . . וָחָי *and it was* if a serpent had bitten a man, *he looked . . . and lived*; Jud. 6. 3 וְהָיָה אִם־זָרַע יִשׂ' וְעָלָה מִדְיָן *and it was when* Israel had sown, Midian *used to come up.* Gen. 24. 14; 27. 40, 44. 31, Ex. 1. 10; 4. 8, 9; 17. 11; Deu. 17. 18, Jud. 4. 20, 1 S. 3. 9; 16. 16, 1 K. 1. 21; 11. 38.—Gen. 30. 41; 38. 9, Jud. 19. 30, 1 S. 16. 23, 2 S. 14. 26; 15. 5. If *and* be disjoined from verb the impf. must be used, Gen. 12. 12; 30. 42. But frequently impf. without *and* is employed, Gen. 4. 14, Ex. 33. 7–9, 1 S. 2. 36; 17. 25, 2 S. 15. 35, 1 K. 2. 37; 19. 17, 2 K. 4. 10, Is. 2. 2; 10. 27; 14. 3, 4.

Rem. 1. In § 56 the time designations are sometimes very terse; Ex. 16. 6 עֶרֶב וִידַעְתֶּם *at evening, then ye shall know.* Cf. Nu. 16. 5 בֹּקֶר וְיֹדַע *in the morning he will show.* Jud. 16. 2. Pr. 24. 27 אַחַר וּבָנִיתָ afterwards, *then build* thy house, 1 K. 13. 31. The causal connection also may be very slightly expressed. Gen. 20. 11 there is no fear of God here וַהֲרָגוּנִי *and* they will kill me. Ru. 3. 9 I am Ruth וּפָרַשְׂתָּ *therefore* spread thy skirt. 2 K. 9. 26 I saw the blood of Naboth yesterday וְשִׁלַּמְתִּי *and* I will requite thee. Is. 5. 8 till there be no place וְהוּשַׁבְתֶּם *and ye be let dwell alone.* 2 S. 7. 9, 14; 14. 7, Gen. 26. 10, 22, Deu. 6. 5, Jud. 1. 15, Pr. 6. 11; 24. 33, 34. Am. 5. 26, 27, *and* (therefore) ye shall

take up (the unexpressed ground is the exaggerated cultus in contrast to *v.* 25).

Vav perf., however, has acquired the force of a representative of the impf., and may occur in a fut. or freq. sense in any connection. Josh. 22. 28, Is. 2. 2, Jud. 13. 3, 1 S. 15. 28, 1 K. 2. 44. Ex. 6. 6, 2 S. 16. 13. Peculiar Am. 7. 4 וְאָכְלָה and it *would* (or *will*, is in act to—the imminent act made pres.) *devour*. The act was not begun.

Rem. 2. The two most common forms of § 57 are Hos. 1. 5 וְהָיָה בַּיּוֹם הַהוּא וְשָׁבַרְתִּי *I will break*; and Hos. 2. 23 וְהָיָה בַּיּוֹם הַהוּא אֶעֱנֶה *I will answer*, cf. *v.* 18. The latter common in Is. (see exx. at end of § 57). Am. 8. 9, Zeph. 1. 8, with 12.

Rem. 3. In later style וְהָיָה sometimes agrees with *subj.* Nu. 5. 27, Jer. 42. 16; cf. *v.* 17, instead of being used impersonally.

PERF. AND IMPF. WITH SIMPLE VAV (COPULATIVE)

§ 58. In the more ancient and classical language *vav* with perf. is almost invariably conversive. In the declining stages of the speech the *vav* of the form וְקָטַל is often simply copulative, *and he killed*; while in post-biblical language the vav convers. disappears. In the classical language, however, vav with perf. occasionally expresses an action not consequential or successive to what precedes, but co-ordinate with it.

(*a*) When the second verb merely repeats the idea of the first, being synonymous, or in some way parallel with it. 1 S. 12. 2 וַאֲנִי זָקַנְתִּי וָשַׂבְתִּי *I am old and grey*; Is. 1. 2 בָּנִים גִּדַּלְתִּי וְרוֹמַמְתִּי *I have nourished and brought up children*. Gen. 31. 7 he has cozened me, *and changed* (changing) my hire. Deu. 2. 30, Nu. 23. 19, 1 K. 8. 47, 2 K. 19. 22, Is. 29. 20; 63. 10, Ps. 20. 9; 27. 2; 38. 9, Job 1. 5, Lam. 2. 22, 1 Chr. 23. 1. This differs little from the asyndetous construction. Jos. 13. 1, Lam. 2. 16, Jud. 5. 27.

(*b*) When the second verb expresses a contrast. 1 K.
3. 11 וְשָׁאַלְתָּ ... לֹא שָׁאַלְתָּ יָמִים thou hast not asked long
life ... *but hast asked*, &c.   Jer. 4. 10, thou saidst, Ye shall
have peace וְנָגְעָה חֶרֶב עַד־הַנֶּפֶשׁ *whereas the sword reaches*
to the life.   1 S. 10. 2 he has lost thought of the asses
וְדָאַג לָכֶם *and is concerned* about you.   2 K. 8. 10, Pr. 9. 12.
And, in general, when an action is thrown out of the
stream of narrative, and invested with distinct importance
and independence.   Gen. 21. 25 וְהוֹכִחַ אב׳ and Abr. *chid*
with Abimelek.   Gen. 34. 5 *held his peace*, so 2 K. 18. 36.
1 K. 21. 12 (the *two* points in Jezebel's letter are carried out).
2 K. 18. 4, where, perhaps, each of the acts is emphasised.
Is. 1. 8 *and is left*, 22. 14; 28. 26.

(*c*) But there are many cases where *vav* with perf.
appears in simple narrative, and is merely copulative.   1 K.
12. 32; 13. 3; 14. 27; 2 K. 14. 7, 10; 21. 4; 23. 4, and often.
The usage becomes more common as the language declines,
and comes under the influence of Aramaic.   Even in early
style the form וְהָיָה *and it was* is not quite rare.   Am. 7. 2,
1 S. 1. 12; 10. 9; 17. 48; 25. 20, 2 S. 6. 16.   In Gen. 38. 5
rd. וְהִיא with Sep.

Rem. 1. The perf. with *vav* seems occasionally to resume
and restate briefly an event previously described in detail;
Jud. 7. 13 ונפל, 1 K. 20. 21, Gen. 15. 6?   The two cases of
וְנַעַל Jud. 3. 23, 2 S. 13. 18 are curious.   In 2 S. *v.* 18 states
how the *two* injunctions of *v.* 17 were literally carried out.
In 1 K. 11. 10 וְצִוָּה has almost plup. sense.   In 1 K. 6. 32,
35 וְקָלַע is freq., distributing the act over several objects;
§ 54 *b*.   In 2 S. 16. 5 the consn. is unusual, two nominal
clauses might have been expected.   In some cases the text
is faulty, as Is. 38. 15 ואמר.

§ 59. The impf. with simple *vav* (copulative) is common
in all periods of the language, especially in animated speech.
The use of the simple impf., and especially its repetition,

gives the various actions more independence and force than
if the ordinary secution with *vav perf.* had been adopted.
Gen. 49. 7 וַאֲפִיצֵם ... אֲחַלְּקֵם *I will divide them ... and I
will scatter them*; Hos. 5. 14 אֶטְרֹף וְאֵלֵךְ. Sometimes with
force of contrast, Hos. 6. 1 טָרָף וְיִרְפָּאֵנוּ he has torn, *but
he will heal us.* 8. 13; 13. 8, Is. 5. 29. The asyndetous
consn. is only slightly more vivid. Ex. 15. 9, Hos. 5. 15;
6. 3; 9. 9; 10. 2 (common in Hos.). In later style impf.
with simple vav is used where earlier style would have used
vav perf., Ps. 91. 14; and in conditional sentences, Is. 40. 30.

THE MOODS. IMPERATIVE, JUSSIVE, AND COHORTATIVE.

§ 60. The imper. is used, as in other languages, to
express a *command, advice* (often *ironical,* 1 K. 2. 22, Am.
4. 4), *permission,* or *request.* Besides the ordinary form one
strengthened by ה may be used, to which or to the ordinary
form the precative particle נא is often added; Gen. 27. 26
גְּשָׁה־נָּא וּשֲׁקָה־לִּי *come here and kiss me !* 24. 23 הַגִּידִי נָא לִי
tell me ! Ex. 20. 12, 2 S. 18. 23, Nu. 23. 7.

The imper. is only used in 2nd pers.; for other persons
the impf. (juss., coh.) must be employed; Gen. 18. 4 יֻקַּח־נָא
מְעַט מַיִם *let some water be brought.* Even for the 2nd pers.
the impf. is often used, § 45, R. 4. Gen. 44. 33, 1 K. 1. 2.

The imper. cannot be used with negative particles. The
impf. must be used, whether with לֹא, expressing a *command,*
or with אַל, expressing oftener *dissuasion, deprecation.* In
the latter case the juss. is very common. Gen. 45. 9 וּרְדָה
אֵלַי אַל־תַּעֲמֹד *come down* to me, *delay not*; Deu. 9. 7 זְכֹר
אַל־תִּשְׁכַּח *remember, forget not.* Gen. 18. 3; 26. 2; 37. 22,
Deu. 31. 6, 2 K. 18. 26–32, Is. 6. 9, Jer. 4. 3, 4. Ex. 20. 3 *seq.*

Rem. 1. While the lengthened imper. originally expressed some subjective emphasis on the part of the speaker,

it is often dificult to see any difference between the forms in usage, comp. Jud. 9. 8 with *v.* 14, 1 S. 9. 23.   The extended form seems more courteous than the abrupt shorter form, but euphony always exerts an influence.   In some cases the longer form has become fixed, as חוּשָׁה *hasten*, עוּרָה *awake*, הַגִּישָׁה *bring near*, הִשָּׁבְעָה *swear*, הַקְשִׁיבָה *listen* (exc. Job 33. 31), and others.

Rem. 2. The imper. is sometimes interjected in descriptions of the fut., the speaker himself taking part in the events described, and directly addressing the subject of them.   This imper. is equivalent to a strong subjective expression of fut., *e.g.* Is. 54. 14 רְחָקִי *be far = thou shalt be far*, Ps. 110. 2, Job 5. 22, 1 S. 10. 7, Is. 37. 30; 65. 18.

Rem. 3. In higher style the plur. imper. is used when no definite subj. is addressed : Is. 13. 2 שְׂאוּ־נֵס *lift up a signal!* = let a signal be lifted up! 14. 21, and often.

Rem. 4. A number of imper. may follow one another, particularly in animated speech.   Gen. 27. 19, Jer. 5. 1. Various forms appear.   1. לֵךְ אֱמֹר *go, say*, Deu. 5. 27, 2 S. 7. 3, 1 K. 18. 8, 19, 41, 44; 19. 5, Hos. 1. 2.   2. לֵךְ וְאָמַר *go and say*, 1 K. 22. 22, &c.   3. לֵךְ וְאָמַרְתָּ, Deu. 12. 28, Jud. 4. 6, 2 S. 7. 5, 1 K. 19. 11, Is. 6. 9.   4. הָלוֹךְ ואמרת, Jer. 2. 1 ; 3. 12, and often in Jer., 2 S. 24. 12, 2 K. 5. 10.

Not uncommon formulas are, 1 K. 20. 7 דְּעוּ־נָא וּרְאוּ, *v.* 22 sing., Jer. 2. 19.   Different order, Jer. 5, 1 וּרְאוּ־נָא וְדְעוּ, cf. both forms, 1 S. 23. 22, 23.

§ 61. Jussive and Cohortative.[1]—Besides the ordinary impf. there are two modified forms of it, the so-called Cohortative and the Jussive.   The former, used in the *first* person, expresses the *desire, will*, or *intention* of the speaker when he himself is subj. of the action ; the juss., used in second and third pers., expresses the speaker's *desire, will*, or *command* when others are the subj. of the action.   The

---

[1] The impf. &c. of an Ar. verb. in 3rd pers. is as follows :—

	Impf.	*Subj.*	*Juss.*	*Energic.*
3 s.	yaqtul*u*	yaqtul*a*	yaqtul	yaqtul*anna*, yaqtul*an*,
3 pl.	yaqtul*ûna*	yaqtul*â*	yaqtul*û*	*p.* yaqtul*a*,

first form is called by some the Intentional; others embrace both under the name Voluntative.

When special cohort. and juss. forms exist they are generally used to express the senses just noted, but by no means uniformly, the simple impf. being often found where the modified forms might have been employed. Job 3. 9 אַל־יֵרָא with 20. 17 אַל־יִרְאֶה.

§ 62. Use of Cohort.—The coh. or intentional is used to express the *will* of the speaker in ref. to his own action, Deu. 12. 20 אֹכְלָה בָשָׂר *I would eat* flesh; 17. 14 אָשִׂימָה עָלַי מֶלֶךְ *I will set* a king over me; 13. 7 ' א נֵלְכָה וְנַעַבְדָה אֲחֵרִים *we will go and serve* other gods. The particle נא is often added, Gen. 18. 21 אֵרְדָה־נָא *I will go down*, Ex. 3. 3, Jud. 19. 11, 13, Is. 5. 1. The cohort. form is only occasional with neg., 2 S. 24. 14 נִפְּלָה־נָא בְיַד־י' וּבְיַד אָדָם אַל־אֶפֹּלָה . . . but into the hand of man *let me not fall*; Jer. 17. 18; 18. 18, Jon. 1. 14, Ps. 25. 2; 69. 15. When there are several verbs one may have coh. form and the others not, or all may have it. Comp. Is. 1. 24, Gen. 24. 57, Ps. 26. 6 with Gen. 22. 5; 33. 12, 2 S. 3. 21, Hos. 2. 9; 6. 3, Ps. 27. 6.— Thus when the speaker is free the coh. expresses intention or determination, or it may be desire; when he is dependent on others it expresses a wish or request. Gen. 11. 3, 4, 7; 12. 2, 3; 33. 14; 50. 5, Nu. 21. 22, Deu. 2. 27, Jud. 12. 5, 1 S. 28. 22, 2 S. 16. 9, 1 K. 19. 20.

§ 63. Use of Jussive.—The juss. is used—(*a*) to express a command; 1 S. 10. 8 שִׁבְעַת יָמִים תּוֹחֵל seven days *thou shalt wait*. Particularly in neg. sentences, Deu. 3. 26 אַל־תּוֹסֶף דַּבֵּר אֵלַי עוֹד *speak to me no more*; Hos. 4. 4 אִישׁ אַל־יָרֵב וְאַל־יוֹכַח אִישׁ *let none contend and none reprove*. If there be several neg. clauses לֹא is often used after the first, 1 K. 20. 8 אַל־תִּשְׁמַע וְלוֹא תֹאבֶה *listen not, nor consent*, Am. 5. 5; but in impassioned language אל

is retained, Hos. 4. 15, Ob. 12–14.—Gen. 22. 12; 30. 34;
33. 9; 45. 20, Deu. 15. 3.

(*b*) To express advice or recommendation; Jud. 15. 2
her sister is prettier תְּהִי־נָא לְךָ תַּחְתֶּיהָ *have her* instead of
her; Gen. 41. 33 יֵרָא פַרְעֹה אִישׁ וִישִׁיתֵהוּ (so Baer) *let
Ph. look out* a man *and place him*; *v*. 34.   Ex. 8. 25, 1 K.
1. 2; 22. 13.

(*c*) To express a wish, request, or entreaty; 1 S. 1. 23
יָקֶם י' דְּבָרוֹ *may Je. fulfil* his word; 1 K. 17. 21 תָּשָׁב־נָא
נֶפֶשׁ־הַיֶּלֶד הַזֶּה *may the soul* of this child *return*; Gen.
18. 30 אַל־נָא יִחַר לַאדֹנִי *be not angry*, Lord.   Gen. 13. 8;
19. 7; 26. 28; 30. 24; 31. 49; 44. 33; 45. 5, Ex. 5. 21, Nu.
23. 10, 1 S. 24. 16, 2 S. 19. 38, 1 K. 20. 32.

Rem. 1. In a few cases the coh. appears in 3rd pers.,
Deu. 33. 16 (*rd.* תבואה?), Is. 5. 19, Ps. 20. 4, Job 11. 17.
On the other hand a few cases occur of juss. in 1st pers.,
1 S. 14. 36, 2 S. 17. 12, Is. 41. 23 (Kth.), 28.   These
facts might suggest that coh. was at one time a complete
tense-form (like Ar. energic), and that the same was true of
juss.   At present the fragmentary forms supplement each
other.

Rem. 2. Except in neg. sent. the juss. of 2nd pers. is
rare, the imper. being used. in 2nd pers.   1 S. 10. 8, Ez.
3. 3 (Sep. points Ḳal), Ps. 71. 21.   It is also rarely that the
juss. is used after לֹא; Gen. 24. 8, 1 Sam. 14. 36, 2 S.
17. 12; 18. 14 (coh.), 1 K. 2. 6, Ez. 48. 14.   Deu. 13. 1.?

Rem. 3. The form יֹסֵף &c. (hiph. of יסף) occurs with no
juss. sense, *e.g.* Nu. 22. 19, Deu. 18. 16, Hos. 9. 15; Jo. 2. 2,
Ez. 5. 16.   So Gen. 4. 12 (hardly from being apod. of a condition).   There seems a confusion with Ḳal of אסף as a פ'א;
cf. 2 S. 6. 1, Mic. 4. 6, Ps. 104. 29.

On some anomalous uses of juss. and coh. cf. § 65,
R. 5. 6.

THE MOODS WITH LIGHT VAV

§ 64. Imper. with simple vav.—The imper. with simple vav following another imper. expresses the certain *effect* of the first, or it may be its *purpose*. The first imper. in this case virtually expresses a condition which carries with it the second as a consequence. Gen. 42. 18 זֹאת עֲשׂוּ וִחְיוּ *do this and live*; 2 K. 5. 13 רְחַץ וּטְהָר *wash and become clean*; Is. 45. 22 פְּנוּ אֵלַי וְהִוָּשְׁעוּ *look unto me, and be saved.* Sometimes the certain *issue* rather than strict consequence is expressed, as in the ironical concession, Is. 8. 9 הִתְאַזְּרוּ וָחֹתּוּ *gird yourselves, but* (ye shall) *be confounded.* 2 K. 18. 31, Am. 4. 4; 5. 4, 6, Jer. 25. 5; 27. 12, Ps. 37. 27. Without *vav*, Hos. 10. 12, Song 4. 16, Pr. 20. 13.

§ 65. Juss. and coh. with simple vav.—The coh. and juss. with simple vav are greatly used to express *design* or purpose; or, according to our way of thought, sometimes effect. If the purpose-clause be neg. וְלֹא with indic. is almost always used.

(*a*) After an imper., or anything with imper. sense, as coh. or juss. Gen. 27. 4 הָבִיאָה לִי וְאֹכֵלָה *bring to me that I may eat*; Ex. 14. 12 חֲדַל מִמֶּנּוּ וְנַעַבְדָה אֶת־מִצ׳ *leave us alone, that we may serve* Egypt; Jud. 6. 30 הוֹצֵא אֶת־בִּנְךָ וְיָמֹת *bring out thy son, that he may die*; Ex. 32. 10 הַנִּיחָה לִּי וְיִחַר־אַפִּי *let me alone, that my anger may burn*; Gen. 42. 2 שִׁבְרוּ־לָנוּ וְנִחְיֶה וְלֹא נָמוּת *buy corn for us, that we may live, and not die*; 1 S. 5. 11 שַׁלְּחוּ . . . וְיָשֹׁב וְלֹא יָמִית אֹתִי *send away the ark that it may return, and not kill me*; 2 S. 13. 25 אַל־נָא נֵלֵךְ כֻּלָּנוּ וְלֹא נִכְבַּד עָלֶיךָ *let us not all go, that we be not burdensome to thee.* Cf. Rem. 1.

(*b*) After clauses expressing a wish or hope. Jud. 9. 29 מִי יִתֵּן אֶת־הָעָם הַזֶּה בְּיָדִי וְאָסִירָה *would that this people were in my hand, that I might* (then I would) *remove* Abim.

Is. 25. 9, Jer. 8. 23; 9. 1; 20. 10 (after אוּלַי, cf. coh. Ex.
32. 30), Ps. 55. 7, Job 6. 9, 10; 13. 5; 22. 28; 23. 3–5; 16.
20, 21 my eye drops (= a prayer) *that he would vindicate*.

(*c*) After neg. sentences. Nu. 23. 19 לֹא אִישׁ אֵל וִיכַזֵּב
God is not a man, *that he should lie*; cf. inf. 1 S. 15. 29. Ps.
51. 18 לֹא תַחְפֹּץ זֶבַח וְאֶתֵּנָה thou desirest not sacrifice,
that I should give it. 2 K. 3. 11, Is. 53. 2, Ps. 49. 8–10;
55. 13. Without *and*, Job 9. 33 there is no daysman, *that he
might lay his hand* upon us both. So *v*. 32.

(*d*) After interrog. sentences. 1 K. 22. 20 מִי יְפַתֶּה
אֶת־אַחְאָב וְיַעַל who will entice Ahab *to go up*? Am. 8. 5
מָתַי יַעֲבֹר הַחֹדֶשׁ וְנַשְׁבִּירָה שֶּׁבֶר when will the new moon
be over, *that we may sell corn*? Ex. 2. 7, 1 S. 20. 4, 1 K.
12. 9 (cf. inf. *v*. 6), 2 K. 3. 11. Is. 19. 12; 40. 25; 41. 26, 28,
Jer. 23. 18 (*rd.* last word וְיַשְׁמֵעַ, cf. *v*. 22), Hos. 14. 10
(Jer. 9. 11), Jon. 1. 11, Lam. 2. 13, Job 41. 3, Est. 5. 3, 6.

Instead of vav with juss. or coh. the more vigorous imper.
with vav may be found in the above cases, *a–d*. Gen. 20. 7;
45. 18, Ex. 3. 10, 2 S. 21. 3, 1 K. 1. 12, 2 K. 5. 10; 18. 32;
Ps. 128. 5, Job 11. 6, Ru. 1. 9.

Rem. 1. Additional exx. of § 65*a*. Gen. 13. 9; 18. 30;
19. 20; 27. 21; 30. 25, 28; 42. 20, Ex. 8. 4; 14. 15, 16,
Nu. 14. 42; 21. 7; 25. 4, Deu. 1. 42; 5. 28, 1 S. 9. 27;
11. 3; 15. 16; 17. 10; 18. 21; 28. 7, 2 S. 14. 7; 16. 11,
1 K. 13. 6, 18; 18. 27, 2 K. 5. 8; 6. 22, Is. 2. 3; 5. 19;
55. 3, Jer. 37. 20; 38. 24, Hos. 2. 4, Ps. 45. 12; 81. 9, 11;
83. 5; 90. 14, Job 13. 13.

In the cases *a-d*, Ar. uses *fa* with subjun. Occasionally
Heb. uses vav with volunt. to express design even after
the indic. in the past, as Lam. 1. 19 בִּקְשׁוּ אֹכֶל וְיָשִׁיבוּ they
sought food *that they might revive* their soul (cf. inf. *v*. 11).
Is. 25. 9, 1 K. 13. 33, 2 K. 19. 25.

Rem. 2. The idea of *design* expressed by the consn. is
illustrated by its interchange with לְ and inf., *e.g.* 1 K.
12. 6 inf. with *v*. 9 juss., 1 K. 22. 7 with *v*. 8, cf. Deu.

17. 17 with *v.* 20. *Effect* is rather expressed by vav perf., וְהָיָה not וִיהִי, though the distinction is not always apparent; comp. 1 S. 15. 25 coh. with *v.* 30 vav perf. Ex. 8. 12, 1 S. 24. 16, 2 S. 21. 6, 1 K. 1. 2. The juss., however, does not express effect simply *so as that*, apart from design ; though there is a tendency to put design into the action rather than the agent, and this might explain some cases of juss.; cf. § 149, R. 3.—On the other hand, in negative sent. vav perf. often expresses the effect or consequence of the action, the whole compound expression (first verb and its consequence vav perf.) being under the neg.; Deu. 7, 25, 26 וְלָקַחְתָּ וְלֹא־תָבִיא וְהָיִתָ . . . לֹא תַחְמֹד thou shalt not covet *and take*, thou shalt not bring it to thy house *and* so *become* a curse. Ex. 33. 20, Deu. 19 10; 22. 4, Is. 28. 28, Ps. 143. 7.

Rem. 3. The neg. apod. is usually subordinated by וְלֹא (or לֹא) with *ordinary* impf. The form וְאַל rather co-ordinates its clause to the preceding one, Deu. 33. 6, Gen. 22. 12, Jud. 13. 14, Ps. 27. 9, though some cases may seem dubious, Nu. 11. 15, 1 S. 12. 19, Ps. 69. 15, cf. both neg. Pr. 27. 2.

Rem. 4. The *vav* is occasionally omitted. Ps. 61. 8 מַן יִנְצְרֻהוּ (imp. *pi.* מנה) enjoin *that they keep him.* Ex. 7. 9, Is. 27. 4, Job 9. 32, 33, 35, Ps. 55. 7; 118. 19; 119. 17. In Ps. 140. 9 *rd.* perhaps יָרִימוּ and attach to *v.* 10.

Rem. 5. Some uses of coh. are peculiar. (*a*) It is not unnatural that the coh. or intentional should be used to express an action which one resigns himself to do, though under external pressure—a subjective *I must.* Is. 38. 10 אֵלְכָה, Ps. 57. 5, Jer. 3. 25? (*b*) Its use is also natural when a narrator recalls and repeats dramatically his thoughts and resolutions on a former occasion, as the Bride recites the resolutions she formed in her dreams, Song 3. 2, cf. 5. 2. So perhaps Ps. 77. 4, 7, Hab. 2. 1, Job 19. 18? But Ps. 66. 6 שָׁם נִשְׂמְחָה there *did we rejoice*, can hardly be so explained (though impf. might be according to § 45, R. 2). Other cases occur where its usual sense cannot be attached to coh. The form, however, is but a fragment of a mood, which possibly had originally a wider range of meaning. There is also a tendency in the later stages of a language

to use the stronger forms without the special force they
have in earlier times. Thus the coh. seems sometimes to
be merely an emphatic impf., and rhythm may occasionally
have dictated the form. Jer. 4. 19, 21; 6. 10, Ps. 42. 5;
55. 3, 18; 88. 16, Is. 59. 10.—In several cases after עֹד, Pr.
12. 19, Ps. 73. 17. Cf. Lam. 3. 50, where juss. יֵרֶא is parall.
to יַשְׁקִיף, not as Ps. 14. 2.

Rem. 6. The use of juss. forms, especially in later books,
is full of difficulty. According to Mass. pointing (the strict
moods being omitted) the following forms are in use :—

perf. 1a הִקְטִיל. impf. 1b יַקְטִיל simple perf. and impf.
    2a וַיִּקְטֵל.   2b וְהִקְטִיל regular convers. forms.
    3a וְהִקְטִיל.   3b וְיִקְטִיל vav copulative.
            4b וַיִּקְטֵל, יַקְטֵל the modified form

with or without simple vav used in the senses of the simple
impf., e.g. in descriptions of past and present (= 1b), and as
vav perf., &c. (= 2b, 3b). While 3a is in the main late (§ 58),
3b is common at all times in animated speech. The difficulty
lies with 4b; e.g. Job 13. 27 וְתָשֵׂם בַּסַּד רַגְלַי and thou settest
my feet in the stocks (the form preserved in the quotation,
33. 11). Ps. 11. 6, Is. 12. 1, Pr. 15. 25, Job 18. 9, 12;
20. 23, 26, 28; 27. 22, &c. Again, Joel 2. 20 וְעָלָה בָאְשׁוֹ
וְתַעַל צַחֲנָתוֹ his smell shall come up and his stink shall ascend,
where וְתַעַל = וְעָלְתָה or וְתַעֲלֶה; Zeph. 2. 13 וְיֵט יָדוֹ and he shall
stretch his hand, for וְנָטָה or וְיִטֶּה. I K. 8. 1; 14. 5, Mic.
3. 4; 6. 14, Lev. 15. 24; 26. 43, Ez. 14. 7, Is. 35. 1, 2;
58. 10, Dan. 8. 12; 11. 4, 10, 16–19, 25, 28, 30, &c.

It is perhaps well to endeavour to fit some known juss.
sense on each case as it is met with, though it may prove a
waste of ingenuity. Further, while the general principles of
Syntax may be common to all the Shem. languages, appeals
to analogies from cogn. languages are often precarious. The
reader for ex. who calls in the use of Ar. au, or, with subj.
in the sense of unless, or else, to explain the juss. Is. 27. 5
אוֹ יַחֲזֵק or that (unless) he take hold, will be disconcerted to
find in the next verse a juss. יַשְׁרֵשׁ in a plain affirmative
sentence.[1]

---

[1] Appeal to Ar. au in Is. 27. 5 is all the more precarious, inasmuch as
the indic. is permissible after au. Cf. a case Noeld, Carm. Arab. 5, 7.

As many juss. forms cannot be understood in a juss.
sense, many scholars are inclined to go behind the Mass.
tradition, and point according to what is supposed to be
classical usage. Two main lines of emendation present
themselves : 1. to point וֹ or וֹ (vav conv.) in a number of
cases where Mass. has וֹ with juss. forms. *E.g.* Job 34. 37
וַיֶּרֶב for וְיֶרֶב, Is. 63. 3 וַיִּז for יֵז. Pr. 15. 25, Job 15. 33;
20. 23 ; 27. 22, &c.   2. To substitute indicative (defectively
written) for juss. of Mass. *E.g.* Mic. 3. 4 וְיַסְתֵּר for וַיַסְתֵּר.
Deu. 32. 8, Ps. 85. 14, Job 34. 29, &c.   In cases where
there is consonantal shortening in the form only the first
method is available ; in cases where there is mere vowel
difference either method may be used, *e.g.* Job 13. 27 וְתִּישֶׂם
may be read וַתָּשֶׂם or וְתָשֶׂם as may seem necessary.   3. These
two principles may need to be supplemented by more or
fewer of the assumptions referred to, § 51, R. 5.

Unfortunately even these very wide operations on the
Mass. text fail to explain all the instances. Cases like Jo.
2. 20, Dan. 11. 4, 16, Lev. 15. 24, Ez. 14. 7, &c. remain.
In these cases the juss. seems used as an ordinary impf.,
and the question is raised how wide the usage may be.
While therefore it is of course legitimate to subject any case
of Mass. pointing to criticism, sporadic emendations, so
long as uncertainty remains on the *general* question, afford
little satisfaction.

The state of the question being understood the following
cases may be looked into.   Exx. of שׁוּב Is. 12. 1, Job 10. 16,
Ecc. 12. 7, Dan. 11. 10, 18, 19, 28. שִׂים Zeph. 2. 13, Ps.
85. 14, Job 13. 27; 24. 25; 33. 11, Dan. 11. 17. גִיל Is.
35. 1, 2; 61. 10, Zech. 10. 7, Pr. 23, 25, &c. היה Gen.
49. 17, 1 S. 10. 5, Lev. 15. 24, Ps. 72. 16, Job 18. 12; 20.
23; 24. 14. חזק *hiph.* Is. 27. 5; 42. 6, Job 18. 9. רעם
hiph. 1 S. 2. 10, 2 S. 22. 14, Job 37. 4, 5; 40. 9 (nowhere in indic.). שׁלך *hiph.* Job 15. 33; 27. 22, Dan. 8. 12,
cf. Ps. 68. 15. סתר *hiph.* Mic. 3. 4, Job 34. 29. מות Is.
50. 2. Job 36. 14. חוס Ps. 72. 13 and often. מטר *hiph.* Ps.
11. 6, Job 20. 23. רום Nu. 24, 7, 1 S 2. 10, Mic. 5. 8.—
Nu. 24. 19, Deu. 28. 8, 21, 36; 32. 8, 18, 1 K. 8. 1, Is.
27. 6; 63. 3, Hos. 14. 7, Mic. 6. 14; 7. 10, Jer. 13. 10 (cf.

coh. 3 25; 4. 19, 21), Nah. 3. 11, Zech. 9. 5, Mal. 2. 12?
Ez. 14. 7 with Jo. 2. 20, Zeph. 2. 13, Ps. 12. 4; 25. 9;
47. 4; 58. 5; 90. 3; 107. 29, Job 10. 17; 17. 2; 20. 26, 28
(cf. 36. 15); 23. 9, 11; 27. 8; 33. 21, 27; 34. 37; 38. 24;
40. 19, Pr. 12. 26; 15. 25, Lam. 3. 50, Dan. 11. 4, 16,
25, 30.

The frequency with which certain words appear anomalously in the juss., and the place of others in the clause,
suggest that rhythm sometimes dictated the form (Job 23.
9, 11). The fact that the anomalous juss. is often at the
head of the clause has little meaning, as this is the usual
place of the verb.—Pointing like Ex. 22. 4 כִּי יַבְעֶר־אִישׁ seems
due to the accentual rhythm, and no more implies an
intermediate יבער than מִינֶקֶת implies anything but מִינִק. Cf.
Job 39. 26; 22. 28, Ps. 21. 2; 104. 20?

GOVERNMENT OF THE VERB

THE ACCUSATIVE

§ 66. Verbs subordinate other words to themselves in
the *accusative* case. This accus. is of various kinds. Besides
the acc. of the object, verbs may subordinate words to themselves in a freer way, in what may be called the adverbial
accus., *e.g.* in definitions of *place* and *time*. Again, the action
of the verb may reach its object not directly, but through
the medium of a preposition. Very many so-called prepositions, however, are really nouns, and stand themselves in the
adverbial *acc.*

The accus. termination *a* in the Shemitic speeches is
probably the remains of a demonstrative particle (Eth. *ha*
or *a*), which indicated the *direction to* of the verbal action or
the verbal state, and this demonstrative nature of the case
explains its very wide usage.[1]

---

[1] With this idea of *direction to* of the verbal action or *bearing on* of the
condition expressed by the verb is to be compared the use of prep. ל with
obj. in Aram. and later Heb.

The chief accusatives are these—(1) The acc. of *absolute object* or infin. abs., with which may be connected the *cognate* acc. (2) The acc. in definitions of *time, place,* and *measure.* (3) The acc. of *condition,* or state of subject or object of the verbal action, including acc. of *manner* of the action. (4) The acc. of *specification,* or, as it is called, of *respect.* (5) The acc. of the direct *object* of transitive verbs. (6) Certain other accusatives, less common or doubtful in Heb., as the acc. of *motive* or purpose of the action; the acc. after הָיָה *to be,* &c.; and that after certain particles as הִנֵּה *behold,* &c.

I. *The Absolute Object*

§ 67. (*a*) Any verb, transitive or intransitive, may subordinate its own inf. abs. or *nomen verbi* in the acc., with the effect of adding force to the predication. Gen. 2. 17 מוֹת תָּמוּת *thou shalt die;* 18. 18 הָיוֹ יִהְיֶה לְגוֹי גָּדוֹל *he shall be* a great nation; Is. 6. 9 שִׁמְעוּ שָׁמוֹעַ *hear ye indeed.* This acc. mostly precedes the verb, but may follow it, and does so always in the case of *imper.* and *ptcp.* See Inf. Abs. § 86.

(*b*) Cognate accus. The cognate noun may be sub ordinated in the same way as an inner acc. in order to strengthen the verb; 1 S. 1. 6 וְכִעֲסַתָּה צָרָתָה גַּם־כַּעַס *and* her rival (fellow-wife) *continually aggrieved her;* Lam. 1. 8 חֵטְא חָטְאָה יְרוּשָׁלַם Jer. *sinned* (a sin); Is. 42. 17 יֵבֹשׁוּ בֹשֶׁת הַבֹּטְחִים בַּפָּסֶל *they shall be ashamed* (with shame). 1 K. 1. 12, Is. 21. 7, 24. 16; 66. 10, Mic. 4. 9, Hab. 3. 9, Ez. 25. 12, Zech. 1. 2, Job 27. 12, Ps. 14. 5; 106. 14.

More frequently the cognate acc., instead of strengthening the action absolutely, expresses a concrete instance of the effect or product of the action; 2 K. 12. 21 וַיִּקְשְׁרוּ־קֶשֶׁר *and* they *made a conspiracy,* so 15. 30; Gen. 40. 8 חֲלוֹם חָלַמְנוּ *we have dreamed a dream.* Ex. 22. 5, Josh. 7. 1; 22. 20, 31. Usually this acc. is strengthened either (1) by a *gen.,* or (2) by one or more *adj.* 1 S. 20. 17 אַהֲבַת נַפְשׁוֹ אֲהֵבוֹ

he loved him with his love for his own soul; Jer. 22. 19 קְבוּרַת חֲמוֹר יִקָּבֵר *he shall be buried with the burial of an ass*; 2 K. 13. 14 חָלָה אֶת־חָלְיוֹ *he was sick of his disease.* Lev. 26. 36, Deu. 16. 18, Josh. 9. 9, 2 S. 4. 5, Is. 14. 6; 27. 7; 45. 17, Jer. 30. 14, Zech. 7. 9, *cf.* Ps. 139. 22. With *adj.*, Gen. 27. 34 וַיִּצְעַק צְעָקָה גְּדֹלָה וּמָרָה עַד־מְאֹד *he cried with an exceeding loud and bitter cry.* Gen. 12. 17; 50. 10, Deu. 7. 23, Josh. 22. 31, Jud. 21. 2, 1 S. 17. 25, 2 S. 13. 15, 36, 1 K. 1. 40, 2 K. 4. 13, Jer. 8. 5; 14. 17, Zech. 1. 14, 15; 8. 2, Jon. 1. 10, Neh. 2. 10.

Rem. 1. When abs. obj. is inf. cons. it is generally introduced as a comparison, with בְּ, Is. 19. 14; 34, 4, cf. noun, 30. 14; but acc. simply (as Ar.) also occurs, Is. 24. 22; 33, 4.

Rem. 2. The cognate acc. may be *plur.*, Gen. 12. 17; 30. 8, 37, Ez. 16. 38. Occasionally too a noun from a different root but cognate in sense is used, Is. 14. 6 (clause instead of *gen.*), Jer. 20. 11; 31. 7, Zech. 8. 2. Cf. Ps. 13. 4 *sleep* (the sleep of) *death*; Ps. 76. 6, Pr. 3. 23.

Rem. 3. Perhaps it should be considered a form of cognate acc. when verbs of *expression* (speak, cry, weep, &c.) or of conduct subordinate the organ of expression or acting in the acc., 2 S. 15. 23 all the land בֹּכִים קוֹל גָּדוֹל *were weeping with a loud voice*, Prov. 10. 4 עֹשֶׂה כַף־רְמִיָּה *he who works with a slack hand.* Deu. 5. 19, 1 K. 8. 55, Is. 19. 18, Ez. 11. 13, Ps. 12. 3; 63. 6; 109. 2, Ezr. 10. 12. Cf. Jer. 25. 30 with a *hêdad*.

2. *Free Subordination to the Verb of Words in the Acc.*

§ 68. Acc. of time.—Definitions of time are put in acc. (*a*) In answer to the question *when?* Hos. 7. 5 יוֹם מַלְכֵּנוּ *on the day* of our king; 2 S. 21. 9 תְּחִלַּת קְצִיר שְׂעֹרִים *in the beginning* of barley harvest; Ps. 127. 2 יִתֵּן לִידִידוֹ שֵׁנָא *he giveth to his beloved in sleep.* Gen. 14. 15; 27. 45; 40. 7, Hos. 1. 2; 7. 6, Ps. 91. 6 (*at noon*; elsewhere with prep. *b*);

7

Ps. 119. 62 חֲצוֹת לַיְלָה *at midnight*; Ps. 5. 4; 6. 11. (*b*) In answer to *how long?* Gen. 3. 14 כָּל־יְמֵי חַיֶּיךָ *all the days* of thy life; Hos. 3. 4 יָמִים רַבִּים יֵשְׁבוּ *many days* shall they abide. Or, *how many?* of time; Gen. 7. 4, 24; 14. 4; 15. 13.— Gen. 21. 34; 27. 44.

§ 69. Acc. of place.—Definitions of place are put in acc. (*a*) In answer to the question *where?* In prose this is usual with the words בַּיִת *house*, פֶּתַח *door*, and some others, but chiefly when the definition of locality is general, prepositions being used when it is more precise. This acc. is also generally defined more fully by a following *gen.* Gen. 24. 23 הֲיֵשׁ בֵּית־אָבִיךְ מָקוֹם is there room *in thy father's house?* 2 S. 9. 4 הִנֵּה־הוּא בֵּית מָכִיר he is *at the house of* M.; Gen. 18. 1, 10 וְהוּא יֹשֵׁב פֶּתַח־הָאֹהֶל as he sat *at the door of* the tent.—Gen. 38. 11; 45. 16, Ex. 33. 10, Josh. 1. 4, 15; 12. 1; 23. 4, 1 K. 19. 13, 2 K. 2. 3, Is. 3. 6, Jer. 36. 10. Gen. 28. 11 *at the place of his head*, 1 S. 26. 7; Ru. 3. 8, 14 *at the place of his feet*. Without a following *gen.*, Ru. 2. 7. Proper names compounded with בַּיִת are similarly construed, 2 S. 2. 32, Hos. 12. 5. Comp. Jer. 27. 18 with *v.* 21.

(*b*) In answer to *whither?* Gen. 27. 3 צֵא הַשָּׂדֶה go out *to the field*; 45. 25 וַיָּבֹאוּ אֶרֶץ כְּנַעַן and they came *to the land of* C. The ה of direction is frequently appended, Gen. 24. 16 וַתֵּרֶד הָעַיְנָה and she went down *to the fountain*; 12. 5; 39. 1, 12; 42. 38; 43. 17. Of course prepp. (אֶל, עַד, &c.) may be used before noun of *place*, and must be used with names of *persons*, to which, too, the ה local cannot be appended; Gen. 45. 25 וַיָּבֹאוּ אֶרֶץ כְּנַעַן אֶל־יַעֲקֹב *to the land* of C. *to Jacob* (cf. Jer. 27. 3). The prep. is used also with creatures, Gen. 31. 4 הַשָּׂדֶה אֶל־צֹאנוֹ *to* the field *to his flock*.—Gen. 13. 10; 24. 27, Ex. 4. 9; 17. 10, Josh. 6. 19, 24, Jud. 1. 26; 19. 18, 1 S. 1. 24; 17. 17, 20, 2 S. 20. 3, Is. 14. 11,

Jer. 16. 8; 18. 2, 3, Nah. 2. 6.—In Ez. 11. 24; 23. 16 כַּשְׂדִּים
is now name of the country; Jer. 50. 10; 51. 24, 35.

(c) In answer to *how far?* Gen. 7. 20, 1 K. 19. 4, Ez. 41. 22, Jon. 3. 4.

Rem. 1. In elevated speech and poetry words are put in acc. in answer to *where?* more freely, 1 K. 8. 43 *in heaven*, Is. 16. 2 *at* the fords, 15. 8; 45. 19 *in a waste* (in vain), 2 Chr. 33. 20.   In 1 S. 2. 29 מעון is corrupt in some way. Job 22. 12, Ps. 92. 9, *height* is scarcely acc. of place but concrete for adj. as predicate, thou *art height* = high; cf. Ps. 10. 5, Is. 22. 16.   In the frequent אֶת־פְּנֵי, 1 S. 1. 22; 2. 11, 17, 18, Ex. 34. 23, &c., את is prep.

Rem. 2. The acc. *whither?* is also used freely; Gen. 31. 4 *called* Rachel *to the field*, 31. 21 set his face *to mount* Gilead, Is. 10. 32 wage his fist *toward the mount*, Is. 40. 26, Ps. 55. 9, Job 5. 11, Ps. 134. 2, Lam. 5. 6.—The force of the ה of direction has in many cases become enfeebled, *e.g.* שָׁמָּה = *there*; so it is used with prep. of motion *to* Josh. 13. 4, Ez. 8. 14, Ps. 9. 18; and even with prep. *in* and *from*, Josh. 15. 21, Jer. 27. 16.   In later style it becomes a mere ornate ending, Ps. 116. 14, 15, 18; 124. 4; 125. 3, though perhaps for sake of rhythm earlier, Hos. 8. 7; 10. 13, Ps. 3. 3.

Rem. 3. When questions *how long? how far?* &c. are answered in *numbers*, it is strictly the numeral that is in acc.   The case of the thing enumerated will depend upon the numeral, being *e.g.* in gen. after numeral, עֲשֶׂרֶת מֹנִים *ten times*, Gen. 31. 7, or in apposition with it, or possibly in the acc. of specification after it, as אַרְבָּעִים יוֹם *forty days*.   See § 37, R. 6.   Possibly under this acc. comes the use of מִסְפַּר *according to the number*, Job 1. 5, Jer. 2. 28, Ex. 16. 16. Or it is acc. of limitation.

Rem. 4. The verb בוא *to come*, when = *come upon* in a hostile sense, has often acc. *suff.* of person in poetry and later style, Is. 28, 15, Job 15. 21; 20. 22, Ps. 35. 8; 36. 12. With *noun* Is. 41. 25 (though יָבֵם has been suggested), Ez. 38. 11.   In a favourable sense, Ps. 119. 41, 77. Similarly אתה *to come upon*, Job 3. 25.

§ 70. Acc. of condition.—Any word describing the *condition* of the subject or object of an action during the action is put in the acc.; and so words describing the *manner* of the action. (*a*) Gen. 15. 2 וְאָנֹכִי הוֹלֵךְ עֲרִירִי seeing *I go childless*; Is. 20. 3 הָלַךְ עַבְדִּי עָרוֹם וְיָחֵף *my servant has walked naked and barefoot*; Prov. 1. 12 נִבְלָעֵם חַיִּים *let us swallow them up alive* (1 K. 20. 18).   Or even when no verb is used, 2 S. 12. 21 בַּעֲבוּר הַיֶּלֶד חַי *for the sake of the child when alive* (1 K. 14. 6 her feet *as she came*).   In general an indef. adj. or ptcp. descriptive of a definite word (pron. or def. noun) may be considered in the acc. of condition.   Exx. with subj., Gen. 25. 8, 25; 37. 35, Deu. 3. 18, Josh. 1. 14, 1 S. 19. 20, 1 K. 22. 10, 2 K. 18. 37; 19. 2, Am. 2. 16, Job 1. 21; 19. 25; 24. 10, Ps. 109. 7, Ru. 1. 21.   Exx. with obj. Gen. 3. 8; 21. 9; 27. 6, 1 K. 11. 8, Is. 20. 4; 57. 20, Hag. 1. 4, Ps. 124. 3, Job 12. 17.—So even nouns that approach the nature of adj., Gen. 38. 11 abide *a widow* (in widowhood), 44. 33 let him abide *as a servant*; perhaps Is. 21. 8 he cried *like a lion*, Job 24. 5, *as wild-asses*.—With Jon. 1. 6 מַה־לְּךָ נִרְדָּם what meanest thou *sleeping*? cf. Kor. 74. 50.

(*b*) Words describing the *manner* of the action are in acc. Certain words have become real adverbs, as מְאֹד *very* (lit. in strength), חִנָּם *in vain, for nought*, הַרְבֵּה *much, very*, הֵיטֵב *well, very*, &c.   But *adjs.* in general may be used adverbially, and (in poetical style particularly) nouns.   Zeph. 1. 14 וְרֹזְעֵק מַר צֹרֵחַ גִּבּוֹר *bitterly* crieth the hero; Ez. 27. 30 וַתִּשְׁבּוּ בֶּטַח מָרָה and they shall cry *bitterly*; 1 S. 12. 11 וַתֵּשְׁבוּ בֶּטַח and ye dwelt *in confidence*, Hos. 14. 5 אֹהֲבֵם נְדָבָה I will love them *freely*, 1 S. 15. 32 וַיֵּלֶךְ אֵלָיו אֲגַג מַעֲדַנֹּת and Agag came to him *cheerfully*.

§ 71. Acc. of specification.—When to the general statement of the action there is added the point of its incidence, or the respect in which it holds, this secondary limitation is put in the acc., Gen. 3. 15 הוּא יְשׁוּפְךָ רֹאשׁ he shall bruise

thee *on the head*; 37. 21 לֹא נַכֶּנּוּ נֶפֶשׁ let us not smite him *as to life* (mortally), 1 K. 15. 23 חָלָה אֶת־רַגְלָיו he was diseased *in his feet*. Gen. 17. 25; 41. 40, Deu. 33. 11; 19. 6, 11, Jud. 15. 8, 2 S. 21. 20 (1 K. 19. 21), Jer. 2. 16, Ps. 3. 8; 17. 11, Job 21. 7. Prov. 22. 23.

Rem. 1. In § 70a the Ar. consn. is assumed as the type. For ex. (a) רָאוּ אִישׁ יֹצֵא they saw *a man coming out*. (b) רָ' הָאִישׁ הַיֹּצֵא they saw *the man who was coming out*. (c) רָ' הָאִישׁ יֹצֵא they saw *the man coming out*. In a, b, *coming out* is adj. in agreement with *a man*, *the man*, but in c it is acc. of condition to the obj. *the man*. It is possible, however, that in such cases as Job 27. 19 he lieth down *rich*, *rich* might be nom. in appos. to subj. in *lieth down*; Job 15. 7; 19. 25, 2 S. 19. 21 (so Hitz.). Eth. seems to use App. while Ar. has acc. The sing. in such cases as Is. 20. 4, Job 12. 17; 24. 10 (cf. pl. Jer. 13. 19) favours acc. of condition.—The word of condition is naturally an adj. or ptcp. expressing a temporary state, or at least a state which might have been different, and so some nouns as Gen. 38. 11; 44. 33 may be similarly used. With Is. 21 8, cf. karra zeidun 'asadan, Zeid charged *like a lion*. With Gen. 38. 11 cf. Kor. 11. 75, and with 2 S. 12. 21 Hamas. 392, l. 3. Other exx. of nouns, Gen. 15. 16 *as the fourth generation*, Deu. 4. 27 *as a few men*, 2 K. 5. 2 *in bands*, Am. 5. 3, Is. 65. 20 *a hundred years old*, Jer. 31. 8 *as* a great assembly, Zech. 2. 8 *as* open villages, Ps. 58. 9. The text of 1 S. 2. 33 die אֲנָשִׁים *as men* (in manhood) is doubtful; Sep. *by the sword of men*.

Rem. 2. The acc. of *manner* of the action of an adj. may be *mas.* or *fem.*, Is. 5. 26 (Joel 4. 4), sing. or plur., esp. fem. plur. Ps. 139. 14, Job 37. 5. If a noun: (1) in principle any noun may be used, Mic. 2. 3 רוֹמָה, Ps. 56. 3 מָרוֹם *haughtily*,[1] Is. 60. 14 שְׁחוֹחַ *bowing down*, Prov. 31. 9 צֶדֶק *in*

---

[1] Ye shall not walk רוֹמָה *to height, i.e.* so that there shall be height (to your walking), rather than *so that ye shall be high* (be height to you). Heb. refers such adverbial modifications rather to the *action* (Ar. more to the *subj.*).

righteousness, Jud. 5. 21 עֹז *in power*; Lev. 19. 16, Nu. 32. 14, Is. 57. 2. (2) The noun may be *plur.*, Lam. 1. 9 פְּלָאִים she came down *wonderfully*, Hos. 12. 15 תַּמְרוּרִים *bitterly*, Ps. 58. 2; 75. 3, cf. 1 S. 15. 32 above. (3) The acc. may extend to a phrase, Josh. 9. 2, 1 K. 22. 13 פֶּה אֶחָד *unanimously*, cf. Zeph. 3. 9; Lev. 26. 21, 23, 24, Pro. 7. 10, 2 S. 23. 3 ruling יִרְאַת א' *in the fear* of God. Ps. 83. 6 is a mixed consn. for לֵב אֶחָד (1 Chr. 12. 38). See § 140, R. 1. This usage of the noun is mostly poetical, prose rather employs a prep., לָבֶטַח *confidently*, but בטח Jud. 8. 11, &c., Lam. 1. 5 שְׁבִי *into captivity*, elsewhere בַּשְּׁבִי; Ps. 119. 78, 86 שֶׁקֶר *falsely*, *in vain*, usually לַשֶּׁקֶר 1 S. 25. 21. Jer. 23. 28, Ps. 73. 13, 119. 75, Job 21. 34. Comp. Is. 30. 7 with 49. 4; 65. 23. Ps. 119. 75 אֱמוּנָה with 2 K. 12. 16.

Rem. 3. The acc. of restriction (§ 71) is usually an indef. noun, Gen. 3. 15; 37. 21, Ps. 3. 8. The phrase *smite in the bowels* is usually אֶל־הַחֹמֶשׁ, 2 S. 2. 23; 4. 6; 20. 10. In 3. 27 אֶל may have fallen out. The acc. 1 K. 15. 23 *in his feet* is בְּרַגְלָיו, 2 Chr. 16. 12, as is usual, cf. 2 S. 2. 18, Am. 2. 15 (so Arab. *fi rijlaihi*). The acc. of respect is little used after adjs. in Heb., the gen. consn. being employed; cf. § 24, R. 5. The place of acc. of resp. is often taken by a prep., 1 K. 22. 24 עַל־הַלֶּחִי, Mic. 4. 14.

Rem. 4. The acc. of *motive*, so common in Arab., perhaps appears Is. 7. 25 יִרְאַת שָׁמִיר *for* (out of) *fear* of thorns. —Possibly also הָיָה when = *become*, takes acc. after it, Hos. 8. 6 the calf of Sam. שְׁבָבִים יִהְיֶה *shall become splinters*. The frequent use of prep. *l* makes this consn. probable; cf. Jer. 26. 18. So Eth.; the Ar. use is wider. And so perhaps verbs of similar meaning, as הפך *to turn* (also niph.), Jer. 2. 21, Lev. 13. 3, 4, 10.

3. *The Acc. of the direct Object*

§ 72. Many verbs govern the direct acc. in Ḳal; and many of those intrans. in Ḳal govern acc. in the Caus. (hiph. &c.). Of the latter kind are בוֹא *come*; hiph. *bring*, &c. Before the direct acc., when also *def.*, the particle אֵת is

common. It is greatly used before persons, and especially before pronouns, which it assumes as suff. in the case of the pers. pron. It is also used, however, before things. Gen. 2. 15 וַיִּקַּח אֶת־הָאָדָם he took *the man*; 2. 24 יַעֲזֹב אֶת־אָבִיו וְאֶת־אִמּוֹ shall leave *his father and his mother*; 4. 11 לָקַחַת אֶת־דְּמֵי אָחִיךָ to receive *thy brother's blood*; 40. 4 וַיְשָׁרֶת אֹתָם and he served *them*; 41. 10 וַיִּתֵּן אֹתִי and he put *me*. Though the use of אֵת is common, it is very often wanting, and is much less employed in poetry and elevated condensed style than in the broader prose writing. It is altogether wanting for ex. in the poems, Ex. 15., Deu. 32., Jud. 5., 1 S. 2., and other poetical passages.

Rem. 1. The direct obj. when a pron. is often appended to the verb. as suff., esp. in earlier style, Gen. 4. 8 וַיַּהַרְגֵהוּ and slew *him*; in later style אֵת with suff. has greater currency. But אֵת must be used in these cases: (*a*) when for the sake of emphasis the obj. is to be placed before the verb; Jud. 14. 3 אֹתָהּ קַח־לִי get *her* for me. Gen. 7. 1; 24. 14; 41. 13, 1 S. 8. 7; 21. 10, Hos. 2. 15. (*b*) When obj. is governed by inf. abs., which is too inflexible to receive suff.; Gen. 41. 43 וְנָתוֹן אֹתוֹ and set *him* over, &c., 1 S. 2. 28, Jer. 9. 23, Ez. 36. 3. (*c*) When the verb, whether fin. or infin., has already a nearer suff. either of subj. or obj.; 2 S. 15. 25 וְהִרְאַנִי אֹתוֹ he will let *me* see *it*; Gen. 29. 20 בְּאַהֲבָתוֹ אֹתָהּ because of *his* loving *her*. Gen. 19. 17; 38. 5, Deu. 7. 24, 1 S. 1. 23; 18. 3, 2 K. 8. 13—the form Deu. 31. 7 is unusual, cf. 1. 38; 19. 3. Similarly when subj. of inf. cons. is a noun, Deu. 22. 2. In Ar. and Eth., as in Ital., the verb can have two suff., a nearer and more remote.

Rem. 2. When several obj. under the same verb are coupled with *and* אֵת is usually repeated before each of them, esp. if they be distinct from one another, Gen. 1. 1. But usage fluctuates, the newer broader style multiplying אֵת. Gen. 8. 1; 10. 15–18; 12. 5, 20; 15. 19–21; 21. 10.

Rem. 3. The use of אֵת with any acc. except that of direct obj. is rare. (*a*) Of time, *how long?* Ex. 13. 7, Deu.

9. 25; *when?* Lev. 25. 22.   (*b*) Of place, *whither?*   Nu.
4. 19, Jud. 19. 18, Ez. 21. 25.   (*c*) Of restriction, Gen. 17.
11, 14, 25 (not 24), 1 K. 15. 23.

Rem. 4. To the rule that את is used only before def. obj.
there are apparent exceptions.   First, it is used with undefined obj.   (*a*) In poetry, which greatly dispenses with the
art.; *e.g.* in the case of words denoting a *class*, Is. 41. 7;
50. 4, Pr. 13. 21.   (*b*) In prose with words which are of the
nature of pronoun, *e.g.* כל all, Deu. 2. 34, 2 S. 6. 1; אַחֵר
another, Jer. 16. 13.   So with אֶחָד *one*; and Num. in general
have a certain definiteness of their own, Gen. 21. 30, Nu.
16. 15, 1 S. 9. 3, 2 S. 15. 16.   Comp. the usage with *man*,
woman, in the sense of *any one*, Ex. 21. 28, Nu. 21. 9,
cf. Lev. 20. 14.   In some other cases the phrase though
put indefinitely has a particular reference, *e.g.* 2 S. 4. 11 *a*
righteous man (Ishbosheth), 1 S. 26. 20 *a flea* (one who is,
&c.), *i.e.* David.   In 2 S. 5. 24 a *known* kind of divine
rustling is referred to, and *art.* of 1 Chr. 14. 15 might be
accepted were it not the habit of Chron. to correct anomalies.
2 S. 18. 18 *pillar* might be cons. before rel., but text is
uncertain (Sep.).   1 S. 24. 6 *of the robe* has prob. fallen out
after *skirt* (Sep.).   On 1 K. 12. 31; 16. 18, cf. § 22, R. 3.

Secondly, את seems used otherwise than before the obj.
(*a*) Some of the cases are only apparent.   For ex. a neut.
verb used impersonally with prep. and subj. is felt to have
the force of an act. vb.; 2 S. 11. 25 אַל־יֵרַע בְּעֵינֶיךָ אֶת־הַדָּבָר =
take not amiss the thing; so 1 S. 20. 13 (*rd.* יִיטַב)   Neh.
9. 32 אַל־יִמְעַט לְפָנֶיךָ אֵת כָּל־הַתְּלָאָה *regard not as little;* so even
the noun מְעַט with prep. לְ, Josh. 22. 17.   Similarly הָיָה לְ =
to have, Josh. 17. 11; cf. the Eth. usage with prep. *ba*, in,
with, as *baya* is *with me* = *I have*, followed by acc. (Dill.
p. 343).   (*b*) In some cases a particle like *behold*, or a verb
like *thou hast*, *seest*, may float before the writer's mind under
whose regimen the noun falls, as Ez. 43. 7 אֶת־מְקוֹם כִּסְאִי
behold (Sep. *thou seest*) the place of my throne.   But in
many cases את seems merely to give emphasis or demonstrative distinctness to the subj., particularly the emph. which
an *additional* or new thing has, or which is natural in
resuming things already spoken of.   1 S. 26. 16 where is

the spear וְאֶת־צַפַּחַת *and the cruse?* 1 S. 17. 34 there came
the lion וְאֶת־הַדּוֹב *and the bear too* (the verbs are frequent.).
Ex. of resumption, Jud. 20. 44, 2 S. 21. 22, 1 K. 2. 32, Ez.
14. 22, Zech. 8. 17.   Other ex. Nu. 3. 26 ; 5. 10, 2 K. 6. 5,
Jer. 27. 8 ; 36. 22, Ez. 17. 21 ; 35. 10 ; 44. 3 (47. 17–19 ?),
Neh. 9. 19, 34, Hag. 2. 17, Zech. 7. 7, Ecc. 4. 3, Dan. 9. 13.
Cf. Ez. 43. 17 after prep. ; 1 S. 30. 23 text obscure (Sep.).

§ 73. Classes of verbs governing acc. of obj.—(*a*) As in
other languages active verbs take acc. of obj., as נתן *give*,
לקח *take*, שׂים *put*, רדף *pursue*. But so also many verbs
properly *stative*, as אהב *love*, שׂנֵא *hate*, חפֵץ *desire*, and
even יכל *to be able* (Is. 1. 13, *prevail over* Ps. 13. 5). So
בכה *to weep for, bewail*.

(*b*) The causative of verbs intrans. in Ḳal, as בּוֹא *come*,
hiph. *bring*, יָצָא *go out*, hiph. *bring out*, עָלָה *ascend*, hiph.
bring up, יָרַד *go down*, hiph. *bring down*, &c.

(*c*) Verbs of *fulness* and *want*, as מָלֵא *be full of*, שָׂבַע
be satisfied with, חָסֵר *to want*, שָׁכֹל *be bereaved of*. Is. 1. 11
שָׂבַעְתִּי עֹלוֹת אֵילִים I am sated with *burnt-offerings of*
rams ; v. 15 יְדֵיכֶם דָּמִים מָלֵאוּ your hands *are full of*
blood; Deu. 2. 7 לֹא חָסַרְתָּ דָּבָר *thou didst want nothing*.
Gen. 18. 28 ; 27. 45, Ex. 15. 9. The acc. here is perhaps
properly one of specification.—Pr. 25. 17 שׂבע with acc. of
person, so מלא Ex. 15. 9.

(*d*) Verbs of *putting on* and *putting off* clothes, as לָבַשׁ
put on, פָּשַׁט *strip*, עָטָה *be clothed with* (more poetical). 1 K.
22. 30 וְאַתָּה לְבַשׁ בְּגָדֶיךָ but *don thou thy robes*; 1 S. 19. 24
וַיִּפְשַׁט גַּם־הוּא בְּגָדָיו he, too, stripped himself *of his clothes ;*
28. 14 וְהוּא עֹטֶה מְעִיל *wearing a robe.*   Gen. 38. 19, Deu.
22. 5, 1 S. 28. 8, Is. 49. 18, Lev. 6. 4, Song 5. 3. Is. 59. 17,
Ps. 109. 29. For *put off* הֵסִיר is often used.

(*e*) Verbs signifying to *inhabit, dwell in*, as ישׁב *dwell in*,
שכן *id.*, גּוּר *dwell with*, Is. 44. 13, Jer. 17. 6, Ps. 37. 3, Jud.

5. 17, Is. 33. 14, 16, Ps. 94. 17.   In poetry even acc. of person,
Ps. 5. 5; 120. 5.—The consn. with prep. is more usual in prose.

(*f*) Verbs of *speaking*, as דִּבֶּר *speak to*, עָנָה *answer, hear*,
קָרָא *call*, צִוָּה *command*, &c.   But consn. with prep. is also
common in most of these cases.

Rem. 1. The verbs בוֹא *go in*, יָצָא *come out*, may also be
construed with acc., Jer. 10. 20 בָּנַי יְצָאֻנִי my children *have
gone out from me*, 2 K. 20. 4, Jos. 8. 19.   So הָלַךְ in the sense
of *go through, walk in* (different from acc. of goal, *whither?*)
Deu. 1. 19; 2. 7, Is. 50. 10 (darkness), Job 29. 3.

Rem. 2. Under (*c*) may be classed such verbs as שָׁרַץ *to
swarm with*, Ex. 7. 28, פָּרַץ *to multiply greatly*, cf. Pr. 3. 10.
נָזַל *to flow with*, Jer. 9. 17, and similar verbs, as שָׁטַף *to over-
flow with*, Is. 10. 22; יָרַד *go down* (flow) *with*, Jer. 13. 17,
Lam. 3. 48, Ps. 119. 136; הָלַךְ *go* (flow) *with*, Jo. 4. 18;
נָטַף *to drop*, Jud. 5. 4, Jo. 4. 18, Song 4. 11; and others.
Also עָלָה *to come up* (be overgrown) *with*, Is. 5. 6 וְעָלָה שָׁמִיר
וָשַׁיִת it shall come up *in thorns and briars*; 34. 13.

Rem. 3. Under (*d*) come such verbs as אָזַר *to gird* (oneself) *with*, 1 S. 2. 4; חָגַר *to gird on*, 1 S. 25. 13, Is. 15. 3;
עָדָה *to deck* (oneself) *with*, Hos. 2. 15, Is. 61. 10, Job 40. 10;
and others which mostly occur with two acc.

Rem. 4. The pron. suff. is usually direct obj., but sometimes indirect, Zech. 7. 5 צַמְתֻּנִי אָנִי did ye fast *for me?* Job
31. 18 גְּדֵלַנִי כְאָב grew up *to me* as a father.   This kind of
consn. (instead of prep.) is easier with suff., *e.g.* Job 6. 4
array *against me*, Neh. 9. 28 cry *unto thee*, Is. 44. 21 forgotten *of me*, Jer. 20. 7, 1 K. 16. 22, 2 Chr. 28. 20.   In
Is. 65. 5 *rd. pi.* קִדַּשְׁתִּיךָ stand back! *I shall sanctify thee!*
cf. Ez. 44. 19.—So with reflex. vb. Ps. 109. 3, though such
verbs may take direct acc., Gen. 37. 18, Jos. 18. 5, Jud.
19. 22, Is. 14. 2.   Ps. 42. 5 אֲדַדֵּם is explained by Hitz. *in
Rücksicht auf sie* ; perhaps *pi.* אַדְרֵם.

Rem. 5. The pron. obj. is often omitted contrary to our
idiom, particularly after vbs. of *giving, bringing, putting,
telling*, and others.   Gen. 2. 19 וַיָּבֵא and brought *them*, 1 S.
17. 31 וַיַּגִּדוּ they told *them*, 1 S. 19. 13 וַתָּשֶׂם she put *them*.
Gen. 12. 19; 18. 7; 27. 13, 14; 38. 18, Deu. 21. 12.—Different

is the case where certain verbs by a brachylogy may omit their obj. *e.g.* נשׂא *lift up*, sc. קוֹל, Is. 3. 7; 42. 2. נשׂא ל *forgive*, sc. עֲוֹן, Is. 2. 9, Gen. 18. 24. כרת sc. בְּרִית 1 S. 20. 16, 2 Chr. 7. 18. הִפִּיל sc. גּוֹרָל *lot*, 1 S. 14. 42, Job 6. 27, cf. Jud. 18. 1. שׂים sc. לֵב Job 4. 20, so בּוֹנֵן Job 8. 8. שׁמר, נטר *to retain*, sc. אַף *anger*, Jer. 3. 5, Ps. 103. 9. שׁלח sc. יָד 2 S. 6. 6. הִקְשָׁה sc. עֹרֶף *neck*, Job 9. 4, cf. Jer. 7. 26. So מִלֵּא אַחֲרֵי sc. לָלֶכֶת *to go*, Jos. 14. 14. In 1 S. 24. 11 *eye* seems om., but perh. *rd.* 1st pers. with Sep. Syr. Cf. 2 K. 10. 13.

Rem. 6. Sometimes the obj. is regarded as the *instrument* or *means* by which the action is realised, and construed with prep. בּ. Ex. 7. 20 הֵרִים בַּמַּטֶּה to lift up *with* the rod, Lam. 1. 17 פֵּרְשָׂה בְיָדֶיהָ she stretches out *with* her hands. Jer. 18. 16 to wag *with* the head; Job 16. 10 to open *with* the mouth, Ps. 22. 8; Job 16. 9 to gnash *with* the teeth; Jer. 12. 8 to give forth *with* the voice. Cf. Pr. 6. 13. So the phrase קרא בְשֵׁם to call *with* the name = *invoke* Gen. 4. 26, *proclaim* Ex. 34. 5, &c.

Rem. 7. The direction of the action upon obj. is sometimes indicated by prep. ל, particularly with ptcp. and inf. whose rection is weaker than that of fin. vb. Is. 11. 9 לַיָּם מְכַסִּים *covering the sea*, cf. différent order, Hab. 2. 14. Am. 6. 3, Is. 14. 2. The caus. (hiph., pi.) not uncommonly reaches its obj. by ל, Nu. 32. 15, 1 S. 23. 10 (2 S. 3. 30), Is. 29. 2, Am. 8. 9, Hos. 10. 1, cf. Jer. 40. 2, Ps. 69. 6; 73. 18, Job 11. 6.—In later style ל is used in all the senses of את, *e.g.* (*a*) direct obj. 1 Chr. 16. 37; 25. 1; 29. 22, Ezr. 8. 16, 24. (*b*) resumptive (or appos.) 1 Chr. 5. 26, 2 Chr. 2. 12; 23. 1, Ps. 136. 19, 20. (*c*) giving prominence to preposed subj.

4. *Verbs with two Acc. of the Object*

§ 74. Many verbs and forms of verbs govern two objects. There are several cases. First, when the two obj. (generally a pers. and a thing) have no relation to one another, and could not stand as subj. and pred. in a simple proposition, as, he showed *him the place*. Secondly, when the two obj.

are so related that in a simple sentence the one might be pred. of the other, as *man is dust*; he made *man* (of) *dust*. Thirdly, in a wider way, when the action is performed upon the main obj. through the medium of some other thing, this *means* as coming also under the action of the verb is considered a remoter *obj.*, as, they stoned *him* (with) *stones*.

§ 75. To the first class belong—(*a*) The causatives of verbs transitive in the Ḳal; Deu. 8. 3 וַיַּאֲכִלְךָ אֶת־הַמָּן he fed *thee with manna*; Jud. 4. 19 הַשְׁקִינִי־נָא מְעַט־מַיִם give *me a little water* to drink; 4. 22 אַרְאֶךָ אֶת־הָאִישׁ I will show *thee the man.* So הוֹדִיעַ *to show*, 1 S. 14. 12; הָבִין, הוֹרָה, *to show* Is. 28. 9; הנחיל *make to inherit*, Deu. 3. 29; 31. 7; לְמַּד *to teach*, Jud. 3. 2, Deu. 4. 5; השמיע *cause to hear*, 2 K. 7. 6, Song 2. 14. 2 K. 6. 6; 11. 4. An ex. of three acc. 2 K. 8. 13 showed *me thee king*, &c.

(*b*) The caus. of verbs of plenty and want (§ 73 *c*). Gen. 42. 25 וַיְמַלְאוּ אֶת־כְּלֵיהֶם בָּר they filled *their sacks with corn*; 26. 15. 1 K. 18. 13 וָאֲכַלְכְּלֵם לֶחֶם וָמַיִם I supported *them* with *bread and water*, Gen. 47. 12, Is. 50. 4. השביע *to satisfy with*, Ps. 132. 15. חסר *to make want*, Ps. 8. 6. רִוָּה *to water with*, Is. 16. 9. Cf. Jud. 19. 5, Ps. 51. 14; 104. 15, Lam. 3. 15. Some cases may belong to *a*.

(*c*) The caus. of verbs of *clothing with, stripping off* (§ 73 *d*). Under this may come verbs of *covering, girding, surrounding with, overlaying* or plating *with, crowning*, &c. 1 S. 17. 38 וַיַּלְבֵּשׁ אֶת־דָּוִד מַדָּיו he put *his garments on David*, Gen. 41. 42, Ps. 132. 16, 18. Gen. 37. 23 וַיַּפְשִׁיטוּ אֶת־יו׳ אֶת־כֻּתָּנְתּוֹ they stripped *Joseph of his coat.* Nu. 20. 26, 28, Is. 22. 21. If the action be performed on oneself one acc. may be represented by reflex., 1 S. 18. 4 וַיִּתְפַּשֵּׁט אֶת־הַמְּעִיל he stripped *himself of the robe.* Comp. § 73, R. 4.

(*d*) Verbs of *asking, answering, calling*, commanding in

the sense of *intrusting to*, &c. (§ 73 *f*). Is. 58. 2 וִשְׁאָלוּנִי
מִשְׁפְּטֵי־צֶדֶק they ask *me for judgments* of righteousness.
I K. 12. 13 וַיַּעַן אֶת־הָעָם קָשָׁה he returned *the people a
harsh answer*, I S. 20. 10. So the phrase הֵשִׁיב דָּבָר, Gen.
37. 14 וַהֲשִׁבֵנִי דָּבָר and return *me an answer* (or, bring *me
word*), 2 S. 24. 13, I K. 12. 6. I S. 21. 3 הַמֶּלֶךְ צִוַּנִי דָבָר
intrusted *me with a matter*. So שלח in this sense, Ex.
4. 28, I K. 14. 6. To *call*, Gen. 41. 51, 52. Is. 45. 11, Ps.
137. 3. I K. 18. 21.

Similarly the verbs in § 73, R. 1; הוֹלִיךְ Hos. 2. 16, Deu.
8. 2, Lam. 3. 2.

§ 76. When two nouns might form the subj. and pred. in
a simple affirmation they become under a verb a double
obj. acc. There are two cases: e.g. *man* is *dust*;—he made
man of *dust* (so-called acc. of *Material*); and, *the stones* are
an altar;—he built *the stones* into *an altar* (so-called acc. of
Product). The nearer obj. is usually *def*. and the more
remote indef. Such verbs are those of *making, placing,
putting, appointing*, and verbs of the mind as to *see, know,
consider, think, find*, &c. Gen. 2. 7 וַיִּיצֶר אֶת־הָאָדָם עָפָר
he made *the man* (out of) *dust* of the ground. Deu. 27. 6
אֲבָנִים שְׁלֵמוֹת תִּבְנֶה אֶת־מִזְבַּח י (of) *whole stones* shalt
thou build *the altar* of Je. Gen. 27. 9, Ex. 20. 25; 25. 18, 28;
38. 3, I K. 7. 15, 27.—I K. 18. 32 וַיִּבְנֶה אֶת־הָאֲבָנִים מִזְבֵּחַ
he built *the stones* into *an altar*. Is. 3. 7 לֹא תְשִׂימֵנִי קְצִין עָם
appoint *me* not *a ruler* of a people, 5. 6; 28. 15, Gen. 28. 18,
Ex. 32. 4, I S. 28. 2, Mic. 4. 13; 6. 7. Deu. 1. 15 וָאֶתֵּן אֹתָם
רָאשִׁים and I made *them heads*, I K. 14. 7, Is. 3. 4. Gen.
15. 6 וַיַּחְשְׁבֶהָ לּוֹ צְדָקָה he counted *it righteousness* to him.

The same consn. occurs with adj. and ptcp., which then
forms a predicate acc. (tertiary pred.). Gen. 7. 1 אֹתְךָ רָאִיתִי
צַדִּיק *thee* have I perceived *righteous*, Deu. 28. 25 יִתֶּנְךָ י' נִגָּף

Je. shall make *thee defeated, v.* 7.   Jer. 22. 30, Is. 53. 4; 26. 7.
2 K. 14. 26.

§ 77.   More generally, when in reaching the main obj. the
verb brings some other thing under its action, both are put
in acc. of obj.   Is. 5. 2 וַיִּטָּעֵהוּ שֹׂרֵק he planted *it* with
choice vines, Jud. 9. 45 וַיִּזְרָעֶהָ מֶלַח he sowed *it* with *salt.*
Mic. 7. 2 hunts *his brother* with *a net,* Mal. 3. 24 smite *the
earth* with (into) *a curse,* Ps. 64. 8 shoot *at them* with *arrows*;
Ps. 45. 8 anointed *thee* with *oil*; 2 K. 19. 32 (קדם *pi.*); Ps.
88. 8.   Jos. 7. 25 וַיִּרְגְּמוּ אֹתוֹ אֶבֶן they stoned *him* with
stones, Lev. 24. 23, 2 Chr. 24. 21; also with בְ *instrum.,* and
so סקל *to stone* always, Jos. 7. 25, Deu. 13. 11, 1 K. 21. 13.—
Pr. 13. 24.

§ 78.   Besides the double obj. verbs may have two acc. of
different kinds, as obj. and *cog.* acc., 1 K. 2. 8 קִלְלַנִי קְלָלָה
נִמְרֶצֶת cursed *me* with a bitter *curse,* 2 K. 17. 21, 1 K. 8. 55;
acc. of *condition,* Gen. 27. 6 שָׁמַעְתִּי אֶת־אָבִיךָ מְדַבֵּר I heard
thy father speaking; acc. of *restriction,* Gen. 37. 21 smite *him*
as to *life* (mortally); acc. *loci,* 37. 24 they cast *him* הַבּוֹרָה
into the pit, &c.

Rem. 1.   Under § 75 *b* may come verbs of *giving, granting,* &c., נתן, חנן *to grant* Gen. 33. 5; to *bless with* Gen.
49. 25, 28; *to requite with* שׁלם 1 S. 24. 18, Ps. 35. 12.

Rem. 2.   Under § 75 *c* might be classed כסה *pi. to cover,*
Mal. 2. 13, Ps. 104. 6; אזר *pi. to gird* Ps. 18. 33, חגר *to gird*
Ex. 29. 9; סבב *surround with* 1 K. 5. 17, עטר *pi. to surround
with, crown* Ps. 5. 13; 8. 6; 103. 4; ספן *to ciel with* 1 K.
6. 9; צפה *pi.,* חפה *pi. to overlay with* 1 K. 6. 20, 21, 22, Ex.
25. 11, 28, 2 Chr. 3. 4–9; טוח *to daub with* Ez. 13. 10.   Song
3. 10 paved *with love.*   Some of these cases might be classed
under § 77.

Rem. 3.   Under § 76 come such verbs as עשׂה *make,* בנה
build, נתן *make, put,* Jos 9. 27; 11. 6, 1 K. 14. 7.   שׂים
put, 1 S. 28. 2, 2 K. 10. 8, Is. 28. 15, Ps. 80. 7; 105. 21.
שׁית *put* Is. 5. 6, Ps. 21. 7; 88. 9; 110. 1.   ברא *create,* Is. 65.

18. הָפַךְ *to turn into* Ps. 114. 8.   Ex. of so-called acc. of product, 1 K. 11. 30 rent *it* into 12 *pieces*, Am. 6. 11, smite *the
house* into *fissures*, Hab. 3. 9 cleave *rivers* into *dry ground*, Ps.
74. 2.   Ar. Gram. regards such cases as acc. of specification.

Rem. 4. The affinity of the consn. § 76 to the usage
of Apposition (§ 29) is evident.   The two obj. are virtually
in Appos. 2 Chr. 2. 15.

Rem. 5. For second obj. לְ is frequently used, esp. with
persons, Gen. 2. 22 built the rib לְאִשָּׁה into a woman ; 12. 2
I will make thee לְגוֹי a nation.   With שִׂים Is. 14. 23 ; 23. 13 ;
28. 17.   So חָשַׁב *to reckon* Gen. 38. 15, 1 S. 1. 13, and
usually ; *to turn into* Am. 6. 12, &c.   And prep. for 2nd acc.
is common in other cases, as *to satisfy with* בְּ Is. 58. 11,
Lam. 3. 15 ; *to smite on the cheek* עַל, Mic. 4. 14 ; *to overlay
with* בְּ, Jer. 10. 4, 2 K. 19. 1.

Rem. 6. Ecc. 7. 25 לָדַעַת רֶשַׁע בֶּכֶסל *to know wickedness* (to
be) *folly*, is an ex. of verb of the mind.   The consn. with
כִּי *that* is more usual.   Ar. Gr. draws a distinction between
verbs like *to see*, &c. as verbs of *sense* and as verbs of the
mind.   In both cases they take 2 acc., but the 2nd acc.
differs.   I saw *him sleeping* (verb of sense), *sleeping* is acc.
of condition ; in the other case it is 2nd *obj.*, *perceived him*
(to be) *sleeping* = that he was sleeping, pred. acc.

Rem. 7. Two acc. appear in the phrase עָשָׂה כָלָה *to make*
(to be) a *full end*, utterly destroy, Neh. 9. 31 לֹא עֲשִׂיתָם כָּלָה,
Nah. 1. 8, Jer. 30. 11, though אֵת seems prep. Jer. 5. 18.
Strong consns. occur in poetry, Ps. 21. 13, put *them the
back* שְׁכֶם, 18. 41 make *them* the *back* עֹרֶף, *i.e.* cause them to
turn the back (in flight) to one.   Ex. 23. 27.

Rem. 8. Sentences beginning with כִּי, אֲשֶׁר, אֵת אֲשֶׁר *that*,
how that, after *tell*, *show*, &c. form virtually a 2nd obj.
§ 146.   And so words with כְּ *as*, *for*, Gen. 42. 30 held us
כִּמְרַגְּלִים *spies*, Ps. 44. 12.—Unique perhaps is הַגִּיד with 2 acc.,
Ez. 43. 10. 2 S. 15. 31 *rd.* וּלְדוד. ; 2 K. 7. 9 בַּיִת is acc. *loci* ;
Job 26. 4 אֶת־מִי = *by whose help* (inspiration), as Gen. 4. 1,
according to parallel clause.

5. *Construction of the Passive*

§ 79. When *one obj.* is governed by the act. this may become subj. of the pass., as in other languages. But frequently the pass. is used, as we say, impersonally (3 sing. mas.), and governs in the same way as the act.—the idea being that the pass. expresses an action of which the agent is unknown, or, not named. 1 K. 2. 21 יִתֵּן אֶת־אֲבִישַׁג *let* Abishag *be given*; Jer. 35. 14 הוּקַם אֶת־דִּבְרֵי יְהוֹנָדָב the commands of Jon. *are performed*; Gen. 40. 20 יוֹם הֻלֶּדֶת אֶת־פַּרְעֹה the day Ph. *was born* (inf.). Ex. 21. 28 לֹא יֵאָכֵל אֶת־בְּשָׂרוֹ its flesh *shall not be eaten.* Gen. 4. 18; 27. 42, Ex. 10. 8, Deu. 12. 22, Jos. 9. 24, 2 S. 21. 6, 11, 1 K. 18. 13, 2 K. 5. 17, Hos. 10. 6, Am. 4. 2, Jer. 38. 4.

§ 80. When *two obj.* are governed in the act. the nearer of the two usually becomes subj. of the pass., and the more remote is retained in accus. Is. 6. 4 וְהַבַּיִת יִמָּלֵא עָשָׁן *and the house was filled with smoke*; Ex. 1. 7, Is. 2. 7, 8; 38. 10. Gen. 31. 15 הֲלוֹא נָכְרִיּוֹת נֶחְשַׁבְנוּ לוֹ *are we not counted for strangers* by him? Cf. 15. 6, Is. 40. 17. Mic. 3. 12 צִיּוֹן שָׂדֶה תֵחָרֵשׁ Zion shall be ploughed *into a field*; Is. 6. 11; 24. 12. 1 K. 6. 7 the house אֶבֶן שְׁלֵמָה נִבְנָה *was built of unhewn stones*, Ezr. 5. 8, cf. Deu. 27. 6.—Gen. 17. 11, Ex. 13. 7; 25. 31, Lev. 6. 9, Jud. 18. 11, 1 K. 7. 14; 14. 6 (cf. Ex. 4. 28); 22. 10, Ps. 80. 11, Pr. 24. 31. So cog. acc. Jer. 14. 17.

§ 81. The connexion between the real personal agent and pass. vb. is usually expressed by prep. לְ. Gen. 14. 19 בָּרוּךְ לְאֵל עֶלְיוֹן *blessed by God*; 31. 15 נֶחְשַׁבְנוּ לוֹ *we are counted by him*; Is. 65. 1 נִמְצֵאתִי לְלֹא בִקְשֻׁנִי *I was to be found by those who sought me not.* Gen. 25. 21, Ex. 12. 16, Jos. 17. 16, 1 S. 15. 13, Jer. 8. 3, Neh. 6. 1. More rarely by מִן (*from*, of source), Hos. 7. 4 תַּנּוּר בֹּעֵרָה מֵאֹפֶה *an oven heated by a baker* (text doubtful), Lev. 21. 7; cf. Jud. 14. 4,

Mal. 1. 9, Job 4. 9, 1 Chr. 5. 22.   Prep. מִן is usual of *cause* or means, not personal.   Gen. 9. 11 יִכָּרֵת מִמֵּי הַמַּבּוּל be cut off *by the waters* of the flood, Ob. 9, Job 7. 14.   Prep. בְ (*through*, of instrum.) is also used of persons, Gen. 9. 6 בָּאָדָם דָּמוֹ יִשָּׁפֵךְ *through men* shall his blood be shed.

Rem. 1. More rarely the remoter obj. becomes subj. of pass., Lev. 13. 49 וְהָרְאָה אֶת־הַכֹּהֵן and it shall be shown *to the priest*, cf. Ex. 26. 30. So Ar. can say, 'u'ṭiya zeid*an* dirham*un*, a dirhem was given Zeid, though usually, Zeid was given a dirhem (zeid*un* dirham*an*).

Rem. 2. It is seldom that both acc. of act. are retained in pass., Nu. 14. 21, Ps. 72. 19. Such impers. use of pass. is easier when the act. governs one acc. and prep., Gen. 2. 23 לְזֹאת יִקָּרֵא אִשָּׁה *this shall be called woman* (acc.), Is. 1. 26, Nu. 16. 29. Of course all acc. except that of the *obj.* must be retained in pass.

Rem. 3. The exx. given above show that the use of acc. after pass. is classical, though the usage perhaps increased in later style. It is common with ילד *to bear*, Gen. 4. 18 (J); 21. 5; 46. 20, Nu. 26. 60. The consn. of this word in some cases is uncertain, Gen. 35. 26 (Sam. *pl.*), cf. 36. 5, 1·Chr. 2. 3, 9; 3. 1, 4. Other exx. Gen. 21. 8, Nu. 7. 10. Ex. 25. 28; 27. 7, Lev. 16. 27. Nu. 11. 22; 26. 55 (cf. *v.* 53); 32. 5. Gen. 17. 5; 35. 10. Gen. 17. 11, 14, 24, 25 (acc. of restriction). In some cases where noun with את precedes the pass. the את may merely give definiteness to the subj., Jud. 6. 28; and in other cases את may be resumptive, Jos. 7. 15.

Rem. 4. The pass. *be heard* in sense of *answered* is niph. of ענה, Job 19. 7, Pr. 21. 13. Pass. of שמע does not seem used in this sense with personal subj. (cf. Del. N.T. Matt. 6. 7).

SUBORDINATION OF ONE VERB TO ANOTHER

§ 82. There are two cases—(*a*) When the first verb expresses the *mode* of the action denoted by the second. In this case the second verb expresses the real action, and the first has to be rendered adverbially.   Gen. 31. 27 נֶחְבֵּאתָ

8

הִקְשִׁיתָ לִשְׁאוֹל לִבְרֹחַ thou hast fled away *secretly*; 2 K. 2. 10
thou hast asked *a hard thing* (lit. *done hardly as to asking*);
Ex. 8. 24 לֹא־תַרְחִיקוּ לָלֶכֶת ye shall not go *far away*; Ps.
55. 8.   Jer. 13. 18 הַשְׁפִּילוּ שֵׁבוּ sit down *low*.   1 S. 1. 12;
2. 3; 16. 17, 2 S. 19. 4, 1 K. 14. 9, 2 K. 21. 6, Is. 23. 16;
29. 15; 55. 7, Jer. 1. 12; 16. 12, Hos. 9. 9, Am. 4. 4, Jon.
4. 2, Ezr. 10. 13, 2 Chr. 20. 35.   The consn. is common with
שׁוּב, יָסַף *to do again*, הִרְבָּה, הִגְדִּיל &c.

(*b*) When the two verbs express distinct ideas.   Gen.
11. 8 וַיַּחְדְּלוּ לִבְנוֹת הָעִיר and they *gave up building* the
city; 1 S. 18. 2 וְלֹא נְתָנוֹ לָשׁוּב he did not *allow* him *to
return*.   1 S. 17. 39 *rd.* perhaps וַיֵּלֶא לָלֶכֶת.

§ 83. Modes of connection.—(*a*) The second verb is subordinated to the first in *inf. cons.*, with, or less commonly
without, לְ, or still less commonly in *infin. abs.*   See exx.
above, and cf. § 90 *c*.

(*b*) The verbs are *co-ordinated* in the same tense-form
with *vav*.   Gen. 24. 18 וַתְּמַהֵר וַתֹּרֶד כַּדָּהּ *she hasted to let
down* her pitcher; 44. 11.   2 K. 6. 3 הוֹאֶל־נָא וְלֵךְ *consent
to go*; Jud. 19. 6.   Gen. 25. 1 וַיֹּסֶף אַב׳ וַיִּקַּח אִשָּׁה and
Abr. *took another wife*; 1 K. 19. 6 וַיָּשָׁב וַיִּשְׁכָּב and he *lay
down again*; 2 K. 1. 11, 13.   Instead of the same tense the
equivalent *vav conv.* form may be used, Hos. 2. 11 אָשׁוּב
וְלָקַחְתִּי *I will take back again*.   Gen. 27. 42, 2 S. 7. 29, 1 S.
20. 31, Is. 6. 13, Mal. 1. 4, Job 6. 9.—Jos. 7. 7, Is. 1. 19, Est.
8. 6, Dan. 9. 25.

(*c*) The verbs are co-ordinated without *vav*, asyndetously.
Esp. in imper.; 2 K. 5. 23 הוֹאֶל קַח כִּכָּרַיִם *please take* two
talents; 1 S. 3. 5 שׁוּב שְׁכַב *lie down again*; *v*. 9, Gen. 19. 22,
Deu. 2. 24.   Jos. 5. 2, Is. 21. 12, Jer. 13. 18, Ps. 51. 4.
—*Impf.* Hos. 1. 6 לֹא אוֹסִיף עוֹד אֲרַחֵם *I will no more
pity*; Gen. 30. 31 אָשׁוּבָה אֶרְעֶה צֹאנְךָ *I will keep* thy flock
again; 1 S. 2. 3 אַל־תַּרְבּוּ תְדַבְּרוּ *speak not always*.   Mic.

7. 19, Lam. 4. 14, Ps. 50. 20; 88. 11; 102. 14, Job 10. 16; 19. 3; 24. 14. Or with equivalent *vav conv.*, Is. 29. 4 וְשָׁפַלְתְּ מֵאֶרֶץ תְּדַבֵּרִי thou *shalt speak low* out of the ground (1 S. 20. 19 *rd.* וְשִׁלַּשְׁתָּ תִּפָּקֵד *shalt be* greatly *missed a third time*, cf. *v.* 18).—*Perf.* Ps. 106. 13 מִהֲרוּ שָׁכְחוּ *speedily* they forgot. Hos. 5. 11; 9. 9, Zeph. 3. 7, Zech. 8. 15.—*Ptcp.* Hos. 6. 4; 13. 3.—The vigorous הָיִיתִי . . . אֲכָלַנִי Gen. 31. 40 reminds of Ar. *kuntu . . . ya'kuluni*;—more usually with inchoative *pendens*, as Gen. 24. 27.   § 106.

Rem. 1. The second verb is occasionally subordinated in *impf.*, Is. 42. 21 חָפֵץ לְמַעַן צִדְקוֹ יַגְדִּיל ' Je. was pleased *to make great*; Job 32. 22 לֹא יָדַעְתִּי אֲכַנֶּה I am not good *at flattering*; Is. 47. 1 לֹא תוֹסִיפִי יִקְרְאוּ לָךְ thou shalt no more *be called*. Lev. 9. 6, Nu. 22. 6, Lam. 1. 10. The consn. is more common in Syr., Noeld. § 267.

Rem. 2. In a few instances the ptcp. or an adj. is subordinated (*acc.*). Is. 33. 1 כַּהֲתִימְךָ שׁוֹדֵד when thou art done *destroying*; 1 S. 3. 2 וְעֵינָו הֵחֵלּוּ כֵהוֹת his eyes had begun *to be dim.* 1 S. 16. 16, Hos. 7. 4, Jer. 22. 30, Neh. 10. 29. So probably a noun, Gen. 9. 20, N. began (as) *a husbandman* (acc.). The consn., and N., the husbandman, *began and planted* (was the first to plant, or, planted for the first time, Gen. 10. 8, 1 S. 14. 35; 22. 15), is rather unnatural, though cf. the appos. Gen. 37. 2. In this sense "begin" is usually followed by *inf.*, but cf. Ezr. 3. 8.—"One of them" says—

> "Or (nae reflection on your lear),
> Ye may commence a shaver," &c.

Rem. 3. The asyndetic consn. § 83 *c* is very common in Syr., Noeld. § 337. In Ar. the older and classical consn. was with *fa, and*, Wr. ii. § 140; de Lag. *Uebersicht*, p. 209 *seq.*, does not alter this fact.

Rem. 4. Such words as לֵךְ לְךָ, לְכָה *come*, קוּם *arise*, are used almost as interjections though construed regularly, Is. 22. 15 לֶךְ־בֹּא, 1 K. 1. 13 לְכִי וּבֹאִי, *v.* 12, Gen. 19. 15, 1 S. 9. 5. The *mas.* לְכָה is even used to a woman, Gen. 19. 32. Both verbs often merely confer liveliness on the real action, Hos. 5. 15; 6. 1, Gen. 19. 35, Ps. 88. 11. Some fixed compound

phrases express only a *single* idea, as וַיַּעַן וַיֹּאמֶר *answered and said*, וַתַּהַר וַתֵּלֶד *conceived and bore* = *she bore*, Gen. 21. 2. Text 1 S. 1. 20 is probably quite right. Comp. 1 Chr. 4. 17 where ותהר alone is used for the whole phrase.

Rem. 5. In some instances the modifying verb stands second, Jer. 4. 5 קִרְאוּ מַלְאוּ cry *with full voice*, cf. 12. 6 קִרְאוּ מָלֵא. Is. 53. 11, Jo. 2. 26.

THE *NOMEN ACTIONIS* OR INFINITIVE

1. *Infinitive Absolute*

§ 84. The infin. abs. as an abstract noun expresses the bare idea of the verbal action, apart from the modifications which subject-inflèctions or tense-forms lend to it. Used along with the inflected form it gives emphasis to the expression of the action, and, when used alone, graphically represents the action in its exercise, continuance, prevalence, and the like, sometimes almost with the force of an exclamation.

Construction of inf. abs.—Expressing the bare nction of the verb the inf. abs. refuses to enter into close construction, receiving neither suffixes nor prep. It may, however—

(*a*) Be the subj. in a nominal sent., esp. when the pred. is טוב *good*, or לֹא טוב (in poet. בַּל טוב) *not good*, but also otherwise. Pr. 28. 21 הַכֵּר־פָּנִים לֹא־טוב *to be partial* is not good. 1 S. 15. 23, Jer. 10. 5, Pr. 24. 23; 25. 27, Job 25. 2. In Job 6. 25 it is subj. to a verbal sent.

(*b*) Or the obj. of a verb. Is. 1. 17 לִמְדוּ הֵיטֵב learn *to do well*; 42. 24 לֹא אָבוּ הָלוֹךְ they willed not *to walk*. Is. 7. 15; 57. 20, Pr. 15. 12, Job 9. 18; 13. 3. Rarely in gen. Is. 14. 23 בְּמַטְאֲטֵא הַשְׁמֵד with the besom of *destruction*. Pr. 1. 3; 21. 16. Cf. Rem. 1.

(*c*) It may govern like its own finite verb, *e.g.* acc., Hos. 10. 4 כָּרֹת בְּרִית *making covenants*; Is. 22. 13 הָרֹג בָּקָר וְשָׁחֹט צֹאן killing *oxen* and slaying *sheep*. Is. 5. 5; 21. 5;

59. 4, 13, Pr. 25. 4, 5. Or prep., Is. 7. 15 מָאוֹס בָּרָע וּבָחוֹר בַּטּוֹב to refuse *evil* and choose *good*. It is not followed by *gen.* either of noun or pron.

Rem. 1. 1 S. 1. 9 is the only ex. of inf. abs. with prep. (text dubious). The inf. abs. tends, however, to become a real noun (Job 25. 2, Lam, 3. 45), and may take prep. when so used, Is. 30. 15, and also when used adverbially, Neh. 5. 18. The inf. cons. hiph. is occasionally pointed like inf. abs., *e.g.* Deu. 32. 8, Jer. 44. 19, 25, which introduces some uncertainty (Deu. 26. 12, Neh. 10. 39 should perhaps be read *pi.*). Inf. abs. as obj. seems to occur first in Is.

§ 85. Use of inf. abs.—The inf. abs. is used *first*, along with the forms of its own verb, to add emphasis. In this case it stands chiefly before its verb, but also after it. *Secondly*, it is used adverbially to describe the action of a previous verb. And, *thirdly*, it is used instead of the finite or other inflected forms of the verb.

§ 86. Use along with its own verb.—(*a*) When *before* its verb the kind of emphasis given by inf. abs. may be of various kinds, *e.g.* that of strong *asseveration* in promises or threats ; that of *antithesis* in adversative statements ; the emphasis natural in a *supposition* or *concession*; and that of *interrogation*, particularly when the speaker is animated, and throws into the question an intonation of surprise, scorn, dislike, &c. Such shades cannot be reproduced in translation. Occasionally such a word as *indeed, surely* (Gen. 2. 17), *forsooth* (37. 8), *of course* (43. 7), *at all* (Hos. 1. 6), &c., may bring out the sense, but oftenest the kind of emphasis is best expressed by an intonation of the voice.

Ex. of *asseveration*: Gen. 2. 17 מוֹת תָּמוּת *thou shalt* (surely) *die !* 16. 10; 18. 10, 2 S. 5. 19. Frequently in injunctions; Ex. 21. 28 סָקוֹל יִסָּקֵל הַשּׁוֹר *the ox shall be stoned*, 23. 4, Deu. 12. 2, and often. *Antithesis*: Jud. 15. 13 לֹא כִּי אָסֹר נֶאֱסָרְךָ וְהָמֵת לֹא נְמִיתֶךָ *nay, we will bind*

thee, but we will not kill thee. 2 S. 24. 24, Deu. 7. 26; 13. 10;
21. 14, and often, 1 S. 6. 3, 1 K. 11. 22, Am. 9. 8, Is. 28. 28,
Jer. 32. 4; 34. 3. *Supposition* (very common): Ex. 21. 5
וְאִם אָמֹר יֹאמַר הָעֶבֶד but *if the slave should say.* Jud.
11. 30, Ex. 22. 3, 11, 12, 16, 22, Jud. 14. 12, 1 S. 1. 11; 20. 6,
9, 21, 2 S. 18. 3. So *concession*: Gen. 31. 30 וְעַתָּה הָלֹךְ
הָלַכְתָּ *well, thou hast gone off* because, &c. (but why steal
my gods?). 1 S. 2. 30. In *questions*: Gen. 24. 5 הֶהָשֵׁב
הַמֵּלֹךְ אָשִׁיב אֶת־בִּנְךָ *am I, then, to bring back?* 37. 8, 10
הֲיָדֹעַ תִּמְלֹךְ עָלֵינוּ *shalt thou rule* (forsooth) over us? 43. 7
נֵדַע כִּי יֹאמַר *were we* (then) *to know?* Nu. 22. 30, 37, 38,
Jud. 11. 25, 1 S. 2. 27, 2 K. 18. 33, Is. 50. 2, Jer. 26. 19, Ez.
14. 3; 18. 23, Zech. 7. 5.

The peculiar emphasis of inf. abs. is well felt when a
speaker gives a report regarding circumstances, or repeats
(directly or indirectly) the words of another, or his own
thoughts. Gen. 43. 3, 7, Jud. 9. 8; 15. 2, 1 S. 10. 16; 14.
28, 43; 20. 3, 6, 28; 23. 22, 2 S. 1. 6. Also when restrictive
particles, אַךְ, רַק, are used, Gen. 27. 30; 44. 28, Jud. 7. 19.

(*b*) In negative sent. inf. abs. precedes the neg. Is. 30. 19
בָּכוֹ לֹא־תִבְכֶּה *thou shalt not weep.* Jud. 15. 13 above, Ex.
8. 24; 34. 7, Deu. 21. 14, Jud. 1. 28, 1 K. 3. 27, Am. 3. 5, Jer.
6. 15; 13. 12. With אַל, 1 K. 3. 26, Mic. 1. 10. Exceptions
occur mostly when a denial is given to previous words, Gen.
3. 4, Am. 9. 8, Ps. 49. 8.

(*c*) When placed after its verb inf. abs. has often the
same force as when before it. 2 K. 5. 11 אָמַרְתִּי אֵלַי יֵצֵא
יָצוֹא *I thought, He will* (certainly) *come out unto me.* Nu.
23. 11, 2 S. 3. 24; 6. 20, Jer. 23. 39, Dan. 11. 10, 13. In this
case inf. abs. is sometimes strengthened by גַם. Gen. 46. 4
וְאָנֹכִי אַעַלְךָ גַם־עָלֹה *I will also bring thee up*; 31. 15, Nu.
16. 13. Inf. abs. always stands after *imper.* and *ptcp.*, Nu.
11. 15 הָרְגֵנִי־נָא הָרֹג *kill me rather* (at once); Jer. 22. 10

בְּכוּ בָכוֹ לְהֹלֵךְ *weep, indeed,* for him that is gone away. Jud. 5. 23, Is. 6. 9. With ptcp. Jer. 23. 17, Is. 22. 17, Jud. 11. 25?

But inf. abs. after its verb suggests an indefinitely prolonged state of the action, and therefore expresses continuance, prevalence, &c. Nu. 11. 32 וַיִּשְׁטְחוּ לָהֶם שָׁטוֹחַ *and they went spreading them out* (the quails). Jer. 6. 29. This use is clearer when another inf. abs. is added; Jud. 14. 9 וַיֵּלֶךְ הָלוֹךְ וְאָכֹל *he went on, eating as he went;* Gen. 8. 7 וַיֵּצֵא יָצוֹא וָשׁוֹב *and it went* (always) *out and back.* 1 S. 6. 12, 1 K. 20. 37, 2 K. 2. 11, Is. 19. 22. This use is akin to the adverbial use, cf. 2 K. 21. 13, where *rd.* probably מָחֹה וְהָפֵךְ, with larger accent at *dish.* This inf. *before* the verb, Is. 3. 16, cf. Ps. 126. 6.

Rem. 1. Exx. like Gen. 43. 3, 7, Am. 9. 8 hardly prove that infin. abs. intensifies the action in the same sense as the *pi.* With 1 S. 20. 6 cf. *v.* 23. In Gen. 19. 9 the inf. after verb may emphasise the assumption *to be judge* on the part of one who was a stranger rather than the *habit* of judging. Jos. 24. 10.

Rem. 2. The inf. abs. is oftenest of the same conjug. as the finite, whether before or after it, *e.g. Kal* Gen. 2. 16, *niph.* Ex. 22. 3, *pi.* Gen. 22. 17, *pu.* 40. 15, *hiph.* 3. 16, *hoph.* Ez. 16. 4, *hith.* Nu. 16. 13. But as the *nomen actionis* of the Kal expresses the abstract idea of the verb in general, it may be joined with any other conjug., *e.g.* with *niph.* Ex. 21. 20; *pi.* 2 S. 20. 18; *pu.* Gen. 37. 33; *hiph.* 1 S. 23. 22, Gen. 46. 4; *hoph.* Ex. 21. 12 (and always in this phrase *shall be put to death*); *hithpo.* Is. 24. 19. Other combinations are rarer, *e.g.* inf. *hoph.* with *niph.* 2 K. 3. 23, and with *pu.* Ez. 16. 4; inf. *pi.* with *hiph.* 1 S. 2. 16. Occasionally the inf. is from another verb, cognate and similar in sound, Is. 28. 28, Jer. 8. 13; 48. 9 (Zeph. 1. 2?). If text right in Jer. 42. 10, שׁוֹב, the weak *yod* has fallen away, cf. Jud 19. 11, 2 S. 22. 41.

Rem. 3. Instead of inf. abs. the abstract noun is some-

times used; Is. 35. 2, Jer. 46. 5, Mic. 4. 9, Hab. 3. 9 (last
two cognate stems), Job 27. 12, cf. Is. 29. 14, both inf. and
noun.—Occasionally the form of inf. cons. is used, Nu.
23. 25, Ru. 2. 16, Jer. 50. 34, Pr. 23. 1 (all due to assonance
with following verb), Ps. 50. 21, Neh. 1. 7.—2 K. 3. 24 והכות
text amiss (but cf. § 96, R. 4), Ez. 11. 7 *rd.* אוציא. Cf.
however, Jos. 4. 3; 7. 7, Ez. 7. 14.

Rem. 4. The verb הלך with its inf. abs. is followed:
(*a*) mostly by another inf. abs. as above in *c*, *e.g.* 2 S. 3. 16.
וילך הלוך וּבָכֹה, Jos. 6. 9, 2 K. 2. 11; but (*b*) also by ptcp.
2 S. 18. 25 וילך הלוך וְקָרֵב, Jer. 41. 6, cf. 2 S. 16. 5; and (*c*)
by a finite tense, 2 S. 16. 13 וילך הלוך וִיקַלֵּל, Jos. 6. 13, 1 S.
19. 23, 2 S. 13. 19, cf. Is. 31. 5.

But הלך is often used in a metaphorical sense to express
progress, continuance, &c. in an action or condition, which
is expressed by ptcp. or adj. Gen. 26. 13 וילך הלוך וְגָדֵל *he grew
ever greater.* Jud. 4. 24, 1 S. 14. 19, 2 S. 5. 10, 1 Chr. 11. 9.
In the same sense the ptcp. הֹלֵךְ is used in a predication.
2 S. 3. 1 וְדָוִד הֹלֵךְ וְחָזֵק *D. waxed stronger and stronger.*
Ex. 19. 19 *always waxed louder.* 1 S. 2. 26 (17. 41
in a literal sense), 2 S. 15. 12, 2 Chr. 17. 12, Est. 9. 4,
Pr. 4. 18.

Used adverbially with inf. abs. of other verbs inf. abs.
of הלך expresses the same idea of progress or endurance.
Gen. 12. 9 וַיִּסַּע הָלוֹךְ וְנָסוֹעַ *he continued always journeying;*
8. 3 *always receded more and more,* cf. *v.* 5.

§ 87. Adverbial use of inf. abs.—The inf. abs. is used to
describe adverbially the manner, degree, &c., of the action
expressed by a previous verb. This inf. is itself without
and, but other inf. may be subjoined to it. Deu. 9. 21 וָאֶכֹּת
אֹתוֹ טָחוֹן הֵיטֵב and *I beat* it, *grinding it small;* 1 S. 3. 12
אָקִים את כל־אשר דִּבַּרְתִּי הָחֵל וְכַלֵּה I will *fulfil* all that
I have spoken, *from beginning to end.* Gen. 21. 16; 30. 32,
Nu. 6. 23, Jos. 3. 17; 6. 3, 11, 1 S. 17. 16, 2 S. 8. 2, Is. 57. 17,
Mic. 6. 13, Zech. 7. 3, Jer. 3. 15; 12. 17; 22. 19. Cf. Gen.
30. 37 מַחְשֹׂף. Some inf. abs. (chiefly hiph.) have become

almost simple adverbs, as הֵיטֵב *well, very,* הַרְבֵּה *much, very,* הַרְחֵק *far,* Gen. 21. 16, Jos. 3. 16.

Rem: 1. Here belongs the phrase of Jer., *e.g.* 7. 13 וָאֲדַבֵּר . . . הַשְׁכֵּם וְדַבֵּר I spoke, *earnestly speaking,* in which inf. of first verb is repeated; 11. 7; 25. 4; 29. 19; 32. 33; 35. 14, 15. As adverbial inf. is without *and,* delete vav in 26. 5.—Instead of inf. of first verb there is finite form, Is. 57. 17, cf. 31. 5. In Hos. 10. 4 the inf. might exegese דִּבְּרוּ דברים, giving examples of their idle or swelling words; or they may express actions on the same line as their talk.

§ 88. Inf. abs. instead of inflected forms.—(*a*) When circumstances, personal relations, &c., have already been suggested by an inflected verbal form, it is often thought sufficient to subjoin further actions in the bare inf. form. This inf. may follow any inflected form, and, unlike the adverbial inf., is introduced by *and.* Jud. 7. 19 וַיִּתְקְעוּ בַּשּׁוֹפָרוֹת וְנָפוֹץ הַכַּדִּים they blew with the trumpets, *and broke* the pitchers; 1 K. 9. 25 וְהֶעֱלָה שׁ׳ וְהַקְטִיר and Solomon offered sacrifices (freq.) *and burnt incense;* Jer. 14. 5 גַּם־אַיֶּלֶת בַּשָּׂדֶה יָלְדָה וְעָזוֹב even the hind calves, *and forsakes* (her young); Jer. 32. 44 שָׂדוֹת יִקְנוּ וְכָתוֹב בַּסֵּפֶר וְחָתוֹם וְהָעֵד עֵדִים they shall buy fields, *and subscribe deeds, and seal them, and take witnesses.* The usage becomes more common in later style. Cf. Rem. 1.

(*b*) The bare inf. abs. is used without a preceding inflected form when the verbal action or state in itself, apart from modifications of time, person, &c., is to be forcibly presented, *e.g.* in injunctions which are general; in descriptions of prevailing conduct or condition of things; but also in any case where the action in itself, apart from its conditions, is to be vividly expressed. Ex. 20. 8 זָכוֹר אֶת יוֹם הַשַּׁבָּת *remember* the sabbath day!—Hos. 4. 2 אָלֹה וְכַחֵשׁ וְרָצֹחַ וְגָנֹב וְנָאֹף *false swearing, and murder, and theft, and adultery* (they

practise)!—1 K. 22. 30 הִתְחַפֵּשׂ וָבֹא בַמִּלְחָמָה *disguise myself* (will I), *and go* into the battle! 2 K. 4. 43 כֹּה אמר יְ' אָכוֹל וְהוֹתֵר thus saith Je., *Eat* (shall ye) *and leave over!*

(*c*) So in other cases where the action in itself, apart from its circumstances, is to be stated, the inf. abs. is sufficient. Is. 20. 2 וַיַּעַשׂ כֵּן הָלֹךְ עָרוֹם וְיָחֵף he did so, *walking naked and barefoot*, Is. 5. 5. Particularly when the action is first indicated by *this*. Jer. 9. 23 בְּזֹאת יִתְהַלֵּל הַמִּתְהַלֵּל הַשְׂכֵּל וְיָדֹעַ אֹתִי *in this* let one glory, *in understanding and in knowing me*; Is. 58. 6 is not *this* the fast that I like, פַּתֵּחַ חַרְצֻבּוֹת רֶשַׁע *to loose* the bonds of wickedness, &c. (three inf., cf. *v.* 7). Gen. 17. 10; Deu. 15. 2, Is. 37. 30, Zech. 14. 12.

Rem. 1. Exx. of *a*. After perf., 1 S. 2. 27, 28, Hos. 10. 4, Jer. 19. 13; 22. 14, Hag. 1. 6, Zech. 3. 4; 7. 5, 1 Chr. 5. 20, 2 Chr. 28. 19, Ecc. 4. 1, 2; 9. 11, Est. 9. 6, 12, 16, cf. 17, Dan. 9. 5.—After impf., Jer. 32. 44; 36. 23. With אֹ *or*, Lev. 25. 14, Nu. 30. 3, Deu. 14. 21.—After vav impf., Gen. 41. 43, Ex. 8. 11, Jer. 37. 21, 1 Chr. 16. 36, Neh. 8. 8.—Vav perf., Zech. 12. 10.—Inf., 1 S. 22. 13, Jer. 7. 18, cf. 32. 33.—Ptcp., Hab. 2. 15, Est. 8. 8.

Rem. 2. Exx. of *b*. Inf. abs. as imper., Ex. 12. 48; 13. 3, Deu. 1. 16; 5. 12; 31. 26, Jos. 1. 13, 2 K. 3. 16, Zech. 6. 10. So הָלֹךְ *go!* 2 S. 24. 12, 2 K. 5. 10, and often in Jer., 2. 2; 3. 12, &c. Is. 14. 31? (נָמוֹג inf. abs.).—Of prevailing conduct or condition, Is. 21. 5; 22. 13; 59. 4, 13, Jer. 7. 9; 8. 15; 14. 19, Ez. 21. 31, Hag. 1. 9.—Exx. of *c*, Jer. 3. 1 (וְשׁוֹב), Ez. 23. 30, 46, Job 40. 2, Pr. 17. 12; 25. 4, 5.

Rem. 3. Like inf. cons. (§ 96), inf. abs. when used for finite may be continued by fin. form, Is. 42. 22; 58. 6.

Rem. 4. A force akin to that of inf. abs. is sometimes obtained by repeating the verb in another form. Ps. 118. 11, Zeph. 2. 1, Hab. 1. 5, Is. 29. 9 (Hos. 4. 18). But in some of these places text is doubtful.

Rem. 5. When inf. abs. is used for finite verb the *subj.*

is occasionally expressed with it, Deu. 15. 2, Lev. 6. 7; Nu. 15. 35, 1 S. 25. 26, Is. 42. 22, Ps. 17. 5, Job 40. 2, Pr. 17. 12, Ecc. 4. 2, Est. 9. 1.   Gen. 17. 12, 13 make it probable that כָּל־זָכָר *v.* 10 is subj. and not acc. after pass.

Rem. 6. In § 86 (cf. § 67) and § 87 the inf. abs. is no doubt in acc. ; possibly also in § 88, cf. Kor. 2. 77.

2. *The Infinitive Construct*

§ 89. The inf. cons. has the qualities both of noun and verb, being used like a gerund, admitting prepp. and suffixes, and yet having the government of its verb.   As *nomen verbi* it does not of itself express tense; the time is either indefinite or suggested by the context and circumstances.   It is too little of a noun to take the *art.*, § 19.

§ 90. Cases of inf. cons. itself.—(*a*) The inf. cons. may be *nom.* as subject to a nominal sentence, especially when the pred. is " good " or " not good " (§ 84 *a*), but also otherwise, Gen. 2. 18 לֹא טוֹב הֱיוֹת הָאָדָם לְבַדּוֹ *man's being alone* is not good ; Is. 7. 13 הַמְעַט מִכֶּם הַלְאוֹת אֲנָשִׁים is *wearying men* too little for you?   Gen. 29. 19; 30. 15, Ex. 14. 12, Jud. 9. 2; 18. 19, 1 S. 15. 22; 23. 20; 29. 6, 2 S. 18. 11, Is. 10. 7, Mic. 3. 1, Ps. 118. 9, Pr. 10. 23; 13. 19; 16. 6, 12, 16, and often.

(*b*) It may be in *gen.* by a noun or prep.   Gen. 2. 4 בְּיוֹם עֲשׂוֹת יהוה in the day *of Jehovah's making* ; 14. 17 אַחֲרֵי שׁוּבוֹ מֵהַכּוֹת *after his returning from smiting.*   Gen. 2. 17 ; 21. 5; 24. 30; 29. 7, Is. 7. 17, Hos. 2. 5, 17.   Also, though rarely, after an adj. or ptcp. in *cons.*, Is. 56. 10, Jer. 13. 23, Ps. 127. 2, Pr. 30. 29.   In a few instances כֹּל *all* precedes inf. cons., Gen. 30. 41, 1 K. 8. 52, Ps. 132. 1, 1 Chr. 23. 31.

(*c*) It may be in *acc.* as obj. to an active verb.   1 K. 3. 7 לֹא אֵדַע צֵאת וָבֹא I know not *how to go out or come in.* Gen. 8. 10, Ex. 2. 3, Deu. 2. 25, 2 K. 19. 27, Is. 1. 14; 11. 9, Jer. 15. 15, Am. 3. 10, Ps. 101. 3.   The acc. sign אֵת occurs before inf.   2 K. 19. 27 (Is. 37. 28).   The inf. cons. with

prep. לְ, which expresses the direction of the action of governing verb, has in usage greatly superseded the simple inf. when *obj.*; Gen. 18. 29 וַיֹּסֶף עוֹד לְדַבֵּר, 11. 8; 13. 16. This inf. with לְ has become almost a simple verbal *form*, and appears often as subj. in the nominal sent., 1 S. 15. 22, 2 S. 18. 11, Is. 10. 7 with 28. 19, Mic. 3. 1, Ps. 118. 8, Pr. 21. 9 with 25. 24. Cf. Hab. 2. 14.

Rem. 1. It is usually the whole clause rather than the mere inf. that is grammatical subj. ; comp. the forcible phrase 2 S. 14. 32. The inf. cons. is too little nominal to be subj. to a verb : in 2 S. 22. 36 *rd.* with Ps. 18. 36 וְעַנְוָתְךָ ; 1 K. 16. 31 הֲנָקֵל is ptcp., cf. 1 S. 18. 23. In 2 S. 24. 13 נְסָךְ is loosely appended to preceding words. Is. 37. 29 שַׁאֲנַנְךָ if text right may be an ex., or adj. used substantively (vocalisation varies). Ps. 17. 3 זַמֹּתִי if inf. is scarcely subj. to following verb. On the other hand the fem. inf. tends to be a real noun, and may be subj. to a verb, Pr. 10. 12.— It is rare that the mas. form of inf. is construed as fem. (neut.), 1 S. 18. 23, Jer. 2. 17 with 2. 19.

Rem. 2. Deu. 25. 2 בִּן הַכּוֹת *worthy of a beating* (adjudged the bastinado) is peculiar, cf. 1 S. 20. 31.

§ 91. Government by inf. cons.—(*a*) The agent or subj., which usually immediately follows inf., is in the *gen.* Gen. 2. 4 בְּהֵעָלַת י' עָשׂוֹת יהוה *Jehovah's making*; 19. 16 עָלָיו *in Jehovah's pitying* him. Gen. 16. 16; 24. 11, Ex. 17. 1, Deu. 1. 27, 1 K. 10. 9. So with suff., Gen. 3. 19 עַד שׁוּבְךָ אֶל־הָאֲדָמָה *until thy returning* to the ground, 3. 5 ; 39. 18.

When separated from inf. by intervening words the subj., with a looser construction, must be supposed to be in the *nom.*; Is. 20. 1 בִּשְׁלֹחַ אֹתוֹ סַרְגוֹן *when Sargon sent* him. Gen. 4. 15, Nu. 24. 23, Deu. 4. 42, Jos. 14. 11, Jud. 9. 2, 1 S. 16. 16, 2 S. 18. 29, Is. 5. 24, Jer. 21. 1, Ez. 17. 10, Ps. 51. 2 ; 56. 1 ; 76. 10; 142. 4, Pr. 1. 27 ; 25. 8, Job 34. 22.

(*b*) The inf. cons. puts its *obj.* in the same case as the verb does from which it is derived, *i.e.* acc. or gen. through

a prep. 1 S. 19. 1 לְהָמִית אֶת־דָּוִד *to kill David*; Deu.
10. 15 לְאַהֲבָה אֹתָם *to love them*; Nu. 22. 11 לְהִלָּחֶם בּוֹ
to fight with him. Gen. 2. 4, Deu. 2. 7, 1 K. 12. 15; 15. 4,
Gen. 19. 16, Deu. 30. 20, Is. 7. 1. The inf. may take two acc.
like its verb, Gen. 41. 39, Deu. 26. 19, Jos. 10. 20.

(*c*) When subj. and obj. are both expressed the usual
order is: inf., subj., obj.   Gen. 41. 39 אַחֲרֵי הוֹדִיעַ אֱ אֹתְךָ
after God's showing thee; Hos. 3. 1 כְּאַהֲבַת י אֶת־בְּנֵי יִשׂ
as Je. loveth the children of Israel; and with pron. as subj.
Gen. 39. 18 כַּהֲרִימִי קוֹלִי *when I lifted up my voice.* Gen.
11. 11, 13; 13. 10; 24. 30; 39. 19, 1 K. 11. 24; 13. 23, 31,
Is. 10. 15, Am. 1. 3, 6, 9, 11, 13, &c.

Rem. 1. The subj., especially when a pron., is often
omitted: (*a*) when clear from the context, Gen. 24. 30 כִּרְאֹת
when he saw; 19. 29, Deu. 4. 21, 1 K. 20. 12, Ez. 8. 6.
(*b*) When general and indeterminate, Gen. 33. 10 כִּרְאֹת *as
one sees*; Jud. 14. 6, 1 S. 2. 13; 18. 19, 2 S. 3. 34; 7. 29,
Is. 7. 22; 10. 14.—Gen. 25. 26, Ex. 27. 7; 30. 12, Nu.
9. 15; 10. 7, Zeph. 2. 2, Zech. 13. 9, Ps. 42. 4 with *v.* 11,
Job 13. 9; 20. 4. The *obj.* is also often omitted, when a
pron., in the same circumstances.   § 73, R. 5.

Rem. 2. The subj. is probably *nom.* in some cases where
it is not separated from inf. (*a* above), *e.g.* when לְ of inf.
has pretonic *qameç*; 2 S. 19. 20 לָשׂוּם הַמֶּלֶךְ with Gen. 16. 3
לְשֶׁבֶת אַבְרָם, 1 K. 6. 1, Job 37. 7.   The inf. hiph. of עי verbs
is never shortened except with suff. (Gen. 39. 18 in *c* above),
e.g. Is. 10. 15 כַּהֲנִיף שֵׁבֶט, 14. 3 בְּיוֹם הָנִיחַ י, 2 S. 17. 14,
Ps. 46. 3.

Rem. 3. The obj. of inf. when a *noun* is probably acc.
and not gen. objecti.   When inf. has suff. this is clear, Gen.
39. 18, Deu. 9. 28.   Also the particle את is frequently expressed, Gen. 14. 17; 25. 26, Deu. 10. 12, 15; 11. 22, 1 S.
18. 19; 25. 2, Zech. 13. 9.   Cases in which neither of these
marks is present are probably to be decided on the same
analogy, *e.g.* Jud. 14. 6 כְּשַׁסַּע הַגְּדִי *as one rends a kid*, Is.
10. 14 *as one gathers eggs*, 17. 5, 1 K. 18. 28, Ps. 66. 10;

101. 3, Pr. 21. 3. The fem. inf., while it may take acc., is occasionally construed with gen. *obj.*, Ps. 73. 28 קִרְבַת אֱלֹהִים *to draw near to God*, Mic. 6. 8, so Aram. Ezr. 4. 22. So the common לִקְרָאתִי *to meet me*, לִקְרַאת דָּוִד *to meet David*, &c. Similarly fem. verbal noun, Deu. 29. 22, cf. acc. Ez. 17. 9, Am. 4. 11, and with mas. noun, Nu. 10. 2 (Hab. 3. 13?). In Nu. 23. 10 *rd.* perhaps מִי סָפַר. Others consider cases like Is. 10. 14 ; 17. 5 as gen. obj. (Hitz. on Is. 1. 7).

Rem. 4. Though inf. has a distinct suff. for acc. only in 1 *p. s.* and occasionally in others, *e.g.* 3 *s.* לְהוֹצִאֵהוּ, Jer. 39. 14, and 1 *pl.* לְהוֹצִיאָנוּ, Ex. 14. 11, there seems no reason to doubt that the suff. of all the persons are often in acc. There is no syntactical reason why inf. should govern acc. of 1 *p. s.* and not of the other persons, as it does govern acc. of all persons with אֵת. A gen. obj. would in many cases be awkward, as Gen. 37. 4 דַּבְּרוֹ *to speak to him*, and where the suff. is parallel to אֵת as 37. 22, Deu. 1. 27. In Deu. 23. 5 the suff. has verbal *n* demons. Comp. exx. like Nu. 22. 23, 25, Deu. 9. 28 ; 26. 19 with Ps. 89. 28, Jud. 13. 23 ; 14. 8 ; 18. 2, 1 S. 2. 25 ; 19. 11, 1 K. 20. 35, 2 K. 9. 35, Ps. 106. 23, 26, 27. When prep. לְ precedes inf. the suff. is mostly acc. ; also often when מִן precedes, and even when other prepp. are prefixed.—Nu. 22. 13 לְתִתִּי = לְתִתֵּנִי, and Jer. 27. 8 תֻּמִּי seems used as trans., though cf. Sep.

§ 92. Usage of inf. cons.—The inf. cons. with prepp. has all the meanings of the finite forms with conjunctions. Gen. 4. 8 בִּהְיוֹתָם בַּשָּׂדֶה *when they were* in the field ; 3. 19 עַד שׁוּבְךָ *until thou return*, cf. Hos. 10. 12 עַד יָבוֹא *until he come*, Gen. 39. 16, 2 S. 10. 5. Gen. 39. 18 בַּהֲרִימִי קוֹלִי *when I lifted up*, cf. 37. 23 כַּאֲשֶׁר בָּא *when he came*. The prepp. become conjunctions, taking finite forms, by combination with the rel. אֲשֶׁר, which, however, is often omitted, as Hos. 10. 12 above, 5. 15. Gen. 18. 12 with Jud. 11. 36, 2 S. 19. 31 ; Am. 1. 11 with 2 S. 3. 30 ; 2 S. 3. 11 with Is. 43. 4.—Gen. 13. 10 ; 34. 7 ; 35. 1, 1 S. 9. 15, 2 S. 12. 6, Ex. 19. 18. Cf. § 145.

§ 93. The prep. לְ, which properly expresses the direction

of the action of previous verb, is used with inf. cons. in a weaker sense (like gerund in *do*) to explain the circumstances or nature of a preceding action. This gerundial (adverbial) use is very common.   1 S. 14. 33 הָעָם חֹטִאים לֶאֱכֹל עַל־הַדָּם the people are sinning *in eating* with the blood; 1 K. 5. 23 תַּעֲשֶׂה אֶת־חֶפְצִי לָתֵת לֶחֶם בֵּיתִי thou wilt do my desire *in giving* (so as to give) bread for my house.   Gen. 18. 25; 19. 19; 29. 26; 34. 7; 43. 6, 1 S. 12. 17, 19; 19. 5; 20. 20, 2 S. 14. 20, 1 K. 8. 32; 14. 8; 16. 19. So the frequent לֵאמֹר *saying*.   Similarly in explanation of a comparison, Gen. 3. 22, 2 S. 14. 25, Is. 21. 1, Ez. 38. 16, Pr. 26. 2, 1 Chr. 12. 8.—Jos. 22. 26 is peculiar if text right. Is. 44. 14 לִכְרָת text dubious.

§ 94. The inf. with ל is also used as a circumscription in various senses of the imperfect.   (*a*) As a periphrastic fut. Gen. 15. 12 וַיְהִי הַשֶּׁמֶשׁ לָבוֹא and it was, *the sun was about to set*, Jos. 2. 5.   Is. 38. 20 י' לְהוֹשִׁיעֵנִי *Je. is* (ready, about) *to save me*.   Is. 10. 32, Jer. 51. 49, Ps. 25. 14; 49. 15, Pr. 19. 8, Ecc. 3. 15, 1 Chr. 9. 25.—In 1 S. 14. 21 *rd.* סָבְבוּ גַם־הֵמָּה *they also turned to be*.   (*b*) As a gerundive, in the sense of *is to be, must be, ought to be.*   2 K. 4. 13 מֶה לַעֲשׂוֹת לָךְ הֲיֵשׁ לְדַבֶּר־לָךְ *what is to be done for thee? should one speak for thee* to the king?   2 K. 13. 19 לְהַכּוֹת חָמֵשׁ אוֹ־שֵׁשׁ פְּעָמִים *percutiendum erat*.   Is. 5. 4, Hos. 9. 13, Ps. 32. 9; 49. 15, Job 30. 6, 2 S. 4. 10.   Or in the sense of *can be*, Jud. 1. 19, 2 S. 14. 19 (יֵשׁ = אִשׁ).—The consn. in Gen. 15. 12, Jos. 2. 5 appears to be as 1 S. 7. 10, 2 S. 2. 24, 1 K. 20. 40, 2 K. 2. 11, and often, the vb. *was* being understood.

§ 95. The *negative* inf. is formed—(*a*) Usually by particle בִּלְתִּי with ל, as Gen. 3. 11 צִוִּיתִיךָ לְבִלְתִּי אֲכָל־מִמֶּנּוּ I commanded thee *not to eat of it*, Deu. 4. 21, 1 K. 11. 10. This particle negatives inf. in its various uses, *e.g.* when it expresses purpose, Gen. 4. 15; 38. 9, and frequently in its

gerundial or explicative sense, Gen. 19. 21, Ex. 8. 25, Deu.
3. 3; 8. 11; 17. 12, Jos. 5. 6, Jud. 2. 23; 8. 1, Jer. 16. 12; 17.
23, 24, 27.

(*b*) The inf. as periphrastic fut. or gerundive (§ 94) is
negatived by לֹא לְ or לְ לֹא or אֵין לְ. Am. 6. 10 לֹא לְהַזְכִּיר בְּשֵׁם יְ
the name of Je. *must not be mentioned*; Jud. 1. 19 (could not
dispossess), 1 Chr. 5. 1. Est. 4. 2 כִּי אֵין לָבוֹא אֶל־הַשַּׁעַר
the gate *must not be gone to.* Ezr. 9. 15, 2 Chr. 5. 11; 20.
6, 17; 22. 9, Est. 8. 8, Ps. 40. 6, Ecc. 3. 14. There seems no
difference in sense between לֹא לְ and אֵין לְ, though the
latter is common in the later style; cf. 1 Chr. 15. 2 with
23. 26. Jer. 4. 11 does not belong here.

§ 96. In the progress of the discourse, when new clauses
are added with *and*, the inf. is very generally changed into
the finite construction. Gen. 39. 18 כַּהֲרִימִי קוֹלִי וָאֶקְרָא
lifted up my voice *and cried*; 2 K. 18. 32 עַד בֹּאִי וְלָקַחְתִּי
אֶתְכֶם till I come *and take you.* Gen. 27. 45, Jud. 6. 18, 1 S.
24. 12, Is. 5. 24; 10. 2; 13. 9; 30. 12, 26; 45. 1, Am. 1. 9, 11,
Ps. 104. 14, 15. This resolution is necessary with a neg.
clause, Am. 1. 9. Cf. Rem. 2.

Rem. 1. The pleonastic neg. לְבִלְתִּי לְ (§ 95) occurs 2 K.
23. 10 (cf. לְמַעַן לְ Ez. 21. 20), and מִבַּלְתִּי Nu. 14. 16 *because
Je. was not able.*—The inf. is sometimes negatived by prep.
מִן *away from*, as Is. 5. 6 מֵהַמְטִיר command *not to rain.* So
after *to swear* Is. 54. 9, cf. Deu. 4. 21, and *to beware* Gen.
31. 29 (cf. *v.* 24), 2 K. 6. 9. Occasionally a periphrasis of
לֵאמֹר *saying* and direct speech is employed, Gen. 3. 11 with
v. 17, Am. 2. 12.

Rem. 2. The finite tense consecutive to the inf. (§ 96)
will show the *nuances* of time, relation, &c., in which the
inf. was used. Thus Gen. 39. 18, 1 S. 24. 12, the inf. referred to a past act; 2 K. 18. 32, Jud. 6. 18 to a future one,
and Am. 1. 11 to a frequentative action. Loose constructions
occasionally arise in the process of resolution, *e.g.* Hos.
9. 7 וְעַל־אֲשֶׁר רבה עַל רֹב עֲוֺנְךָ וְרַבָּה *i.e.* *and because . . . is great*;

so Jer. 30. 14, 15. So perhaps 1 S. 4. 19 וּמֵת . . . אֶל־הִלָּקַח,
i.e. וְאֶל־(עַל־) אֲשֶׁר מֵת and regarding the fact that he was dead.

Rem. 3. Sometimes, esp. in later style, the inf. with
suff. appears used for finite form, Job 9. 27 אִם אָמְרִי *if I
think* (my thought be).   Jer. 9. 5, Zeph. 3. 20, Dan. 11. 1.
Comp. also the consn. Ex. 9. 18, 2 S. 19. 25.

Rem. 4. The inf. cons. with *and* is used, particularly in
later style, in continuation of a preceding finite or other
form (cf. inf. abs. § 88).   Several times וְלָתֵת, Ex. 32. 29,
Jer. 17. 10; 19. 12, Dan. 12. 11.   Originally and in the
older passages the inf. stood perhaps under the influence of
a *will* or *purpose* implicitly contained in preceding clause,
but in many cases this cannot any more be discovered; the
inf. is merely a shorter way of indicating the action.   Am.
8. 4, Hos. 12. 3 (Sep. wants *and*), 1 S. 8. 12, Jer. 44. 19,
Ez. 13. 22, Is. 44. 28, Lev. 10. 10, 11, Neh. 8. 13, Ps. 104. 21,
Job 34. 8, 1 Chr. 6. 34; 10. 13, 2 Chr. 7. 17; 8. 13, Ecc.
9. 1, Dan. 2. 16, 18.   In Gen. 42. 25 *and to restore* is under
" commanded," the preceding clause being brachylogy usual
with " command."   Prep. omitted 1 Chr. 21. 24, cf. 2 S.
24. 24.

Rem. 5. Though the *pass.* inf. is quite common the act.
is often used where pass. might be expected.   Gen. 4. 13,
Ex. 19. 13, 1 S. 18. 19, Is. 18. 3, Hos. 10. 10, Jer. 6. 15;
25. 34; 41. 4, Hag. 2. 15, Ps. 42. 4; 67. 3, Job 20. 4,
Ecc. 3. 2.

Obs.—In composition, if doubt arise, it is safe to use
prep. לְ before inf., as the bare inf. being a noun can be
governed properly only by a trans. verb.   The prep. must
be used: 1. After verbs expressing *purpose* and verbs of
motion, Gen. 2. 15, Ex. 3. 4.   2. After a nominal sent.,
pos. or neg., Gen. 2. 5; 24. 25.   3. After an adj., Gen.
19. 20, Is. 5. 22 (Job 3. 8 a rare exception).   4. After a
noun, Hos. 8. 11; 10. 12, Is. 5. 22, unless the inf. be gen.,
Gen. 29. 7.   Such verbs, however, as יָכֹל *to be able*, מֵאֵן *to
refuse*, are trans. in Heb. and may take bare inf., Deu. 1. 9,
Hos. 8. 5, Is. 1. 13, Nu. 22. 14, Jer. 3. 3; so נִלְאָה *to be
weary*, Is. 1. 14, Jer. 15. 6.

9

THE *NOMEN AGENTIS* OR PARTICIPLE

§ 97. The ptcp. or *nomen agentis* partakes of the nature both of the noun (adj.) and the verb. It presents the person or subj. in the continuous exercise or exhibition of the action or condition denoted by the verb. The *pass.* ptcp. describes the subj. as having the action continuously exercised upon him, or at least differs from the adj. in presenting the state of the subj. as the result of an action.

Rem. 1. The ptcp. carries the notion of action, opera-tion, like the verb, while the quality expressed by the adj. inheres in the subj. as a mere motionless characteristic. On the other hand the ptcp. differs from the impf. in that the continuousness of the impf. is not unbroken, but mere repetition of the action. The ptcp. is a line, the impf. a succession of points.

It is but natural, however, that act. ptcps. expressing conditions or operations which are habitual should come to be used as nouns, as אהב *friend*, א׳ב *enemy*, שׁפט *judge*, שׁמר *watchman*, חזה *seer*, &c., and that pass. ptcps. should in usage become adjectives. The ptcp. *niph.* in particular has the sense of the Lat. gerundive and adj. in *bilis*, as נוֹרָא *to be feared*, terrible, נֶחְשָׁב *æstimandus*, נֶחְמָד *desirable*, נִתְעָב *detestable*, נִכְבָּד *honourable*. Occasionally ptcp. *Pu.*, מְהֻלָּל *laudandus*, Ps. 96. 4. Possibly Ḳal, Ps. 137. 8 (some point שְׁדוֹדָה). Jer. 4. 30, Is. 23. 12, are real or imagined pasts. See Is. 2. 22, Ps. 18. 4; 19. 11; 22. 32; 76. 8; 102. 19, Job 15. 16. In like manner the difference between ptcp. and impf. is often scarcely discernible in usage. Gen. 2. 10, Ex. 13. 15, Lev. 11. 47, Nu. 24. 4, 16. Cf. Jud. 4. 22 with 2 K. 6. 19.

§ 98. Construction of ptcp.—The ptcp. is construed— (*a*) Verbally, taking the government of its verb, *acc.* or *prep.* Gen. 32. 12 יָרֵא אָנֹכִי אֹתוֹ *I fear him*; 25. 28 רִבְקָה אֹהֶבֶת אֶת־יַעֲקֹב *Reb. loved Jacob*. Gen. 27. 8; 37. 7, 16; 40. 8, 17; 41. 9; 42. 29, 1 S. 11. 3, 2 S. 14. 18, 1 K. 18. 3, Am. 5. 8, 9, 18.

With prep. Gen. 16. 13; 26. 11, 1 S. 17. 19; 23. 1, 2 S. 23. 3,
Ps. 89. 10.   The ptcp. may take any acc. taken by its verb;
Deu. 6. 11 מְלֵאִים כָּל־טוּב *full of every good*, Am. 2. 13;
cogn. acc. 1 K. 1. 40; or two acc., 2 S. 1. 24 הַמַּלְבִּשְׁכֶם שָׁנִי
who clothed you with crimson.   Zeph. 1. 9.

(*b*) Or, nominally, being in cons. with following gen.
Gen. 3. 5 יֹדְעֵי טוֹב וָרָע *knowing good and evil*; Hos. 2. 7
נֹתְנֵי לַחְמִי וּמֵימַי *who give my bread and water*.   This consn.
is very common: the *act.* ptcp. of verbs governing a direct
obj. take this obj. in gen.; and the *pass.* ptcp. of such verbs
take the subj. of the verbs in the gen.   Gen. 22. 12 יָדַעְתִּי
אִשָּׁה אֲהֻבַת רֵעַ *'א כִּי־יְרֵא* thou fearest God*; Hos. 3. 1
a woman *loved by a paramour*.   Gen. 19. 14, 25, Ex. 15. 14;
23. 31, Jud. 1. 19; 5. 6, 2 S. 4. 6; 6. 13, 1 K. 2. 7; 12. 21,
Is. 5. 18, Hos. 6. 8.   So ptcp. of other act. conjugations,
Is. 5. 8; 19. 8, 9, 10; 28. 6; 29. 21, Jer. 23. 30, 32, Hos.
5. 10; 11. 4, Ps. 19. 8, 9; cf. 136. 4–7.   Pass. ptcp., Gen.
24. 31 *blessed by Je.*, 2 S. 5. 8 *hated by*, Is. 53. 4, Job 14. 1.
Frequently the *cause* or instrument takes the place of the
subj., Is. 1. 7 שְׂרֻפוֹת אֵשׁ *burnt with fire*.   Gen. 20. 3; 41. 6,
Deu. 32. 24, Is. 14. 19; 22. 2; 28. 1 *stricken down with wine*,
Jer. 18. 21, Hos. 4. 17.

(*c*) In like manner suff. to ptcp. may be *acc.* or *gen.*   Deu.
8. 16 הַמַּאֲכִלְךָ מָן *who fed thee* with manna.   Deu. 8. 5
(*n* demons.); 13. 6, 11; 20. 1, Is. 9. 12; 10. 20; 47. 10; 63. 11,
Jer. 9. 14 (cf. 23. 15), Ps. 18. 33; 81. 11, Job 31. 15; 40. 19.
Often in *gen.*; Gen. 27. 29 מְבָרְכֶיךָ *they who bless thee* (thy
blessers), 4. 14, Ex. 20. 5, 6, 1 S. 2. 30, Is. 50. 8, Ps. 7. 5;
55. 13, Job 7. 8.

Rem. 1. The mixed consn., gen. and acc. (for 2 acc.),
Am. 4. 13 is curious.—The verbs בא *to go into* and יצא *to
come out of*, may be consd. with acc. (Gen. 44. 4, Deu.
14. 22, 2 K. 20. 4, Lam. 1. 10, Ps. 100. 4), and so their
ptcp. with. gen.   Gen. 9. 10; 23. 10, 18; 34. 24; 46. 26,

Ex. 1. 5, Jud. 8. 30.   Similarly other kinds of acc., as that
of *direction*, Is. 38. 18 יְרִדֵי־בוֹר *gone down to the pit*, 1 Chr.
12. 33, 36, or of *respect*, Is. 1 30 fading *in its leaf*.   In
poetry this brief forcible consn. of gen. represents prose
consn. with prep.; Ps. 88. 6 *lying in the grave*, though cf.
57. 5 ; Mic. 2. 8, Is. 22. 2.   Particulary with suff., Ps. 18. 40
קָמַי *those rising up against me*, cf. Ps. 3. 2.   Deu. 33. 11,
Is. 22. 3, Ps. 53. 6 ; 73. 27 ; 74. 23 ; 102. 9, Pr. 2. 19.   Is.
29. 7 *who war against her and her stronghold* is so condensed
as to be suspicious.

The pass. ptcp. also may retain the acc. of act. verb, as
1 S. 2. 18 חָגוּר אֵפוֹד *girt with an ephod*, Jud. 18. 11, Ez.
9. 2, 3, Neh. 4. 12; or take the gen., Is. 3. 3 ; 51. 21, Joel
1. 8, Ez. 9. 11.   Particularly when the gen. explains the
extent of application of ptcp. (§ 24 *d*).   Is. 3. 3. נְשׂוּא פָנִים
he whose face is lifted up.   Ps. 32. 1 כְּסוּי חֲטָאָה *he whose sin
is covered*.   2 S. 13. 31, Is. 33. 24, Pr. 14. 2.   In 2 S. 15. 32
קָרוּעַ כֻּתָּנְתּוֹ כ' is not acc. of respect, *as to* his garment, but
subj. to *rent*, though *rent* at the same time is acc. of condition to Hushai.   On the other hand Jud. 1. 7 is rather an
ordinary circ. cl., *cut off* being pred. to *thumbs*, although
elsewhere this word is fem.   Ex. 12. 11, Jer. 30. 6.

§ 99. The ptcp. becomes virtually a noun, as Is. 19. 20
מוֹשִׁיעַ one who saves, *a saviour*, and may be subj. or obj. of
a sentence.   When in apposition with a noun it is used as
an adj., Deu. 4. 24 אֵשׁ אֹכְלָה *a devouring fire*, 4. 34 *an out-*
stretched arm, Gen. 22. 13, Is. 18. 2, 5, Jud. 1. 24 וַיִּרְאוּ אִישׁ
יֹצֵא they saw *a man coming out*.   Am. 5. 3, Is. 2. 13 ; 10. 22.
With the art. the ptcp. may like the adj. designate a class.
Am. 5. 13, Is. 14. 8 ; 28. 16, Mic. 4. 6 ; or have the sense of
he who . . ., whoever, Gen. 26. 11 הַנֹּגֵעַ בָּאִישׁ הַזֶּה *whoever*
touches, 2 S. 14. 10 ; and so with gen., Gen. 9. 6, Ex. 21. 12,
15, 16.

When in appos. with a preceding def. subj. the ptcp. with
art. has the meaning very much of a relative clause.   Gen.
12. 7 הַנִּרְאָה אֵלָיו י' Je. *who had appeared to him* ; 1 S.

1. 26 אֲנִי הָאִשָּׁה הַנִּצֶּבֶת I am the woman *who stood*, cf. Jud.
16. 24. This usage is very common: Gen. 13. 5; 27. 33;
35. 3; 43. 12, 18; 48. 15, 16, Ex. 11. 5, Jud. 8. 34, 1 S. 4. 8,
2 S. 1. 24, 2 K. 22. 18, Is. 8. 6, 17, 18; 9. 1, Am. 4. 1; 5. 3,
Mic. 3. 2, 3, 5. With pass. ptcp., Nu. 21. 8, Jud. 6. 28 the
altar *that had been built*, 20. 4 the woman *who was murdered*,
1 K. 18. 30, Ps. 79. 10.—Ps. 19. 11 resumes *v.* 10 (they) *which
are more desirable.* Ps. 18. 33; 49. 7.

Rem. 1. Of course the ptcp. with art. is not to be used
as an ordinary rel. clause after an *indef.* noun, only after def.
words as pron., proper name, or other defined word. In later
style exceptions occur, Jer. 27. 3; 46. 16, Ez. 2. 3; 14. 22,
Ps. 119. 21, Dan. 9. 26, though in most of these cases the
preceding word is really def. though formally undetermined.
In other cases the preceding subj. receives a certain definiteness from being connected with *all*, Gen. 1. 21, 28, or a
numeral, Jud. 16. 27, cf. 1 S. 25. 10, or from standing in a
comparison, Pr. 26. 18 (Ps. 62. 4 *rd.* perhaps גְּדֵרָה דּ), or
from being described by an adj., Is. 65. 2, cf. *v.* 3.

Rem. 2. When another ptcp. follows one with art. it is
often without art., as predicate, Is. 5. 20, Am. 6. 4, Job
5. 10. But in vigorous speech the clauses are made parallel
and the art. used, Is. 40. 22, 23, Mic. 3. 5. Occasionally
the rel. pron. takes the place of the art. as more distinct,
Deu. 1. 4, Jer. 38. 16, Ez. 9. 2, Ps. 115. 8. Both are used
1 K. 12. 8; 21. 11.

Rem. 3. When the ptcp. as direct pred. receives the art.
it becomes coextensive with the subj. Gen. 2. 11 it is
that which goeth round. 45. 12 my mouth is *that which
speaketh.* Deu. 3. 21 thine eyes were *they which saw.* Gen.
42. 6, Deu. 3. 22, 1 S. 4. 16, Is. 14. 27.

§ 100. (*a*) The ptcp. as pred., unlike the finite verb, does
not contain the subj., which must be expressed. 1 S. 19. 11
מָחָר אַתָּה מוּמָת to-morrow *thou shalt be slain*; Gen. 38. 25
הִוא מוּצֵאת *she was brought forth*; 1 S. 9. 11 הֵמָּה עֹלִים
they were going up. The pron., however, is often omitted if

the subj. has just been mentioned, particularly after הִנֵּה
Gen. 24. 30 וַיָּבֹא אֶל־הָאִישׁ וְהִנֵּה עֹמֵד he came to the
man, *and, behold, he was standing.* Gen. 37. 15; 38. 24,
41. 1, 1 S. 30. 3, 16, Am. 7. 1, Is. 29. 8. With גַם Gen. 32. 7.
Occasionally the pron. is omitted anomalously, Jos. 8. 6, Ps.
22. 29 (*he* is ruler), Neh. 9. 3, 5. In 1 S. 6. 3 אַתֶּם has
probably dropped out. On ptcp. with general subj. § 108 *c.*

(*b*) Owing to the emphasis thrown by the idea and usage
of ptcp. on the subj. the latter usually precedes. Gen. 2. 10
וְנָהָר יָצָא *and a river went forth*; 24. 21 וְהָאִישׁ מִשְׁתָּאֵה לָהּ
and the man gazed at her, 24. 13, 37 (see above in *a*). This
order is usual with הִנֵּה and in rel. clauses, 18. 17; 24. 37;
28. 20; 31. 43. On the other hand, if emphasis fall on ptcp.,
and in clauses beginning with כִּי *for, that*, אִם *if*, which give
prominence to the pred., the ptcp. precedes the subj. Gen.
30. 1 וְאִם אַיִן מֵתָה אָנֹכִי and if not *I die*; 3. 5 כִּי יֹדֵעַ א׳
for *God knoweth*, 15. 14; 19. 13; 25. 30; 29. 9; 32. 12; 41. 32.
With interrog., Gen. 4. 9; 18. 17, Nu. 11. 29. After אַךְ Jud.
3. 24.

(*c*) The ptcp. does not indicate time, its colour in this
respect being taken from the connection in which it stands.
The pass. ptcp. refers chiefly to the past, though not
exclusively. The act. ptcp. is mainly descriptive of something present, *i.e.* either actually present to the speaker, or
present to him in idea, as the *fut. instans*; or, as in circums.
clauses, present to the main action spoken of, though this
may be in the past. Gen. 4. 10 דְּמֵי אָחִיךָ צֹעֲקִים thy
brother's *blood crieth.* Gen. 19. 13, 14 כִּי מַשְׁחִיתִים אֲנַחְנוּ
for *we are destroying* (going to des.). 1 S. 1. 12 she *prayed*
long וְעֵלִי שֹׁמֵר אֶת־פִּיהָ *Eli watching her mouth.* See exx.
in Rem. 1.

(*d*) Owing to its nominal character the ptcp. is negatived
by אַיִן. The place of the neg. varies. Gen. 41. 8 אֵין פּוֹתֵר

אֹתָם *there was none interpreting* them ; cf. different order, 40. 8; 41. 15.   Ex. 5. 16 תֶּבֶן אֵין נִתָּן *straw is not given*; 1 K. 6. 18 אֵין אֶבֶן נִרְאָה *no stone was seen*.   The אֵין often takes suff. of subj., Gen. 43. 5 אִם אֵינְךָ מְשַׁלֵּחַ *if thou dost not let go*, Ex. 5. 10.—Gen. 20. 7; 39. 23; 41. 24, Ex. 3. 2, Deu. 4. 22 ; 22. 27, Jos. 6. 1, Jud. 3. 25, 1 S. 3. 1 ; 22. 8; 26. 12, 1 K. 6. 18, Hos. 5. 14, Am. 5. 2, 6, Is. 5. 27 ; 17. 2 ; 22. 22, Jer. 9. 21.   See Rem. 3.

(*e*) When additional clauses are joined by *and* to a participial consn. the *finite* tense is usually employed, though not always.   Gen. 35. 3 לָאֵל הָעֹנֶה אֹתִי וַיְהִי עִמָּדִי the God *who answered me, and was* with me; 27. 33 הַצָּר צַיִד וַיָּבֵא *who hunted* venison, *and brought* it.   In animated speech without *and*, Is. 5. 8 מַגִּיעֵי בַיִת בְּבַיִת שָׂדֶה בְשָׂדֶה יַקְרִיבוּ *who join* house to house, *lay* field to field ; cf. Ps. 147. 14–16.—Gen. 7. 4 ; 17. 19 ; 48. 4, Deu. 4. 22, 1 S. 2. 6, 8, 31 ; 2 S. 20. 12, Is. 5. 23 ; 14. 17 ; 29. 21 ; 30. 2 ; 31. 1 ; 44. 25, 26 ; 48. 1, Am. 5. 7–12, Hos. 2. 16, Jer. 13. 10, Ps. 18. 33.   This change to the finite is *necessary* when the additional clause is neg.   See Rem. 4.

(*f*) As the ptcp. presents the subj. as in the continuous exercise of the action, it is greatly employed in describing scenes of a striking kind and in circumstantial clauses (§ 138 *b*).   Much of the picturesqueness of prose historical writing is due to it.   So it is used with such particles as הִנֵּה *behold*, עוֹד *still, while*.   1 K. 22. 10 the kings יֹשְׁבִים אִישׁ עַל־כִּסְאוֹ מְלֻבָּשִׁים בְּגָדִים וְכָל־הַנְּבִיאִים מִתְנַבְּאִים *were sitting, each on his throne, clothed in their robes, and all the prophets were prophesying* before them ; so *v.* 12, 19. 2 S. 15. 30 David's ascent of Olivet, cf. *v.* 18, 23.   Is. 6. 2, 2 S. 12. 19, 1 S. 9. 11, 14, 27, Is. 5. 28, Nu. 11. 27, 1 K. 12. 6, 2 K. 2. 11.   With הנה, Gen. 25. 32 ; 37. 7 ; 41. 1–3, 1 S. 10. 22 ; 12. 2, 2 K. 17. 26.   With עוד, Gen. 18. 22, Ex. 9.

2, 17, 1 K. 1. 14, 22, 42, 2 K. 6. 33, Jer. 33. 1, Job 2. 3.   So
with יֵשׁ and אֵין.   Gen. 24. 42, 49; 43. 4, Deu. 29. 14, Jud.
6. 36.

Rem. 1. The *time* of ptcp., § 100 c.   Exx. of present
time: Gen. 16. 8; 19. 15; 32. 12; 37. 16; 43. 18, Deu.
4. 1; 12. 8 and often, Jud. 7. 10; 18. 3, 1 S. 14. 11, Is. 1. 7,
Hos. 3. 1.   Exx. of past time: Gen. 39. 23 וַאֲשֶׁר הוּא עֹשֶׂה
' מַצְלִיחַ whatever *he did Je. prospered*, 37. 7, 15; 40. 6;
41. 1 seq., Ex. 18. 5, 14, Deu. 4. 12, Jud. 4. 22; 14. 4;
19. 27, 1 S. 2. 13; 9. 11, 1 K. 3. 2; 4. 20; 6. 27, 2 K.
13. 21.   Exx. of fut. time: Gen. 7. 4; 17. 19; 41. 25, 28;
49. 29, Ex. 33. 15, Jud. 11. 9; 15. 3, 1 S. 20. 36, 2 S.
12. 23, 2 K. 4. 16, Ps. 22. 32; 102. 19.   Particularly with
הִנֵּה, as Gen. 15. 3; 20. 3; 24. 13; 1 S. 3. 11, 1 K. 13. 2,
Is. 3. 1; 7. 14, Am. 8. 11.   The ptcp. with הנה however
may refer to any time, as pres., Gen. 38, 24 *is with child*,
Jud. 9. 36, 1 S. 10. 22, 1 K. 1. 25; 17. 12; or past, Gen.
40. 6; 41. 1, Am. 7. 1, 4, 7.

The ptcp., even without copula, may express *juss.* sense;
Gen. 3. 14 אָרוּר אַתָּה *cursed be thou*, 9. 26; 24. 27, 1 K.
2. 45, cf. Ru. 2. 19.

Rem. 2. In order to express more distinctly the idea of
duration, particularly in past, the verb היה is sometimes
used with the ptcp., generally in a clause of circumstance
explicative of the main narrative, but also in an independent
statement.   Gen. 37. 2 יוֹסֵף הָיָה רֹעֶה Jos. *was herding*; Jud.
16. 21 וַיְהִי טוֹחֵן בְּבֵית הָאֲסוּרִים *and he continued to grind*; 1 S.
2 11 וְהַנַּעַר הָיָה מְשָׁרֵת אֶת־י' and the child *continued to minister*.
Gen. 4. 17; 39. 22, Ex. 3. 1, Deu. 9. 7, 22, 24; 28. 29,
Jud. 1. 7, 1 S. 18. 29, 2 S. 3. 6, 17; 7. 6, 2 K. 17. 25–41;
18. 4, Is. 2. 2; 59. 2, Jer. 26. 18, 20, Hos. 9. 17, Ps.
122. 2, Job 1. 14.   Pass. ptcp. Lev. 13. 45, 1 K. 22. 35,
Jer. 14. 16; 36. 30, Zech. 3. 3.   The usage is more common
in the later style (occurring sometimes with almost no
emphasis).   Neh. 1. 4; 2. 13. 15, 1 Chr. 6. 17; 18. 14,
2 Chr. 30. 10; 36. 16, Est. 2. 15, Dan. 1. 16; 5. 19; 10. 9.

Rem. 3. The ptcp. is negatived by לא when an attributive.
Jer. 2. 2 אֶרֶץ לֹא זְרוּעָה a land *not sown* (cf. adj. Deu. 32. 6,

Hos. 13. 13). Jer. 18. 15, Hab. 1. 14 in an attributive clause, Job 29. 12. Cf. 2 S. 1. 21, Hos. 7. 8. But also in a number of cases when *pred.*, perhaps with rather more force, Nu. 35. 23 (= Deu. 19. 4), Deu. 28. 61, 2 S. 3. 34, Jer. 4. 22, Ez. 4. 14; 22. 24, Zeph. 3. 5, Ps. 38. 15, Job 12. 3. The double neg. of 1 K. 10. 21 is wanting in 2 Chr. 9. 20. The accents show Is. 62. 12, Jer. 6. 8, to be perf.; Zeph. 2. 1 is doubtful. Of course לֹא רֻחָמָה Hos. 1. 6, לֹא נֶחָמָה Is. 54. 11, are perfs.

Rem. 4. The finite tense which *continues* ptcp. will vary (cf. on inf. § 96, R. 2). It will be *vav conv. impf.* when ptcp. referred to a fact in the past, Gen. 27. 33; 35. 3, or was equivalent to a perf. of experience, Am. 5. 7, 8; 9. 5. It will be simple impf. or *vav conv. perf.* when ptcp. expressed a thing habitual or general, 2 S. 20. 12, Am. 8. 14, Is. 5. 8, Mic. 3. 5, 9, or referred to fut., 1 K. 13. 2, 3.

Rem. 5. The ptcp. being of weaker force than finite tense, sometimes uses prep. לְ instead of acc. to convey the action, particularly when obj. precedes. Is. 11. 9 לַיָּם מְכַסִּים waters *covering the sea*. Nu. 10. 25, Deu. 4. 42, Am. 6. 3 (cf. Is. 66. 5), Is. 14. 2. So in Ar., *limâlihi* fîha *muhîna*, making light of his money, Am. b. Kelth. *v.* 4.

Rem. 6. The ptcp. without subj. tends to be used in later style for 3rd pers. like finite verb. Jos. 8. 6, Neh. 6. 6; 9. 3. 5, Is. 13. 5, and in Psalms. So occasionally for inf., Jer. 2. 17 עֵת מוֹלִכֵךְ the time when he led thee. Gen. 38. 29 (comp. Mal. 1. 7 with 8; 1. 12; 2. 17; also 2. 15). In Ez. 27. 34 *rd.* עַתְּ נִשְׁבֶּרֶת. Both uses are common in post-biblical Heb.

Rem. 7. The pass. ptcp. appears in some cases to express a state which is the result of the subject's own action. Is. 26. 3 בָּטוּחַ *trusting*, Ps. 103. 14 זָכוּר *mindful*, Is. 53. 3 יָדוּעַ *acquainted with*. Cf. 1 S. 2. 18, Jud. 18. 11, Ez. 9. 2, 3, Song 3. 8.

SUBORDINATION OF NOUNS TO THE VERB BY MEANS
OF PREPOSITIONS

§ 101. The action of the verb often reaches the obj. through the medium of a prep. The prepp. may be assumed to be—1. Words expressing *locality*. 2. Then they are transferred to the sphere of *time*. 3. And, finally, they are used to express relations which are intellectual or ideal.

When several words are coupled together under the regimen of the same prep. it is often repeated before each, as Hos. 2. 21 בְּצֶדֶק וּבְמִשְׁפָּט וּבְחֶסֶד וּבְרַחֲמִים Gen. 12. 1; 40. 2, 2 S. 6. 5, Hos. 1. 7. But usage varies, Hos. 2. 20; 3. 2. Sometimes, in poetry especially, the prep. exerts its influence over a second clause without being repeated, Is. 28. 6 for לִמְשִׁיבֵי, Job 15. 3 for וּבְמִלִּים, Is. 30. 1 *from* my spirit, 48. 9 *for the sake of* my praise.

Certain prepp. of motion, chiefly אֶל and מִן, are used with verbs that do not express motion, and, on the other hand, a prep. of rest such as בְ may be used with a verb of motion. This *pregnant* consn., as it has been called, permits the ellipse of a verb. 1 S. 7. 8 אַל־תַּחֲרֵשׁ מִמֶּנּוּ *be not silent* (turning away) *from* us. Ps. 22. 22 מִקַּרְנֵי רֵמִים עֲנִיתָנִי *heard* (and delivered) *me from* the horns. 1 S. 24. 16 וִישַׁפְּטֵנִי מִיָּדֶךָ, cf. 2 S. 18. 19. Is. 38. 17, Ez. 28. 16 *profane* (and cast) *thee from* the mount, Ps. 28. 1; 18. 22; 73. 27, Ezr. 2. 62.—Gen. 19. 27 אֶל־הַמָּקוֹם . . . וַיַּשְׁכֵּם *he rose early* (and went) *unto* the place, Song 7. 13. Gen. 42. 28 וַיֶּחֶרְדוּ אִישׁ אֶל־אָחִיו *they trembled* (and looked) *unto* one another; and often with verbs of *fear, wonder*, &c., Gen. 43. 33, Is. 13. 8, Hos. 3. 5 *come trembling unto*, Mic. 7. 17, cf. Is. 41. 1, Ps. 89. 40 *profaned* (and cast) *to* the ground, 74. 7. Is. 14. 17, Gen. 14. 3. With 1 S. 21. 3 (if text יודעתי right) cf. Gen. 46. 28. 1 S. 13. 7 *rd*. prob. מֵאַחֲרָי *trembled from after* him

(left him from fear). So the brief language, 1 S. 15. 23,
rejected thee מִמֶּלֶךְ *from* (being) *king*, cf. *v.* 26 מִהְיוֹת מ' ;
1 K. 15. 13 removed her מִגְּבִירָה *from being* queen-mother.
Is. 7. 8; 17. 1, Hos. 9. 12, Jer. 48. 2, Ps. 83. 5.   Ps. 55. 19
פָּדָה בְשָׁלוֹם *redeemed* (so as to he) *in peace*, Ps. 23. 6?   1 S.
22. 4 וַיַּנְחֵם אֶת־פְּנֵי מֶלֶךְ מ' *led them* (so that they were)
in the presence of the king of Moab.

Rem. 1. The prepp. are either, (*a*) of rest *in*, as בְּ; (*b*)
of motion in the direction of, as אֶל, לְ, עד ; (*c*) of motion
away from, as מִן ; or (*d*) of the expression of other relations,
as עַל *over, above, upon*, תחת *under*, &c.   In addition there
are compound prepp., mostly with אל or מן as first element.
See the Lexx.   Only a few points can be noticed.

(*a*) Prep. בְּ is either *in, within* (Ar. *fî*), or, *at, on* of contact
(Ar. *bi*).   Most of its uses are reducible to these two senses,
e.g. בַּבַּיִת *in the house*, בָּאָרֶץ, בָּהָר *in, on* the mountain ; of time,
בַּבֹּקֶר.   Hence its use with verbs *to touch* נָגַע, *to cleave to* דָּבַק, *to
hold* תָּמַךְ, אָחַז.   From the sense of *in* (in the sphere of, em-
bodied in) comes its use with pred. (*beth essentiæ*), as Ps.
68. 5 בְּיָהּ שְׁמוֹ (in) *Jah is his name*, Ex. 18. 4 God בְּעֶזְרִי *is* (in)
my help, Ps. 35. 2.   And otherwise, Ex. 6. 3 I appeared בְּאֵל
שַׁדָּי *as* El shaddai, Is. 40. 10 בְּחָזָק *as* a strong one, Ps. 39. 7
as an image ; Ps. 37. 20 ; 146. 5, Pr. 3. 26, Job 23. 13, Lev.
17. 11.   With ptcp. the plur. is used, though ref. be to a
single person, Jud. 11. 35 בְּעֹכְרָי *among* my troublers = *my
troubler*, Ps. 54. 6 ; 118. 7 ; 99. 6 *as* (being) his priests, cf.
Hos. 11. 4.   So other allied senses, *e.g.* where we use *with*,
בְּחַיִל כָּבֵד *with* a great army (in, in the element of ; less
naturally of contact, and so accompaniment), בְּמַקְלִי *with* my
staff, Gen. 32. 11 ; so *with* of instrument, Mic. 4. 14 בַּשֵּׁבֶט
with the rod, Is. 10. 24, 34 ; of persons, *in, through*, Hos.
1. 7 בַּיהוה *through Je.*, Gen. 9. 6.   Similar is בְּ of *price*, Gen.
30. 16, בְּדוּדָאֵי בְנִי *for* (with) the mandrakes, *v.* 26, 33. 19 ;
37. 28, 1 K. 10. 29.   Finally בְּ has partitive sense, Job 7. 13
my bed יִשָּׂא בְשִׂיחִי will bear *of* (in) *my* complaint, Nu. 11. 17,
Ez. 18. 20.   On בְּ with obj., § 73, R. 6.

(*b*) Prep. אל expresses motion *towards*, in the direction of,

whether the goal be reached or not. Gen. 2. 19 brought them אֶל־הָאָדָם *unto* the man, 3. 19 *unto* the dust, 6. 18 *into* the ark, 19. 3, 2 S. 5. 8. Then less literally, Gen. 39. 7 lifted up her eyes אֶל־יוֹסֵף *towards* (upon) Jos., Deu. 24. 15; Gen. 32. 31 פָּנִים אֶל־פָּנִים face *to* face, Nu. 12. 8 mouth *to* mouth. So after verbs *to speak*, דִּבֶּר אֶל (mostly with this verb). After verbs of speaking, in the sense of *of, in reference to*, Gen. 20. 2, 1 S. 1. 27; 3. 12, 2 S. 7. 19, Is. 29. 22, Ps. 2. 7. Naturally *unto* may mean *in addition to*, 1 S. 14. 34 eat אֶל־הַדָּם *with* the *blood*, Lev. 18. 18, 1 K. 10. 7, Lam. 3. 41, Ez. 7. 26 (עַל is more common in this sense, and the two prepp. are often confounded). The verb may give to *unto* the complexion of *hostility*, Gen. 4. 8 rose up אֶל־הֶבֶל *against* Abel, Gen. 22. 12, Jud. 1. 10, Is. 2. 4; 3. 8.

Prep. לְ *to* may like אֶל imply motion to, Gen. 24. 54; 27. 14, 25, 1 S. 25. 35, Is. 53. 7, Jer. 12. 15 (perhaps oftener in later style, 2 Chr. 1. 13), but oftenest expresses *direction to*, and greatly in an ideal sense. Hence with verb *to say* אמר; and after verbs of *speaking, remembering,* &c., in the sense of *in reference to*, Gen. 20. 13 אִמְרִי־לִי say *of me*, Ps. 3. 3; 132. 1, Jer. 2. 2, Ez. 18. 22; 33. 16, 1 K. 2. 4; 20. 7, Gen. 17. 20; 19. 21; 27. 8; 42. 9; 45. 1, Is. 5. 1. So Is. 8. 1 לְמַהֵר, though the לְ is not to be translated. In particular, לְ is used to introduce the indirect obj. (dat.), Jud. 1. 13 וַיִּתֶּן־לוֹ gave *him*, and in the various senses of the dat., Gen. 24. 29 וּלְרִבְקָה אָח R. *had a brother*, 13. 5. The so-called *dat. commodi* (or, incommodi, Jer. 2. 21, Mic. 2. 4, Ez. 37. 11, Ps. 137. 7), Is. 6. 8 מִי יֵלֶךְ־לָנוּ, Jud. 1. 1, Deu. 30. 12, 13; particularly in the form of the *ethical dat.*, when the action is reflected back upon the agent and done *for* him. Mostly with imper.: Gen. 12. 1 לֶךְ־לְךָ *get thee*, 22. 5 שְׁבוּ־לָכֶם *sit you* here, 21. 16 וַתֵּשֶׁב לָהּ she *sat her down*; Deu. 1, 7, 40; 2. 3; 5. 27, Jos. 7. 10; 22. 19, 1 K. 17. 3, Is. 2. 22; 36. 9; 40. 9, Am. 2. 13; 7. 12, Ps. 120. 6; 122. 3; 123. 4. On use of לְ to express second obj. after *to make, put,* &c., § 78, R. 5; with agent of pass., § 81; to circumscribe the gen., § 28, R. 5.—Prep. לְ also expresses the norm, *according to* (perh. allied to *in ref. to*), Is. 11. 3 לְמַרְאֵה עֵינָיו *according to* the sight of his eyes, Gen. 33. 14; 13. 3, 1 S.

25. 42, Hos. 10. 12? Comp. such phrases as 1 S. 1. 18 וַתֵּלֶךְ לְדַרְכָּהּ *went her way*, 1. 17 לְכִי לְשָׁלוֹם *go in peace*; to smite לְפִי חֶרֶב *with the edge*, Is. 1. 5 לַחֳלִי, 50. 11. On לְ with obj. cf. § 73, R. 7.

The prep. עַד *unto, as far as to*, often includes the limit, 1 S. 17. 52 ; esp. the form (וְעַד) עַד . . . מִן, Gen. 31. 24 מִטּוֹב עַד־רָע *good or evil* (from g. to e.), 14. 23 ; 19. 11, Ex. 22. 3, 1 K. 6. 24, Is. 1. 6. The form לְמִן is common, Deu. 4. 32, Jud. 19. 30, 2 S. 7. 6, cf. Is. 7. 17, Am. 6. 14. In later style the compound עַד לְ is common, 2 Chr. 28. 9 ; 29. 28, cf. 1 K. 18. 29 ; Jud. 3. 3 in the phrase " unto the entering in of Hamath," 1 Chr. 13. 5, cf. 5. 9. The sense *up to* becomes = *even* (cf. Ar. ḥatta), Nu. 8. 4, 1 S. 2. 5, Hag. 2. 19, Job 25. 5, cf. Ex. 9. 7, Deu. 2. 5.

(*c*) Prep. מִן may be a noun = *a part*. Its various senses follow from this, *e.g.* (1) the partitive, Gen. 30. 14 מִדּוּדָאֵי בְנֵךְ *some of* thy son's mandrakes, 28. 11 ; 45. 23, Ex. 4. 9 ; 6. 25 ; 16. 27 ; 17. 5, Lev. 5. 9, 1 K. 1. 6, Job 27. 6, Neh. 5. 5, Ps. 137. 3 (§ 11, R. 1 *a*). So perhaps such passages as Lev. 4. 2, Deu. 15. 7 (§ 35, R. 2), 1 S. 14. 45, 2 S. 14. 11, Ex. 12. 4, unless such cases belong to (3) below, *e.g.* 1 S. 14. 45 *from* (beginning with, starting from) *a hair*. Cases like Gen. 6. 2 ; 7. 22 ; 9. 10 ; 17. 12, where מן seems to particularise, are explainable in the same way.

(2) The sense *from, away from*, naturally follows. Hence use of מן in comparison, Ex. 12. 4, 1 S. 15. 22, 2 S. 20. 6, Hos. 6. 6 (§ 33 *seq.*). Hence also *privative* sense, *away from, without*, Gen. 27. 39 מִטַּל *away from* the dew, Job 11. 15 מִמּוּם *without spot*, 19. 26 ; 21. 9, Is. 22. 3, Hos. 9. 11, Jer. 10. 14 ; 48. 45, Mic. 3. 6, Zech. 7. 11, Ps. 109. 24, Pr. 20. 3. So after verbs of *delivering, saving, redeeming from, restraining, ceasing from, fearing* and *being ashamed* to do, &c. And in pregnant consns. (§ 101 above); Gen. 27. 1, 1 S. 8. 7 ; 15. 23, 1 K. 15. 13, Is. 7. 8, Hos. 4. 6 ; 9. 12, Ps. 102. 5, cf. 1 S. 25. 17 *so that there is no* speaking to him. (3) The sense *from* may refer to *source*, point of starting from, *e.g.* frequently in the local (and temporal) sense, Gen. 12. 1 ; 13. 11 ; 15. 4, Ex. 15. 22, 1 S. 17. 33 ; 20. 1 ;

but then, naturally, in a *causative* sense (influence coming from), *from, because of, by*, as Gen. 48. 10 his eyes were set מִזֹּקֶן *from* old age, Is. 53. 5 pierced מִפְּשָׁעֵינוּ *because of* our transgressions. Gen. 9. 11; 16. 10; 49. 12, Ex. 6. 9, Deu. 7. 7, 1 S. 1. 16, 1 K. 14. 4, Is. 28. 7; 40. 26, Ob. 9, 10, Hos. 11. 6. Cf. § 81.

(*d*) Prep. עַל has the meaning *above, over, upon*; *e.g.* locally whether of motion or rest, as Gen. 2. 5 had not rained עַל־הָאָרֶץ *upon* the earth, 2 K. 4. 34 he laid himself עַל־הַיֶּלֶד *upon* the child, Gen. 24. 30 he saw the bracelets עַל־יְדֵי אֲחֹתוֹ *upon the hands* of his sister, Gen. 1. 20 let fowl fly עַל־הארץ *above* the earth. And in a figurative sense, Gen. 16. 5 חֲמָסִי עָלֶיךָ my wrong be *upon thee*, 41. 33 set him עַל־הָארץ *over* the land, Jud. 3. 10, 1 S. 15. 17.

From these senses comes the use of עַל with verbs to *cover*, as כִּסָּה, *to pity, spare* חוּס, חָמַל, *to burden*, as Is. 1. 14 הָיוּ עָלַי לָטֹרַח they are *a burden upon me*, 2 S. 15. 33, Job 7. 20. So to express *obligation*, 2 S. 18. 11 עָלַי לָתֶת לְךָ *it would have lain upon me* to give thee, Gen. 30. 28, Jud. 19. 20, Pr. 7. 14. With words expressing the idea of *addition*, Gen. 31. 50 if thou take wives עַל־בְּנֹתַי *in addition to* my daughters, 32. 12 אֵם עַל־בָּנִים mother *with* children, Gen. 28. 9; 48. 22, Hos. 10. 14, Am. 3. 15. Other uses of עַל are similar, as Jud. 9. 17 נִלְחַם עֲלֵיכֶם fought *for you* (*over*, protecting), but also in a hostile sense *against*, Gen. 43. 18 *to fall upon*, Gen. 34. 30 to gather themselves *against*, 50. 20 plot *against*, Nu. 10. 9, Am. 7. 9, Is. 7. 5, Ps. 2. 2. From the sense *over* (being higher) comes the meaning *beside, by* after *to stand, sit*, &c. Ps. 1. 3 עַל־פַּלְגֵי־מַיִם *by* the rivers of water, 2 S. 9. 10 עַל־שֻׁלְחָנִי *at* my table (also אֶל), Gen. 18. 2 standing *beside him*, 16. 7; 29. 2; 41. 1; Ex. 14. 2, Is. 6. 2.

From the sense *upon* comes the use of עַל to express the condition, circumstances in which an action is performed, on which it rests or which underlie it. Here עַל seems more general than בּ and has such meanings as *amidst, although, notwithstanding, according to*, &c. Jer. 8. 18 עָלַי יָגוֹן *amidst* trouble, Job 10 7 עַל־דַּעְתְּךָ *though* thou knowest, Is. 53. 9 עַל לֹא־חָמָס עָשָׂה *notwithstanding that* he had done no evil, Job 16. 17. 2 K. 24. 3, Ps. 31. 24, Jer. 6. 14, Is. 38. 15; 60. 7.

Ps. 50. 5. So perhaps Ex. 12. 8 עַל־מְרֹרִים *with* bitter herbs
(the idea *in addition to* is less expressive), Nu. 9. 11.[1]

Prep. עִם is *with* of accompaniment. Hence the sense of
beside, near locally, Gen. 25. 11 ; 35. 4, Jud. 9. 6, 1 S. 10. 2.
So its use in comparisons, Job 9. 26 עִם־אֳנִיּוֹת אֵבֶה *like* ships
of reed, Ps. 88. 5 ; and in the sense *as well as*, 1 Chr. 25. 8,
Ecc. 2. 16. In 1 S. 16. 12 ; 17. 42 עִם seems used adverbially, unless יְפֵה be employed nominally, *along with beauty*
of eyes.

Prep. תַּחַת *under, below* ; hence such usage as 1 S. 14. 9
תַּחְתֵּינוּ *where we stand* (under us), on the spot, Jos. 5. 8 ;
6. 5, Jud. 7. 21, 2 S. 2, 23. So the sense *instead* ; and ת' אֲשֶׁר
because.

The particle כְּ *like, as*, is either a prep. or an undeveloped
noun, *instar*. If the latter, it may be in appos. with a
previous word or in acc. of condition. If a prep. it is used
in a pregnant sense ; in either case it governs the gen.
Ps. 95. 8 harden not your hearts כִּמְרִיבָה as *at* M., 83. 10 do
to them כְּסִיסְרָא as *to* S., Gen. 34. 31 הַכְזוֹנָה as *with* a harlot ?
Hos. 2. 5 כְּיוֹם הִוָּלְדָהּ as *on* the day. Is. 1. 25 ; 5. 17 ; 10. 26 ;
23. 15 ; 28. 21 ; 51. 9, Hos. 2. 17 ; 9. 9 ; 12. 10, Am. 9. 11,
Ps. 35. 14, Job 28. 5 ; 29. 2.

The first element of the compound prepp. is chiefly מִן or
אֶל. The form מִפְּנֵי in earlier writings is mostly a prep. *incommodi* ; in later style it is used for *because of, for the sake
of*, even in a favourable sense.

---

[1] From the sense *upon* comes the general use of עַל as a prep. *incommodi*,
opposed to לְ. Particularly in the expression. of feelings and mental states
with such words as *heart, soul, spirit*, the prep. suggests the pressure *upon*
the subject of the feeling or state. Jer. 8. 18 עָלַי לִבִּי דַוָּי my heart *is sick
upon me*, Hos. 11. 8, Lam. 3. 20, Job 10 1 ; 14. 22 ; 30. 16, Ps. 42. 6, 7, 12 ;
43. 5 ; 131. 2 ; 142. 4 ; 143. 4, Jon. 2. 8. In translation *in* must often be
used, and sometimes the prep. is almost untranslatable, *e.g.* Gen. 48. 7
Rachel *died* עָלַי, cf. Nu. 11. 13, Jud. 14. 16. The primary sense may become
weakened in usage, Neh. 5. 7.

SYNTAX OF THE SENTENCE

THE SENTENCE ITSELF

§ 102. A sent. consists of a subj. and pred. The subj. may be expressed separately, as אֲנִי יוֹסֵף *I am Jos.*, or in the case of the verbal sent. contained in the form, as מְכַרְתֶּם *ye sold.* Besides the mere subj. and pred. sentences usually contain additional elements, such as an obj. under the regimen of the pred., or some amplifications descriptive either of subj. or pred.

The subj. may be a pron., or a noun, or anything equivalent to a noun as an adj. or adverb used nominally, or a clause. Gen. 39. 9 אַתְּ אִשְׁתּוֹ *thou* art his wife; 3. 3 אָמַר לֹא טוֹב הֱיוֹת הָאָדָם לְבַדּוֹ 18 .2 ;said has God אֱלֹהִים *that man be alone* is not good. So 2 K. 9. 33 וַיִּז מִדָּמָהּ *some of her blood* spirted. Ex. 16. 27, 2 S. 1. 4; 11. 17, 2 K. 10. 10.

The pred. may be a pron., Jud. 9. 28 מִי שְׁכֶם *who* is Shechem? A noun, Gen. 39. 9 (above), an adj. or ptcp., Gen. 2. 10 נָהָר יֹצֵא a river *went out*, Is. 6. 3 קָדוֹשׁ יהוה *holy* is Je.; a finite verb, Gen. 3. 3 (above); or an adverbial or prepositional phrase, Gen. 2. 12 שָׁם הַבְּדֹלַח *there* is bdolach; Ps. 11. 4 בַּשָּׁמַיִם כִּסְאוֹ *in heaven* is his throne. The noun as pred. is very common, because the adj. is little developed in the earlier stages of the Shemitic languages. See Nom. Appos. § 29 *e.*

The simple sent. is either nominal or verbal. A verbal sent. is one whose pred. is a *finite* verb. All other sentences

are nominal.—This definition, though only partially exact, is sufficient.

1. *The Nominal Sentence*

§ 103. In the nominal sent., which expresses a constant and enduring condition, the subj. is the most prominent element. In general the emphatic word is placed first, hence in this sent. the order is—subj., pred. The subj. in the nominal sent. is very generally definite, but not always. Gen. 2. 12 וּזֲהַב הָאָרֶץ הַהִיא טוֹב *and the gold* of that land is good; 13. 13 וְאַנְשֵׁי סְדֹם רָעִים *and the men* of S. were wicked; 2. 10 וְנָהָר יֹצֵא *and a river* went forth; 29. 17 וְעֵינֵי לֵאָה רַכּוֹת *the eyes* of L. were tender, 12. 6; 13. 7. Esp. after הִנֵּה, and when ptcp. is pred., 16. 6 הִנֵּה שִׁפְחָתֵךְ בְּיָדֵךְ *thy maid* is in thy hand. 20. 15, 16; 27. 42; 28. 12; 41. 3, 5, 6; 48. 1.

§ 104. This order is not invariable. There is considerable freedom in the disposition of the parts of the sent., and emphasis on the pred. may give it the first place. (*a*) A simple adj. when pred. often stands first, particularly if the subj. be also simple, though when the subj. is of some heaviness the adj. may be put at the end, cf. Gen. 2. 12 above. Jer. 12. 1 צַדִּיק אַתָּה יהוה *righteous* art thou, Je. Particularly if the adj. be in the comparative, 1 S. 24. 18 צַדִּיק אַתָּה מִמֶּנִּי thou art *more righteous* than I; Gen. 29. 19 טוֹב תִּתִּי אֹתָהּ לָךְ *it is better* that I give her to thee. Gen. 4. 13, Hos. 13. 12, Ps. 111. 2, 4; 116. 5; 118. 8, 9.

(*b*) In dependent sentences, *e.g.* after כִּי *that, for*, the pred. has a certain emphasis, and stands first. Gen. 3. 5 כִּי יֹדֵעַ אלהים for God *knows*, 3. 6; 22. 12. Esp. if subj. be a pron.; 3. 10 כִּי עֵירֹם אָנֹכִי because I was *naked*; 3. 19; 20. 7; 25. 30; 29. 9; 42. 33, Am. 7. 13. And in general the pronominal subj. is without emphasis, 24. 34; 26. 9; 30. 1, Am. 7. 14; though, of course, it may be otherwise, as when

10

God speaks solemnly of Himself, Gen. 15. 1 ; 26. 24; 28. 13. After nom. *pendens* the resumptive pron. with indef. pred. is unemphatic; 34. 21 ; 40. 12, 18; 41. 25–27 ; 42. 11.

(*c*) Naturally the pred. is emphatic in interrogative sentences of whatever kind. Gen. 24. 65 הַלָּזֶה הָאִישׁ מִי *who* (pred.) is yonder man? 1 S. 17. 43 אָנֹכִי הַכֶלֶב am I *a dog*? Gen. 18. 17. אֲנִי הַמְכַסֶּה *shall* I *hide*? Gen. 4. 9, Jud. 2. 22, 1 S. 16. 4; though emphasis may alter this order, Ex. 16. 7, 8 מָה וְנַחְנוּ what are *we*? In answers the order of question is generally retained; Gen. 29. 4 . . . אַתֶּם מֵאַיִן אֲנַחְנוּ מֵחָרָן *from where* are ye? *from Haran* we, 24. 23, 24, 2 K. 10. 13. But great variety appears in use of the pron.; cf. Gen. 24. 65.

The prep. לְ with noun or pron. when meaning *to be to*, *to have*, often stands first; Gen. 26. 20 הַמַּיִם לָנוּ the water *is ours*; 29. 16 בָנוֹת שְׁתֵּי וּלְלָבָן *and L. had* two daughters. 19. 8; 31. 16; 48. 5, Ex. 2. 16, Jud. 3. 16, 1 S. 1. 2; 17. 12; 25. 2, 2 S. 14. 6. And so adverbial expressions, Gen. 2. 12.

In the nominal sentences above the predication is expressed by the mere juxtaposition of subj. and pred. without any copula. The time also to which the predication belongs is left unexpressed.

2. *The Verbal Sentence*

§ 105. In the verbal sent. the idea expressed by the verb is the emphatic element, and in ordinary calm discourse the order is—pred., subj. Gen. 4. 26 יֻלַּד־בֵּן וּלְשֵׁת a son *was born*. And with the conversive tenses universally, which must stand at the head of the clause, Gen. 3. 2 וַתֹּאמֶר הָאִשָּׁה *and* the woman *said*. This kind of sentence is far the most common in prose narrative.

When, however, any emphasis falls on the subj. it may precede the verbal pred. This emphasis may be of various kinds, though generally due to some kind of antithesis,

latent or expressed. Gen. 3. 13 הַנָּחָשׁ הִשִּׁיאַנִי *the serpent* beguiled me; 37. 33 כְּתֹנֶת בְּנִי חַיָּה רָעָה אֲכָלָתְהוּ *it is my son's coat, an evil beast* hath devoured him; 37. 27 וְיָדֵנוּ אַל־תְּהִי־בוֹ but let not *our hand* be upon him. Often the antithesis is expressed: Is. 1. 3 יָדַע שׁוֹר קֹנֵהוּ יִשְׂרָאֵל לֹא יָדַע the ox knoweth his owner, *Israel* does not know; Gen. 4. 2 Abel was a shepherd וְקַיִן הָיָה עֹבֵד אֲדָמָה *but Cain* was a tiller of the ground; 1 S. 1. 22 ... וַיַּעַל הָאִישׁ וְחַנָּה לֹא עָלָתָה the man went up, *but Hannah* did not go up. Gen. 6. 8; 18. 33; 33. 17; 35. 18; 37. 11, Hos. 2. 23, 24; Is. 1. 2 and *they*; Am. 7. 17. A new subject in distinction from others is thus introduced, *e.g.* Jud. 1. 29 *and Ephraim*; sometimes without *and*, Jud. 1. 30, 31, 33. Or any new point that is to be somewhat signalised, Gen. 2. 6 *and a mist* went up. 1 K. 2. 28 *and the report* came to Joab. But rhythm and style must also be taken into account.

In the circumstantial sent. (§ 137) the subj. is prominent, and precedes the verbal pred. Gen. 24. 31 why stand outside וְאָנֹכִי פִּנִּיתִי הַבַּיִת *when I* have made ready the house? Job 21. 22 הַלְאֵל יְלַמֶּד־דָּעַת וְהוּא רָמִים יִשְׁפּוֹט shall one teach *God* knowledge when *he* judges those on high? Ex. 23. 9; 33. 12, Jud. 4. 21.

Rem. 1. As stated above, there is a departure from the ordinary prose narrative style with *vav impf.* when a *new* subject has to be introduced or any important point signalised which is the beginning of a new development, *e.g.* Gen. 4. 1, the new history after the fall. In these cases the subj. is placed first even in the verbal sent. This is particularly the usage when the event to be signalised was anterior to the events in the current of the narrative. Jud. 1. 16 וּבְנֵי קֵינִי עָלוּ *now the Kenites* had gone up with Judah. Gen. 16. 1; 24. 62; 31. 19, Jud. 4. 11. See exx. § 39 c.

Rem. 2. It is a point of style, however, especially in prophetic parallelism, and even otherwise, to vary the consn.,

and after a conversive tense to use the simple tense and
subj. before it with no emphasis. Is. 6. 7 וְסָר עֲוֹנֶךָ וְחַטָּאתְךָ
תְּכֻפָּר. Is. 11. 13; 14. 25; 28. 18; 31. 3, Ps. 78. 64.

3. *The Compound Sentence. Casus pendens*

§ 106. In such a sent. as *Cain's father is dead* the
language often prefers to say, *Cain, his father is dead*,
קַיִן מֵת אָבִיהוּ instead of מֵת אֲבִי־קַיִן. So for: the way of
God is perfect, הָאֵל תָּמִים דַּרְכּוֹ Ps. 18. 31. While a certain
prominence is thus given to the main subject it is slight, and
the rendering *as for God,* his way, &c., is an exaggeration.
Such sentences are composite; the subj. is placed at the
head in an isolated position as *casus pendens,* and the
predication regarding it follows in a distinct sent., which
may be nominal or verbal. The effect of this consn. is
sometimes to give real emphasis to the chief subj., but often
merely to give emphasis or vividness and lightness to the
sentence as a whole. The consn. is common in sentences
where the subj. is encumbered with complementary elements,
so that it needs to be disentangled and restated. Gen. 3. 12
הָאִשָּׁה . . . הִיא נָתְנָה *the woman* whom thou gavest, &c.,
she gave me; 15. 4 אֲשֶׁר יֵצֵא . . . הוּא יִירָשֶׁךָ *he who* shall
come out of thy loins, *he* shall be thine heir; 24. 7 יְ' אֱלֹהֵי
הַשָּׁמַיִם . . . הוּא יִשְׁלַח *Je. the God of heaven* who took me,
and who, &c., *he* shall send.

The subj. placed as an isolated inchoative is resumed by
a pron. in the same case as the subj. would have had in a
simple sent.

(*a*) Nom.—Gen. 42. 11 כֻּלָּנוּ בְּנֵי אִישׁ אֶחָד נָחְנוּ *we are
all* sons of one man; Is. 1. 13 קְטֹרֶת תּוֹעֵבָה הִיא לִי
incense (sacrificial smoke) is an abomination to me. Jer.
12. 6 גַּם־אַחֶיךָ . . . גַּם־הֵמָּה בָּגְדוּ בָךְ *even thy brethren* have
acted treacherously. Gen. 14. 24; 22. 24; 30. 33; 31. 16;

34. 21 ; 41. 25 ; 44. 17 ; 45. 20, Ex. 12. 16, Jud. 4. 4, 2 S. 5. 1,
Deu. 1. 30, 38, 39.

(*b*) Gen.—Jud. 17. 5 וְהָאִישׁ מִיכָה לוֹ בֵּית אֱ *the man
Micah had* a house of God. 2 K. 1. 4 הַמִּטָּה אֲשֶׁר עָלִיתָ
שָׁם לֹא־תֵרֵד מִמֶּנָּה *from the bed* which thou hast gone up
into *thou shalt not come down*. Is. 4. 3 קָדוֹשׁ ... וְהַנִּשְׁאָר
יֵאָמֶר לוֹ *he that is left shall be called holy*. The prep. is
sometimes placed before the main subj., and repeated with
the pron. Gen. 2. 17 וּמֵעֵץ הַדַּעַת ... לֹא תֹאכַל מִמֶּנּוּ *but*
thou shalt not eat *of the tree of knowledge.* 2 S. 6. 23.—Gen.
17. 4, 15 ; 48. 7, 1 S. 12. 23, 1 K. 1. 20; 12. 17, Is. 3. 12 ; 9. 1 ;
11. 10, Hos. 9. 8, 11, Ps. 10. 5 ; 11. 4 ; 125. 2, Jon. 2. 7.

(*c*) Acc.—Gen. 24. 27 אָנֹכִי בַּדֶּרֶךְ נָחַנִי יְ *Je.* led *me in
the way.* Gen. 28. 13 הָאָרֶץ ... לְךָ אֶתְּנֶנָּה *the land* on
which thou liest will I give thee. Is. 1. 7 אַדְמַתְכֶם זָרִים
אֹכְלִים אֹתָהּ *your land* strangers devour in your sight. The
main subj. may be acc., which is resumed: Gen. 47. 21
וְאֶת־הָעָם הֶעֱבִיר אֹתוֹ *and the people* he removed. Gen.
13. 15 ; 49. 8, Nu. 22. 35, Jud. 11. 24, 1 S. 9. 13 ; 25. 29, 1 K.
15. 13 ; 22. 14, 2 K. 9. 27, Is. 8. 13, Ps. 125. 5, Deu. 13. 1 ; 14. 6.

(*d*) In the verbal sent. the expression of the resumptive
pron. throws emphasis upon the subj., the place of which at
the head gives it prominence. The same is the case in the
nominal sent. when the pred. is definite, as 1 K. 18. 39
יהוה הוּא הָאֱלֹהִים *Jehovah* is God ! Deu. 18. 2 יהוה הוּא
נַחֲלָתוֹ *Jehovah* is his inheritance. In this case the pron.
precedes the pred. Gen. 2. 14 ; 9. 18 ; 42. 6, Deu. 10. 17 ;
12. 23 ; 31. 6, 8, Is. 9. 14 ; 33. 6, 1 S. 17. 14.

When the pred. of the nominal sent. is indefinite the
pron. usually follows the pred., and there is a balance of
emphasis on subj. and pred., the resumptive pron. sinking
almost to the rank of a copula. Gen. 41. 25 חֲלוֹם פַּרְעֹה
אֶחָד הוּא *the dream* of Ph. is *one*; 47. 6 אֶרֶץ מִצְרַיִם לְפָנֶיךָ

הוּא. Gen. 34. 21 ; 45. 20, Ex. 3. 5 ; 32. 16, Nu. 11. 7, Deu. 1. 17 ; 4. 24, Jos. 5. 15, 2 S. 21. 2, 1 K. 20. 31, Mic. 7. 3. Cf. Ps. 76. 8.

The sent. is also compound when *cas. pend.* is resumed by convers. tenses, *e.g.* 1 K. 12. 17.

Rem. 1. When the *cas. pend.* is to be resumed in acc. (*c* above) it may be put in acc. also in Ar.   And in other languages—

> Den König Wiswamitra,
> Den treibt's ohne Rast und Ruh . .

Rem. 2. The fact that the pron. agrees with subj. in gend. and numb., *e.g.* הָדָם הוּא הַנֶּפֶשׁ, seems to show that properly it is a resumption of the subj. and not an anticipation of the pred.   Its occasional agreement with pred. (*e.g.* in Eth. &c.) is a familiar case of attraction, cf. Jer. 10. 3.

The consn. is probably different when the pron. stands after a pron. of 1st or 2nd pers., as 2 S. 7. 28 אַתָּה הוּא הָאלֹהִים. Here the 3rd pers. pron. strengthens the other, *thou* art God.[1] Is. 37. 16, Jer. 14. 22, Ps. 44. 5, Neh. 9. 6, 2 Chr. 20. 6, cf. Is. 51. 9, 10, and with 1st pers. Is. 43. 25 ; 51. 12 ; 52. 6. So 1 Chr. 21. 17 *I* am *he-who* (אֲשֶׁר) has sinned, Ez. 38. 17, cf. Jer. 49. 12.   Others (Ew. Dr.) regard הוּא in these cases as pred., 2 S. 7. 28 *thou* art *he*—God.   The same seems the consn. with זֶה הוּא Ecc. 1. 17, 1 Chr. 22. 1, and אֵלֶּה הֵם Gen. 25. 16, Lev. 23. 2, Nu. 3. 20, 21, 27, 33, &c., though the emphasis here is very slight.

In some cases הוּא appears to be pred., Is. 41 4 אֲנִי הוּא I am *he* (43. 10, 13 ; 46. 4 ; 48. 12, Ps. 102. 28), where *he* (it) expresses the divine consciousness of himself, cf. the

---

[1] This use of the *third* pers. pron. seems secondary.   Naturally it would be used to strengthen only words in the 3rd pers., *e.g.* Is. 7. 14, Nu. 18. 23, Ex. 12. 42, Ezr. 7. 6, 2 Chr. 32. 30.   The same use of 3rd pers. pron. appears in the so-called Ar. " pron. of separation " (a mere empirical phrase).   This 3rd pers. pron. should properly be used only after a subj. in 3rd pers., its use after *I, thou*, &c., is no doubt secondary and analogical, and is less classical.   *E.g.* John 14. 6 ana *hua* elṭarîq (van Dyck), *I am the way*, in the more classical trans. of the Jesuits is ana elṭarîq, ana elbâb, *I am the door*, &c.

beginning of 43. 11 and end of 43. 12.   In sense, *it is I*, or
I am (what I am) is nearly the same.

When the sent. is transposed with pred. first the pron.
anticipates the subj., Lam. 1. 18 צַדִּיק הוּא יהוה; Song 6. 8, 9
אַחַת הִיא יוֹנָתִי *one* is she, my dove ; Pr. 30. 24, 29.   Cf. Pr.
6. 16 ; 30. 15, 18.   Peculiar is 1 S. 20. 29 וְהוּא צִוָּה לִי אָחִי (Sep.
otherwise), cf. Ps. 87. 5.

EXPRESSION OF SUBJECT IN VERBAL SENTENCE

§ 107. In the verbal sent. the subj. is expressed by the
inflectional element of the form, except in 3rd pers., as יָדַעְתִּי
I know, מְכַרְתֶּם *ye* sold (where *tem* and *ti* express the subj.).
In the nominal sent. the subj. has to be expressed.   On its
omission with ptcp. cf. § 100.

1. *Emphasis on Subject*

When emphasis falls on the pronom. subj. in verbal sent.
it is expressed separately, being then placed chiefly before,
but also after, the verb.   The emphasis is often slight, and
due to contrast.   Gen. 42. 8 וְהֵם לֹא הִכִּרֻהוּ *but they* did
not recognise him ; 33. 3 ; 42. 23, Jud. 4. 3 ; 13. 5, Is. 1. 2,
Hos. 2. 10, Am. 2. 9.   After the verb, Jud. 8. 23 לֹא־אֶמְשֹׁל
אֲנִי בָּכֶם *I* will not rule over you.   Gen. 24. 60, Ex. 18. 19,
1 S. 20. 8 ; 23. 22, 2 S. 12. 28 ; 17. 15, 2 K. 10. 4, Is. 20. 6,
Jer. 17. 18.   The pron. is often strengthened by גַּם
whether before the verb or after.   Gen. 20. 6 ; 38. 11 ; 48. 19,
Jud. 1. 3, 22 ; 3. 31, Hos. 4. 6.

Rem. 1. These additional exx. of pron. may be turned up.
Gen. 30. 26 ; 31. 6 ; 42. 19 ; 43. 9 ; 45. 8, Ex. 20. 19, Deu.
3. 28 ; 5. 24, Jud. 8. 21 ; 15. 12.   In many cases, however,
the emphasis is not on the mere pron. ; the expression of
the pron. gives force or solemnity to the whole phrase,
which is emphatic.   Particularly in *responses* to preceding
statements or requests, as Gen. 21. 24 *I will swear*, 38. 17 ;
47. 30, Jud. 6. 18 (11. 9), 2 S. 3. 13 ; 21. 6, 1 K. 2. 18 ;

5. 22, 2 K. 6. 3. But also in other cases, Jud. 5. 3 *I will sing, I will sing to the Lord.* Pr. 24. 32. And in prayers the *thou* is merely part of the solemnity of the sentiment, 1 K. 3. 6. And so in earnest appeals, as in the phrases *thou knowest, ye know,* the emphasis is not on the mere pron. but belongs to the whole expression. Gen. 44. 27, Jos. 14. 6, 1 S. 28. 9, 2 S. 17. 8, 1 K. 2. 5, 15; 5. 17, 20 (2 K. 9. 11), 2 K. 4. 1, cf. 2 K. 19. 11. Many languages whose inflected verb does not need the pron. show a tendency to express 1st and 2nd pron. So Moab. St. l. 21 seq. Pleonastic expression of אֲנִי after verb is a peculiarity of Eccles., *e.g.* 1. 16; 2. 1, 11, 15, &c., cf. Song 5. 5.

2. *The Indefinite Subject*

§ 108. The indefinite, unnamed subj. (Eng. *they, one*) is expressed in various ways. (*a*) By 3 pers. sing. of verb, *e.g.* in the phrase *they called the name,* &c. Gen. 11. 9 עַל־כֵּן קָרָא שְׁמָהּ בָּבֶל *they called* its name Babel. Gen. 16. 14; 21. 31, Ex. 15. 23. The 3 plur. is also used, 1 S. 23. 28, 1 Chr. 11. 7; 14. 11. But in other cases 3 sing. is of frequent use. Is. 7. 24 בַּחִצִּים וּבַקֶּשֶׁת יָבֹא שָׁמָּה with arrows and bow *shall one go* there; Ex. 10. 5 וְלֹא יוּכַל לִרְאֹת הָאָרֶץ so that *one shall not be able* to see the earth. Gen. 38. 28; 48. 1, Deu. 15. 2, 1 S. 16. 4; 23. 22; 26. 20, 2 S. 15. 31; 16. 23, 1 K. 18. 26, 2 K. 5. 4, Is. 6. 10; 8. 4; 14. 32, Am. 6. 12, Mic. 2. 4.

(*b*) By 3 plur. Gen. 29. 2 מִן־הַבְּאֵר הַהִוא יַשְׁקוּ הָעֲדָרִים from that well *they watered* the flocks; 1 S. 27. 5 יִתְּנוּ־לִי מָקוֹם *let them give* me a place. Gen. 41. 14; 49. 31, 1 S. 1. 25, 1 K. 1. 2; 15. 8, Hos. 11. 2, 7; 12. 9, Jer. 8. 4; 16. 6 (sing. and pl.), Job 6. 2, 2 Chr. 25. 16.

(*c*) By ptcp., in plur. Gen. 39. 22 וְאֵת כָּל־אֲשֶׁר עֹשִׂים שָׁם הוּא הָיָה עֹשֶׂה and whatever *they did there.* Is. 32. 12, Jer. 38. 23, Ez. 13. 7, Neh. 6. 10, 2 Chr. 9. 28. More rarely sing., Is. 21. 11 אֵלַי קֹרֵא *one calleth* unto me from Seir.

Rem. 1. The 3-sing. *fem.* seems used Num. 26. 59, 1 K. 1. 6. The real subject in *a*, *b* is the ptcp. sing. or plur., קָרָא קֹרֵא *a caller*, or הַקֹּרֵא *the caller*, called. The ptcp. is often expressed : Is. 28. 4 אֲשֶׁר יִרְאֶה הָרֹאֶה אֹתָהּ which *one* (the seer) *sees*; *v.* 24. Nu. 6. 9, Deu. 22. 8, 2 S. 17. 9, Is. 16. 10, Jer. 9. 23; 31. 5, Ez. 33. 4, Am. 9. 1, Mic. 5. 2, Nah. 2. 3, Ps. 129. 3. In 2 K. 12. 10 אִישׁ is used for *one*, cf. 23. 8. Am. 6. 10 הַעוֹד עִמָּךְ are there *any* still beside thee? the subj. is rather understood.

Rem. 2. The 3 plur. is sometimes used where human agents cannot be supposed, in the sense of *pass.* Job 7. 3 and wearisome nights מִנּוּ לִי *are appointed* me ; 6. 2 ; 19. 26 ; 34. 20, Ez. 32, 25, Pr. 9. 11. The usage is common in Aram., Dan. 2. 30 ; 4. 22. So ptcp. 4. 28, 29. Peculiar ptcp. sing., Jud. 13. 19 וּמַפְלִא לַעֲשׂוֹת and something marvellous was done.

Rem. 3. The use of 2nd person for the indeterminate subj. is rare, except in the phrase בֹּאֲךָ, עַד־בֹּאֲךָ (בֹּאֲכָה) *till thou comest* = *as far as*, 1 K. 18. 46, Gen. 10. 19, 30 ; 13. 10. Apparently, Is. 7. 25 לֹא תָבוֹא שָׁמָּה *thou shalt not come there.* In the injunctions of the Law *thou* is the community personified or each person, and in Prov. *thou* is the pupil of the Wiseman, though cf. Pr. 19. 25 ; 26. 12 ; 30. 28.

3. *Impersonal Construction*

§ 109. The verb is also used impersonally in 3 sing., perf. and impf., chiefly mas. but also fem. Jud. 2. 15 וַיֵּצֶר לָהֶם מְאֹד *they were greatly distressed*; Gen. 32. 8. 1 S. 30. 6 מְאֹד, וַתֵּצֶר לְדָוִד מְאֹד, Jud. 10. 9. So mas. in וַיְהִי *and it was*, וְהָיָה *and it shall be.* So many words followed by prep. לְ; as רַע לְ to be amiss to, Nu. 22. 34, Gen. 21. 12, 2 S. 19. 8 ; Jer. 7. 6. טוֹב לְ 1 S. 16. 16, Hos. 10. 1, Jer. 7. 23. מַר לְ *bitter*, Ru. 1. 13, Lam. 1. 4. חַם לְ to have heat, 1 K. 1. 1, 2, Hag. 1. 6. Job 3. 13 אָז יָנוּחַ לִי *I should have had rest*, Is. 23. 12, Neh. 9. 28. Cf. Gen. 4. 5, 1 S. 16. 23.

The fem. seems used in reference to the phenomena of

nature.   Job 11. 17 תֶּעְפָּה (cohort.) *should it be dark.*   Am.
4. 7 תַּמְטִיר *it rained* (freq.).   Mic. 3. 6 *it shall be dark*, Ps.
50. 3; 68. 15.   (But cf. 1 S. 29. 10 *when it is light* (mas.),
2 S. 2. 32, see Gen. 44. 3, Jer. 13. 16.)   And of an unseen
power, Job 18. 14 *it* brings him (he is brought) to the king
of terrors.   The *pass.* is also used impersonally in the *mas.*
Gen. 4. 26 אָז הוּחַל לִקְרֹא   then *it was begun* to invoke;
Ez. 16. 34 וְאַחֲרַיִךְ לֹא זוּנָּה *there was no whoring* after thee.
The pass. in this case often governs like the act. (§ 79),
Am. 4. 2 וְנִשָּׂא אֶתְכֶם *ye shall be taken away.*   Nu. 16. 29,
Deu. 21. 3, 4, 2 S. 17. 16, Is. 14. 3; 16. 10; 27. 13; 53. 5, Jer.
16. 6, Am. 9. 9, Mal. 1. 11 (ptcp.), Ps. 87. 3.

Rem. 1.   The forms טוֹב, רַע, מַר, &c., might be adjectives,
but the use of impf. and inf. makes it more probable that
they are perfs.   Peculiar is Prov. 13. 10, by pride יִתֵּן מַצָּה *there
comes* strife (es giebt).   Rarely with suff., Job 6. 17 בְּחֻמּוֹ
when it is hot.

Rem. 2.   It is scarcely impersonal use of fem. when it is
employed of a subject suggested by some statement preceding, where we say *it.*   Is. 7. 7 לֹא תָקוּם *it* shall not stand
(the purpose); 14. 24, Jud. 11. 39, 1 S. 10. 12.   The fem.
is often, however, used for *neut.*—Comp. these cases of
fem.: Gen. 24. 14 (*thereby*), 1 S. 11. 2 וּשְׂמְתִיהָ (*it,* putting
out their eye), Gen. 15. 6 counted *it* (the *fact* that he believed)
Ex. 30. 21, Jos. 11. 20 הָיְתָה, 2 S. 2. 26; 3. 37, 1 K. 2. 15, 2 K.
19. 25; 24. 3, 20, Is. 22. 11; 30. 8, Mic. 1. 9, Jer. 4. 28;
5. 31; 7. 31; 10. 7; 19. 5, Ez. 33. 33, Job 4. 5; 18. 15.

Rem. 3.   In poetry a peculiar consn. occurs in which the
verb seems to have a double subj., one personal and the
other the organ or member, &c., by which the action is
actually performed.   This neuter subj. has always a suff.
of the same person as the personal subj., and may precede
or follow the verb.   Ps. 3. 5 קוֹלִי אֶל־י' אֶקְרָא *my voice, I cried,*
i.e. I cried aloud; Is. 10. 30 צַהֲלִי קוֹלֵךְ *shout aloud!*   Is. 26. 9,
Hab. 3. 15, Ps. 17. 10, 13, 14; 32. 8; 44. 3; 60. 7; 66. 17;
69. 11; 108. 2, 7; 142. 2.   In a nominal sent. Ps. 83. 19.

—Others consider קוֹלִי, &c., to be acc., but the presence of the suff. distinguishes the present case from that in § 67, R. 3.

COMPLEMENT OF THE VERBAL SENTENCE

§ 110. The sent. does not usually consist of mere subj. and pred.; the verbal sent. has usually an obj., and all sentences may have additional elements which are the complements of the two chief parts of the sentence. These complements usually follow the parts, subj. or pred., which they amplify. The order of the verbal sentence is: verb, subj., obj., or complement of the verb. But emphasis may alter this order. Gen. 3. 14 עַל־גְּחֹנְךָ תֵלֵךְ וְעָפָר תֹּאכַל *on thy belly* shalt thou go, *and dust* shalt thou eat. 1 S. 20. 8 וְעַד־אָבִיךָ לָמָּה־זֶּה תְבִיאֵנִי but why bring me *to thy father*? 1 K. 2. 26 עֲנָתֹת לֵךְ *to Anathoth* with you! Gen. 15. 10; 20. 4; 38. 9, Deu. 5. 3, Jos. 2. 16, Is. 6. 5, Hos. 5. 6, Job 1. 12; 34. 31.

The adverb usually follows the verb, except negatives; and so longer designations of time. But short words of time, like אָז *then*, עַתָּה *now*, בְּרֵאשִׁית *at first*, &c., precede.

§ 111. Out of this principle of emphasis may arise a variety of order, *e.g.*—

(*a*) Obj., verb, subj. 1 S. 2. 19 וּמְעִיל קָטֹן תַּעֲשֶׂה־לּוֹ אִמּוֹ *and a little robe* his mother used to make him. Gen. 42. 4, 1 S. 17. 36, 1 K. 14. 11. And very often when subj. is contained in the verb. Jud. 14. 3, 2 K. 22. 8, Is. 4. 1, Hos. 1. 7; 10. 6.

(*b*) Verb, obj., subj. 1 S. 15. 33 כַּאֲשֶׁר שִׁכְּלָה נָשִׁים חַרְבֶּךָ as thy sword *has bereaved women.* Gen. 21. 7, Nu. 19. 7, 18, 1 K. 8. 63; 19. 10, Is. 19. 13.

(*c*) Subj., obj., verb. Is. 1. 15 יְדֵיכֶם דָּמִים מָלֵאוּ. This collocation brings the subj. and obj. into very close relation. Jud. 17. 6 *every man what was right in his own sight* used to

do.   Jer. 32. 4 *and his eyes his eyes* shall see, cf. 34. 3.   Is. 11. 8 ; 32. 8.

Rem. 1.   Other forms are occasional, as obj., subj., verb. 2 K. 5. 13, Is. 5. 17 ; 28. 17.   This order is usual in nominal sent. with participial pred.   Gen. 41. 9 אֶת־חֲטָאַי אֲנִי מַזְכִּיר *my faults* I call to remembrance.   Gen. 37. 16, Jud. 9. 36 ; 14. 4, 2 K. 6. 22, Jer. 1. 11.

Rem. 2.   Aramaic shows a liking for placing the verb at the end of the clause, the obj. and complement of the verb preceding it, as in *c.*   Dan. 2. 16, 18 ; 3. 16 ; 4. 15.   Cf. inf. Is. 49. 6.   Jud. 6. 25.   2 Chr. 31. 7, 10.

Rem. 3.   It is a point of style, however, particularly in prophetic and poetic parallelism, to vary the order of words.   So even in ordinary prose.   Ex. 3. 7 רָאִיתִי אֶת־עֳנִי עַמִּי . . . וְאֶת־צַעֲקָתָם שָׁמַעְתִּי, Is. 5. 24 ; 11. 8 ; 31. 1.   Cf. 1 K. 20. 18 the double *take them alive.*

AGREEMENT OF SUBJECT AND PREDICATE IN RESPECT OF GENDER AND NUMBER

§ 112.   There is less precision in the matter of agreement than there is in classical or other languages.   Several general peculiarities appear—

1.   When the pred. stands first the speaker's mind is fixed on the act in itself, and clear consciousness of the coming subj. is not yet present to him, and he puts the pred. in the most general form, mas. sing.[1]

2.   There is a great tendency to construe according to *the sense* rather than strict grammatical law, hence gramm. singulars, such as collectives and words that suggest a plurality, are often joined with plur. pred., especially when they refer to persons.

3.   On the other hand, there is a tendency to group things that resemble one another, or belong to the same class, under one conception, and construe them with a sing. verb.

---

[1] Ar. grammarians have a more ingenious explanation of this usage.

The plur. of lifeless objects and living creatures, not persons, may be treated as gramm. collect., and joined with sing. fem.

1. *Agreement of Simple Subject*

§ 113. (*a*) When subj. precedes the pred. there is in general agreement in gend. and numb., whether the subj. be person or thing. Gen. 15. 12 נָפְלָה וְתַרְדֵּמָה and *a sleep fell*; *v.* 17 הַשֶּׁמֶשׁ בָּאָה the *sun was gone down*; 16. 1. But exceptions occur; Mal. 2. 6 עַוְלָה לֹא־נִמְצָא *evil was not found.* Gen. 15. 17, Ex. 12. 49, Jer. 50. 46, Zech. 6. 14, cf. *v.* 7, Job 20. 26.

(*b*) When pred. precedes, while agreement in gend. and numb. is usual, esp. when subj. is personal, the verb is often in 3 sing. mas., even though the subj. be plur. or fem. This is common with הָיָה *to be*. The subj. having once been mentioned, however, following verbs are in proper agreement. Gen. 1. 14 יְהִי מְאֹרֹת וְהָיוּ *let there be* lights, and *let them be* signs. Is. 17. 6 וְנִשְׁאַר־בּוֹ עֹלֵלֹת there *shall be left gleanings*; 2 K. 3. 26 חָזַק מִמֶּנּוּ הַמִּלְחָמָה *the battle was too strong* for him, cf. *v.* 18. Deu. 32. 35, Is. 13. 22; 24. 12, Jer. 36. 32. Nu. 9. 6 וַיְהִי אֲנָשִׁים אֲשֶׁר הָיוּ, 1 K. 11. 3 וַיְהִי־לוֹ נָשִׁים שָׂרוֹת *he had wives, princesses*, 700. The *mas.* is apt to be used for 3 pl. fem. impf.; 1 K. 11. 3 וַיַּטּוּ נָשָׁיו אֶת־לִבּוֹ his *wives perverted* his mind; 2 S. 4. 1 יָדָיו his hands *were paralysed* (cf. Zeph. 3. 16), Jud. 21. 21, Jos. 11. 11, Is. 19. 18, Jer. 13. 16, Ez. 23. 42, Hos. 14. 7. Gen. 20. 17; 30. 39. Song 6. 9. Imper., Is. 32. 11, Hos. 10. 8, Zeph. 3. 16.—1 S. 1. 2, Jud. 20. 46, Gen. 35. 5, 1 Chr. 2. 22; 23. 17, 22.

(*c*) Subjects in dual are necessarily joined with plur pred., verb or ptcp. Gen. 48. 10 עֵינֵי יש׳ כָּבְדוּ מִזֹּקֶן the eyes of Israel *were dim* from age. 2 K. 21. 12; 22. 20. Is. 1. 15, Mic. 7. 10. Ptcp., 1 S. 1. 13, 2 S. 24. 3, Is. 30. 20, Hos.

9. 14, 2 Chr. 16. 9.   Cf. § 31, and on 1 S. 4. 15, Mic. 4. 11.
§ 116.

2. *Agreement of Compound Subject*

§ 114. When the subj. is compound, consisting of several
elements joined by *and*.—(*a*) When subj. is first the verb is
usually plur., and so the pred. in nominal sent.   2 S. 16. 15
וְאַבְשָׁלוֹם וכל־הָעָם בָּאוּ Abs. and all the people *came*; Gen.
8. 22; 18. 11.   But sometimes the verb is sing., agreeing
either with the word next it or with the chief element of the
complex subj., or the several parts of subj. all forming one
conception: 2 S. 20. 10 Joab and Abishai his brother רָדַף
pursued.   Hos. 4. 11 whoredom and wine and new wine
יִקַּח־לֵב *take away* the understanding.   Hos. 9. 2, Deu. 8. 13.
Neh. 5. 14 אֲנִי וְאַחַי לֹא אָכַלְתִּי.   2 S. 3. 22, Est. 4. 16.[1]
If parts of the subj. be of different genders pred. is usually
mas., Gen. 18. 11, but cf. Jer. 44. 25.

(*b*) When the pred. is first it perhaps oftenest agrees in
gend. and numb. with the element of the subj. which is next
it; but it may be in plur.   When the subj. has once been
mentioned following verbs are in plur.   Gen. 31. 14 וַתַּעַן
רָחֵל וְלֵאָה וַתֹּאמַרְנָה R. and L. *answered and said*; Nu.
12. 1 וַתְּדַבֵּר מִרְיָם וְאַהֲרֹן . . . וַיֹּאמְרוּ Mir. and Aaron *spoke
and said*; Gen. 3. 8 וַיִּתְחַבֵּא הָאָדָם וְאִשְׁתּוֹ *hid themselves*.
Gen. 7. 7; 9. 23; 21. 32; 24. 50, 55; 33. 7; 44. 14, Jud. 5. 1;
8. 21, 1 S. 11. 15; 18. 3; 27. 8, 1 K. 1. 34, 41.—Pl. Gen. 40. 1,
Nu. 20. 10; 31. 13, Ex. 5. 1; 7. 20.   Or it may be mas. sing.
(§ 113 *b*), Joel 1. 13.

(*c*) When the subj. is a pron. and noun, the pron. must
be expressed whether verb be sing. or plur.   Gen. 7. 1
בֹּא־אַתָּה וכל־בֵּיתְךָ go *thou* and all thy house, Jud. 7. 10, 11.
Jud. 11. 38 וַתֵּלֶךְ הִיא וְרֵעוֹתֶיהָ *she* and her companions

---

[1] The *and* before "maids," Est. 4. 16, and before "brethren," Neh.
5. 14, recalls Ar. *waw* of concomitance.

went.   1 K. 1. 21 וְהָיִיתִי אֲנִי וּבְנִי *I* and my son shall be.
Gen. 14. 15; 20. 7; 24. 54 (pl.); 31. 21; 1 S. 20. 31; 28. 8,
2 S. 19. 15.   In 1 S. 29. 10 אַתָּה is missed before *servants*.

Even when two nouns are subj. a pron. referring to the
first must be expressed if any words separate it from the
second, unless the words be a mere apposition.   Gen. 13. 1;
35. 6; 38. 12; 50. 14, 22, Jud. 9. 48, Neh. 2. 12, cf. Jos. 22. 32.
The pron. *may* be expressed in any case, 1 S. 29. 11; 30. 9.

When compound subj. is of different persons 1st pers.
precedes 2nd and 2nd the 3rd.   1 K. 1. 21 above, *I and my
son.*   1 S. 14. 40; 20. 23, Nu. 20. 8, Gen. 43. 8.

3. *Agreement of Collectives*

§ 115.   With sing. nouns having a collective meaning the
pred. is often construed in the plur. according to sense:
particularly when the collective term refers to persons, but
sometimes also when it refers to lower creatures, or even to
things.   Grammatical agreement in sing. is also common,
and the two consns. often interchange.   When the pred. is
first it may be in sing. while following verbs are in plur.
Hos. 4. 6 נִדְמוּ עַמִּי my people *are destroyed*, cf. Is. 5. 13
גָּלָה עַמִּי *is gone away*; Is. 9. 8 וְיָדְעוּ הָעָם כֻּלּוֹ the people
shall know all of *it*.   1 K. 18. 39 וַיַּרְא כָּל־הָעָם וַיִּפְּלוּ.   Ex.
1. 20; 4. 31, Jud. 2. 10.   Gen. 41. 57 וְכָל־הָאָרֶץ בָּאוּ all the
world *came*; 1 S. 14. 25; 17. 46, 2 S. 15. 23.   Nu. 14. 35
הָעֵדָה הַזֹּאת הַנּוֹעָדִים this congregation *that are met
together.*   With creatures: Gen. 30. 38 תָּבֹאנָה הַצֹּאן the
flock *used to come*, Ps. 144. 13.   So fem. pl. with בָּקָר Job
1. 14; mas. pl. 1 Chr. 27. 29, cf. 1 K. 8. 5.   With things:
Jer. 48. 36 יִתְרַת עָשָׂה אָבָדוּ the gain he has made *is lost*.
Is. 15. 7, Hos. 9. 6, Hag. 2. 7, Ps. 119. 103.   Comp. 1 S. 2. 33
increase in a personal ref.—Ex. 15. 4, Jud. 9. 36, 37 *people*
sing. and pl., so 1 S. 13. 6, cf. *vv.* 15, 16.   Jud. 1. 22; 9. 55,

2 K. 25. 5, Am. 1. 5, Hos. 10. 5 ; 11. 7, Is. 16. 4 ; 19. 13.   Gen. 34. 24.   Nu. 20. 11 ; 21. 7, Job 8. 19.

§ 116. On the other hand, plur. of inanimate objects that may be grouped under one conception, of the lower creatures, and abstract plurals are frequently construed with fem. sing. of pred.   1 S. 4. 15 קָמָה וְעֵינָיו *and his eyes were set*, Mic. 4. 11.   Jo. 1. 20 אֵלֶיךָ תַּעֲרֹג שָׂדֶה בַּהֲמוֹת *the beasts* of the field *pant* unto thee.   Ps. 103. 5 כַּנֶּשֶׁר תִּתְחַדֵּשׁ נְעוּרָיְכִי *thy youth is renewed* like the eagle.   Gen. 49. 22, Is. 34. 13 ; 59. 12, Jer. 4. 14 ; 12. 4, Mic. 1. 9, Ps. 18. 35 ; 37. 31, Neh. 13. 10, Job 12. 7 ; 14. 19 ; 20. 11.   Cf. 2 S. 24. 13.   2 K. 3. 3 מְמֵנָּה (*sins* of Jeroboam) ; 13. 11, Is. 59. 8.   There is no reason for Ḳ'ri Ps. 73. 2, שְׁפכה.   Deu. 21. 7 is more unusual.—Sometimes when subj. precedes it is treated almost as *casus pendens*, and its general idea becomes subj.; Gen. 47. 24 *the four fifths* יְהִיָה *it shall be*.   Ex. 12. 49, Ecc. 2. 7.   Cf. Is. 16. 8, Hab. 3. 17.

Rem. 1. General plurals are sometimes construed with sing. pred. from a tendency to individualise and distribute over every individual, or apply it to any individual supposed. Gen. 27. 29 אָרוּר אֹרְרֶיךָ *they that curse thee shall be cursed.* Nu. 24. 9, Jer. 22. 4.   Ex. 31. 14, Lev. 17. 14 ; 19. 8, Zech. 11. 5, Ps. 64. 9, Pr. 3. 18, 35 ; 14. 9 ; 27. 16 ; 28. 1, 2 Chr. 10. 8 (*rd.* יְעָצֻהוּ).   In particular a sing. suff. frequently refers back to a plur.   Is. 2. 20 עָשׂוּ־לוֹ אֲשֶׁר which *they made* each *for himself*, Hos. 4. 8.   Deu. 21. 10 ; 28. 48, Is. 1. 23 ; 2. 8 ; 5. 23 ; 8. 20, Jos. 2. 4, Ex. 28. 3, Zech. 14. 12, Or sing. and plur. interchange, Is. 30. 22 ; 56. 5, Ps. 62. 5 ; 141. 10. Cf. Deu. 4. 37 ; 7. 3, Jud. 1. 34, 2 K. 19. 14.   Sometimes sing. pron. refers back to plur. as a collective unity, Is. 17. 13, Jer. 31. 15 אֵינֶנּוּ (of Rachel's children), 2 S. 24. 13, Jos. 13. 14, and perhaps some of the exx. above.   Or the pron. expresses a generalised *it*, Jud. 11. 34 בֵּן מִמֶּנּוּ אֵין־לוֹ אוֹ־בַת he had not *besides it* (her) son or daughter.   Ex. 11. 6 *like it*.

Rem. 2. When the compound subj. is a noun with its

gen. agreement may be with gen. as expressing the main idea of the phrase ; or pred. being next gen. may agree with it by a kind of attraction. 1 K. 17. 16 וְצַפַּחַת שֶׁמֶן לֹא חָסֵר the cruse of *oil did not fail*. Is. 2. 11, 1 S. 2. 4, Lev. 13. 9; Job 21. 21 ; 29. 10 ; 38. 21. Attraction of gend. Jer. 10. 3, Lev. 25. 33 ; in the case of verb *to be* attraction by pred. Gen. 31. 8, Pr. 14. 35. The pred. usually agrees with gen. after כֹל *all*, Hos. 9. 4, Gen. 5. 5, Ex. 15. 20, but not universally, Hos. 10. 14, Is. 64. 10.

Rem. 3. In nominal sent. the pred. adj. when first is sometimes uninflected, Ps. 119. 137 יָשָׁר מִשְׁפָּטֶיךָ *upright* are thy judgments, cf. *v.* 155 ; but this is rare, except with the word טוֹב ; Jud. 8. 2, Gen. 49. 15, 1 S. 19. 4, 2 K. 5. 12, Ps. 73. 28; 119. 72; 147. 1, Pr. 17. 1; 20. 23.—Gen. 47. 3 רֹעֵה is collec., cf. Deu. 14. 7, Ezr. 3. 9, Neh. 2. 16.

Rem. 4. Plurals of Eminence such as אלהים *God*, אדנים בְּעָלִים *lord*, *owner*, when referring to a single person, are usually in concord with sing., Ex. 21. 29 בְּעָלָיו יוּמַת *its owner shall be killed*, Is. 19. 4 אֲדֹנִים קָשֶׁה *a cruel lord*. When אלהים means *gods* it is construed with pl., and in a few cases even when it is God, Gen. 20. 13 ; 35. 7, Ex. 22. 8, Jos. 24. 19 (E.), and sometimes in the phrase *living God*, Deu. 5. 23, 1 S. 17. 26, Jer. 10. 10; 23. 36. Words only used in pl. are occasionally joined to sing., *e.g.* 2 S. 10. 9 פָּנִים as fem. sing., cf. Job 16. 16.

Rem. 5. Names of nations are construed in three ways : (*a*) with mas. sing., the name being that of the personal ancestor, Ex. 17. 11, Is. 19. 16, Am. 1. 11, 1 Chr. 18. 5; 19. 15, 16, 18, 19. (*b*) Or with plur., 2 S. 10. 17, 1 K. 20. 20, 2 K. 6. 9, 1 Chr. 18. 2, 13. (*c*) Or with fem. sing., when the ref. is to the country or when the population is treated as a collective, often personified ; 2 S. 8. 2, 5, 6 ; 10. 11 ; 24. 9, Is. 7. 2, Jer. 13. 19, 1 Chr. 19. 12, Job 1. 15. The consns. *a*, *b*, *c* may interchange in the same passage. Jer. 48. 15, Am. 2. 2, 3, Hos. 14. 1, Mal. 2. 11. Peculiar, Is. 18. 1, 2.

Rem. 6. When there are several predicates one may be in agreement and the other left uninflected. Is. 33. 9, Mic. 1. 9, Eccli. 3. 11 ; cf. on adj § 32. R. 4. But irregularity

in gend. and numb. is common, *e.g.* Jer. 31. 9 בָּהּ ... דֶּרֶךְ יָשָׁר,
Zech. 6. 7. Sometimes text may be at fault, Jud. 4. 20
עָמֹד, inf. abs. ? 1 S. 2. 20 *rd.* שָׁאַל; 25. 27 הֵבִיאָה, cf. *v.* 35.
In particular, vowel terminations of verbs were not always
expressed in ancient texts, and are sometimes given or
omitted wrongly by Mass. Ez. 18. 29 יִתָּכֵנוּ as *v.* 25. With
20. 38 יבוא cf. Is. 45. 24. In Lam. 5. 10 נִכְמָרוּ may be due
to plur. suff. in *our skin*, cf. 1 Chr. 24. 19, 2 Chr. 17. 14,
Jer. 2. 34.

　　Exx. of mas. for 2 fem. impf., Is. 57. 8, Jer. 3. 5, Ez.
22. 4; 23. 32; 26. 14.

PARTICULAR KINDS OF SENTENCE

INTERJECTIONAL SENTENCE

　§ 117. Words in direct address (the voc.) are of the form
of interj. as הַמֶּלֶךְ *O king!* אֲדֹנִי הַמֶּלֶךְ my lord the king!
and such phrases of entreaty as בִּי אֲדֹנִי. But any words
may be uttered as exclamations, 2 K. 4. 19 רֹאשִׁי רֹאשִׁי *my
head!* 11. 14 קֶשֶׁר קָשֶׁר *treason! treason!* Jer. 4. 19 *my
bowels!* 37. 14 שֶׁקֶר it's *a lie!* 2 K. 9. 12. Is. 29. 16 הַפְכְּכֶם
your perversity! Jer. 49. 16. Hab. 2. 19 הוּא יוֹרֶה *it* reveal!
Hos. 8. 1 to thy mouth the trumpet! 2 S. 13. 12 אַל־אָחִי
don't! my brother! Gen. 49. 4. So adverbs: לֹא *no!* הֵן
well, yes! טוֹב *good! well!* Also the imper. of some verbs,
as הָבָה (יהב) *go to!* Gen. 38. 16, Ex. 1. 10; לְכָה, לֵךְ (even
to a woman, Gen. 19. 32) *come!*

　More strict interjections are הַס *hush! silence!* Jud. 3. 19,
Am. 6. 10, Zeph. 1. 7, Hab. 2. 20, Zech. 2. 17. A verb הסה
is denom. from הַס Neh. 8. 11, Nu. 13. 30.—אֵיךְ *how!* in
the Elegy, 2 S. 1. 25, 27, Hos. 11. 8 (elegiac measure), more
commonly אֵיכָה Is. 1. 21, Lam. 1. 1.—אוֹי *woe!* with prep. לְ,
Is. 6. 5 אוֹי־לִי, 3. 9, 11, Jer. 4. 31; without prep. Ez. 24. 6.

In Ps. 120. 5 אוֹיָה לִי, so אַלְלַי לִי Mic. 7. 1, Job 10. 15.—
הוֹי‎ *woe! alas!* in lament for the dead, 1 K. 13. 30 הוֹי אָחִי;
fuller form for the king, Jer. 22. 18. In the form הוֹ Am.
5. 16. In a more general sense, Jer. 48. 1; 50. 27. Also in
threatening remonstrance, Is. 1. 4 הוֹי גּוֹי חֹטֵא *Ha!* sinful
nation, and often in Is.—Other forms, Jo. 1. 15 אֲהָהּ לַיּוֹם
alas! for the day. Ez. 30. 2 הָהּ לַיּוֹם, 6. 11 אָח.—An
exclamation of *delight*, הֶאָח Is. 44. 16; by the horse in
battle, Job 39. 25; of malicious delight, Ps. 35. 21; 40. 16;
70. 4, Ez. 25. 3; 26. 2.

The pron. מָה *how! what!* is used in the expression of
a variety of feelings, as wonder, awe, Gen. 28. 17; scorn,
sarcasm, 2 S. 6. 20; dislike, Mal. 1. 13 הִנֵּה מַתְּלָאָה *Oh
what a bore!* And so מִי *who!* Mic. 7. 18, &c.

The particle הִנֵּה also, as הִנֵּנִי *here I am!* Gen. 18. 9
הִנֵּה בָאֹהֶל *there! in the tent* (is she). 16. 11 הִנָּךְ הָרָה
see thou art with child! Very passionately Job 9. 19, is it
a question of strength? הִנֵּה! perhaps, *of course!* (*he* is
irresistible).

Rem. 1. The adj. חָלִילָה *profane* (absit)! is construed with
לְ of person and מִן of the act repudiated. The full phrase
is found 1 S. 26. 11 חָלִילָה לִּי מֵיהוה מִשְּׁלֹחַ, 24. 7, 1 K. 21. 3
(so *rd.* 2 S. 23. 17), but oftener without מִי', Gen. 44. 7, 17.
The phrase acquires the force of an oath, and may be followed by אִם (§ 120). 1 S. 24. 7, 2 S. 20. 20, Job 27. 5. Cf.
Jos. 22. 29; 24. 16.

Rem. 2. In Gen. 16. 11, &c., the consn. is הִנָּךְ אַתְּ הרה.
So in Ar. with def. pred., Kor. 2. 11, 12, 122.

Rem. 3. In exclamatory sentences there is omission of
subj. as Gen. 18. 9, or of pred. as Hos. 8. 1, to the mouth the
trumpet (set ye!), 1 K. 22. 36 *every man to his city* (get ye!),
Hos. 5. 8 אַחֲרֶיךָ בִנְיָמִין perhaps, *thy rear!* Benj. (sc. guard!),
or *behind thee* B. (is the danger). The word קוֹל *voice,
sound of*, is nearly *hark!* Is. 13. 4; 66. 6.

AFFIRMATIVE SENTENCE

§ 118. Affirmative force is given in various ways, *e.g.*—
(1) By *casus pendens*, Gen. 3. 12 the woman . . . *she gave me*,
42. 11 (§ 106). (2) By expression of pron. either alone or
with *vav*, גַּם, &c. Gen. 4. 4; 20. 5, Is. 14. 10. (3) By inf.
abs. (§ 86). (4) By repetition of words, Is. 38. 19, *the living*,
the *living*. Ecc. 7. 24 *deep*, *deep*, who shall find it? Is. 6. 3,
Jer. 7. 4.

Affirmative particles are אֲבָל *truly*, Gen. 42. 21
אֲשֵׁמִים אֲנַחְנוּ *verily* we are guilty; 2 S. 14. 5, 1 K. 1. 43;
later a particle of contrast, Dan. 10. 7, 21.— אַךְ *truly*,
surely, Gen. 26. 9 אַךְ אִשְׁתְּךָ הִוא *in truth* she is thy wife.
1 S. 16. 6, Hos. 12. 9. So אָכֵן, Ex. 2. 14 אָכֵן נוֹדַע הַדָּבָר
verily the thing is known. Gen. 28. 16, 1 S. 15. 32, Is. 53. 4.

Rem. 1. Also various derivatives of אמן, *e.g.* אָמְנָם *verily*,
in truth, 2 K. 19. 17; ironically Job 9. 2; 12. 2 *verily* ye are
the people. Also אֻמְנָם *id.* (always with interrog.), Nu.
22. 37, Gen. 18. 13, 1 K. 8. 27. So אָמְנָה, Gen. 20. 12,
Jos. 7. 20.

The word כִּי often strengthens. Gen. 18. 20 the cry of
Sodom כִּי רָבָּה (surely) *it is great*. Particularly in antithesis
after neg.: Gen. 18. 15 לֹא כִּי צָחַקְתְּ *nay*, thou *didst* laugh.
1 K. 3. 22 לֹא כִּי בְנִי הַחַי no! *my child is the live one*. And
so usually, Jos. 5. 14; 24. 21, Jud. 15. 13, 1 S. 2. 16 (לֹא = לוֹ),
2 S. 16. 18 (לוֹ=לֹא last cl.), 1 K. 2. 30, 2 K. 3. 13 אַל;
20. 10, Is. 30. 16, Ps. 49. 11.

§ 119. The oath.—אֵל, יהוה, אלהים, חַי אָנִי *as I live*,
as God, Je. liveth; but חֵי נַפְשְׁךָ, פַרְעֹה *as thy soul, Phar.*,
&c., *liveth*. With pron. *I* and divine names the form is חַי,
otherwise חֵי, cf. the curious חֵי אֱלֹהֶיךָ דָן Am. 8. 14 *as thy
god*, O Dan, *liveth*.—Jud. 8. 19 חַי יהוה. 2 S. 2. 27
חַי הָאֱלֹהִים, Jer. 44. 26 חַי אֲדֹנָי י׳, Job 27. 2 חַי אֵל, 1 K.

18. 10, 15.—Nu. 14. 21, 28 אָנִי חַי; usually this shorter form
(Deu. 32. 40 אָנֹכִי) and invariably so pointed.—1 S. 20. 3
חַי י' וְחֵי נַפְשֶׁךָ, 25. 26; Gen. 42. 15, 2 S. 15. 21.

§ 120. The oath of *denial* is made by אִם *if = that not ;*
of affirmation by אִם לֹא *if not = that,* or כִּי *that.* 1 S. 19. 6
וַיִּשָּׁבַע־לִי חַי י' אִם יוּמַת *he shall not be put to death,* 1 K. 1. 51
בַיּוֹם אִם יָמִית let him swear to me first *that he will not kill*
me. Gen. 42. 15, 1 S. 24. 22 ; 30. 15.—1 K. 18. 15 חַי י' כִּי
הַיּוֹם אֶרָאֶה אֵלָיו *I will show myself* to him to-day; Is.
45. 23 בִּי נִשְׁבַּעְתִּי כִּי לִי תִכְרַע כָּל־בֶּרֶךְ *I have sworn by*
myself that to me every knee shall bow. 1 S. 14. 44; 20. 3;
29. 6. Job 1. 11 אִם לֹא יְבָרֲכֶךָ (I swear) *he will disavow*
thee. Jos. 14. 9, 2 K. 9. 26.

Rem. 1. The word אַךְ has also restrictive force, *only,*
Gen. 18. 32 *only* this once, 1 S. 18. 8 *only* the kingdom. So
in sense of *utterly* with adj. Deu. 16. 15, Is. 16. 7. Similarly
רַק, § 153.

Rem. 2. חַי אַתָּה is not said ; חַיֶּךָ *by thy life,* 2 S. 11. 11,
if text right. Cf. Dr. or Well. *in loc.*

Rem. 3. Exx. of אִם Gen. 21. 23, Nu. 14. 23, 1 S. 3. 14,
17; 14. 45; 17. 55; 28. 10, 2 S. 11. 11 ; 14. 11, 2 K. 2. 2;
3. 14; 6. 31, Is. 22. 14, Ps. 89, 36; 132. 3, 4. Of כִּי 1 S.
14. 39; 26. 16; 29. 6, 2 S. 3. 9, 1 K. 18. 15, 2 K. 5. 20,
Jer. 22. 5. Of אִם לֹא Nu. 14. 28, 2 S. 19. 14, 1 K. 20. 23,
Is. 5. 9; 14. 24, Jer. 15. 11.—In many cases there is no
formal oath, and the particles merely express strong denial
or affirmation. Ps. 131. 2.

Rem. 4. The full formula כֹּה יַעֲשֶׂה־לִּי אֱלֹהִים *God do so to*
me, &c., occurs only in 1, 2 S., 1, 2 K., and Ru., *e.g.* 1 S.
3. 17; 14. 44, 1 K. 2. 23, 2 K. 6. 31, Ru. 1. 17. The
formula is followed by pos. or neg. statement. Usually
לִי or the speaker's own name is used (1 S. 20. 13, 2 S. 3. 9) ;
therefore in 1 S. 25. 22 *rd.* לְדָוִד with Sep., and possibly לִי
has fallen out 1 S. 14. 44 (Sep.), but cf. 1 K. 19. 2. In 1 S.
3. 17 לְךָ of person adjured.

Rem. 5. When a clause intervenes before the thing

sworn כִּי is often repeated, 2 S. 2. 27; 3. 9; 15. 21, 1 K.
1. 30, Jer. 22. 24, Gen. 22. 16.   In כִּי אִם the אִם is sometimes merely conditional, *that*, *if*, 1 S. 14. 39, Jer. 22. 24,
cf. Deu. 32. 40.   In other cases the use of כִּי אִם is peculiar.
(1) 2 S. 3. 35 with 2 K. 3. 14 seems to show that the use
of כִּי in the oath was customary without ref. to the pos. or
neg. nature of the thing sworn (apod.).   The כִּי, which may
be repeated, merely adds force to the whole statement.   (2) On
the other hand, in such passages as Jud. 15. 7, 1 K. 20. 6,
2 S. 15. 21, the אִם seems pleonastic.   Its idiomatic use may
in some way add force to the כִּי, though the origin of the
idiom is difficult to trace.   It can scarcely be the same use
of אִם as occurs after a neg. or exception, *but* (= " yes, if ").

INTERROGATIVE SENTENCE

§ 121. The interrog. sent. may be nominal or verbal. See
exx. below.—The interrogation may be made without any
particle, by the mere tone of voice.   2 S. 18. 29 שָׁלוֹם לַנַּעַר
is the child well?   2 S. 11. 11 וַאֲנִי אָבוֹא אֶל־בֵּיתִי *and shall*
I *go to my house?*   1 S. 21. 16 חֲסַר מְשֻׁגָּעִים אָנִי *am* I *in*
want of madmen?   Gen. 18. 12; 27. 24, Jud. 14. 16, 1 S.
16. 4; 22. 7, 15; 25. 11, 2 S. 9. 6; 16. 17; 19. 23; 23. 5, 1 K.
1. 24; 21. 7, Jon. 4. 11, Song 3. 3.   Less frequently in *neg.*
sent., 1 S. 20. 9, 2 K. 5. 26, Job 2. 10.   Omission of the
particle is most common in animated speech, as when any
idea is repudiated, and particularly when pron. is expressed ;
cf. Jud. 14. 16, 2 S. 11. 11, 2 K. 19. 11, Jer. 25. 29, Ez. 20. 31,
Jon. 4. 11.

§ 122. When a particle is used it is generally put at the
head of the clause, Gen. 3. 11.   The simple question is
oftenest made by הֲ (Gr. § 49).   Gen. 4. 9 הֲשֹׁמֵר אָחִי אָנֹכִי
am I *my brother's keeper?*   24. 58 הֲתֵלְכִי עִם הָאִישׁ הַזֶּה
wilt thou go with this man?   Gen. 18. 17; 43. 27, 29; 45. 3,
2 S. 7. 5.—So before יֵשׁ and אַיִן; Gen. 24. 23 הֲיֵשׁ בֵּית אָבִיךְ
מָקוֹם לָנוּ לָלִין *is there room* for us to lodge in the house of

thy father? Jud. 14. 3 הַאֵין בִּבְנוֹת אַחֶיךָ אִשָּׁה *is there not a woman* among the daughters of thy brethren? Gen. 43. 7 ; 44. 19, Ex. 17. 7, Jud. 4. 20, 1 S. 9. 11, 2 K. 4. 13 ; 10. 15. —1 K. 22. 7, 2 K. 3. 11, Jer. 7. 17.

Sometimes אִם (= *num*) is used as a lively denial, or when the idea in the question is repudiated or disapproved, Jud. 5. 8, 1 K. 1. 27, Is. 29. 16, Lam. 2. 20, Job 6. 12, 28; 39. 13 ; though in some cases the first half of a disjunctive question may be unexpressed, Am. 3. 6.

§ 123. The *neg.* question is put by הֲלֹא, Gen. 13. 9 הֲלֹא כָל־הָאָרֶץ לְפָנֶיךָ *is not all the land* before thee? 4. 7 ; 20. 5 ; 44. 5, Ex. 14. 12, Nu. 23. 26, Deu. 31. 17. Or by הַאֵין when the existence of the subj. is questioned, or when the pred. is a ptcp. (§ 100 *d*). 1 K. 22. 7, Jud. 14. 3 (§ 122 above), Am. 2. 11, Jer. 7. 17. Occasionally the elements of הֲלֹא are separated for the sake of emphasis, Gen. 18. 25.

Rem. 1. The interrog. particle, pos. or neg., may be strengthened by other particles, as אַף Gen. 18. 13, 24, Am. 2. 11, Job 40. 8, or גַּם Gen. 16. 13.

Rem. 2. The part. הֲלֹא implying an affirmative answer is often = הִנֵּה, Gen. 37. 13, Deu. 3. 11 and often. In Chr. הנה is sometimes used for הלא of earlier Books, comp. 2 Chr. 16. 11 with 1 K. 15. 23. See 1 Chr. 29. 29, 2 Chr. 27. 7; 32. 32, and Sep. ἰδού for הלא, Deu. 3. 11, Jos. 1. 9, Jud. 6. 14, Est. 10. 2, cf. 2 K. 15. 21. So Ar. *'alà*, which may be used with imper. Jud. 14. 15 is hardly to be read הֲלֹם *here* (Targ.).

§ 124. The disjunctive or alternative question is put by הֲ in first clause, and אִם or וְאִם in second. Jos. 5. 13 הֲלָנוּ אַתָּה אִם לְצָרֵינוּ *art thou for us or for* our enemies? 1 K. 22. 15 הֲנֵלֵךְ אִם נֶחְדָּל *shall we go or forbear?* Or if neg. by אִם לֹא in second clause (or אִם אַיִן if יֵשׁ be in the first), Gen. 27. 21 הַאַתָּה זֶה בְּנִי אִם־לֹא *art thou* my son *or not?* (cf. § 7 *c*). Ex. 17. 7 הֲיֵשׁ י' בְּקִרְבֵּנוּ אִם־אָיִן *is Je.*

in our midst *or not?* Nu. 13. 20.—Gen. 17. 17, Jud. 9. 2;
20. 28, 1 K. 22. 6, 15, 2 K. 20. 9 (§ 41 *c*), Am. 6. 2, Is. 10. 9,
Jer. 2. 14; 18. 14, Job 7. 12.—2 S. 24. 13, Jo. 1. 2, Job 11. 2;
21. 4; 22. 3, cf. Pr. 27. 24. The second half of the alternative
is often merely the first in a varied form. Nu. 11. 12, Job
8. 3; 22. 3. Gen. 37. 8, Jud. 11. 25, 2 S. 19. 36.

§ 125. The indirect interrogation is made just as the
direct, with no effect upon the tense. Gen. 8. 8 לִרְאֹת הֲקַלּוּ
הַמַּיִם to see *whether the waters were abated.* 21. 26 לֹא
יָדַעְתִּי מִי עָשָׂה I do not know *who did it.* Deu. 13. 4
לָדַעַת הֲיִשְׁכֶם אֹהֲבִים to know *whether ye love.* Gen. 24. 21
לָדַעַת הַהִצְלִיחַ י' דַּרְכּוֹ אִם לֹא to know *whether Je. had
prospered* his way *or not.* Gen. 42. 16; 43. 7, 22, Jud. 3. 4;
13. 6, 1 S. 14. 17, 1 K. 1. 20. Exx. of disjunctive sent., Gen.
37. 32, Ex. 16. 4, Nu. 11. 23, Deu. 8. 2, Jud. 2. 22.—In the simple
indirect sent. אִם occurs (after *to see, inquire,* &c.), 2 K. 1. 2,
Jer. 5. 1; 30. 6, Mal. 3. 10, Lam. 1. 12, Ezr. 2. 59, Song 7. 13.

§ 126. The *answer* is usually made by repeating part of
the question, or by the use of some word suggested by it.
Gen. 29. 6 הֲשָׁלוֹם לוֹ ... שָׁלוֹם *is he well?* ... *well.* 24. 58
הֲתֵלְכִי ... אֵלֵךְ *wilt thou go?* ... *I will go.* 1 S. 26. 17
הֲקוֹלְךָ זֶה בְּנִי ... קוֹלִי *is it thy voice,* my son? it is *my
voice.* Gen. 27. 24 אַתָּה זֶה בְּנִי ... אָנִי *art thou* my son?
I am! 2 S. 9. 2 הַאַתָּה צִיבָא ... עַבְדְּךָ *art thou* Ziba?
thy servant! Jud. 13. 11, 1 S. 17. 58; 23. 11, 12, 2 S. 2. 20;
9. 6; 12. 19, 1 K. 21. 20.

To הֲיֵשׁ *is there?* &c., the pos. reply is יֵשׁ, 2 K. 10. 15
(וְיֵשׁ begins the next clause, § 132, R. 2), Jer. 37. 17; and the
neg. אַיִן, Jud. 4. 20. The neg. reply to הַעוֹד *is there any
more?* is אֶפֶס *no more,* Am. 6. 10, cf. 2 S. 9. 3. The neg.
reply to a simple question may be לֹא *no,* Jud. 12. 5, Hag.
2. 12, 13. In Jos. 2. 4 כֵּן = *yes,* and Gen. 30. 34 הֵן = *well,
yes* (cf. Ar. *'inna* in the story Kos. *Aghani,* pp. 13, 14). In

the reply the word that takes up the point of the question usually stands first, being emphatic. Gen. 24. 23; 27. 19, 32; 29. 4, 1 S. 17. 58.

Interrog. sentences are made also by interr. pron. (§ 7, and the exx.), and by various particles. See Rem. 6.

Rem. 1. The disjunctive question very rarely has הֲ in second clause, Nu. 13. 18; sometimes אִו Job 16. 3; 38. 28, 31, Mal. 1. 8, Ecc. 2. 19; and sometimes simple וְ Job 13. 7; 38. 32.

Rem. 2. In animated questions particles of interr. are sometimes accumulated, Gen. 17. 17 *or shall Sarah—shall one* 90 years old bear? Jud. 14. 15, Ps. 94. 9; or repeated 1 S. 14. 37; 23. 11; 30. 8, 2 S. 5. 19.

In Job 6. 13, Nu. 17. 28 the double הַאִם seems = *nonne?* In Nu. תַּמְנוּ לִגְוֺעַ means *we are finished dying* = *are all dead* (Jos. 4. 11, 1 S. 16. 11, 2 S. 15. 24), therefore: *are we not dead to a man?* (cf. *v.* 27). If הַאִם were a stronger form of ה, the sense would be: *are we to die* (have died) *to a man?* but such a meaning of הַאִם does not suit Job 6. 13.

Rem. 3. In the forms הֲכִי *is it that?* הֲלֹא כִי *is it not that?* כִי adds force to the question. 2 S. 9. 1; 13. 28, Job 6. 22, cf. Deu. 32. 30. Sometimes הֲכִי vividly posits a fact as ground for a real or supposed inference. Gen. 27. 36 *is it that* they called his name Jacob? = *well has he been called,* &c.; 29. 15, cf. 1 S. 2. 27, 1 K. 22. 3.

Rem. 4. The interrogation often co-ordinates clauses when other languages would subordinate; Is. 50. 2 *why am I come and there is no man?* = *why, when I am come, is there,* &c. 2 S. 12. 18, 2 K. 5. 12, Is. 5. 4, Am. 9. 7, Job 4. 2, 21; 38. 35.

Rem. 5. The form of question is much used as a strong expression of declinature, repudiation of an idea, or deprecation of a consequence. Gen. 27. 45, 1 S. 19. 17, 2 S. 2. 22; 20. 19, 1 K. 16. 31, 2 Chr. 25. 16, Ecc. 5. 5.

Rem. 6. Some other interrog. particles:

(*a*) *Why? wherefore?* לְמָה ,וְלָמָּה ,לָמָּה; לָמֶה ,מַדּוּעַ; וּמַדּוּעַ ,מַדוּעַ; *why not?* לְמָה לֹא ,מַדּוּעַ לֹא.—1 S. 19. 17 לָמָה כָּכָה רִמִּיתָנִי *why hast*

thou cheated me thus? Gen. 12. 18 לִי הִגַּדְתָּ לֹא לָמָּה *why didst thou not tell me?* 1 S. 26. 15, 2 S. 16. 17; 19. 26. Ex. of מדוע Gen. 26. 27; 40. 7, Ex. 2. 18, 1 S. 20. 2; with neg. 2 S. 18. 11, Job 21. 4.—Ex. of לָמֶה *why?* Gen. 27. 45, Ex. 32. 11, Nu. 20. 4, Jud. 12. 3, 1 K. 2. 22. See Rem. 7.

Like the pronouns, לָמָּה is often strengthened by זֶה (but not מדוע). Gen. 18. 13 צָחֲקָה שׂ' זֶה לָמָּה *wherefore did Sarah laugh?* Gen. 25. 22, 32, Ex. 5. 22, 2 S. 18. 22; 19. 43, Job 27. 12, cf. Jud. 18. 24, 1 K. 21. 5, 2 K. 1. 5. See Rem. 8.—The simple מה or עַל מה and the like are often used in the same sense, Nu. 22. 32, Is. 1. 5, Jer. 9. 11, Job 13. 14, and all these interr. particles are used as words of remonstrance, surprise, &c., and as interjections.

(b) *Where?* אֵי (cons. of אַי), אַיֵּה, זֶה אֵי, אֵיפֹה, &c.; *whither?* אָנָה, זֶה אֵי; *whence?* מֵאַיִן, מִזֶּה אֵי. Gen. 4. 9 הָבֶל אָחִיךָ אֵי *where is* Abel? Deu. 32. 37, 1 S. 26. 16. With suff. Ex. 2. 20 אַיּוֹ *where is he?* &c. Gen. 3. 9, Is. 19. 12, Mic. 7. 10, Nah. 3. 17.—Gen. 19. 5 הָאֲנָשִׁים אַיֵּה *where are* the men? 18. 9; 22. 7; 38. 21, Jud. 9. 38, 2 S. 17. 20, 2 K. 2. 14.— Ex. of אֵיפֹה *where?* Gen. 37. 16, 2 S. 9. 4, Is. 49. 21.— Ex. of מֵאַיִן *whence?* Gen. 42. 7; 29. 4, Nu. 11. 13, Jos. 2. 4, Jud. 17. 9, Is. 39. 3, Job 1. 7, Ps. 121. 1.—Ex. of מִזֶּה אֵי *whence?* Gen. 16. 8, Jud. 13. 6, 1 S. 25. 11, 2 S. 1. 3, 13.— Ex. of אָנָה *whither?* Gen. 16. 8; 37. 30, 2 S. 2. 1, Is. 10. 3; cf. 1 K. 22. 24.

(c) *How?* אֵיךְ, אֵיכָה; בַּמֶּה (*by what?* Gen. 15. 8); *how not?* אֵיךְ לֹא, 2 S. 1. 5 שׂ' כִּי־מֵת יָדַעְתָּ אֵיךְ *how dost thou know* that Saul is dead? 2 S. 1. 14 *how not?* Deu. 18. 21, Jud. 20. 3, 1 K. 12. 6, 2 K. 17. 28, Ru. 3. 18. These particles are used in remonstrance, Gen. 26. 9, Jer. 2. 23; repudiation or refusal, Gen. 39. 9; 44. 8, 34, Jos. 9. 7; the expression of hopelessness, &c., Is. 20. 6. The form אֵיכָה *how!* usually raises the elegy, Is. 1. 21, Lam. 2. 1; 4. 1; but also אֵיךְ, 2 S. 1. 19, 25, 27.

(d) *How many?* בַּמֶּה. 2 S. 19. 35 חַיַּי שְׁנֵי יְמֵי כמה. Gen. 47. 8, 1 K. 22. 16, Zech. 7. 3, Job 13. 23. Also *how much?* Zech. 2. 6; *how long?* Job 7. 19, Ps. 35. 17; *how often?* Job 21. 17, Ps. 78. 40, 2 Chr. 18. 15.

Rem. 7. The form לָמֶה is generally used before words

beginning with any of the letters אהע, in order to avoid the hiatus, see the ex. Rem. 6 a. There are some exceptions, e.g. 1 S. 28. 15, 2 S. 2. 22; 14. 31, Jer. 15. 18, Ps. 49. 6.

Rem: 8. The particle אֵיפֹא is likewise used to strengthen the question *who?* or *where?* &c. Gen. 27. 33, Ex. 33. 16, Jud. 9. 38, Hos. 13. 10, Is. 19. 12; 22. 1, Job 17. 15; 19. 23.

NEGATIVE SENTENCE

§ 127. The neg. particles are לֹא, אַל *not*, אַיִן *there is, was, not*, פֶּן *lest, that not*, טֶרֶם *not yet*, אֶפֶס *no more*, לְבִלְתִּי *not* (with infin.), and some others, chiefly poetical.

(*a*) The neg. לֹא is used in objective statements and in commands. Gen. 45. 1 וְלֹא יָכֹל יוֹסֵף לְהִתְאַפֵּק and J. *was unable* to restrain himself. 3. 1 לֹא תֹאכְלוּ מִכֹּל עֵץ הַגָּן *ye shall eat of no tree* of the garden. On neg. interrog. הֲלֹא cf. § 123.—The particle אַל is the subjective neg., used sometimes in commands, oftener in dissuasion, deprecation, expression of a wish, &c. (see Juss. § 63). Gen. 19. 7 אַל־נָא אַחַי תָּרֵעוּ *do not* my brethren *do wrong*, cf. v. 8. Gen. 43. 23, 1 S. 17. 32; 26. 20, 2 K. 18. 31, Jer. 7. 4; 9. 22, Ps. 51. 13.

The usual place of the neg. is before the verb, but it may be placed before the emphatic word in the neg. clause. Gen. 45. 8 לֹא אַתֶּם שְׁלַחְתֶּם אֹתִי *it was not you* that sent me. Gen. 32. 29, Ex. 16. 8, 1 S. 2. 9; 8. 7, Nu. 16. 29, Neh. 6. 12, 1 Chr. 17. 4.

Both לֹא and אַל are used only with perf. and impf., cf. e.g. Is. 5. 27. On imper. with neg. § 60; ptcp. § 100 *d*: infin. § 95.

On mode of expressing *no, none*, cf. § 11, R. 1 *b*.

(*b*) The particle אַיִן is a noun which embraces the idea of *to be, being*, meaning therefore *not-being* (opposite of יֵשׁ *being*), i.e. *there is, was, not*. Its natural place is before the word (noun or pron.) which it denies, and in cons. state.

Gen. 20. 11 אֵין יִרְאַת א׳ בַּמָּקוֹם הַזֶּה *there is not the fear of God*, &c.   Gen. 37. 29; 39. 11; 41. 8, Nu. 14. 42, Jud. 21. 25.   The word denied may stand for emphasis before אֵין, in which case the neg. is properly in the abs. in apposition.   Gen. 2. 5 וְאָדָם אַיִן לַעֲבֹד and *man was not* to till. 2 K. 19. 3 וְכֹחַ אַיִן לְלֵדָה *there is not strength* to bring forth, Nu. 20. 5.   But the cons. form, being now habitual, mostly remains in any place except at the end of a clause.   Gen. 40. 8 וּפֹתֵר אֵין אֹתוֹ *there is no interpreter* of it; 37. 24; 47. 13, Jer. 30. 13, Pr. 30. 27.—Mic. 7. 2 וְיָשָׁר בָּאָדָם אָיִן one upright among men *there is not*.   Ex. 17. 7; 32. 32, Lev. 26. 37, Jud. 4. 20; 9. 15, 1 S. 10. 14, 1 K. 18. 10.

When pers. pron. is subj. it appears as suff.   Ex. 5. 10 אֵינֶנִּי נֹתֵן לָכֶם תֶּבֶן *I will not give* you straw.   2 K. 17. 26 אֵינָם יֹדְעִים *they do not know*.   Gen. 20. 7; 31. 2; 39. 9, Jud. 3. 25, Jer. 14. 12.   So when existence is denied absolutely, Gen. 5. 24 וְאֵינֶנּוּ *and he was not*, Jer. 31. 15; but a subst. is put in *casus pendens*, and resumed by suff., Gen. 42. 36 יוֹסֵף אֵינֶנּוּ *J. is not;* cf. v. 13; 37. 30.   With a clause, Gen. 37. 29 אֵין יוֹסֵף בַּבּוֹר *Jos. was not* in the pit.   44. 31, Nu. 14. 42.

(c) The telic neg. פֶּן *that not, lest*, is usually joined to impf. and prefixed immediately to the verb.   It expresses the *motive* of action in previous clause, and hence is much used: 1. After imper. (juss., coh.) and neg. clause.   Gen. 3. 3 לֹא תִגְּעוּ בּוֹ פֶּן־תְּמֻתוּן *ye shall not touch it lest ye die*. 19. 17; 38. 23, Ex. 5. 3, Jud. 18. 25, 2 S. 1. 20, Is. 6. 10. 2. After words of *fearing*, expressed or understood.   Gen. 32. 12 I fear him פֶּן־יָבוֹא וְהִכַּנִי *lest he come* and smite me, 26. 7, 9.   Gen. 3. 22 וְעַתָּה פֶּן־יִשְׁלַח יָדוֹ, 19. 19.   Frequently in this sense after אָמַר *to say, think*.   Gen. 38. 11 כִּי אָמַר פֶּן־יָמוּת גַּם הוּא for he thought, *Lest he die too*, 31. 31; 42. 4, Nu. 16. 34, Deu. 32. 27.—Also after *beware*, Gen. 31. 24 הִשָּׁמֶר לְךָ פֶּן־תְּדַבֵּר *beware not to speak*; 24. 6, Deu. 4. 23,

and often in Deu.—Sometimes in the sense of Lat. *ne* in an
independent sent., Ex. 34. 15 פֶּן־תִּכְרֹת בְּרִית *ne ineas pactum*.
Is. 36. 18, Jer. 51. 46, Job 32. 13 *say not!*

(*d*) The neg. טֶרֶם *not yet* is usually joined to impf. even
when referring to the past. Gen. 19. 4 טרם יִשְׁכָּבוּ *they were
not yet lain down*. Gen. 2. 5; 24. 45, Ex. 10. 7, Jos.
2. 8, 1 S. 3. 3 (in *v*. 7 *rd.* perhaps יֵדַע).—The word אֶפֶס
(אָפֵס *to be done*) means *ceasing, being done, no more, nothing*.
Is. 5. 8 עַד אֶפֶס מָקוֹם *till there be no more place*. 2 S. 9. 3
הַאֶפֶס עוֹד אִישׁ *is there none still remaining?* Am. 6. 10
הַעוֹד עִמָּךְ . . . אָפֵס *are there any still there? no more!*
With prep. Is. 52. 4 *for nothing*, 40. 17 *of nothing*. Cf. Is.
45. 14; 46. 9, Pr. 26. 20 (prep.). In Zeph. 2. 15, Is. 47. 8, 10
אַפְסִי has junctive vowel (not suff.), I am, *and none besides* (me).

§ 128. The double neg. adds force to the negation. Zeph.
2. 2 בְּטֶרֶם לֹא־יָבוֹא *before it does not come*. Ex. 14. 11
הַמִבְּלִי אֵין קְבָרִים *is it because there are no graves* (מִן *is
causative*), 2 K. 1. 3, 6, 16. The prep. מִן *away from, so as
not* to be, &c., has neg. force, and is often joined with
pleonastic אֵין. Is. 6. 11 מֵאֵין יוֹשֵׁב *so that there shall be no*
(=*without*) *inhabitant*, Is. 5. 9; Jer. 4. 7. Cases like Is.
5c. 2 מֵאֵין מַיִם, Jer. 7. 32 מֵאֵין מָקוֹם *are different: from
there being* (because there is) *no water*, &c., comp. Rem. 5.
The text of 1 K. 10. 21 is not above suspicion, owing to use
of לֹא with ptcp. (2 Chr. 9. 20 omits לֹא).

Rem. 1. The neg. לֹא is used as privative in forming
compounds : (*a*) with nouns, לֹא אֵל a *no-god*, Deu. 32. 21,
cf. *v*. 17; לֹא אִישׁ (one) *not-man*, Is. 31. 8; לֹא עֵץ (what is)
not-wood, Is. 10. 15 ; לֹא דָבָר a *no-thing*, Am. 6. 13, cf. Hos.
1. 9; 2. 25. (*b*) With adj., as לֹא חָכָם *unwise*, Hos. 13. 13,
לֹא חָסִיד *impious*, Ps. 43. 1, cf. Pr. 30. 25 *not-strong*, 2 K.
7. 9.—With prep. בְּלֹא *without*, Nu. 35. 22, 23 (inf.), Ez.
22. 29, cf. Isa. 55. 1, 2, Lev. 15. 25.—Job 26. 2 לְלֹא כֹחַ

the *not-strength, strengthless,* abstract noun for adj. (or to be resolved into לוֹ (לַאֲשֶׁר לֹא־בֹחַ לוֹ), Is. 5. 14.

Rem. 2. The neg. אַל with juss. &c., sometimes expresses merely the subjective feeling and sympathy of the speaker with the act.   Is. 2. 9 וְאַל־תִּשָּׂא לָהֶם and *thou canst not forgive* them.   Jer. 46. 6, Ps. 41. 3 ; 50. 3 ; 121. 3 ; 141. 5, Job 5. 22 ; 20. 17, Pr. 3. 25, Song 7. 3, cf. the strong ex. Ps. 34. 6.   In strong deprecation with אַל the verb is occasionally suppressed or deferred to a second clause, 2 S. 13. 12 אַל־אָחִי *don't!* my brother, *v.* 25 אַל־בְּנִי *nay!* my son.   Gen. 19. 18, Jud. 19. 23, 2 S. 1. 21, 2 K. 4. 16, Ru. 1. 13, Is. 62. 6.   In other cases the verb has to be supplied from the previous clause, Am. 5. 14 seek good וְאַל־רָע *and not evil*! Jo. 2. 13, Pr. 8. 10 ; 17. 12.   The word is used absolutely, in deprecation of something said, 2 K. 3. 13, Gen. 33. 10. —2 K. 6. 27 אַל־יוֹשִׁעֵךְ י' perhaps, *if Je. help thee not!* For אַל 1 S. 27. 10 *rd.* אֶל־מִי (Sep.) or אָן *whither?* — In composition אַל is little used, Pr. 12. 28 אַל־מָוֶת *not-death,* immortality.

Rem. 3. The particle אֵין frequently forms abbreviated circums. clauses, as אֵין מִסְפָּר (there is) *no number, without number, countless,* § 140.   In this sense לֹא in poetry, 2 S. 23. 4 בֹּקֶר לֹא עָבוֹת a morning *without clouds* ; Job 10. 22 *without order,* 12. 24 ; 38. 26, Ps. 59. 4 ; in prose, 1 Chr. 2. 30, 32 לֹא בָנִים *childless.* — Ps. 135. 17 the stronger אֵין יֵשׁ, 1 S. 21. 9, cf. Job 9. 33.—From the semiverbal force of אֵין a late writer can say אֵין אֶתְכֶם, Hag. 2. 17.   In two passages, Jer. 38. 5, Job 35. 15, אֵין seems used with finite verb.—A contracted form is אִי in composition, 1 S. 4. 21 אִי־כָבוֹד *not-glory,* inglorious, Job 22. 30 אִי־נָקִי *not innocent.* This is the usual form of neg. in Eth.   On אֵין לְ with inf. § 95.

Rem. 4. The form פֶּן־יֵשׁ occurs owing to the verbal force of יֵשׁ, Deu. 29. 17, 2 K. 10. 23.   With *perf.* פֶּן expresses what is feared *may have* happened, 2 K. 2. 16 ; 10. 23, 2 S. 20. 6.

Rem. 5. In Poetry.   בַּל = לֹא *not,* Hos. 7. 2 וּבַל יֹאמְרוּ *and they say not.*   9. 16, Is. 14. 21 ; 26. 10, 11, 14, 18.   Often with niph. of מוֹט, Ps. 10. 6 ; 16. 8 ; 21. 8, &c.   With inf.

Ps. 32. 9 בַּל קְרֹב (when) *there is not coming nigh* (they do not come)—בְּלִי־ = לֹא or אֵין. With finite vb. Is. 14. 6, Hos. 8. 7; 9. 16 (Cod. Petrop. בל), Job 41. 18 (once in prose, Gen. 31. 20). With adj. 2 S. 1. 21, בְּלִי מָשִׁיחַ *un-anointed,* Hos. 7. 8 ptcp., Ps. 19. 4. With noun = *without,* Job 8. 11 בְּלִי־מַיִם *without* water, 24. 10; 30. 8; 31. 39, Ps. 59. 5; 63. 2, Is. 28. 8.

With a preceding prep. Deu. 4. 42 בִּבְלִי דַעַת *without know-ledge* (unawares), cf. Is. 5. 14, Job 38. 41; 41. 25.—מִבְּלִי *from lack of,* Deu. 9. 28 מִבְּלִי יְכֹלֶת *from not being able.* Is. 5. 13, Hos. 4. 6, Lam. 1. 4. With another neg., cf. § 129 above.—In the same sense as מֵאֵין *so that there is not,* Jer. 2. 15; 9. 9, Zeph. 3. 6. In other cases = *without* Job 4. 20; 6. 6; 24. 8.—The form בִּלְתִּי once with adj., 1 S. 20. 26 *not clean.* With noun, Is. 14. 6 *without* cessation; suff. 1 S. 2. 2, Hos. 13. 4 *except* me, thee.

Rem. 6. The neg. without being repeated often exerts its force over a succeeding clause, 1 S. 2. 3, Nu. 23. 19, Is. 23. 4; 28. 27; 38. 18, Mic. 7. 1, Ps. 9. 19; 44. 19, Pr. 30. 3.

THE CONDITIONAL SENTENCE

§ 129. The conditional sent. is compound, consisting of two clauses, the former stating the supposition, and the second the result dependent upon it (the answer to the supposition). Conditional sentences may be nominal or verbal, or partly nominal and partly verbal. The apodosis, in particular, may assume many forms.

In conditional sentences the verbal form will be used which would have been used if the sentence had been direct. The verbal forms vary according as the mind presents to itself the condition as fulfilled and actual (perf.), or to be fulfilled, and merely possible (impf.). In ordinary speech the impf. is most common both in the protasis and apodosis, but the mind may present to itself the condition as realised, in which case the perf. is used. This happens particularly in animated speech, and in the higher style. And, naturally,

when the condition is conceived as realised and actual, the
result depending on it may appear carried with it, so that
two perfs. may be used.

The conditional particles are chiefly אִם *if,* כִּי *when, if,*
supposing that, לוּ *if;* less common אֲשֶׁר *when, if,* and הֵן *if;*
neg. אִם אַיִן, אִם לֹא *if not,* לוּלֵא *if not, unless.* These
may be strengthened by other particles, גַּם כִּי, כִּי אִם
(גַּם אִם *rare,* Eccl. 8. 17).

§ 130. (*a*) When the supposition expresses a real con-
tingency of any degree of possibility, the most common
form is impf. in prot. and vav conv. perf. or simple impf. in
apod., the impf. having any of the shades of sense proper
to it (§ 43 *seq.*). The impf. must be used in apod. when the
verbal form cannot stand first in the clause, as in a neg. sent.,
or when apod. precedes the protasis, cf. Am. 9. 2–4.—Jud.
4. 8 אִם תֵּלְכִי עִמִּי וְהָלָכְתִּי וְאִם־לֹא תֵלְכִי לֹא אֵלֵךְ *if thou*
wilt go with me *I will go, but if thou wilt not go* with me
I will not go. 2 K. 4. 29 כִּי תִמְצָא־אִישׁ לֹא תְבָרֲכֶנּוּ *if thou*
meetest anyone thou shalt not salute him. Gen. 18. 28
לֹא אַשְׁחִית אִם־אֶמְצָא *I will not destroy if I find.* 13. 16
אִם יוּכַל אִישׁ לִמְנוֹת... גַּם זַרְעֲךָ יִמָּנֶה *if one could count*
the dust, thy seed also *might be counted.* Of course a ptcp.
may take the place of impf., Gen. 43. 4, 5 אִם־יֶשְׁךָ מְשַׁלֵּחַ
גֵּרְדָה וְאִם־אֵינְךָ מְשַׁלֵּחַ לֹא נֵרֵד *if thou wilt let go* our
brother *we will go down, but if thou wilt not let him go,* &c.
Gen. 24. 42, Ex. 8. 17, Jud. 6. 36, 37, 1 S. 19. 11. So without
יֵשׁ Deu. 5. 22, Jud. 9. 15; 11. 9, 1 S. 6. 3; 7. 3, 1 K. 21. 6,
2 K. 10. 6. But the prot. may be a purely nominal sent.,
and the apod. may take almost any form; 1 K. 18. 21
אִם יהוה הָאֱלֹהִים לְכוּ אַחֲרָיו *if Jehovah be God, follow*
him; Ex. 7. 27 אִם מָאֵן אַתָּה הִנֵּה אָנֹכִי נֹגֵף *if thou refuse,*
behold, I will smite. Gen. 42. 19; 44. 26, Ex. 1. 16; 21. 3, Jos.
17. 15, Jud. 6. 31, 2 K. 1. 10; 10. 6, Mal. 1. 6.

(*b*) Perf. in prot.—The mind may conceive or imagine the condition as realised and actual, in which case perf. stands in prot. with the same apod. as in (*a*): Jud. 16. 17 אִם גֻּלַּחְתִּי וְסָר כֹּחִי *if I be shaved my strength will depart;* 2 S. 15. 33 אִם עָבַרְתָּ אִתִּי וְהָיִתָ עָלַי לְמַשָּׂא *if thou go on* with me *thou shalt be* a burden to me. Comp. Gen. 43. 9 with 42. 37. Deu. 32. 41, 2 K. 7. 4, Is. 4. 4; 16. 12, Mic. 5. 7, Jer. 14. 18; 23. 22; 37. 10; 49. 9, Obad. 5, Job 7. 4; 10. 14; 11. 13; 21. 6, Ru. 1. 12. Comparison of cases like Lev. 13. 53, 56, 57 shows that the use of perf. or impf. is merely a matter of mental conception. Comp. Lev. 17. 4 with 9, Num. 30. 6 with 9. Job 17. 13, 14. Probably the difference of use had become a mere matter of style, although the perf. has in it something more forcible and lively. Cf. Job 31 throughout.

In many cases the supposition refers to an actual past *fact* anterior to the speaker's position, or to the main action spoken of; or refers to something which shall have come to light through inquiry or inspection. In all such cases the *perf.* will be used in the protasis. 1 S. 26. 19 אִם י' הֱסִיתְךָ יָרַח מִנְחָה *if Je. has set thee on, let him smell* an offering (=if it be Je. that has); Jud. 9. 19 אִם בֶּאֱמֶת עֲשִׂיתֶם שְׂמָחוּ *if ye have dealt justly, rejoice.* Ex. 22. 1, 2 אִם . . . אִם יִמָּצֵא הַגַּנָּב זָרְחָה הַשֶּׁמֶשׁ *if the thief be found* in the act . . . *if the sun have risen,* &c. Deu. 17. 2, 3 . . . כִּי יִמָּצֵא אִישׁ אֲשֶׁר יַעֲשֶׂה וַיֵּלֶךְ *if a man be found who does evil . . . and has gone* and served (having gone). With Ex. 22. 2 cf. 21. 36 (אוֹ). Lev. 4. 23; 5. 1, Nu. 5. 19, 20, 27; 15. 24; 22. 20, Deu. 22. 20, 21, 1 S. 21. 5, Is. 28. 25, Am. 3. 3, 4; 7. 2, Ps. 41. 7; 44. 21; 50. 18, Job 8. 4; 9. 15, 16; 31. 5, 9, 21, 24, 33; 34. 32.

Narratives of past frequentative actions are also often introduced by אִם with perf. (§ 54, R. 1). Gen. 38. 9, Nu. 21. 9, Jud. 2. 18; 6. 3. More rarely אִם and impf., Gen. 31. 8, Ex. 40. 37.

12

(c) The protasis is often of considerable length, and has a tense-secution within itself which must be distinguished from the apod. of the whole sentence. This tense-secution is the usual one.　Gen. 28. 20　אִם יִהְיֶה א׳ עִמָּדִי וּשְׁמָרַנִי וְנָתַן וְשַׁבְתִּי . . . וְהָיָה י׳ *if God will be* with me, *and keep me, and give me, and I return . . . then shall Je. be* my God.　Deu. 13. 2　כִּי יָקוּם נָבִיא וְנָתַן אוֹת וּבָא הָאוֹת . . . לֹא תִשְׁמַע *if a prophet shall arise and give a sign, and the sign come true . . . thou shalt not listen.*　Nu. 5. 27　אִם נִטְמְאָה וַתִּמְעֹל וּבָאוּ . . . *if she has been defiled and trespassed . . . then shall come,* &c.　Gen. 43. 9 (secution of fut. perf. of imagination is that of impf., § 51, R. 2); 46. 33, 34, Jud. 4. 20, 1 S. 1. 11; 12. 14, 15; 17. 9, 2 S. 15. 34, 1 K. 9. 6; 11. 38; 12. 7.

Rem. 1. Additional exx.—אִם and impf. in prot., with vav perf. in apod. : Gen. 24. 8; 32. 9, Ex. 13. 13; 21. 5, 6; 21. 11, Nu. 21. 2, Jud. 14. 12, 13; 21. 21, 1 S. 12. 15; 20. 6, 1 K. 6. 12; coh. after אם Job 16. 6.　With impf. in apod. : Gen. 30. 31; 42. 37, Ex. 20. 25, 1 S. 12. 25, 1 K. 1. 52, Is. 1. 18–20; 7. 9; 10. 22, Am. 5. 22; 9. 2–4, Ps. 50. 12.　With כי in prot. : Gen. 32. 18; 46. 33, Ex. 21. 2, 7, 20, 22, 26, 28; 22. 4, 6, 9, Deu. 13. 13; 15. 16; 19. 16 *seq.*, Josh. 8. 5, 1 S. 20. 13, 2 S. 7. 12, 1 K. 8. 46, 2 K. 18. 22, Jer. 23. 33, Hos. 9. 16, Ps. 23. 4; 37. 24; 75. 3, Job 7. 13.　With אֲשֶׁר, Lev. 4. 22, Josh. 4. 21, 1 K. 8. 31.— Various forms of apod. : Gen. 4. 7; 24. 49; 27. 46; 30. 1; 31. 50, Ex. 8. 17; 10. 4; 33. 15, Jud. 9. 15, 1 S. 19. 11; 20. 7, 21; 21. 10, Is. 1. 15; 43. 2, Jer. 26. 15, Ps. 139. 8. Ex. 8. 22 (הֵן in prot.).

Rem. 2. Impf. with simple vav in apod. is less common, Gen. 13. 9, Josh. 20. 5.

Rem. 3. The prot. is often strengthened by inf. abs., but only with אם and impf., not with כי nor with perf. Ex. 21. 5; 22. 3, 11, 12, 16, Nu. 21. 2, Deu. 8. 19, Jud. 11. 30, 1 S. 1. 11; 20. 6, 7, 9, 21 (§ 86).　So with הֵן Is. 54. 15.　The אם may be strengthened by כי.—Inf. abs.

with perf. after לוּא 1 S. 14. 30.—The apod. is also many times strengthened by כִּי, Is. 7. 9, Jer. 22. 24.

Rem. 4. Instead of the natural calm apod. with vav perf. or impf. the more animated perf. (of certainty, § 41) may occur, expressing the immediateness or certainty of the result; 1 S. 2 16 וְאִם־לֹא לָקַחְתִּי and if not, *I will take it.* Nu. 32. 23, Jud. 15. 7, Job 20. 14, Ps. 127. 1. Comp. vav conv. impf., Ps. 59. 16, Job 19. 18. Two perfs. Pr. 9. 12; with כַּאֲשֶׁר Gen. 43. 14, Est. 4. 16; cf. Mic. 7. 8.—Cases like Nu. 16. 29, 1 S. 6. 9, 1 K. 22. 28 are different, being elliptical. 1 S. 6. 9 if it go up by Beth. הוּא עָשָׂה *he has done it* = ye shall know *that he*, &c.; cf. next clause.

Rem. 5. The conditional particle usually stands first, the order being, particle, verb, subj.; but words may come between part. and verb if emphatic, and oftener with אם than כי. In the casuistry of the Law (P) the *subj.* curiously precedes the particle in the principal clause. Lev. 4. 2 נֶפֶשׁ כִּי־תֶחֱטָא, Lev. 5. 1, 4, 15; 7. 21; 12. 2; 13. 2 and often; Num. 9. 10; 27. 8; 30. 3, 4; cf. Ez. 14. 9, 13; 18. 5, 18; 33. 2, 6, 9. In subordinate clauses the usual order is found, Lev. 13. 42, &c. Comp. the older order Ex. 22. 4, 5, 6, 9, 13, and often; but cf. Is. 28. 15, 18, 1 K. 8. 37, Ps. 62. 11. In the group of Laws Ex. 21 *seq.* the principal supposition is made by כי and the subordinate details follow with אם or וְאִם, Ex. 21. 2–5, 7–11, &c.

§ 131. Hypothetical sent.—Actions not realised in the past, or considered not realisable (or unlikely) in the pres. or fut. may be made the subject of supposition. In this case לוּ (לְא) *if*, and (לוּלֵא) לוּלֵי *if not, unless*, are used. (*a*) In the case of past actions the perf. stands both in prot. and apod. (§ 39 *d*). Jud. 13. 23 לוּ חָפֵץ לַהֲמִיתֵנוּ לֹא לָקַח *if he had wished* to kill us *he would not have taken*, 8. 19; Gen. 31. 42 לוּלֵי אֱלֹהֵי אָבִי הָיָה לִי כִּי עַתָּה שִׁלַּחְתָּנִי *unless* the God of my father *had been* for me, surely *thou hadst sent me away* empty, 43. 10.—Nu. 22. 33 (*rd.* לוּלֵי), Jud. 14. 18, 1 S. 14. 30 (apod. interrog.); 25. 34, 2 S. 2. 27, Is. 1. 9, Ps.

94. 17; 119. 92 (both nominal prot.); 106. 23.   Nu. 22. 29
may be opt., or, *if there had been . . . I would have slain.*
See Opt. sent.

(*b*) When supposition refers to pres. or fut. the apod. is
usually impf., 2 S. 18. 12 לֹא־אֶשְׁלַח יָדִי . . . לֹא אָנֹכִי שֹׁקֵל
if I weighed 1000 shekels on my palms *I would not put forth
my hand,* 2 K. 3. 14; Deu. 32. 29 לוּ חָכְמוּ יַשְׂכִּילוּ *if they
were wise they would perceive* this, Job 16. 4; Mic. 2. 11, Ps.
81. 14.   2 S. 19. 7 (nominal prot. and apod.).

Rem. 1.   Ez. 14. 15 אִם=לוּ, just as לוּ=אִם Ps. 73. 15.—
Ps. 44. 21 perhaps, *if we forgot would he not search?* Job
10. 14.   Gen. 50. 15 לוּ impf., ot action feared but depre-
cated.   Deu. 32. 27 לוּלֵי impf. in prot. may be action
generalised in past, or extending into pres.   Ps. 124. 1, 2
seems to approach the Ar. *laula, but for* with a noun ; at
anyrate the rel. here is not a conj. as in Aram. *ellu lo d,
unless that.*

Rem. 2.   The אָז, עַתָּה in the apod., originally temporal,
have become often merely logical.   Both are good, Gen.
31. 42; 43. 10, 2 S. 2. 27, cf. Job 11. 15. 16, Pr. 2. 5.
The כִּי strengthens, Job 8. 6; but in some cases this כִּי seems
resumption of כִּי of oath, 1 S. 25. 34, 2 S. 2. 27.   This kind
of apod. occurs with no formal prot., the prot. having to be
supplied from the connection ; *e.g.* after neg., 1 S. 13. 13
thou hast not kept; (if thou hadst) *then he would have estab-
lished;* or an interr., Job 3. 13 *why breasts that I should suck?*
(if not) *then I should have lain down;* or a gerundive inf.,
2 K. 13. 19 *percutiendum erat sexies, then thou* wouldst *have
smitten* Aram.   Ex. 9. 15, Job. 13. 19.   This kind of apod.
with אָז, כִּי אָז, כִּי עַתָּה is common in Job.

§ 132. What is equivalent to a cond. sent. often occurs
without any cond. particle.   (*a*) An idiomatic sent. of this
kind is made by vav conv. perf. both in prot. and apod.
This is chiefly in subordinate clauses.   Gen. 44. 22 וְעָזַב
אֶת־אָבִיו וָמֵת *if he leave* his father *he will die* (lit., and he

will leave, and he will die). Ex. 4. 14 וְרָאֲךָ וְשָׂמַח בְּלִבּוֹ *when he sees thee he will be glad* in his heart. Gen. 33. 13; 42. 38; 44. 4, 29, Ex. 16. 21, Nu. 14. 15; 23. 20, 1 S. 16. 2; 19. 3; 25. 31, 2 S. 13. 5, 1 K. 8. 30; 18. 10 (if they said No, he took an oath of them), 2 K. 7. 9, Is. 21. 7, Jer. 18. 4, 8; 20. 9, Pr. 3. 24. This vav perf. may have any of the senses proper to it, *e.g.* frequentative, Ex. 16. 21; 33. 10, 1 S. 14. 52, 1 K. 18. 10, Jer. 20. 9.—Of course if vav cannot be joined to the verb, impf. will be used in either clause, Nu. 23. 20 וּבֵרַךְ וְלֹא אֲשִׁיבֶנָּה *if he blesses I cannot reverse it*; 2 K. 18. 21 אֲשֶׁר יִסָּמֵךְ אִישׁ עָלָיו וּבָא *on which if one lean it goes* into his hand. Deu. 22. 3, 1 S. 20. 13, Jos. 22. 18, Is. 29. 11, 12, Prov. 6. 22 (no *and* in apod.). More vigorously an imper. for second perf., 1 S. 29. 10.

(*b*) Two corresponding imper. often form a virtual cond. sent., Gen. 42. 18 זֹאת עֲשׂוּ וִחְיוּ *this do and live* (if ye do, ye shall), Is. 8. 9 הִתְאַזְּרוּ וָחֹתּוּ *though ye gird yourselves ye shall be broken*. Juss. or coh. may take place of imp., Gen. 30. 28, Is. 8. 10. Two juss. are less usual, Ps. 104. 20: 147. 18, Job 10. 16; 11. 17, cf. Is. 41. 28.

Rem. 1. In the case of two imper. of course both are expressions of the will of the speaker ; he wills the first and he wills the second as the consequence of the first. Similarly in the case of two jussives (§ 64 *seq.*). It is only to our different manner of thought that a condition seems expressed.

Rem. 2. Such words as אֲשֶׁר *he - who, whoever,* מִי, מִי אֲשֶׁר *whoever,* and similar phrases form virtually conditional sentences, Jud. 1. 12; 6. 31, Mic. 3. 5. And the conj. *and* without any particle may introduce a cond. sent., *e.g.* with יֵשׁ, לֹא, עוֹד, &c. Jud. 6. 13 וְיֵשׁ י' עִמָּנוּ *if then Je. be* with us. So 2 K. 10. 15 וְיֵשׁ *if it be* (a larger accent should be on first יֵשׁ). Similarly the neg. וְלֹא *if not,* 2 S. 13. 26, 2 K. 5. 17.—Is. 6. 13 וְעוֹד בָּהּ *if there be still in it* a tenth. 2 K. 7. 9 וְאֲנַחְנוּ מַחְשִׁים. Cf. 2 S. 19. 8 כִּי אֵינְךָ יֹצֵא.

But in lively speech aided by intonation almost any direct

form of expression without particles may be equivalent to
what in other languages would be a conditional.   1. Impf.—
Hos. 8. 12 נֶחְשָׁבוּ . . . אֶכְתֹּב *though I wrote* . . . they would
be considered; so Is. 26. 10.   Ps. 139. 18 אֶסְפְּרֵם *were I to
count them*;   141. 5 *should the righteous smite*;   104. 22, 27–
30, Jud. 13. 12, Pr. 26. 26; two impf. Song 8. 1.   Coh., Ps.
40. 6 אַגִּידָה *if I would declare*, Ps. 139. 8, 9, Job 19. 18.
With הנה, 1 S. 9. 7 *behold we will go* (= if we go), Ex 8. 22.
—Cf. Ps. 46. 4; 109. 25; 146. 4, Is. 40. 30.

2. Perf.—Am. 3. 8 אַרְיֵה שָׁאָג *if the lion roars*.   Job 7. 20
חָטָאתִי *be it I have sinned*.   Ps. 139. 18 *if I awake*.   Pr.
26. 12 רָאִיתָ *seest thou*.   Nu. 12. 14, Ps. 39. 12, Job 3. 25;
19. 4; 23. 10.   With הנה, 2 S. 18. 11, Hos. 9. 6, Ez. 13. 12;
14. 22; 15. 4.   And if perf. naturally also vav impf., Jer.
5. 22, Ps. 139. 11.   Ex. 20. 25, Job 23. 13, Pr. 11. 2.   Two
perf., Pr. 18. 22, Mic. 7. 8.

3. The ptcp.—Is. 48. 13 קֹרֵא אֲנִי *if I call* they stand up.
2 S. 19. 8.   Ptcp. with *art.* (or in consn.) *whoever*, 2 S.
14. 10, Gen. 9. 6, Ex. 21. 12, 16 and often.   Frequently in
Prov., *e.g.* 17. 13; 18. 13; 27. 14; 29. 21, &c.   Particularly
ptcp. with כֹל *all*; 1 S. 2. 13, Ex. 19. 12, Nu. 21. 8, Jud.
19. 30, 2 S. 2. 23, 2 K. 21. 12.   With הנה 1 K. 20. 36,
2 K 7 2, Ex. 3. 13.

4. Inf. abs.—Pr. 25. 4, 5 הָגוֹ סִינִים *if dross be removed*,
12. 7.   Inf. cons. with prep., Pr. 10. 25 (2 S. 7. 14, 1 K.
8. 33, 35).   Ps. 62. 10 בְּמֹאזְנַיִם לַעֲלוֹת *to go up* (or, *at going up*
= if they are put) upon the balance.

THE OPTATIVE SENTENCE

§ 133. The *wish* may be expressed by impf. (juss., coh.),
2 S. 18. 32 יְהִיּוּ כַנַּעַר אֹיְבֵי אֲדֹנִי *may* the enemies of my
lord *be as that young man*.   With or without נָא, 2 S. 24. 14
נִפְּלָה־נָא *let us fall*; 1 S. 1. 23 יָקֵם י' דְּבָרוֹ *may Je. establish*.
By imper., or part. (without cop.), Gen. 3. 14 אָרוּר אַתָּה
mayest thou be cursed, Is. 12. 5 מוּדַעַת זֹאת *may this be
known*.   With omission of verb, Gen. 27. 13 *on me be thy
curse!*   1 S. 25. 24, Ps. 3. 9.

§ 134. Opt. particles.—The common opt. part. is לוּ, less usually אִם. The perf. or impf. will be used according to reference. Nu. 14. 2 לוּ־מַתְנוּ בְּאֶרֶץ מ׳ *would we had died* in the land of Egypt; Nu. 20. 3, Jos. 7. 7. Is. 63. 19 לוּא קָרַעְתָּ שָׁמַיִם *would thou hadst rent* (*i.e.* wouldst rend,— perf. caused by the importunity. So 48. 18—hardly a real *past*).—With impf., Gen. 17. 18 לוּ יִשׁ׳ יִחְיֶה *O that* Ishmael *might live*; Job 6. 2 לוּ שָׁקוֹל יִשָּׁקֵל כַּעֲשִׂי *O that* my trouble *were weighed* (apod. כִּי עַתָּה). With imper., Gen. 23. 13; ptcp., Ps. 81. 14.—Ps. 139. 19 אִם תִּקְטֹל רָשָׁע *O that thou wouldst kill* the wicked. Ps. 81. 9; 95. 7; Pr. 24. 11.

§ 135. An interrog. sent. with מִי *who?* expresses a wish. 2 S. 23. 15 מִי יַשְׁקֵנִי מַיִם *O that I had water to drink!* (lit., who will let me drink!). Ps. 4. 7 מִי יַרְאֵנוּ טוֹב *O that we saw* some success! Nu. 11. 4, 2 S. 15. 4, cf. Mal. 1. 10.— Particularly the phrase מִי יִתֵּן *who will give?* 2 S. 19. 1 מִי יִתֵּן מוּתִי אֲנִי תַחְתֶּיךָ *would that I had died* for thee! Ex. 16. 3. With impf., Job 6. 8 מִי יִתֵּן תָּבוֹא שֶׁאֱלָתִי *O that* my request *might come!* Job 13. 5; 14. 13.

Rem. 1. The opt. sense of לוּ, אִם, has arisen out of the *conditional* use; cf. Gen. 24. 42, Ex. 32. 32, where the transition is seen.

Rem. 2. A rare opt. part. is אַחֲלַי, אַחֲלִי (out of אָח and לוּ=לִי), 2 K. 5. 3, Ps. 119. 5 (אָז in apod.).

Rem. 3. The consn. of מִי יִתֵּן varies. (1) One acc., Jud. 9. 29, Deu. 28. 67, Ps. 14. 7; 55. 7, Job 14. 4; 29. 2 (suff.), 31. 31, 35 (ptcp.). (2) Two acc., Nu. 11. 29, Jer. 8. 23; 9. 1 (verbs of *granting*, 2 acc. § 78, R. 1; unless the consn. be *who will set me in* the wild, (*in*) a lodge, as Jos. 15. 19, Jud. 1. 15 where אֶרֶץ might be acc. of place). (3) inf. cons. 2 S. 19. 1, Ex. 16. 3; acc. and inf., Job 11. 5 מִי יִתֵּן אֱלוֹהַּ דַּבֵּר *that God would speak* (anomalous order perhaps due to emph. on *God*). (4) Simple impf., Job 6. 8; 13. 5; 14. 13; impf. with vav, Job 19. 23; vav conv. perf., Deu. 5. 26

O that this mind of theirs might be to them (always), to fear, &c. With perf. Job 23. 3 (stative v.).

CONJUNCTIVE SENTENCE

§ 136. The uses of the conjunction *and* are various. On vav conv., § 46 *seq.* On vav of purpose after imper. &c., § 64 *seq.* On vav apod. in conditional sent., § 130 *seq.*; after *casus pendens*, &c., § 50, 56. On various senses of vav in circumstantial cl., § 137. On vav of equation, § 151.

The conjunc. vav, used to connect words, sometimes stands before each when there is a number of them: Gen. 20. 14; 24. 35, Deu. 12. 18; 14. 5, Jos. 7. 24, 1 S. 13. 20, Hos. 2. 20, 21, Jer. 42. 1; or only with the concluding words of a series, Gen. 13. 2, 2 K. 23. 5, *e.g.* with the last of three; or only with second, Deu. 29. 22, Job 42. 9; or sometimes the words are disposed in pairs, Hos. 2. 7.

Both . . . and is expressed by גַּם . . . גַּם or גַּם . . . וְגַם. Gen. 24. 25 גַּם־תֶּבֶן גַּם־מִסְפּוֹא *both* straw *and* provender. Or with several words, 43. 8 גַּם־אֲנַחְנוּ גַם־אַתָּה גַּם טַפֵּנוּ *both* we *and* thou *and* our children. Jud. 8. 22.—1 S. 2. 26 גַּם עִם־יְ וְגַם עִם־אֲנָשִׁים *both* with Je. *and* with men.—Gen. 44. 16; 47. 3, 19, Nu. 18. 3, Zeph. 2. 14.—Gen. 24. 44, 1 S. 12. 14; 26. 25. When influenced by a *neg.* this *both . . . and* becomes *neither . . . nor*, Nu. 23. 25, 1 S. 20. 27; 21. 9, 1 K. 3. 26, cf. 1 S. 16. 8 *neither* this one, &c. Less commonly and mainly later וְ . . . וְ is *both . . . and.* Ps. 76. 7 נִרְדָּם וְרֶכֶב וָסוּס *both* chariot *and* horse are sunk into sleep. Nu. 9. 14, Jer. 32. 20 *both* in Isr. *and*, &c., Dan. 8. 13, Job 34. 29.

Rem. 1. For the various uses of *and* the Lexicon must be consulted. (*a*) It occasionally has the sense of *also*, Hos. 8. 6 וְהוּא, 2 S. 1. 23 *also* in their death.

(*b*) There is a dislike to begin a sentence without *and*, hence even Books are commenced with it, Ex. 1. 1, Ru. 1. 1. Hence also speeches begin with it, Jos. 22. 28

וַנֹּאמֶר וְהָיָה and we said, *It shall happen.* Jer. 9. 21, so probably Is. 2. 2.

(*c*) The *and* has a sort of exegetical force, with a certain emphasis on the word that explains, Ps. 74. 11 thy hand *and* (even) thy right hand. Ps. 85. 9 to his people *and* to his saints. Zech. 9. 9 *and* on a colt. Ps. 72. 12 the poor *and* *he that* (*i.e.* who) has no helper. Often with the sense *and that*, Am. 3. 11 a foe וְסָבִיב *and that* round about the land ; 4. 10 *and that* into your nostrils. Jud. 7. 22, Is. 57. 11, Jer. 15. 13, Zech. 7. 5, Neh. 8. 13, 1 Chr. 9. 27, 2 Chr. 29. 27, Ecc. 8. 2. Comp. 2 S. 13. 20 וְשֹׁמֵמָה, Ps. 68. 10 וְנִלְאָה, Lam. 3. 26 וְדוּמָם *and that* in silence. Somewhat different 2 S. 3. 39 וּמָשׁוּחַ מֶלֶךְ *though* anointed king.

(*d*) The vav is common to introduce what is consequential or follows from what precedes, *so, then, e.g.* with imper. Jud. 8. 24 I will make a request וּתְנוּ־לִי *Give me,* &c. 2 K. 4. 41 ; 7. 13, Nu. 9. 2, Ez. 18. 32, Ps. 45. 12 *worship him.* Cf. Salkinson Matt. 8. 3 I will, וּטְהָר *be thou clean,* which is better than the bare טְהָר of Del.—Particularly in dialogue the vav attaches to something said (or understood) with various shades of sense, often introducing an interrogation. Jud. 6. 13 the Lord is with thee; וְיֵשׁ י' עִמָּנוּ וְלָמָּה *If Je. be with us, Why* . . . ? Ex. 2. 20 וְאַיּוֹ *Where is he?* Nu. 12. 14 ; 20. 3, 1 S. 10. 12 ; 15. 14, 2 S. 18. 11, 12, 23 ; 24. 3, 1 K. 2. 22, 2 K. 1. 10 ; 2. 9 ; 7. 19. Peculiar 2 S. 15. 34 עֶבֶד אָבִיךָ וַאֲנִי מֵאָז thy father's servant—*that was I* formerly, &c. In the specimens of letters preserved, the salutation and compliments appear omitted, and the letter begins וְעַתָּה *and now,* 2 K. 5. 6 ; 10. 2, as Ar. 'amma ba'du.

CIRCUMSTANTIAL CLAUSE

§ 137. The cir. cl. expresses some circumstance or concomitant of the principal action or statement. Such a circumstance will generally be concerning the chief subject (whether gramm. subj. or obj.) of the main action, but the subj. of cir. cl. may be different, provided what is said of it be circumstantial of the main action—whether modal of it or contemporaneous with it.

The cir. cl. differs from acc. of condition (§ 70) in being a proposition. It forms a real predication, subordinate to the principal sent. in meaning but co-ordinate in construction. Though often corresponding to the classical absolute cases the construction is different.

The cir. cl. may be nominal or verbal, though it is chiefly nominal, and even when verbal the order of words is that of the nominal sent. (§ 103). In such a clause the subj. is naturally prominent, hence it stands first, the order being— *vav, subj., pred.* This simple *vav* may need to be rendered variously, as *if, while, when, seeing, though*, with a verb, or *with* before a noun. Besides the *and* a pron. referring back to the subj. of the principal sent. usually connects the clauses (see exx. below). Occasionally the subj. is repeated from the main clause, Deu. 9. 15 *and the mountain*, Gen. 18. 17, 18, Jud. 8. 11, 1 K. 8. 14.

§ 138. (*a*) The cir. cl. may be nominal. Gen. 11. 4 נִבְנֶה מִגְדָּל וְרֹאשׁוֹ בַשָּׁמַיִם let us build a tower *with its head* in the heavens. 24. 15 behold Rebecca יֹצֵאת וְכַדָּהּ עַל־שִׁכְמָהּ coming out *with her pitcher* on her shoulder (lit. *and her pitcher was*, &c.). 1 S. 18. 23 הֲנְקַלָּה הִתְחַתֵּן בַּמֶּלֶךְ וְאָנֹכִי אִישׁ־רָשׁ is it a light thing to be son-in-law of the king *when I am a poor man*? Jer. 2. 37 תֵּצְאִי וְיָדַיִךְ עַל־רֹאשֵׁךְ thou shalt come out *with thy hands upon thy head*. Gen. 18. 12, 27; 20. 3; 24. 10; 37. 2; 44. 26, 30, Jos. 17. 14, Jud. 19. 27, Hos. 6. 4, Jer. 2. 11, Am. 3. 4–6.

(*b*) Naturally the graphic ptcp. is much used in such descriptive clauses. Is. 6. 1 I saw Adonai sitting וְשׁוּלָיו מְלֵאִים אֶת־הַהֵיכָל *with his train filling* the temple. 1 S. 4. 12 וַיָּרָץ אִישׁ וּמַדָּיו קְרֻעִים there ran a man *with his garments rent.* Gen. 15. 2 מַה־תִּתֶּן־לִי וְאָנֹכִי הוֹלֵךְ עֲרִירִי *seeing I go* childless? Is. 53. 7 נִגַּשׂ וְהוּא נַעֲנֶה he was oppressed, *though he was submissive*; cf. *v.* 12 *though* (while) *he bore.* Is. 11. 6 *a little child leading them.* Gen. 14. 13;

18. 1, 8, 10; 19. 1; 25. 26; 28. 12; 32. 32; 44. 14, Jud. 3. 20;
4. 1; 6. 11; 13. 9, 20, 1 S. 10. 5; 22. 6, 1 K. 1. 48; 22. 10,
Is. 49. 21; 60. 11, Nah. 2. 8.

(c) The cir. cl. may be verbal with subj. first. Gen. 24. 56
אַל־תְּאַחֲרוּ אֹתִי וַיהֹוָה הִצְלִיחַ דַּרְכִּי delay me not *when Je.
has prospered* my journey. 1 K. 1. 41 the guests heard
וְהֵם כִּלּוּ לֶאֱכֹל *as they had just finished dinner.* Gen. 26. 27
why are ye come to me וְאַתֶּם שְׂנֵאתֶם אֹתִי *when ye hate
me?* Ru. 1. 21. Jud. 16. 31 *he having judged.*—Gen. 18. 13;
24. 31, Ex. 33. 12, Jud. 4. 21; 8. 11, Jer. 14. 15. Gen. 34. 5,
Am. 3. 4–6.

§ 139. Small emphatic words like negatives may precede
the subj., *e.g.* in the frequent וְלֹא יָדְעוּ *unawares* (lit. and
they, &c., *do not know*), Is. 47. 11, Job 9. 5, cf. 24. 22, Ps. 35. 8,
Pr. 5. 6. So frequently with אֵין, Is. 17. 2 וְרָבְצוּ וְאֵין מַחֲרִיד
they shall lie down, *none making them afraid*, Lev. 26. 6.
Is. 13. 14 וְאֵין מְקַבֵּץ, Jer. 9. 21 וְאֵין מְאַסֵּף, 4. 4, 2 K. 9. 10,
Pr. 28. 1, Is. 45. 4, 5, cf. Pr. 3. 28. In particular, it is
characteristic to place the pred., when a prep. with suff., or
a prep. with its complement, before the subj. Jud. 3. 16
וַיַּעַשׂ חֶרֶב וְלָהּ שְׁנֵי פֵיוֹת he made a dagger *having two
edges.* 2 S. 16. 1 a pair of saddled asses וַעֲלֵיהֶם מָאתַיִם
לֶחֶם *with 200 loaves upon them.* Is. 6. 6 וַיָּעָף אֶחָד מִן
הַשְּׂרָפִים וּבְיָדוֹ רִצְפָּה there flew one of the S. *with a hot
stone in his hand.* 2 S. 20. 8, Ez. 40. 2, Am. 7. 7, Zech. 2. 5.
But also in other cases, Ps. 60. 13 וְשָׁוְא תְּשׁוּעַת אָדָם *for
vain is the help of man.* But cf. Ps. 149. 6.

Rem. 1. The nominal sent. seems in certain cases in-
verted, pred. standing first, particularly in statements of
weight, measure, &c. Gen. 24. 22 he took a nose ring
בֶּקַע מִשְׁקָלוֹ *its weight a beka.* Jud. 3. 16 he made a dagger
גֹּמֶד אָרְכָּהּ *its length a cubit.* The general rule in the nominal
sent. is that the determined word is subj.; if both be determined the more fully determined is subj. Cf. § 103.

The view of pred. and subj. was perhaps not always the same as ours, cf. Amr, Mu‘all. l. 31.

§ 140. The cir. cl., however, is frequently introduced without *and*. Ex. 12. 11 תֹּאכְלוּ אֹתוֹ מָתְנֵיכֶם חֲגֻרִים ye shall eat it *with your loins girt*. Jer. 30. 6 מַדּוּעַ רָאִיתִי כָל־גֶּבֶר יָדָיו עַל־חֲלָצָיו why see I every man *with his hands upon his loins?* Gen. 12. 8 וַיֵּט אָהֳלֹה בֵּית־אֵל מִיָּם he pitched his tent, *Bethel being on the west*. 32. 12 פֶּן־יָבוֹא וְהִכַּנִי אֵם עַל־בָּנִים lest he come and smite me, *mother with children*. Deu. 5. 4 פָּנִים בְּפָנִים דִּבֶּר *face to face* he spoke. Gen. 32. 31, Jud. 6. 22, Nu. 12. 8 *mouth to mouth*, Jer. 32. 4, 1 S. 26. 13, Jud. 15. 8, Is. 30. 33 ; 59. 19.

Especially with shortened expressions. 2 S. 18. 14 בְּלֵב אַב' עוֹדֶנּוּ חַי into the heart of Absalom *when still alive*. Ex. 22. 9, 13 אֵין רֹאֶה . . . וּמֵת and it die, *none seeing it*, Am. 5. 2, and often, as Ex. 21. 11 אֵין כֶּסֶף *without money*. Is. 47. 1 *throneless*, Jer. 2. 32 *numberless*. Hos. 3. 4 ; 7. 11. Ps. 88. 5. Gen. 43. 3, 5.

> Rem. 1. It is possible that such phrases as *face to face*, אַפַּיִם אַרְצָה *with face to the ground* Gen. 19 1, *mouth to mouth* and the like, may now be adverbial acc. Originally at any rate they were real propositions, *face was to face, faces were groundwards*, &c. So Ar. says, I spoke to him *fûhu* (nom.) 'ila fiyya, *his mouth* (*was*) to my mouth ; but also *fâhu* (acc.) 'ila fiyya, *with his mouth* to my mouth. Similarly in Gen. 43. 3 בִּלְתִּי, בִּלְתִּי אֲחִיכֶם אִתְּכֶם is a conj., not a prep., *except* your brother *be*, &c.

§ 141. The subordinate character of the cir. cl. is generally shown by its place *after* the principal sent. In some cases, however, the concomitant event is placed first, with the effect of greater vividness. Gen. 42. 35 וַיְהִי הֵם מְרִיקִים . . . וְהִנֵּה and it was, *they were emptying* their sacks, *and behold*, &c., *i.e.* as they were emptying, behold. 15. 17 וַיְהִי הַשֶּׁמֶשׁ בָּאָה

וְהִנֵּה and it was, *the sun had gone down, and behold, i.e.* the sun having gone down. 2 K. 2. 11; 8. 5; 13. 21; 19. 37; 20. 4, 1 S. 23. 26; 25. 20 (וַיְהִי = וְהָיָה, so 2 S. 6. 16), 1 K. 18. 7; 20. 39, 40. In ref. to fut. 1 K. 18. 12.

The relation of the two events (concomitant and principal) to one another is still more vividly expressed when the clauses containing them are placed parallel to one another, with no introductory formula like *and it was.* Gen. 44. 3 הַבֹּקֶר אוֹר וְהָאֲנָשִׁים שֻׁלְּחוּ *the morning broke, and the men were let go, i.e.* when the morning broke (had broken) the men, &c. 1 S. 9. 27 הֵמָּה יֹרְדִים וּשְׁמוּאֵל אָמַר *as they were coming down S. said.* Gen. 29. 9 עוֹדֶנּוּ מְדַבֵּר וְרָחֵל בָּאָה *as he was still speaking R. came.* Particularly when the subj. of both clauses is the same. Jud. 18. 3 הֵמָּה עִם־בֵּית מִיכָה וְהֵמָּה הִכִּירוּ *as they were at the house of Mic. they recognised.* Gen. 38. 25, 1 S. 9. 11.

Rem. 1. In some cases the accentuation wrongly makes the following noun or pron. subj. to the introductory וַיְהִי, *e.g.* 2 K. 20. 4, 1 K. 20. 40, Gen. 24. 15, 1 S. 7. 10, 1 K. 18. 7; other passages show that וַיְהִי is impersonal, 1 S. 25. 20, 2 K. 13. 20, 21, cf. 19. 37; 2 S. 13. 30.

Rem. 2. The construction is the same with or without the introductory formula. The second clause in the balanced sent. always begins with *vav*, the first most commonly without. It is the first cl. that to our modes of thought appears circumstantial. 1. When the first cl. has a perf. the two events were contemporaneous or the *circumstance* had *just* occurred when the main event happened. 2. When the first has a ptcp. or a nominal sent. equivalent, the main event occurred during the action expressed by the ptcp. 3. When both clauses have ptcp. the two actions, main and subordinate, were going on simultaneously. Some ex. of perf. in first cl. : Gen. 19. 23, cf. 27. 30 for a more precise way of stating that the circumstance had *jusi* happened (cf. Jud. 7. 19). Gen. 24. 15; 44. 3, 4, Ex. 10. 13, Jos.

2. 8 (טרם with impf. = perf., Gen. 24. 15), Jud. 3. 24 ; 15. 14 ;
18. 22, 1 S. 9. 5 ; 20. 36, 41, 2 S. 2. 24 ; 6. 16 ; 17. 24,
2 K. 20. 4.   Some ex. of ptcp. in first cl. : Jud. 19. 22 (11),
1 S. 7. 10 ; 9. 14, 27 ; 17. 23 ; 23. 26 ; 25. 20, 2 S. 13. 30 ;
20. 8, 1 K. 1. 14, 22 ; 14. 17 (? or, ptcp. = perf.) ; 18. 7 ;
20. 39, 40, 2 K. 2. 11, 23 ; 4. 5 ; 8. 5 ; 9. 25 ; 13. 21 ; 19. 37.
With עוֹד Gen. 29. 9, 1 K. 1. 14, 22, 42, 2 K. 6. 33, cf. Job
1. 16–18.—In 1 K. 13. 20 the consn. is unusual וַיְהִי הֵם יֹשְׁבִים
וַיְהִי דְבַר י, cf. the usual one 2 K. 20. 4.

Rem. 3. On the use of perf. in attributive and circ.
clauses where other languages would use ptcp. cf. § 41,
R. 3 ; on similar use of impf. § 44, R. 3.   The impf. is
much used in circ. cl., cf. Nu. 14. 3, 1 S. 18. 5 went out
prospering, Is. 3. 26 *sitting* on the ground, 5. 11 wine *in-
flaming* them, Jer. 4. 30 *beautifying thyself*, Ps. 50. 20
sattest *speaking*, Job 16. 8 *answering* to my face.   The
finite tense must be used with *neg.*, Lev. 1. 17 *not dividing*,
Job 29. 24 ; 31. 34 *not going out*.   In Ar. the circumstantial
impf. may express an accompanying action of the subj. or
one purposed by him, and Job 24. 14 יִקְטָל־עָנִי. seems = *to kill*,
lit. he will kill.   Perhaps 30. 28 is rather, I stand up *crying
out*, cf. Ps. 88. 11 ; 102. 14.   See § 82.

Obs.—The use of this *and* of circumstance is common
in language.

> And shall the figure of God's majesty
> Be judged, and he himself not present !
>
> How can ye chaunt, ye little birds,
> An' I sae weary, fu' o' care !
>
> Played me sic a trick,
> An' me the El'r's dochter !

RELATIVE SENTENCE

§ 142. The rel. sent. may be nominal or verbal, *e.g.* Deu.
1. 4 the Amorite אֲשֶׁר יוֹשֵׁב בְּחֶשְׁבּוֹן *who dwelt*.   The Engl.
relative sentence embraces various kinds of sentences, as—
(*a*) the proper rel. sent., Gen. 18. 8 he took בֶּן־הַבָּקָר אֲשֶׁר
עָשָׂה *the* calf *which he had made ready*, in which the ante-

cedent is determined; and (*b*) the attributive or descriptive
sent., as Gen. 49. 27 Benj. is זְאֵב יִטְרָף *a* wolf *which ravins*
(a ravining w.), in which the antecedent is indefinite.   In the
former class of sentences the word אֲשֶׁר is expressed, in the
descriptive and circumstantial sentences it is omitted.   But
the language does not strictly adhere to either side of the
rule, *e.g.* Jer. 13. 20 אַיֵּה הָעֵדֶר נִתַּן־לָךְ where is *the* flock
that was committed to thee?   Ex. 18. 20.   The omission of
אֲשֶׁר where it should stand occurs mostly in poetry and
elevated style.   On omission of retrospective pron. cf. § 9 *seq.*
In the following cases of omission of אֲשֶׁר it can be noted
whether the omission be according to the rule *a*, *b*, above,
or not.

§ 143. When the antecedent is expressed.—The אֲשֶׁר
may be omitted—(*a*) When the retrospective pron. is subj.,
and whether this pron. be expressed (implied in the verb)
or not.   Deu. 32. 15 וַיִּטֹּשׁ אֱלוֹהַּ עָשָׂהוּ he forsook God *who
made him*; *v.* 17 new gods *which* had lately come.   Jer.
13. 20; 20. 11; 31. 25, Is. 10. 3, 24; 30. 5, 6; 40. 20; 55. 13;
56. 2, and often in second half of Is., Mic. 2. 10, Song 1. 3,
Zeph. 3. 17, Job 31. 12.   Particularly in comparisons, Jer. 14.
8, 9; 23. 29; 31. 18, Hos. 6. 3; 11. 10, Ps. 38. 14; 42. 2;
49. 13; 83. 15; 125. 1, Job 7. 2; 11. 16, Lam. 3. 1, Hab.
2. 14.—So in nominal sent., Jer. 5. 15 גּוֹי אֵיתָן הוּא a nation
which is ancient.   Gen. 15. 13 בְּאֶרֶץ לֹא לָהֶם in a land
which is not theirs.   Gen. 39. 4, cf. *v.* 5, Hab. 1. 6, Ps. 58. 5,
Pr. 26. 17.

(*b*) When the retrosp. pron. is obj., whether it be expressed
or not.   Deu. 32. 17 אֱלֹהִים לֹא יְדָעוּם gods *whom* they
knew not, cf. Jer. 44. 3.   Is. 42. 16 בְּדֶרֶךְ לֹא יָדְעוּ in a way
which they know not.   Mic. 7. 1, Is. 6. 6; 15. 7; 55. 5, Ps.
9. 16; 18. 44; 118. 22, Job 21. 27.   And in comparisons; Nu.
24. 6 כַּאֲהָלִים נָטַע יהוה like aloes *which* Je. has planted.
Jer. 23. 9, Ps. 109. 19, Job 13. 28.

(c) When the retrosp. pron. is gen. by noun or prep.; Jer.
5. 15 גּוֹי לֹא־תֵדַע לְשׁוֹנוֹ a people *whose speech* thou shalt
not understand. 2. 6 בְּאֶרֶץ לֹא עָבַר בָּהּ אִישׁ *through which*
no one passed. Ps. 49. 14 זֶה דַרְכָּם כֵּסֶל לָמוֹ this is their
fate *who are confident.* Deu. 32. 37, Ex. 18. 20, Ps. 32. 2
with Jer. 17. 7, Job 3. 15. With omission of retrosp. pron.,
Is. 51. 1 הַצּוּר חֻצַּבְתֶּם the rock *out of which* ye were hewn,
cf. Job 38. 26.

§ 144. When אֲשֶׁר means *he-who*, &c., § 10.—In this case
אשר may also be omitted. Is. 41. 24 תּוֹעֵבָה יִבְחַר בָּכֶם
an abomination is *he-who* chooses you. Nu. 23. 8 מָה אֶקֹּב
לֹא קַבֹּה אֵל how shall I curse *him-whom* God has not
cursed! (next clause without pron.). Ps. 12. 6 אָשִׁית בְּיֵשַׁע
יָפִיחַ לוֹ I will set in safety *him-whom* they snort at, Is. 41.
2, 25.—Jer. 2. 8 אַחֲרֵי לֹא־יוֹעִילוּ הָלָכוּ after *those-which*
profit not they have gone, cf. *v.* 11. Ex. 4. 13 שְׁלַח בְּיַד
תִּשְׁלָח send *through* (by the hand of) *him-whom* thou wilt
send. Is. 65. 1 נִדְרַשְׁתִּי לְלוֹא שָׁאָלוּ I was to be inquired
of *by them-that* asked not, Jer. 2. 11.—Ps. 35. 15; 65. 5; 81. 6,
Job 24. 19; 34. 32, 1 Chr. 15. 12, 2 Chr. 1. 4, Jer. 8. 13, 2 Chr.
16. 9, Ps. 144. 2, Song 8. 5 *she that bore.* Lam. 1. 14 בִּידֵי לֹא
אוּכַל קוּם the hands *of those-whom* I cannot withstand.

Rem. 1. Such cases as 1 S. 10. 11 מַה־זֶּה הָיָה, 1 K. 13. 12
אֵי־זֶה הַדֶּרֶךְ הָלַךְ are probably to be construed : what is this
which has happened? which is the way *that* he went? but
in usage אשר is omitted; cf. Jud. 8. 1, Gen. 3. 13, 2 K.
3. 8. So usually Ar. *ma dha* what? The same consn. also
in מִי הוּא, &c., with omission of אשר, cf. 1 S. 26. 14, Job
4, 7 ; 13. 19, Is. 50. 9.

Rem. 2. Words of *time, place,* and occasionally of
manner, are apt to be put in cons. state before a clause,
which takes the place of a *gen.,* אשר being frequently omitted.
See the exx. § 25.

Rem. 3. Phrases like: a man, *whose name* was Job, are

usually made thus : אִישׁ וּשְׁמוֹ אִיּוֹב 1 S. 1. 1 ; 9. 1. 2 ; 17. 12,
2 S. 3. 7, &c. ; but occasionally אִיּוֹב שְׁמוֹ, a transposed
descriptive sentence ; Job 1. 1, 1 S. 17. 4, 23, 2 S. 20, 21.
1 K. 13. 2, Zech. 6. 12.   The antecedent is indefinite (1 S.
17. 4, 23 is doubtful owing to the obscurity of אִישׁ הַבֵּנַיִם),
and אֲשֶׁר seems nowhere expressed, though after a def. antecedent it might be, cf. Dan. 10. 1, and in Aram. 2. 26 ;
4. 5.—In cases of identification, as Gen. 14. 2, 8 Bela, *which*
is Zoar, the usage is בֶּלַע הִיא־צֹעַר, cf. *vv.* 3, 17, and often.
Similarly with persons, Jud. 7. 1, &c.—On the other hand,
in giving the geographical position of a place אֲשֶׁר is used.
Gen. 33. 18 ; 50. 10, 11, Jud. 18. 28, 1 S. 17. 1, 1 K. 15. 27,
1 Chr. 13. 6.

Rem. 4. The אֲשֶׁר is sometimes omitted with *and* and a
verb.   Mal. 2. 16 וְכִסָּה *and* (I hate) *him-who* covers. Is.
57. 3 וַתִּזְנֶה (seed of an adulterer) *and of her-who* committed
whoredom.   Am. 6. 1 וּבָאוּ *and they-to-whom* the house of
Is. comes (freq.).

Rem. 5. Some instances of omission of אֲשֶׁר in later
prose are, Ezr. 1. 5, Neh. 8. 10, 1 Chr. 15. 12 ; 29. 3, 2 Chr.
1. 4 ; 16. 9 ; 20. 22 ; 30. 19.—In 2 K. 25. 10 *rd.* prep. אֵת
before רַב with Jer. 52. 14 ; and 2 Chr. 34. 22 *rd.* אָמַר
after rel.

Rem. 6. The text Zeph. 3. 18 reads : those sorrowing
far away from the assembly will I gather, which (they) are
of thee, (thou) on whom reproach lay heavy (lit. was a
burden).   Well. suggests חרפה . . . מִשְּׂאֵת *so that no reproach
be taken up* against her.

TEMPORAL SENTENCE

§ 145. 1. The prep. (many of which are nouns in cons.
state), *e.g.* בְּ, כְּ, לְ, מִן, לִפְנֵי, אַחֲרֵי, עַד, &c., are joined with
the *nominal* form of the verb, the inf. cons.   2. These prep.
become conjunctions when the rel. כִּי, אֲשֶׁר, is added to
them, and are then joined with the *finite* forms of the verb.
3. The rel. element אֲשֶׁר, however, is often omitted, though
not usually after strict cons. forms like לִפְנֵי, &c.

13

(a) *When* may be expressed by בְּ, כְּ, with inf., or by כִּי, כַּאֲשֶׁר with finite. Gen. 39. 18 כַּהֲרִימִי קוֹלִי *when* I lifted up, 24. 30.—4. 8 בִּהְיוֹתָם בַּשָּׂדֶה *when* they were in the field, 45. 1.—Hos. 11. 1 כִּי נַעַר יִשׂ׳ *when* Isr. *was* a child, Gen. 44. 24, Jos. 17. 13.—Gen. 24. 22 כַּאֲשֶׁר כִּלּוּ לִשְׁתּׂת *when* they had done drinking, Jud. 8. 33; 11. 5. The form כְּמוֹ is more poetical, Gen. 19. 15. After designations of time the simple אֲשֶׁר may be *when*, Hos. 2. 15, Ps. 95. 9, cf. § 9 *c*. Also אִם *if, when*, with freq. actions, Gen. 38. 9.

(b) *After*, by אַחֲרֵי with inf., or אַחֲרֵי אֲשֶׁר with finite. Gen. 14. 17 אַחֲרֵי שׁוּבוֹ מֵהַכּוֹת *after his returning*, 13. 14; 24. 36.—Deu. 24. 4 אַחֲרֵי אֲשֶׁר הֻטַּמָּאָה *after* she has been defiled. Jos. 9. 16, Jud. 11. 36; 19. 23, 2 S. 19. 31.

(c) *Before*, by לִפְנֵי with inf., Gen. 13. 10 לִפְנֵי שַׁחֵת י׳ אֶת־סְדֹם *before* Je. destroyed Sodom, . 36. 31, 1 S. 9. 15, 2 S. 3. 35.—Very often by בְּטֶרֶם, usually with impf. even when referring to past; Gen. 27. 33 בְּטֶרֶם תָּבוֹא *before* thou camest, 37. 18; 41. 50. Of fut., Gen. 27. 4; 45. 28. Occasionally with *perf.*, Ps. 90. 2, Pr. 8. 25 (*inf.* Zeph. 2. 2, text dubious). The simple טֶרֶם properly *not yet* (usually with impf., Gen. 2. 5, Ex. 9. 30; 10. 7), has also sense of *before*, with *impf.*, Ex. 12. 34, Jos. 3. 1, Is. 65. 24.

(d) *Since*, מֵאָז, with perf., Ex. 9. 24 מֵאָז הָיְתָה לְגוֹי *since it became* a nation. Gen. 39. 5, Ex. 5. 23, Jos. 14. 10, Is. 14. 8, Jer. 44. 18. Once with inf., Ex. 4. 10. As prep. with noun, Ru. 2. 7, Ps. 76. 8.—As adv. *formerly, long ago*, &c. Is. 16. 13; 44. 8; 45. 21; 48. 3, 5, 2 S. 15. 34, Ps. 93. 2, Pr. 8. 22.

(e) *Then*, אָז, with perf. 1 K. 8. 12 אָז אָמַר שְׁלֹמֹה *then* said Sol., Gen. 49. 4, Jud. 5. 11, 2 S. 21. 17. Not uncommonly with impf., Deu. 4. 41, 1 K. 8. 1; 9. 11; 11. 7, cf. § 45. On אָז in apod., cf. § 131, R. 2. Jos. 22. 31, 2 K. 5. 3, 1 Chr. 14. 15.

(*f*) *Until*, עַד, with infin., or עַד אֲשֶׁר ,עַד כִּי ,עַד אִם,
עַד אֲשֶׁר אִם with finite, with ref. to past or fut. Gen. 27. 45
עַד־שׁוּב אַף־אָחִיךָ *till* thy brother's anger *turn away*. 27. 44
עַד אֲשֶׁר־תָּשׁוּב חֲמַת אָחִיךָ *till* thy brother's rage *shall turn
away*. Gen. 29. 8, Ex. 23. 30, Deu. 3. 20, Jud. 4. 24, 1 S.
22. 3; 30. 4, 1 K. 17. 17.—Ex. of עַד כִּי Gen. 26. 13; 41. 49;
49. 10, 2 S. 23. 10. Of עַד אִם Gen. 24. 19, 33, Is. 30. 17.
Of עַד אֲשֶׁר אִם Gen. 28. 15, Nu. 32. 17, Is. 6. 11. By falling
away of rel. the simple עַד often stands with finite, Gen.
38. 11, Jos. 2. 22, 1 S. 1. 22, 2 K. 7. 3, Ps. 110. 1, Pr. 7. 23.

(*g*) *As often as*, כְּמִדֵי (דֵּי) with inf., 1 S. 1. 7; 18. 30, 1 K.
14. 28, 2 K. 4. 8, Is. 28. 19; once impf. Jer. 20. 8.

Rem. 1. The word *after* in some cases = *seeing that*
Gen. 41. 39, Jos. 7. 8, Jud. 11. 36, 2 S. 19. 31, cf. Ezr.
9. 13 (common in post-biblical Heb.). *After* has also a
pregnant sense = *after the death of*, or *departure of* (Ar.
ba'd). Gen. 24. 67 אַחֲרֵי אִמּוֹ *after his mother*. Job 21. 21,
Pr. 20. 7. Frequent in Ecc., אַחֲרַי *when I am gone*. Cf.
לְפָנַי *before I came*, Gen. 30. 30. In Lev. 25. 48, 1 S. 5. 9
אַחֲרֵי with finite tense. Jos. 2. 7 אַחֲרֵי כַּאֲשֶׁר *after when*,
pleonastic, if text right.

Rem. 2. Is. 17. 14 בטרם construed with noun. Ps. 129. 6
שֶׁקַּדְמַת *before* is unique.

Rem. 3. Some adverbs of time are : *when?* מָתַי, Gen.
30. 30; *how long, till when?* עַד מָתַי; with *neg.*, *how long . . .
not?* 2 S. 2. 26, Hos. 8. 5, Zech. 1. 12.—*still, yet*, עוֹד.
The noun may be in *casus pend.*, resumed by suff., Gen.
18. 22 ואב' עוֹדֶנּוּ עֹמֵד and Abr. *was still standing*, 1 S. 13. 7,
cf. Gen. 45. 26, 28 ; 25. 6. With ptcp. § 100.

Rem. 4. On the expression of *when, while* by the circums.
clause, cf. § 137. On the expression of sentences like *and
when* thou overtakest them *thou shalt say* (Gen. 44. 4) by
two *vav perfs*. cf. § 132 ; and such sentences as *and when*
he overtook them *he said* (44. 6) by two *vav impfs*. § 51,
R. 1. In general cf. the circums. cl., the conditional sent.,
and sections on vav perf. and vav impf.

SUBJECT AND OBJECT SENTENCE

§ 146. It is usually only clauses containing an infin. that are subject, and mostly to a nominal pred. (§ 90, R. 1). In a few cases a clause introduced by אֲשֶׁר, כִּי *that*, is the subj. to a nominal sent., 2 S. 18. 3, Lam. 3. 27, Ecc. 5. 4 (all with pred. *good, better*).

The object sent. is mostly introduced by כִּי *that*, and may be nominal or verbal. 1 S. 3. 8 וַיָּבֶן עֵלִי כִּי י' קֹרֵא לַנַּעַר and E. perceived *that Je. was calling* the child, Gen. 3. 11; 6. 5.—Gen. 8. 11 וַיֵּדַע כִּי קַלּוּ הַמַּיִם knew *that the waters were abated*; 15. 8; 16. 4; 29. 12; in a long sent. כִּי repeated, 1 K. 20. 31.—Not so commonly in earlier books, but often in later, אֲשֶׁר *that.* 1 S. 18. 15 וַיַּרְא שָׁאוּל אֲשֶׁר הוּא מַשְׂכִּיל מְאֹד and S. saw *that he prospered* greatly. Ex. 11. 7, Deu. 1. 31, 1 K. 22. 16, Is. 38. 7, Jer. 28. 9, Ez. 20. 26, Neh. 8. 14, 15, Est. 3. 4; 4. 11; 6. 2, Ecc. 6. 10; 7. 29; 9. 1, Dan. 1. 8. Also אֶת אֲשֶׁר *the fact, circumstance that, how that.* 2 K. 20. 3 זְכָר־נָא אֵת אֲשֶׁר הִתְהַלַּכְתִּי remember *how that I have walked.* 2 S. 11. 20 הֲלוֹא יְדַעְתֶּם אֵת אֲשֶׁר־יֹרוּ *that they would shoot?* Deu. 9. 7, Jos. 2. 10, 1 S. 2. 22; 24. 19. So 1 K. 19. 1 וְאֵת כָּל־אֲשֶׁר הָרַג, אֵת כל אשר *how all* he had slain.

It is common for the logical subj. of the object sent. to be attracted as obj. into the governing clause. Gen. 49. 15 וַיַּרְא מְנֻחָה כִּי טוֹב he saw *rest that it was good* (that rest was). 1 K. 5. 17 יָדַעְתָּ אֶת־דָּוִד אָבִי כִּי לֹא יָכֹל *that my father D. was unable.* Gen. 31. 5, Ex. 2. 2, 2 S. 17. 8. Gen. 1. 4, 31, Nu. 32. 23.

Rem. 1. After the verb *say*, &c., the words of the speaker are often quoted directly. Gen. 12. 12 וְאָמְרוּ אִשְׁתּוֹ זֹאת they shall say, "this is his wife," *v.* 19; 20. 2, 13; 26. 7; 43. 7, Jud. 9. 48, 1 S. 10. 19, 2 S. 3. 13, 1 K. 2. 8, Ps. 10. 11. Or with some equivalent for *say*, Ps. 10. 4 " there is no

God" are all their thoughts. But there is a tendency to pass into the semi-oblique form, as Gen. 12. 13 אָמְרִי־נָא אֲחֹתִי אָתְּ say, *thou art my sister*. Gen. 41. 15, 2 S. 21. 4, Hos. 7. 2, Ps. 10. 13; 50. 21; 64. 6; Job 19, 28; 22. 17; 35. 3, 14. This is usual in language—

> Die Welt ist dumm, die Welt ist blind,
> Wird täglich abgeschmackter!
> Sie spricht von dir, mein schönes Kind:
> Du hast keinen guten Charakter.

Rem. 2. Even when words are given directly they are often introduced by כִּי (כִי recitativum). 1 K. 1. 30 I sware saying כִּי שְׁ׳ בְּנֵךְ יִמְלֹךְ אַחֲרַי "Sol. thy son shall reign after me." Jud. 6. 16 וַיֹּאמֶר י׳ כִּי אֶהְיֶה עִמָּךְ Je. said, "I will be with thee." Gen. 29. 33, Jos. 2. 24, Jud. 11. 13, 1 S. 13. 11, 1 K. 11. 22; 21. 6, 2 K. 8. 13, 1 Chr. 4. 9; 21. 18; 29. 14. Cf. Gen. 45. 26. Jud. 10. 10, where כי only in second clause. —Rarer אֲשֶׁר recit.; 1 S. 15. 20, 2 S. 1. 4, Neh. 4. 6, Ps. 10. 6 (last words, though the sense, *one-who* shall not have misfortune, is good). Ps. 118. 10—12, 128. 2 are hardly ex. (Hitz.), cf. Is. 7. 9, Job 28. 1. The clause with כי as well as the direct quotation in R. 1 occupies the place of obj. in the sentence.

Rem. 3. The כִי of obj. sent. is sometimes omitted, Ps. 9. 21 may know אֱנוֹשׁ הֵמָּה *that they are men*. Am. 5. 12, Is. 48. 8, Zech. 8. 23, Job 19. 25, cf. 2 K. 9. 25.

Rem. 4. A clause with *and* occasionally takes the place of an obj. sent. Gen. 30. 27 נִחַשְׁתִּי וַיְבָרְכֵנִי י׳ I have divined *and* = *that* Je. has blessed. 47. 6 אִם־יָדַעְתָּ וְיֶשׁ־בָּם if thou knowest *and there be* = *that there are* among them. Dan. 2. 13 the law went out *and* = *that* the wise men were to be slain (ptcp.). Nu. 14. 21, Is. 43. 12.—A usual brachylogy occurs with *command*, Gen. 42. 25 וַיְצַו יו׳ וַיְמַלְאוּ Jos. commanded (to fill) *and they filled*, Jon. 2. 11, cf. Am. 6. 11; 9. 9. In Ar., God decreed *that* the Christians *were defeated*, for, should be defeated and they were defeated.

THE CAUSAL SENTENCE

§ 147. A lighter way of suggesting causality is afforded by *and*, especially in circums. clauses. Ex. 23. 9, ye shall not oppress a stranger וְאַתֶּם יְדַעְתֶּם נֶפֶשׁ הַגֵּר *because your- selves know* the feelings of a stranger; cf. Neh. 2. 3. Cf. § 137.

Commonly used is כִּי *because*, Gen. 8. 9. Similarly, אֲשֶׁר Gen. 30. 18, 1 S. 26. 16, 1 K. 3. 19, 2 K. 17. 4, (both, Zech. 11. 2), Jer. 20. 17.—Also the prep. יַעַן coupled with rel. אֲשֶׁר or כִּי. Is. 7. 5 יַעַן כִּי־יָעַץ רָעָה *because he has purposed* evil. The phrase is affected by Is., 3. 16; 8. 6; 29. 13; elsewhere, Nu. 11. 20, 1 K. 13. 21; 21. 29 (always with perf.). Very common יַעַן אֲשֶׁר לֹא הָלְכוּ עִמִּי 30. 22 S. 1 ;יַעַן אֲשֶׁר *because they went not* with me. Gen. 22. 16, Deu. 1. 36, Jud. 2. 20, 1 K. 3. 11; 14. 7, 15 (always with perf.—except Ez. 12. 12?). Also יַעַן simply as conj., Nu. 20. 12 יַעַן לֹא הֶאֱמַנְתֶּם *because* ye believed not, 1 K. 14. 13, 2 K. 22. 19. As a prep. with inf., Is. 30. 12 יַעַן מָאָסְכֶם *because of your rejecting*, 37. 29, Jer. 5. 14; 7. 13; 23. 38, Am. 5. 11, &c.— only in the prophets and 1 K. 21. 20.

Rem. 1. Several prep. have causal force, as בְּ, מִן, עַל, תַּחַת, mostly in composition with אֲשֶׁר or כִּי. Gen. 39. 9 בַּאֲשֶׁר אַתְּ אִשְׁתּוֹ *because thou art* his wife; *v.* 23. Is. 43. 4 מֵאֲשֶׁר יָקַרְתָּ *because thou art dear.* 2 S. 3. 30 עַל אֲשֶׁר הֵמִית *because he slew.* Deu. 29. 24, 1 K. 9. 9; neg., עַל אֲשֶׁר לֹא 2 K. 18. 12; 22. 13. So עַל כִּי Jud. 3. 12, Deu. 31. 17 (nominal sent.), Ps. 139. 14. With rel. omitted in neg. sent., Gen. 31. 20, Ps. 119. 136. Often עַל with inf., Am. 1. 3, 6, 9, 11, &c.—So תַּחַת אֲשֶׁר, Deu. 28. 47 תַּחַת אֲשֶׁר לֹא עָבַדְתָּ *because thou hast not served.* 1 S. 26. 21, 2 K. 22. 17, Is. 53. 12. So תַּחַת כִּי, Deu. 4. 37.—Of the same meaning is עֵקֶב אֲשֶׁר, Gen. 22. 18; 26. 5, 2 S. 12. 6 (עַל אֲשֶׁר in next clause). So עֵקֶב כִּי, Am. 4. 12, 2 S. 12. 10. Without rel., Nu. 14. 24. For other forms cf. Deu. 23. 5, Jer. 3. 8.

Rem. 2. Repetition of יַעַן for emphasis, Lev. 26. 43, Ez. 13. 10, cf. 36. 3.

FINAL OR PURPOSE SENTENCE

§ 148. Lighter ways of expressing purpose are—(*a*) The use of וְ (simple *vav*) with juss., coh., *e.g.* after an imper., or anything with the meaning of imper., as juss., cohort. Gen. 24. 14 הַטִּי־נָא כַדֵּךְ וְאֶשְׁתֶּה let down thy pitcher *that I may drink*. Cf. Is. 5. 19 after לְמַעַן in first clause. Similarly after optative, neg., and interrog. sentences. See §§ 62, 63. In this case the *neg.* purpose is expressed by וְלֹא with impf., or sometimes לֹא simply (בַּל in poetry, Is. 14. 21).

(*b*) The inf. cons. with לְ. Jud. 3. 1 לְנַסּוֹת בָּם אֶת־יִשׂ׳ *in order to prove* Israel by them. The neg. purpose in this case is expressed by לְבִלְתִּי. Gen. 4. 15 לְבִלְתִּי הַכּוֹת־אֹתוֹ כָל־מֹצְאוֹ *that* whoever found him *might not kill him*. Gen. 38. 9. Cf. § 95.

§ 149. More formal telic particles are—לְמַעַן אֲשֶׁר with impf., Jer. 42. 6 לְמַעַן אֲשֶׁר יִיטַב־לָנוּ *that it may be well with us*; oftener לְמַעַן simply, with impf. or inf. cons., Gen. 27. 25 לְמַעַן תְּבָרֶכְךָ נַפְשִׁי *in order that* my soul may bless thee. Jud. 2. 22 לְמַעַן נַסּוֹת בָּם *in order to prove* by them, cf. simple לְ inf., Jud. 3. 1 (in *b* above). Jud. 3. 2, Jos. 11. 20.—Gen. 18. 19, Lev. 17. 5, 2 S. 13. 5.—Gen. 12. 13, Ex. 4. 5, Deu. 4. 1, Hos. 8. 4, Is. 41. 20.—Gen. 37. 22, 1 K. 11. 36, Am. 2. 7, &c. The simple אֲשֶׁר is also common, Deu. 4. 10 אֲשֶׁר יִלְמְדוּן לְיִרְאָה אֹתִי *that they may learn* to fear me. Nu. 23. 13, Deu. 4. 40; 6. 3 (cf. *v*. 2); 32. 46. The neg. clause is best made by אֲשֶׁר לֹא, Gen. 11. 7, Ex. 20. 26; but also by למען אשר לא, Deu. 20. 18, Nu. 17. 5, and by לְמַעַן לֹא, Ez. 19. 9; 26. 20, Ps. 119. 11, 80; 125. 3, Zech. 12. 7.

In the same sense בַּעֲבוּר אֲשֶׁר with impf., Gen. 27. 10; more usually בַּעֲבוּר simply with impf., Gen. 27. 4, or inf.

cons., 2 S. 10. 3.—Gen. 21. 30; 46. 34, Ex. 9. 14; 19. 9.—
Ex. 9. 16, 1 S. 1. 6, 2 S. 18. 18.

On פֶּן *lest, that not*, cf. § 127 c.

Rem. 1. The form לְמַעַן לְ Ez. 21. 20; so בַּעֲבוּר לְ 1 Chr.
19. 3.   On the other hand לְבַעֲבוּר 2 S. 14. 20; 17. 14.—Jos.
4. 24 *rd.* לְמַעַן יִרְאָתָם inf.

Rem. 2. In Ez. 13. 3 וּלְבִלְתִּי רָאוּ is not telic, but probably
means, *and after that which they have not seen*; possibly
וּגְבֻלֹתַי should be *rd.* = לֹא רָאוּ (1 S. 20. 26).   In Ez. 20. 9, 14,
22 הֵחֵל is inf. niph.—Jer. 27. 18 בֹּאוּ seems euphonic con-
traction for impf., cf. 42. 10; 23. 14 should perhaps be
pointed in the same way שֵׁבוּ = impf.   Ex. 20. 20, 2 S. 14. 14.

Rem. 3. The particles לְמַעַן, &c. are always telic, and do
not express merely result.   But sometimes the purpose
seems to animate the action rather than the agent, Am.
2. 7, Hos. 8. 4, Mic. 6. 16, Ps. 30. 13; 51. 6.

Rem. 4. Peculiar, Deu. 33. 11 מִן־יְקוּמוּן *that they rise not
up* (= מֵאֲשֶׁר).   Ps. 59. 14 וְאֵינֵמוֹ . . . כַּלֵּה consume . . . *that
they be no more*, cf. Job 3. 9 וְאַיִן.

CONSEQUENTIAL SENTENCE

§ 150. Lighter ways of expressing consequence are the
use of *vav impf.* and *vav perf.*   Also use of simple vav וְ
with impf. (juss.) after neg. sent., as Nu. 23. 19 לֹא אִישׁ
אֵל וִיכַזֵּב *God is not a man so that he should lie.*   So
interrog. sent., Hos. 14. 10.

More formal particles of consequence are כִּי *that,* אֲשֶׁר
that, so that.   2 K. 5. 7 הָאֱלֹהִים אָנִי כִּי־זֶה שֹׁלֵחַ אֵלַי *am I
God, that this person sends to me?*   And often in questions,
Gen. 20. 10, Ex. 3. 11, Nu. 16. 11, Job 6. 11; 7. 12, Ps. 8. 5.—
Gen. 40. 15 I have done nothing כִּי־שָׂמוּ אֹתִי בַּבּוֹר *that they
should have put.*   With אֲשֶׁר, 2 K. 9. 37 אֲשֶׁר לֹא־יֹאמְרוּ זֹאת
אִיזָבֶל *so that they shall not say,* This is Jez.   Gen. 22. 14,
Deu. 28. 27, 51, Mal. 3. 19, Ps. 95. 11, 1 K. 3. 12, 13.—Ez.

36. 27 וְעָשִׂיתִי אֵת אֲשֶׁר תֵּלֵכוּ I will cause *that ye shall walk* (sent. of consequence construed as object sent.).

COMPARATIVE SENTENCE

§ 151. This form of sent. has usually כַּאֲשֶׁר in prot. and כֵּן in apod.   Gen. 41. 13 כַּאֲשֶׁר פָּתַר־לָנוּ כֵּן הָיָה *as* he interpreted to us, *so* it was.   Ex. 1. 12, Jud. 1. 7, Is. 31. 4; 52. 14, 15; 65. 8, Ps. 48. 9; cf. transposed order, Gen. 18. 5, Ex. 10. 10, 2 S. 5. 25.—Or כְּ with inf. or noun in prot., Hos. 4. 7 כְּרֻבָּם כֵּן חָטְאוּ־לִי *as* they multiplied, *so* they sinned. Ps. 48. 11; 123. 2, Pr. 26. 1, 8, 18, 19, 1 S. 9. 13 (temporal).

In the prot. כאשר may be omitted.   Hos. 11. 2 קָרְאוּ לָהֶם כֵּן הָלְכוּ *as* (the more) they called them, *so* they went away.   Jud. 5. 15, Jer. 3. 20, Is. 55. 9, Ps. 48. 6.   In vigorous style the compar. particle may be omitted both in prot. and apod., Is. 62. 5.   The two clauses are then often equated by *vav*, especially in proverbial comparisons.   Prov. 26. 14 the door turns on its hinges וְעָצֵל עַל־מִטָּתוֹ *and* (so) a sluggard on his bed.   Pr. 11. 16; 17. 3; 25. 3, 20, 25; 26. 7, 9, 21, Job 5. 7; 12. 11; 14. 11, 12.   And sometimes without *and*, Pr. 25. 26, 28, Job 24. 19.

Rem. 1.   In some passages כֵּן *so* expresses the corresponding immediateness of the result or consequence of the prot. Ps. 48. 6 they saw *so* they feared (as soon as they saw, &c.), cf. Nah. 1. 12, 1 K. 20. 40.

Rem. 2.   With כְּ ... כְּ or וּכְ ... כְּ the first word is usually compared to the second, *so . . . as*.   Gen. 44. 18 כָמוֹךָ כְּפַרְעֹה thou art *as* Ph. (*so* thou *as* Ph.), 18. 25 כַּצַּדִּיק כָּרָשָׁע the righteous *like* the wicked, Hos. 4. 9, 2 Chr. 18. 3. But sometimes the reverse, *as . . . so*, 1 S. 30. 24, Jud. 8. 18, Is. 24. 2, Jos. 14. 11.

DISJUNCTIVE SENTENCE

§ 152. The conj. *and* often expresses our *or, nor, e.g.* after a *neg.*, the neg. denying the whole combination of words.

Gen. 45. 6 אֵין חָרִישׁ וְקָצִיר *neither* earing *nor* harvest.   1 K.
17. 1 אִם יִהְיֶה טַל וּמָטָר *there shall not be* dew *or* rain.
Gen. 19. 35, Nu. 23. 19, Deu. 5. 14, Jud. 6. 4, Is. 10. 14, 2 K.
5. 25, Ps. 37. 25 ; 129. 7.   Or more strongly וְגַם, Jud. 2. 10
לֹא יָדְעוּ אֶת־יְ׳ וְגַם אֶת־הַמַּעֲשֶׂה *nor yet* the work, 1 S.
16. 8, cf. 28. 6.   The conjunctive *both . . . and* becomes disjunctive *neither . . . nor* when preceded by *neg.*, § 136.

The disjunctive *or* is expressed by אוֹ, Gen. 24. 49 עַל־יָמִין
אוֹ עַל־שְׂמֹאל to the right *or* to the left.   44. 8 אֵיךְ נִגְנֹב כֶּסֶף
אוֹ זָהָב how should we steal *silver or gold*?   Gen. 24. 50 ;
44. 19, Ex. 5. 3 ; 21. 18, 28, 32, 33, 37, Deu. 13. 2, Jud. 21. 22,
1 S. 2. 14.

When repeated, אוֹ . . . אוֹ is *whether . . . or* (sive . . . sive).
Ex. 21. 31 אוֹ־בֵן יִגַּח אוֹ־בַת יִגַּח *whether* it gore a boy *or* a
girl, Lev. 5. 2.   In the same sense אִם . . . אִם, Ex. 19. 13
אִם בְּהֵמָה אִם אִישׁ לֹא יִחְיֶה *whether* beast *or* man, it shall
not live.   Deu. 18. 3, 2 S. 15. 21.   So אִם . . . וְאִם, Gen.
31. 52, Jer. 42. 6, Pr. 20. 11.   Less commonly וְ . . . וְ, Ex.
21. 16.

RESTRICTIVE, EXCEPTIVE, ADVERSATIVE SENTENCES

§ 153. Restrictive particles are אַךְ, רַק *only, howbeit.*
Gen. 18. 32 אַךְ הַפַּעַם *only* this time.   Ex. 10. 17, Jud.
6. 39 ; 16. 28.   Gen. 27. 13 אַךְ שְׁמַע בְּקוֹלִי *only, however,*
listen to my voice.   Gen. 20. 12 *only not.*   Ex. 12. 16, Nu.
22. 20, 1 S. 8. 9 (אַךְ כִּי) ; 12. 20 ; 18. 8 ; 20. 39, 1 K. 17. 13.
The use of רַק is similar.   Gen. 6. 5 ; 14. 24 ; 24. 8, Deu. 2. 28,
Jud. 14. 16, 1 S. 1. 13, 1 K. 14. 8, Am. 3. 2.   Both combined,
Nu. 12. 2 הֲרַק אַךְ בְּמֹשֶׁה דִּבֶּר יְ׳.   Similarly אֶפֶס, Nu. 22. 35,
cf. *v.* 20 ; 23. 13.   On the affirmative force of אַךְ &c., cf. § 118.

§ 154. Particles modifying in the way of exception some-
thing preceding are, בִּלְתִּי or בִּלְתִּי אִם *saving that,* אֶפֶס כִּי *saving*
alone, כִּי אִם *except.*   Am. 9. 8 אֶפֶס כִּי לֹא אַשְׁמִיד *saving*

that I will not destroy.   Nu. 13. 28, Deu. 15. 4, Jud. 4. 9.
And אֶפֶס simply, 2 S. 12. 14.[1]—Am. 3. 3 shall two walk
together בִּלְתִּי אִם נוֹעָדוּ *except* they have met?   Gen. 43. 3
בִּלְתִּי אֲחִיכֶם אִתְּכֶם *except* your brother be with you, Is.
10. 4.   There is often ellipse of the verb or its equivalent,
Gen. 47. 18 *except our* bodies, Jud. 7. 14.—Am. 3. 7 Je. doeth
nothing כִּי אִם־גָּלָה סוֹדוֹ *except* he have revealed his
counsel.   Gen. 32. 27 כִּי אִם־בֵּרַכְתָּנִי *except* thou bless me.
Ru. 3. 18, Is. 55. 10, Lev. 22. 6.   And with ellipse or continuation of the verb, Gen. 28. 17 ; 39. 6, 9 *except* the bread,
except thee, 1 S. 30. 17, 2 K. 4. 2.   Naturally *except* chiefly
follows a neg. or interrog. with neg. force, Mic. 6. 8, Is. 42. 19.

§ 155. The simple *vav* is often used where we employ
adversative particles.   Ps. 2. 6 וַאֲנִי נָסַכְתִּי *but* I have set.
Gen. 17. 5 וְהָיָה שִׁמְךָ *but* thy name shall be.   Gen. 2. 17, 20;
3. 3; 37. 30; 42. 10, Ecc. 11. 9 *but know*.   A more pro-
nounced adversative is אוּלָם, וְאוּלָם *but, howbeit*.   Gen.
28. 19, Ex. 9. 16, Nu. 14. 21, 1 K. 20. 23, Mic. 3. 8, Job 2. 5 ;
5. 8; 11. 5 ; 13. 3, 4; 14. 18.   So גַּם is a correlative adversative, Am. 4. 6, 7 וְגַם אֲנִי נָתַתִּי *and I on my part*.   Gen.
20. 6, Jud. 2. 21, Ps. 52. 7, Job 7. 11, Pr. 1. 26.

After a neg. *but* is expressed by כִּי אִם, Gen. 32. 29
לֹא יַעֲקֹב . . . כִּי אִם יִשְׂרָאֵל *not* Jacob *but* Israel.   1 S. 21. 5,
2 K. 23. 9, Jer. 16. 14, 15.   Or simply by כִּי, Gen. 45. 8
לֹא אַתֶּם שְׁלַחְתֶּם כִּי א' *it is not you* who sent *but* God.
1 K. 21. 15, 2 Chr. 20. 15.

---

[1] When כִּי belongs to a phrase it may be omitted before another כִּי with
a different sense, or the one כִּי serves both uses, *e.g.* אַף כִּי *how much more*,
&c. may = אַף כִּי *how much more, when*, 2 S. 4. 11, 1 S. 21. 6; 23. 3,
2 K. 5. 13, Pr. 21. 27.

INDEX OF PASSAGES REFERRED TO

1 SAMUEL	§§	2 SAMUEL	§§	2 SAMUEL	§§
28 14	73	11 11	120 R 2, 121	19 2	51 R 4
16	45 R 1	12	50 b	7	131
29 3	6 R 2	17	29 a, 102	8	40 b, 109, 132 R 2
10	132 a	20	146	20	91 R 2
30 2	41 R 3, 48 c	25	44 a, 72 R 4	21	71 R 1
6	109	12 4	32 R 2	25	9 c, 96 R 3
17	3 R 3	14	154	44	34 R 2
21	37 f	16	54 R 1	20 6	128 R 4
22	24 c, 147	18	53 b, 126 R 4	8	139
24	151 R 2	21	70 a	10	71 R 3, 114
		22	43 R 1	12	100 R 4
2 SAMUEL		13 12	117	19	28 R 6, 126 R 5
1 4	146 R 2	15	67 b	20	117 R 1
6	24 R 3, 86 a	17	4	21 3	65 d
9	22 R 1, 28 R 3	18	58 R 1	4	1 R 1, 41 R 3
21	100 R 3, 128 R 5	20	136 R 1	6	65 R 2, 79
22	44 R 1	25	65 a	9	36 R 4, 68
23	33, 136 R 1	26	132 R 2	22 14	65 R 6
24	98 a, 99	30	141 R 1	24	51 R 7
25	117	31	98 R 1	33	29 R 4
2 9	29 R 6	39	29 R 1	36	90 R 1
23	71 R 3, 101 R d	14 5	47, 118	23 3	71 R 2
27	119, 120 R 5, 131 R 2	10	55 c, 56, 99	4	128 R 3
32	69 a	11	101 R c	5	2
3 1	86 R 4	14	43 c, 149 R 2	6	22 R 3
9	120 R 4, 120 R 5	19	94	11	28 R 5
13	107 R 1, 146 R 1	20	149 R 1	15	135
16	86 R 4	25	93	17	117 R 1
24	86 c	32	90 R 1	24 3	38 R 5, 113, 136 R 1
33	43 b	34	135	13	29 d, 90 R 1, 116 R 1
34	91 R 1, 100 R 3	15 4	135	14	62
35	120 R 5	10	51 R 1	24	29 d, 86 a
39	136 R 1	12	86 R 4	1 KINGS	
4 1	113	21	25, 120 R 5, 152	1 1, 2	109
8	17 R 2	23	67 R 3, 115	2	55 a, 63, 65 R 2, 108
10	94	30	100 f	4	34
11	72 R 4, 154 n.	31	78 R 8	5	37 R 1
5 2	19 R 3	32	98 R 1	6	1 R 1, 101 R c, 108 R 1
8	98 b	33	130 b	12	65 d, 67 b
10	24 R 6, 86 R 4	34	130 c, 136 R 1	13	83 R 4
19	86 a, 126 R 2	37	45 R 2	20	106 b, 125
24	41 c, 72 R 4	16 1	139	21, 34	114
25	151	4	40 b	26	1
6 1	63 R 3, 72 R 4	5	58 R 1, 86 R 4	27	122
6	73 R 5	10	8 R 3	30	120 R 5, 146 R 2
16	58 c, 141	13	57 R 1, 86 R 4	33	28 R 5, 38
20	86 c	18	118	40	98 a
23	106 b	17 3	29 e	41	138 c
7 3, 5	60 R 4	5	1	51	120
7, 8	29 a	8	107 R 1, 146	2 2	55 c
9	10 R 3, 57 R 1	11	11 c, 40 b	5	26, 47, 107 R 1
23	8 R 2	12	63 R 1, 63 R 2	6	63 R 2
28	106 R 2	15	11 R e	8	78, 146 R 1
29	83, 91 R 1	16	109	15, 18	107 R 1
8 2	87, 116 R 5	17	55 c	21	79
8	29 d	18 3	86 a, 146	22	60, 126 R 6 a, 136 R 1
10	23	11	101 R d, 132 R 2, 136 R 1	26	24 R 3, 110
9 1	126 R 3	12	8, 131	28	105
2	126	14	63 R 2, 140	31	24 R 4, 55 a
3	126, 127 d	18	72 R 4	39	27, 28 R 5
4	69 a	23	8, 60	42	40 b, 55 b
10	101 d	25	86 R 4	44	57 R 1
13	24 d	29	91 a, 121		
10 9	116 R 4	32	133		
11, 17	116 R 5	19 1	1, 135		

2 Kings	§§	2 Kings	§§	2 Kings	§§
1 2 .	32 R 3, 125	7 8 .	19 R 1	16 14 .	29 c, 50 b
3 .	128	9 .	78 R 8, 128 R 1,	15 .	29 R 7
4 .	106 b		132 a, 132 R 2	17 .	29 c
8 .	24 R 3	13 .	20 R 4, 136 R 1	17 4 .	29 R 8
11, 13 .	83	16, 18 .	29 d	6 .	38 R 2
13, 14 .	37 R 5	19 .	136 R 1	13 .	28 R 6
2 9 .	136 R 1	8 5 .	141	21 .	78
10 .	82	8, 9 .	32 R 3	26 .	127 b
11 .	86 R 4, 100 f, 141	10 .	58 b	28-41 .	100 R 2
16 .	128 R 4	13 .	22 c, 43 b, 72 R 1,	29 .	29 R 8
17 .	36 a, 37 e		75, 146 R 2	18 4 .	58 b
3 1 .	38	17 .	36 R 3	9, 10 .	38
3 .	116	22 .	45 R 2	17 .	32 R 5
4 .	29 d, 37 d, 54 R 1	25 .	38	21 .	132 a
8 .	8 R 4, 144 R 1	29 .	29 R 1, 44 R 2	23 .	20 R 4, 37 d
11 .	65 c, 65 d, 122	9 1 .	35 R 2	26-32 .	60
13 .	118, 128 R 2	3 .	40 b	31 .	64
14 .	120 R 5, 131	4 .	29 b	32 .	55 b, 65 d, 96
16 .	29 R 8, 88 R 2	5 .	21 f	36 .	58 b
24 .	86 R 3	8 .	17 R 5	37 .	70 a
26 .	113	10 .	129	19 1 .	78 R 5
27 .	43 a	12 .	11 R e, 117	3 .	127 b
4 1 .	19 R 1, 107 R 1	15 .	29 R 1	4 .	9 b, 31, 53 b
8, 11, 18	21 R 2, 145	18 .	1 R 1, 7 b, 8 R 3	11 .	107 R 1, 121
9 .	30	20 .	44 a	14 .	116 R 1
13 .	67 b, 94, 122	25 .	28 R 5, 146 R 3	17 .	118
19 .	117	26 .	57 R 1, 120	22 .	7 a, 58 a
29 .	130 a	32 .	36 R 5	25 .	65 R 1, 109 R 2
41 .	136 R 1	33 .	102	27 .	90
43 .	4 R 1, 7 b, 88	35 .	91 R 4	28 .	56
5 2 .	71 R 1	10 2 .	136 R 1	32 .	77
3 .	135 R 2	2, 3 .	55 b	37 .	141 R 1
4 .	11 R e	4 .	107	20 3 .	146
5 .	29 R 3	6 .	28 R 6, 34	4 .	32 R 2, 73 R 1,
6 .	136 R 1	10 .	102		141 R 1
10 .	60 R 4, 65 d	13 .	73 R 5, 104 c	9 .	41 R 2, 124
11 .	21 R 2, 86 c	14 .	37 c	12 .	16
12 .	116 R 3, 126 R 4	15 .	32 R 5, 126,	13 .	32 R 2
13 .	64, 111 R 1		132 R 2	14 .	45 R 1
17 .	79, 132 R 2	23 .	128 R 4	21 6 .	82
20 .	51 R 2, 120 R 3	25 .	11 R b	12 .	113, 132 R 2
21 .	21 a	11 4 .	28 R 5, 75	13 .	86 c
22 .	6 R 2. 36 a	10 .	17	22 1 .	36 R 3
23 .	29 d, 83	12 .	17 R 4	8 .	111
25 .	152	14 .	117	13 .	9 a
26 .	121	12 10 .	35 R 2, 108 R 1	18 .	99
6 3 .	83, 107 R 1	12-17 .	44 R 2	20 .	17 R 3, 113
5 .	72 R 4	16 .	71 R 2	23 3 .	22 R 3
6 .	75	18 .	51 R 2	8 .	108 R 1
8 .	11 R e	21 .	67 b	9 .	44 b, 155
9 .	96 R 1	13 11 .	116	10 .	96 R 1
10 .	38 R 5	14 .	43 a, 67 b	17 .	20 R 4, 29 c
12 .	35 R 2, 44 a	19 .	39 d, 94, 131 R 2	24 3 .	101 R d, 109
16 .	10	20, 21 .	141 R 1		R 2
19 .	97 R 1	14 7 .	58 c	12 .	38
20 .	4	10 .	53 b	14 .	17, 37 e
22 .	111 R 1	12 .	29 R 6	25 1 .	17, 38 R 2
25 .	38 R 6	23 .	38	5 .	115
31 .	120 R 4	26 .	17 R 5, 76	8, 27 .	38
32 .	45	15 1 .	39 R 1	9 .	32 R 5
33 .	6 R 1, 100 f	13 .	29 d, 38	10 .	144 R 5
7 1 .	29 d	16 .	20 R 4	15 .	29 R 8
3 .	41 c, 145	17, 23, 27	38	16 .	32 R 2
4 .	130 b	21 .	123 R 2	17 .	36 R 3
7 .	1 R 1	30, 32 .	38	19 .	9 R 2

PSALMS	§§	PSALMS	§§	PSALMS	§§
40 6	95, 132 R 2	59 17	25	81 9	134
41 3	128 R 2	60 5	29 e	14	131, 134
7	130 b	10	23	83 5	101
42 2	143	11	41 R 2	6	71 R 2
4	91 R 1, 96 R 5	12	51 R 5	10	101 R d
5	65 R 5, 73 R 4	13	13)	15	143
6, 12	51 R 4	61 8	65 R 4	19	109 R 3
6, 7, 12	p. 143 n.	62 4	32 R 2, 99 R 1	84 4	40 c
43 1	128 R 1	5	116 R 1	85 9	136 R 1
5	p. 143 n.	10	34 R 3, 132 R 2	14	65 R 6
44 3	109 R 3	63 7	17 R 2	87 3	109
5	106 R 2	64 6	146 R 1	5	106 R 2
10, 11	51 R 5	7	27	88 5	101 R d, 140
19	128 R 6	8-10	49 b	6	98 R 1
21	130 b, 131 R 1	9	116 R 1	8	77
45 8	77	65 4	17 R 3	9	17 R 2
9	29 e	5	25, 32 R 5, 144	11	83 R 4, 141 R 3
12	136 R 1	66 6	65 R 5	89 28	91 R 4
13	34	9	19 R 2	40	101
14	28 R 3	10	91 R 3	48, 51	1 R 1
46 3	91 R 2	17	109 R	51	32 R 1
4	132 R 2	67 3	96 R 5	90 2	145
5	17 R 2, 32 R 5	68 5	101 R a	3	65 R 6
7	45 R 2	10	136 R 1	15	25
47 4	65 R 6	15	65 R 6, 109	91 6	68
48 6, 11	151, 151 R 1	16	34 R 6	14	59
49 4	17 R 2	22	28 R 3	92 9	29 e, 69 R 1
7	99	69 5	29 R 4	11	19 R 4
8	86 b	10	23	12	32 R 2
8-10	65 c	11	109 R 3	94 9	126 R 2
11	118	15	62, 65 R 3	17	73, 131
13	22 R 2, 143	22	51 R 5	22, 23	49 b
14	143	33	45 R 2	95 7	134
15	94	71 21	63 R 2	8	101 R d
50 3	109, 128 R 2	72 13, 16	65 R 6	10	22 R 3, 50 a
5	101 R d	19	81 R 2	11	150
10	22 R 3	73 2	116	96 4	97 R 1
16	50 a	10	32 R 5	97 1	39 R 1
18	130 b	13	71 R 2	99 6	101 R a
20	83, 141 R 3	15	131 R 1	101 3	91 R 3
21	86 R 3, 146 R 1	17	45, 65 R 5	5	22 R 3
51 3	28	27	98 R 1, 101	5	101 R c
4	83	28	91 R 3, 116 R 3	9	98 R 1
6	149 R 3	74 7	101	14	83, 141 R 3
14	75	11	136 R 1	28	106 R 2
18	65 c	15	32 R 5	103 5	116
52 5	34 R 2	23	98 R 1	14	100 R 7
9	45 R 3, 50 a, 51 R 4	75 3	71 R 2	104 6	78 R 2
53 6	98 R 1	76 6	67 R 2	6-8	45 R 2
54 6	101 R a	7	136	14, 15	96
55 3	65 R 5	8	97 R 1, 145	15	75
7	65 b, 65 R 4	11	17 R 2	16	34 R 6
9	69 R 2	77 4, 7	65 R 5	18	32 R 2
13	65 c	78 6	44 R 3	20	22 R 3, 65 R 6, 132 b
18	51 R 4, 65 R 5	9	28 R 6	21	96 R 4
19	101	15, 26, 49, 50	51 R 5	22, 27-30	132 R 2
22	29 e	17, 20	45 R 2	25	6 R 1
56 3	71 R 2	49	32 R 5	32	51 R 4, 51 R 6
4, 10	25	79 10	99	33	3 R 1
57 5	65 R 5, 98 R 1	80 5	41 R 2	106 13	83
7	41 R 5	9	45 R 2	14	67 b
58 2	71 R 2	11	34 R 6, 80	18	51 R 5
5	65 R 6, 143	15	6 R 1	23, 26, 27	91 R 4
9	71 R 1	81 6	25, 144	43	44 R 1
59 16	50 b, 130 R 4	7, 8	51 R 5		

Psalms	§§	Psalms	§§	Proverbs	§§
107 6, 13	51 R 5	134 2	69 R 2	8 6	14
26–29	51 R 6	135 17	128 R 3	22, 25	145
29	65 R 6	136 4–7	98 b	30	29 e
108 2, 7	109 R 3	19, 20	73 R 7	32	25
109 2	32 R 5, 67 R 3	137 3	11 R a, 75, 101 R c	9 11	108 R 2
3	73 R 4	8	97 R 1	12	58 b, 130 R 4
4	29 e	8, 9	25	10 1	44 a
7	70 a	138 3	25, 50 b, 51 R 5	4	67 R 3
19	143	139 8, 9	132 R 2	25	132 R 2
24	101 R c	11	48 d, 132 R 2	26	16
28	49 b	12	34 R 2	11 2	48 d, 132 R 2
110 2	60 R 2	13	51 R 5	16	24 R 3 151
3	29 e	14	71 R 2	21	22 R 3
111 7	29 e	18	3 R 1, 132 R 2	12 4	24 R 3
8	32 R 5	19	134	7	132 R 2
114 3	51 R 5	22	67 b	19	65 R 5
8	76, 78 R 3	140 9	65 R 4	26	65 R 6
115 7	3 R 2	12	24 R 3	28	128 R 2
8	99 R 2	141 5	128 R 2, 132 R 2	13 10	109 R 1
116 5	104	10	116 R 1	21	72 R 4
14, 15, 18	69 R 2	142 4	p. 143 n.	24	77
15	28 R 5	143 7	65 R 2	14 2	98 R 1
118 8, 9	33, 104	144 2	144	9	116 R 1
11	88 R 4	3	51 R 3	19	40 c
19	65 R 4	13	115	35	116 R 2
20	28 R 5	146 2	3 R 1	15 12	84
119 5	135 R 2	4	132 R 2	20	24 a
11, 80	65 149	5	101 R a	25	65 R 6
17	65 R 4	147 1	116 R 3	16 4	20 R 4
21	99 R 1	18	132 b	5	22 R 3
41, 77	69 R 4	148 13	22 R 3	19	32 R 5
62	68	149 2	16	29	54 a
72	116 R 3	6	139	17 1	116 R 3
75, 78, 86	71 R 2			3	151
86	29 R 4	**Proverbs**		5	40 b
92	131	1 3	84	12	88 R 2, 88 R 5
103	115	7	40 c	13	132 R 2
136	73 R 2	9	24 c	20	24 R 5
137, 155	116 R 3	12	70 a	18 3	48 d
120 5	73, 117	27	91 a	9	24 R 3
7	29 e	2 5	131 R 2	10, 17	54 a
121 3	19 R 2, 128 R 2	19	98 R 1	13, 22	132 R 2
123 2	151	3 10	73 R 2	22	48 d
4	20 R 4, 28 R 5	17	29 e	19 8	94
124 1, 2	131 R 1	18, 35	116 R 1	25	108 R 3
3	70 a	23	67 R 2	20 3	101 R c
4	69 R 2	24	132 a	7	145 R 1
125 1	143	25	128 R 2	10	29 R 8
4	24 R 5	26	101 R a	13	64
5	22 R 3, 106 c	28	139	21 3, 9	33, 91 R 3
126 5	86 c	4 16	54 a	6	28 R 3
127 1	130 R 4	18	86 R 4	13	81 R 4
2	68, 90	5 6	139	16	84
128 5	65 d	19	24 c	19	24 R 3
129 3	108 R 1	22	29 R 7	22	49 a
6	145 R 2	6 11	57 R 1	22 12, 13	40 c
8	40 b	13	73 R 6	19	1
130 1	40 b	16	106 R 2	21	29 e
2	31	17, 18	31	23	71
131 2	120 R 3, p. 143 n.	22	132 a	24	24 R 3
132 1	90	7 7	51 R 5	23 1	86 R 3
5	17 R 2	10	71 R 2	2	24 R 3
11, 12	6 R 3, 28 R 5	14	101 R d	15	1
15, 16, 18	75	19	21 d	25	65 R 6
133 1	76	26	90 R 1	24 8	31 R 3

15

ECCLESIASTES §§
9 11 . . . 88 R 1
12 4 . . . 24 R 3
7 . . . 65 R 6

ESTHER
1 8, 22 . . . 29 R 8
2 11 . . . 29 R 8
15 . . . 100 R 2
3 4 . . . 146
4 2 . . . 95
14 . . . 43 R 1
16 . . . 114, 130 R 4
5 3, 6 . . . 65*d*
8 6 . . . 83
8 . . . 88 R 1, 95
9 1 . . . 88 R 5
4 . . . 86 R 4
6, 12, 16, 17 . . . 88 R 1
10 2 . . . 123 R 2

DANIEL
1 5, 12, 15 . . . 36*c*
8 . . . 146
16 . . . 100 R 2
17 . . . 36 R 4
20 . . . 38 R 5
2 13 . . . 146 R 4
16, 18 . . . 96 R 4, 111 R 2
26 . . . 144 R 3
30 . . . 108 R 2
37 . . . 9 R 1
3 27 . . . 17 R 4
4 5 . . . 144 R 3
6 . . . 9 R 1
22 . . . 108 R 2
28, 29 . . . 108 R 2
5 19 . . . 100 R 2
7 18 . . . 16
8 1 . . . 22 R 4
6 . . . 24 R 3
12 . . . 65 R 6
13 . . . 20 R 4, 29*e*, 32 R 2, 35 R 1, 136
16 . . . 6
9 5 . . . 88 R 1
13 . . . 72 R 4
23 . . . 29*e*
25 . . . 83
26 . . . 99 R 1
10 1 . . . 144 R 3
9 . . . 100 R 2
11 1 . . . 96 R 3
4, 10 . . . 65 R 6
10, 13 . . . 86*c*
11, 27 . . . 29 R 7
14 . . . 28 R 6
16–19 . . . 65 R 6
25, 28, 30 . . . 65 R 6
31 . . . 32 R 2
12 2 . . . 5
11 . . . 96 R 4

EZRA
1 5 . . . 144 R 5
7 . . . 39 R 1

EZRA §§
2 . . . 37 R 3
59 . . . 125
62 . . . 29 R 4, 101
65 . . . 32 R 3
3 7 . . . 24 R 6
8 . . . 83 R 2
9 . . . 116 R 3
12 . . . 6 R 1, 29 R 7
4 22 . . . 91 R 3
5 8 . . . 80
12 . . . 1 R 1
7 8 . . . 38 R 2
21 . . . 1
8 15 . . . 36*c*
16, 24 . . . 73 R 7
21 . . . 29*a*
25 . . . 22 R 4
29 . . . 20 R 4
9 1 . . . 29*a*, 29 R 7
4 . . . 44 R 2
15 . . . 95
10 12 . . . 67 R 3
13 . . . 29*e*, 82
14 . . . 20 R 4, 22 R 4, 28 R 5, 29 R 8
17 . . . 22 R 4

NEHEMIAH
1 1 . . . 38
4 . . . 100 R 2
7 . . . 86 R 3
2 1 . . . 38 R 2
3 . . . 147
9 . . . 48 R 2
10 . . . 67*b*
12 . . . 29*d*, 114
13, 15 . . . 100 R 2
16 . . . 116 R 3
4 4 . . . 17
11 . . . 35 R 1
12 . . . 98 R 1
17 . . . 1 R 1
5 5 . . . 101 R*c*
7 . . . p. 143*n*.
14 . . . 38 R 2, 114
18 . . . 84 R 1
6 1 . . . 81
2 . . . 17 R 3
6 . . . 100 R 6
12 . . . 127*a*
18 . . . 24 R 3
7 64 . . . 29 R 4
8 8 . . . 88 R 1
10 . . . 144 R 5
11 . . . 117
13 . . . 96 R 4, 136 R 1
9 3, 5 . . . 100*a*, 100 R 6
6 . . . 106 R 2
19, 32, 34 . . . 72 R 4
28 . . . 73 R 4, 109
31 . . . 78 R 7
35 . . . 32 R 2
10 29 . . . 83 R 2
37 . . . 17 R 6
39 . . . 84 R 1

NEHEMIAH §§
13 10 . . . 116
17 . . . 47
21 . . . 22 R 3
23 . . . 1 R 1, 41 R 3
24 . . . 29 R 8

1 CHRONICLES
2 3, 9 . . . 81 R 3
30, 32 . . . 128 R 3
3 1, 4 . . . 81 R 3
1, 5 . . . 28 R 5
20 . . . 36 R 3
4 9 . . . 146 R 2
17 . . . 83 R 4
5 1 . . . 17 R 2, 95
9 . . . 29*a*
26 . . . 29 R 7, 73 R 7
6 17 . . . 100 R 2
34 . . . 96 R 4
7 5 . . . 28 R 5
9 13 . . . 26
22 . . . 1 R 1, 29 R 7
25 . . . 94
27 . . . 136 R 1
10 13 . . . 96 R 4
11 7 . . . 108
8 . . . 44 R 2
23 . . . 37 R 4
12 8 . . . 93
23 . . . 34 R 6
34 . . . 29 R 8
13 5 . . . 101 R*b*
14 15 . . . 72 R 4
15 2 . . . 95
12 . . . 144, 144 R 5
19 . . . 29*c*
27 . . . 20 R 4
16 36 . . . 88 R 1
37 . . . 73 R 7
17 4 . . . 127*a*
21 . . . 8 R 2
18 14 . . . 100 R 2
19 3 . . . 149 R 1
20 3 . . . 44 R 2
21 17 . . . 6 R 1, 106 R 2
18 . . . 146 R 2
22 1 . . . 106 R 2
23 26 . . . 95
24 12–18 . . . 38
16 . . . 38 R 3
25 8 . . . 101 R*d*
18–31 . . . 38
19 . . . 38 R 3
26 13 . . . 29 R 8
27 2–13 . . . 38
29 . . . 115
28 5 . . . 32 R 1
18 . . . 29 R 4
19 . . . 88 R 1
29 3 . . . 144 R 5
4 . . . 29 R 3
8, 17 . . . 22 R 4
14 . . . 146 R 2
22 . . . 73 R 7
29 . . . 123 R 2

2 Chronicles	§§	2 Chronicles	§§	2 Chronicles	§§
1 4 . . .	22 R 4	9 21 . . .	44 b	23 1 . . .	73 R 7
10 . . .	32 R 3	28 . . .	108	25 16 . .	108, 126 R 5
2 12 . . .	73 R 7	10 8 . . .	116 R 1	20 . . .	22 R 3
13, 14 . .	22 d	11 12 . . .	29 R 8		17
3 4-9 . .	78 R 2	16 9 .	113, 144, 144 R 5	26 13 . . .	17
4 10 . . .	32 R 5	11 . . .	123 R 2	27 7 . . .	123 R 2
13 . . .	29 c	12 . - .	71 R 3	28 9 . . .	101 R b
5 11 . . .	95	17 12 . . .	86 R 4	20 . . .	73 R 4
7 17 . . .	96 R 4	14 . . .	116 R 6	29 27 .	25, 136 R 1
18 . . .	73 R 5	18 3 . . .	151 R 2	36 . . .	22 R 4
8 11 . . .	28 R 5	19 5 . . .	29 R 8	30 10 . . .	100 R 2
13 . . .	96 R 4	20 6 .	95, 106 R 2	19 . . .	144 R 5
16 . . .	20 R 4	15 . . .	155	31 7, 10 . .	111 R 2
18 . . .	29 R 3	17 . . .	95	32 32 . . .	123 R 2
9 9, 13 . .	29 R 3	22 . . .	144 R 5	33 20 . . .	69 R 1
20 . . .	128	22 6 . . .	44 R 2	34 22 . . .	144 R 5
				36 16 . . .	100 R 2

CORRECTIONS IN INDEX OF PASSAGES

Ex. 10 7 *read* 11 7.

    32 12 ,, 33 12.

Jud. 9 4, 5 ,, 9 45.

1 K. 12 19 ,, 12 9.

Is. 3 1 *add* 17 R 5, and *delete* ref. Is. 3 5.

    14 21 *read* 14 24.

    52 12, 13 ,, 51 12, 13.

Job 4 19 ,, 4 9.

1 Chr. 28 19 ,, 2 Chr. 28 19.

Delete references Numb. 27 24, Deut. 4 17, Song 2 13.

INDEX OF SUBJECTS

(Figures refer to §§.)

ABSOLUTE object, 67.

Abstract ideas, expressed by *fem.*, 14 ; by *plur.*, 16.

Accentuation of ptcp. with Art. 22 R 4 ; error in, 141 R 1.

Accusative, idea of, 66 ; kinds of, 66 ; acc. of absolute obj., 67 ; cognate acc , 67, in plur., 67 R 2 ; organ of expression as cog. acc., 67 R 3 ; acc. of time, 68 ; of place, 69, 69 R 1, 69 R 2 ; acc. of condition, 70 ; adverbial acc., 70, 71 R 2 ; acc. of specification, 71, 71 R 3 ; of motive, 71 R 4 ; acc. of direct obj., 72 ; verbs governing obj., 73 ; verbs with two acc. of obj., 74-77 ; acc. of product, 76 ; predicate acc., 76, 78 R 6 ; two acc. of different kinds, 78 ; acc. after pass. 79 seq. *Nota acc.* rare in poetry, 72 ; cases where use necessary, 72 R 1 ; rare except with acc. of obj., 72 R 3 ; apparent anomalous use, 72 R 4.

Active infin. for pass., 96 R 5.

Addition, idea of, expressed by prep., 101 R *b*, 101 R *d*.

Adjective, placed exceptionally before noun, 30 R 1 ; concord of, 30 ; with dual, 31 ; with plur. of Eminence, 31, 116 R 4 ; with collectives, 31, 115 ; determination of adj., 30, 32 R 2, demons. adj., 32, 32 R 3 ; adj. used nominally, 32 R 5, 28 R 3 ; the epithet used instead of noun, 32 R 6 ; adj. little developed in early Shemitic, 24, 102. *See* Comparison.

Adverb, 70 *b* ; follows verb, except negatives, 110 ; adverbial use of inf. abs., 87 ; adverbial idea expressed by a verb, 82 ; some adv. of time, 145 R 3.

Adversative Sent., 155.

Affirmative Sent., 118 ; the oath, 119.

Agreement of subj. and pred., 112 ; simple subj., 113 ; dual subj., 113 ; composite subj., 114 ; when consisting of noun and pron., 114 ; when of different genders, 114. Agreement of collectives, 115 ; of plur. of Eminence, 31, 116 R 4 ; of

plur. inhumanus, 116 ; anomalies in agreement, 116 R 1, 116 R 3, 116 R 6 ; agreement with gen., 116 R 2 ; names of nations, 116 R 5.

Answer, in interrog. sent., 126.

Anticipative pron. resumed by noun (permutative), 29 R 7.

Apposition, nominal, 29 seq. ; repetition of prep., &c., before proper name, 29, 29 R 2 ; some apparent cases may be acc. of specification, &c., 29 R 4, and others due to errors of text, 29 R 5 ; the word *all* in appos., 29 R 6 ; appos. (permutative) to pron., 29 R 7 ; various senses of same word repeated in appos., 29 R 8 ; words in appos. as double acc. of obj., 76.

Article, 19 seq. ; numeral *one* for indef. Art., 19 R 1 ; pred. and inf. without Art., 19 ; Art. not used with words determinate in themselves or by consn., 20 ; exceptions to this rule, 20 R 4 ; Art. with vocative, 21 ; with classes and in comparisons, 22, 22 R 2 ; omitted in poetry, 22 R 3 ; used as Rel., 22 R 4 ; with ptcp., 22 R 4, 99.

Attributive (Adj.) circumscribed by gen. of noun, 24 ; especially with the words *man, woman,* &c., 24 R 3, and in neg. clauses, 128 R 3, 128 R 5 ; by perf., 41 R 3, and impf., 44 R 3.

Beth essentiæ, 101 R *a*.

CARDINAL Numbers, 35 seq.

Cases, 18.

Casus pendens, 106.

Causal Sent., 147 ; causal sense of prep., 101 R *c*, 147 R 1.

Circumscription of Gen. by prep., 28 R 5.

Circumstantial Clause, 137 seq. ; order of words in, 137 ; ptcp. greatly used, 138 ; circumstance placed parallel to main action, 141 ; use of impf. in cir. cl., 44 R 3, 141 R 3.

Cognate acc., 67. *See* Acc.